Cultural Heritage Mana

Cultural Heritage Studies

UNIVERSITY PRESS OF FLORIDA

Florida A&M University, Tallahassee
Florida Atlantic University, Boca Raton
Florida Gulf Coast University, Ft. Myers
Florida International University, Miami
Florida State University, Tallahassee
New College of Florida, Sarasota
University of Central Florida, Orlando
University of Florida, Gainesville
University of North Florida, Jacksonville
University of South Florida, Tampa
University of West Florida, Pensacola

Cultural Heritage Management

A Global Perspective

EDITED BY

PHYLLIS MAUCH MESSENGER AND GEORGE S. SMITH

SERIES FOREWORD BY PAUL A. SHACKEL

University Press of Florida

Gainesville/Tallahassee/Tampa/Boca Raton

Pensacola/Orlando/Miami/Jacksonville/Ft. Myers/Sarasota

First cloth printing, 2010
First paperback printing, 2014

Library of Congress Cataloging-in-Publication Data
Cultural heritage management: a global perspective/edited by Phyllis Mauch
Messenger and George S. Smith; series foreword by Paul A. Shackel.
p. cm.—(Cultural heritage studies)
Includes bibliographical references and index.
ISBN 978-0-8130-3460-7 (cloth: alk. paper)
ISBN 978-0-8130-6085-9 (pbk.)
1. Cultural property—Protection—Case studies. 2. Historic sites—
Management—Case studies. 3. Antiquities—Collection and preservation—
Case studies. 4. Historic preservation—Case studies. I. Messenger, Phyllis
Mauch, 1950– II. Smith, George S.
CC135.C845 2010
930.19–dc22   2009051046

The University Press of Florida is the scholarly publishing agency for the State
University System of Florida, comprising Florida A&M University, Florida
Atlantic University, Florida Gulf Coast University, Florida International Uni-
versity, Florida State University, New College of Florida, University of Central
Florida, University of Florida, University of North Florida, University of South
Florida, and University of West Florida.

University Press of Florida
15 Northwest 15th Street
Gainesville, FL 32611-2079
http://www.upf.com

Contents

Figures and Tables

Figures

Tables

Series Foreword

Global Perspective and World Heritage

PAUL A. SHACKEL

Heritage is not always about the truth or authenticity. It can also be about politics and uses of the past. Communities make conscious decisions about what to protect and what to remember. Many see heritage as a tool of the nation-state. It is a way to promote social cohesion through the creation of origin myths and promote moral examples by providing examples of the past. Anything that the state deems worthy of saving eventually enters an arena where its meaning is discussed, debated, and sometimes modified (Harrison 2010). Robert Hewison (1987) suggests that heritage is largely imposed from above to create a nostalgic past, especially during times of economic decline.

This volume, *Cultural Heritage Management: A Global Perspective*, edited by Phyllis Mauch Messenger and George S. Smith, is an important collection of essays that demonstrates the significance of cultural heritage and sometimes the contestations over the meaning of the past. The volume is truly global in nature, as it contains compelling case studies that provide insight into the uses of heritage in local and global contexts. The authors provide important examples of heritage practices and they show the many complicated issues that arise when dealing with real life situations. Topics about ownership of the past, protecting the past, and interpreting the past provide some of the main themes in this volume.

The uses and practices of heritage have become important in the twenty-first century as global issues affect the way we see and use the past. For instance, the transformation of the world's political economy over the past century has endangered many communities and has threatened tangible and intangible forms of heritage that are important for providing a sense of place and identity. Global climate change is affecting communities and their sense of place, and every year millions of people are displaced because of natural disasters. At the beginning of this century, there were twenty-one million refugees who had fled their native lands to other countries to escape violence. The World Bank reports that development projects displace approximately 10 million people a year. Many of these people suffer as their basic human and environmental rights are being violated. Ethnic nationalism, globalized forms of development, energy development, and urban renewal also threaten the heritage of millions of people (Oliver-Smith 2006:45–46).

Representation and inclusiveness on a global scale are increasingly important issues that heritage professionals must face. When the World Heritage List was established in the 1970s, the honored places tended to be European. An initiative launched in 1994 by the World Heritage Centre promoted a global strategy for a more balanced, representative, and credible World Heritage List. By the early twenty-first century, the United Nations Educational, Scientific and Cultural Organization (UNESCO) had produced a list of types of cultural heritage that included tangible and intangible values and new categories for World Heritage sites, such as cultural landscapes, industrial heritage, deserts, coastal-marine, and small-island sites. While nearly 50 percent of the World Heritage sites are in Europe and North America, these broader definitions of heritage have made this designation more inclusive and more sensitive to the world's cultural diversity.

Creating a sense of place while communities, regions, and the world become more homogenized in our new global economy presents a challenge. The recovery, celebration, and interpretation of the past are necessary components of sustaining identity and creating a sense of place. Heritage is about power and the control of a community's collective memory. We make choices about what to conserve, protect, and honor. This volume addresses some of these issues and shows the complexities of creating a diverse and inclusive world heritage.

References Cited

Harrison, Rodney
2010   Introduction. *Understanding the Politics of Heritage.* Manchester University Press, Manchester, England.
Hewison, R.
1987   *The Heritage Industry: Britain in a Climate of Decline.* Methuen, London.
Oliver-Smith, Anthony
2006   Communities after Catastrophe: Reconstructing the Material, Reconstituting the Social. In *Community Building in the Twenty-First Century,* edited by Stanley E. Hyland, pp. 45–70. School of American Research Press, Santa Fe, New Mexico.

Foreword

Being in the Department of Archaeology at the University of Southampton in the early 1980s was exciting. Peter Ucko had arrived as the new professor and department head and had immediately set about dramatically revising the curriculum, introducing new topics and ideas, moving the subject on from a fascinating academic discipline to one that is vibrant, exciting, and, crucially, socially important and *relevant*. Within a few years we were deep in the organization of, what turned out to be, the First World Archaeological Congress (WAC-1), a meeting that most now accept changed dramatically the world of archaeology and heritage management.

WAC-1 was based around themes that broke down academic, chronological, and geographic boundaries, allowing colleagues from around the world to debate with each other on an equal footing. For me, one of the most important and relevant topics discussed was public archaeology and cultural resource management, organized in a series of sessions by Henry Cleere, then the director of the Council for British Archaeology. Cleere had never let his potentially restricting title and role as director for *British* archaeology get in his way of globetrotting, and he traveled, in particular at that time to other parts of Europe and the United States, forging links and seeing how different countries dealt with managing their heritage. Others had worked on heritage management in their own countries, working within their own legal frameworks—one immediately thinks of Charles McGimsey and Hester Davis—but in these sessions came a rallying cry to do more, to compare and contrast, and to learn from each other.

One of the things that had come out of Cleere's travels was, in 1984, the publication of *Approaches to the Archaeological Heritage*—the first published attempt to compare and contrast heritage management in more than one country. The volume certainly influenced the topic's inclusion within the WAC-1 program, and the sessions Cleere organized resulted in the publication of *Archaeological Heritage Management in the Modern World* (1989), the ninth volume of the One World Archaeology series; this volume built upon and broadened the approach and coverage contained in his *Approaches* of 1984.

Sitting in those lecture theaters in Southampton in 1986 and listening to the wide range of experts Cleere had gathered together was little less than a life-changing experience for me. The speakers confirmed that I had found the area of archaeology in which I wanted to specialize. They showed that there were other people who understood that the issues were important, that there were other people who *cared*, not just about the stories held within sites that could be unlocked by archaeological investigation, but also about the relevance of those sites to the present and the future. In his preface to the pre-circulated papers for the WAC-1, Cleere indicated that he hoped the papers would "serve to demonstrate the diversity of problems confronting cultural resource management archaeologists and provide an opportunity to compare and contrast the efficacy of the solutions adopted." They did that and so much more.

However, the world has moved on significantly since the 1980s. For example, few could have predicted the enormous success of the World Heritage Convention, not only in creating an impressive, increasingly representative, list of sites with so-called outstanding universal value but also, and perhaps more importantly, in championing the improved management of World Heritage sites. This has led generally to improved management of large parts of the wider cultural heritage across the globe. Much of this improvement stems from understanding that there are a wide range of frequently conflicting interests affecting the cultural heritage. Working for English Heritage (the government's advisor on all heritage matters) in the 1980s and 1990s, I was struck by the speed of change: from site management based around a quinquennial architectural review of monuments (effectively how to ensure that the historic remains continued to stand for a further five years), to a far more comprehensive style of management. This wider view recognized the importance of a much larger range of professional interests than just those of the specialist archaeologist or architect—for the first time including, as almost equals, those professionals concerned with education, interpretation, and visitor management.

Cleere's focus in 1984 in *Approaches* had been on the legal instruments available to protect the heritage: a heritage essentially identified, ranked in importance, controlled, and managed by archaeologists and architects. Discussions at WAC-1 and since have altered that focus: now the question is not only "What to conserve and how?" but also "Who has the right to decide on what management regime is best for a particular country, landscape, or site?" Suddenly cultural heritage experts, such as those working for English Heritage, were not the only people with control and influence, as the rights and interests of local communities and indigenous peoples grew in importance. In the United Kingdom, Hadrian's Wall was the first World Heritage site to have a management plan (1996) and, as I write this foreword, letters are going out inviting people to the launch of the third iteration of the plan (2009–2014). As the chair of the Hadrian's Wall Management Plan Committee, I can testify, from personal experience, that good heritage management is about prioritizing frequently conflicting demands and trying to anticipate problems before they arise and dealing with them before they turn into threats or disasters. The Management Plan Committee now in-cludes academics and farmers, businesspeople and planners, tourism specialists and bed-and-breakfast owners, regional government officials dealing with eco-nomic regeneration and local community representatives, among others. They all have real and valuable contributions to make to the improved management of the World Heritage site—although on occasion I cannot help but think how easy it must have been when only archaeologists concerned themselves with the monument!

A second issue that has been identified since WAC-1 is that of mass tour-ism, which in the 1980s was only a major problem at a few sites, mostly, but not exclusively, situated in Europe. Since then mass tourism has become a global issue and the demands it places upon heritage sites are now frequently a, if not *the*, starting point in understanding the complexity of their management. Cul-tural heritage experts need to work more closely with organizations such as the World Tourism Organisation if we are to address this issue successfully.

And third, few at WAC-1 could have imagined the purposeful destruction of the Bamiyan Buddhas, nor the wide-ranging devastation—through specific targeted destruction, so-called collateral damage, and the illicit looting of ar-chaeological sites and museums—that has been seen over the last six years in Iraq. In 1986, few cultural heritage experts would have expected the bloodshed following the destruction in 1992 of the Babri Masjid mosque in Ayodhya, nor the central part played in its destruction by a number of senior Indian archae-ologists—a total failure of the heritage community to safeguard the heritage. Cultural heritage experts need to engage more with the protection and manage-ment of cultural heritage in times of conflict if such damage is to be mitigated.

Cultural Heritage Management: A Global Perspective picks up these and many other issues as it follows in the footsteps of those trailblazing speakers at WAC-1 in 1986. It offers a snapshot of how the cultural heritage is managed in a range of different countries and by international agencies in the early twenty-first century. It will not be the final, definitive guide to this work; it cannot be, as the issues and problems will continue to change over time. However, as a contribution, it is a major one.

Peter G. Stone
International Centre for Cultural and Heritage Studies, Newcastle University
Former chief executive officer of the World Archaeological Congress

Preface

The genesis of this book can be traced to events, projects, and publications beginning in the late 1980s. The first was the Save the Past for the Future Working Conference held in Taos, New Mexico, in 1989 under the leadership of the Society for American Archaeology (SAA) with the support of numerous organizations and U.S. federal agencies. The conference addressed three major areas dealing with preventing the destruction of archaeological resources—understanding the problem, preventing the problem, and combating the problem. The resulting publication, *Save the Past for the Future: Actions for the '90s*, addressed these three areas and made recommendations on how to deal with the issues (Society for American Archaeology [SAA] 1990). Key outcomes of those efforts were the establishment of the Public Education Committee of SAA, and enhanced understanding and cooperation among archaeologists, resource managers, and law enforcement agencies in the United States.

In 1994 the SAA again organized a working conference—Save the Past for the Future II—to assess achievements since the working conference of 1989 and make further recommendations for protecting and managing the past. The agenda was expanded beyond the issue of site looting to include not only law enforcement but education and integrated resource management as means of protecting archaeological sites. A conference report, *Save the Past for the Future II: Report of the Working Conference* (SAA 1995), presented the results of the conference and recommendations for the future. Based on several of the recommendations from this working conference, the SAA and partner organizations organized a workshop to assess the needs and opportunities for developing education and training for students and professional archaeologists. The resulting publication, *Teaching Archaeology in the Twenty-first Century* (Bender and Smith 2000), made recommendations for incorporating core principles addressing stewardship, diverse pasts, social relevance, ethics and values, written and oral communication, fundamental archaeological skills, and problem solving using real world issues into the curriculum, beginning with undergraduate education. In a multi-year SAA project, "Making Archaeology Teaching Relevant in the XXI Century" (MATRIX), funded by the National Science Foundation and directed by Anne Pyburn (Indiana University), faculty at eight American colleges and universities developed a set of undergraduate anthropology courses designed to provide a wide range of opportunities for students to learn about archaeology in all its diverse applications. The MATRIX courses have been reviewed and tested and are available online (see Making Archaeology Teaching Relevant in the XXI Century in the references cited). An expansion of the project to include more indigenous and global perspectives is being undertaken.

The ongoing review and rethinking about archaeology in the larger context of cultural heritage led to plans for another gathering in 2005 that would focus on resource management and public policy issues in a more global context. It was clear that a successful dialogue needed to be multidisciplinary and geographically diverse. Invited participants were asked to look at the study, management, and preservation of archaeological and heritage sites around the world from multiple perspectives, taking into account politics, laws, tourism, and economic development among other conditions that make heritage management a global issue that cannot be adequately addressed by means of existing regional or national strategies and practices.

The working conference, Preserving the World's Heritage Resources, was organized by George Smith and Phyllis Messenger and held at Cumberland Island National Seashore, Georgia, in November 2005. Participants were divided into two working groups, focused on public policy and resource management. The public policy group was chaired by William Jansen, with participants including María Luz Endere, Patrick O'Keefe, Barbara Miller, Patty Gerstenblith, Anne Pyburn, and Lori Jahnke (recorder). The resource management group was chaired by Hester Davis, with participants including Willem Willems, Kirk Cordell, David Morgan, Neil Brodie, Brijesh Thapa, and Erin Kuns (recorder). Through the sharing of position papers, dialogues, and informal collaboration, each working group identified and examined areas in which archaeologists can work more effectively with their colleagues in other disciplines and institutions to manage heritage resources and participate in public policy making and implementation.

Outcomes from the working groups included drafts of recommendations, best practices, and proposed action items to be discussed and further refined in multiple venues, including professional conferences and other international gatherings, with the hope that these recommendations might help identify and shape future steps by individuals, organizations, and governmental agencies, as well as influence future research questions and training programs. Papers and symposia related to the Preserving the World's Heritage Resources working conference have been presented at conferences of the SAA, the World Archaeological Congress, the Society for Historical Archaeology, the European Archaeological Society, the Ename Center, and others. In addition, a follow-up working conference on defining, measuring, and teaching heritage values took place at Cumberland Island in November 2007, and a separate volume, *Heritage Values in Contemporary Society*, is being published by Left Coast Press.

Cultural Heritage Management: A Global Perspective is based on papers prepared for the conference in 2005 and additional papers solicited to address cultural heritage management in a global context. In selecting contributions dealing with cultural heritage management, we sought to provide a broad geographic and governmental base for discussion. As a result, contributions from 14 countries and several regions are included, representing Africa, North America, Mesoamerica, South America, Europe, Asia, and Oceania, with various forms of government, including democracies, republics, constitutional monarchies, and communist states. Other authors address public policy issues related to international development and finance, indigenous and postcolonial stakeholders, international law, and tourism. In addition to the workshop participants named above, the editors wish to thank these authors who contributed additional chapters to this volume: Heather Burke, Claire Smith, Paulo DeBlasis, David Pokotylo, Andrew Mason, Chen Shen, Hong Chen, S. B. Ota, Katsuyuki Okamura, Akira Matsuda, Nelly Robles García, Jack Corbett, Jorge Silva, Zbigniew Kobyliński, Nick Petrov, Janette Deacon, Thanik Lertcharnrit, Arlene Fleming, and Ian Campbell. We also wish to thank Peter Stone for graciously agreeing to write a foreword, and Paul A. Shackel, the series editor, and John Byram and the University Press of Florida staff for their support and encouragement.

Without the financial and in-kind support of several institutions, the Preserving the World's Heritage Resources conference and this volume would not have been possible. They include the Southeast Archeological Center (SEAC), Hamline University, Cumberland Island National Seashore, the National Center for Preservation Technology and Training, and SRI Foundation, all in the United States; and Halach Winik Travel Agency in Quintana Roo, Mexico.

The editors wish to thank Jerre Brumbelow, the superintendent of Cumberland Island National Seashore, and his staff for their assistance during the workshop in 2005. Thanks also to Chuck Lawson and Steven Kidd of the SEAC for assistance with logistics, and John Ehrenhard, the former director of the SEAC, for sharing his culinary skills. Elizabeth Tarkenton, a former editor with the SEAC, assisted with preliminary versions of chapters, and Professor Lewis C. "Skip" Messenger of Hamline University provided stellar editorial support during his sabbatical leave in 2007–2008 and beyond. His sharp eye and bibliographic research skills significantly added to the overall quality of the book.

A word about language and terminology is in order. The original title of this project, "Preserving the World's Heritage Resources," became a matter of discussion as we circulated chapter drafts among the expanded group of authors. After reading Burke and Smith's chapter on Australian heritage management, the editors suggested modifying the title phrase to "Cultural Heritage Management" to reflect several major points addressed in Burke and Smith's chapter, as well as in other discussions (see the introduction). Two points in their argument were particularly germane to our consideration of the title. The first was that "heritage" implies conservation, whereas "resource" implies use or even exploitation. The second was that the use of "cultural heritage" represents more than just a change in terms. It encapsulates a shift in attitude about the purposes of management, the inclusion of multiple stakeholders, and the outcomes of managing a system that may be largely composed of someone else's heritage, as is the case in the United States, Australia, and numerous other countries. It is this shift in attitude that we think is an important part of the book. However, as discussion in the introduction attests, there are many nuances to this topic, and in the end we encouraged authors to use language that best reflected their own experience, context, and current thinking.

In keeping with our desire to support the expanding network of colleagues engaged in these conversations, we have assigned all royalties from the sale of this book to the World Archaeological Congress (WAC) in support of travel scholarships to WAC conferences for participants from indigenous communities and developing nations.

References Cited

Bender, Susan J. and George S. Smith (editors)
2000   *Teaching Archaeology in the Twenty-first Century.* SAA, Washington, D.C.
"Making Archaeology Teaching Relevant in the XXI Century (MATRIX)." Electronic
        document, http://www.indiana.edu/~arch/saa/matrix/homepage.html, accessed
        April 19, 2009.
Society for American Archaeology (SAA)
1990   *Save the Past for the Future: Actions for the '90s.* SAA, Washington, D.C.
1995   *Save the Past for the Future II: Report of the Working Conference.* SAA, Washington, D.C.

Introduction

PHYLLIS MAUCH MESSENGER AND GEORGE S. SMITH

This book represents a particular moment in time in the global discussion of issues related to the world's cultural heritage. It captures the voices of a cross-section of archaeologists, anthropologists, and other professionals from 17 nations and every continent who are engaged in the study, management, protection, and interpretation of places and objects that represent histories, traditions, and cultural identities. Some of the contributors work on heritage management at the regional or national level; others work in the international arena in areas of law, development, and policy making.

The project out of which this book emerged seeks to encourage the ongoing discussion about the management, protection, and value of cultural heritage by providing examples of various histories and current approaches, including perspectives not usually heard in the English-language discourse. While the international discussion of heritage management issues has developed only in recent decades, it builds upon the work of many others (for example, Carman 2005; Cleere 1989, 1984; Green 1984; International Council on Monuments and Sites [ICOMOS] 1964; Johnson and Schene 1987; King et al. 1977; Layton 1989a, 1989b; Lipe and Lindsay 1974; McGimsey 1972; McManamon and Hatton 2000; Messenger 1999; Meyer 1973; Schiffer and Gumerman 1977; Smith and McManamon 1988; U.S. House of Representatives, One Hundredth Congress 1988). Until 1984, according to Cleere, there was almost no international debate on heritage management issues; instead, heritage issues were largely organized by each country's laws, administrative traditions, and procedures. As Fairclough notes, "The current more comprehensive scope of heritage has been reached over the past century or so by incremental expansion. In the UK, for example, the first state-endorsed definition of the archaeological heritage [in 1882] . . . was concerned almost only with major prehistoric monuments" (2008:297). The definition has slowly expanded to include standing buildings, non-monumental heritage, landscapes, contemporary, and even intangible heritage.

International conventions have sought to codify common understandings of language and meaning as the scope of heritage expands. Article I of UNESCO's Convention Concerning the Protection of the World Cultural and Natural

Heritage of 1972 provided one definition of what is considered to be tangible "cultural heritage." It included monuments, groups of buildings, and sites of outstanding universal value from the historical, aesthetic, ethnological, or anthropological point of view (see United Nations Educational, Scientific and Cultural Organization [UNESCO] 1972). The Council of Europe Framework Convention on the Value of Cultural Heritage for Society of 2005 states that "cultural heritage is a group of resources inherited from the past which people identify, independently of ownership, as a reflection and expression of their constantly evolving values, beliefs, knowledge and traditions." (See Fairclough et al. 2008, for essays on the widening discussion of what constitutes heritage.)

While there is a growing tendency to use the term "cultural heritage" in referring to the material evidence of culture (cf. Hoffman 2006; Schofield 2008), there are many variations in language that reflect differences in geography, political and colonial histories, professional practice, and tradition. The term "cultural resource management" came into widespread use by archaeologists in the United States, for example, with the passage of legislation in the 1960s (see Davis, this volume). The term "cultural property," widely used in the twentieth century, has been largely replaced by "cultural heritage," as Western notions of "property" and "ownership" are increasingly challenged by indigenous belief systems that view cultural objects as interconnected with society (for example, see Messenger 1999; and Endere, and Morgan, both this volume). In Australia, a move from "cultural resource management" to "cultural heritage management" reflects a paradigm shift from the concept of use and exploitation to one of conservation and acknowledgment of other, nonwestern, ways of viewing the past (see Burke and Smith, this volume). Others intentionally keep the language of "resources" (see Willems, this volume), noting that "heritage" can sometimes become a static concept that argues for in situ preservation at all costs, thus not allowing for the integration and use of the past in the present. And for many, it is the relationship between concepts of resources and heritage that reflect larger issues of identity, economic development, and nationalism (for example, see Petrov, Brodie, and Thapa, all in this volume).

The authors in this volume discuss the history and current status of cultural heritage research and preservation in countries around the world. They discuss strategies in place for enlisting the fiscal and human resources of developers, national and local governments, communities, nongovernmental agencies, professional organizations, funding agencies, researchers, and others for effective resource management. They address the impact of policies and strategies, financing, and development on heritage resources. They contribute to the development and promotion of a cultural sector as an advocate for heritage that insures input at the level where policy crafting, resource allocation, and planning of government assistance and collaboration take place. Their rich and detailed narratives, which uncover both commonalities and disagreements, make an important contribution to the development of a robust theoretical framework that encompasses the broadest conception of heritage, as discussed by Ahmad (2006), Carman (2000), Harvey (2001), and Smith (2000, 2008), among others.

Many of the authors in this volume focus on heritage management at the national level, representing distinct political structures, from democracies and republics to constitutional monarchies and communist governments. Discussion of national and regional histories of heritage management elucidates the impact of cultural, historical, geographic, political, and economic variations in how management practices have developed, and how they are described. The development of heritage management and protection practices in some countries has a history spanning several centuries. Ota discusses India's rich history of heritage laws beginning in the early 1800s; Pokotylo and Mason trace Canada's laws from the late 1800s. The history of cultural resource management in many other countries is much shorter, as discussed by Endere for Argentina, DeBlasis for Brazil, and Silva for Peru. National laws sometimes have unintended consequences. For example, Davis describes how the creation of the field of cultural resource management in the United States in response to new historic preservation laws in the 1960s and 1970s caused a split (real or perceived) among practitioners of archaeology in academic positions and the applied field.

In some countries, heritage management is closely tied to political history or land ownership practices. In Russia, the state continues to assert control over archaeological and heritage sites, even with the recent introduction of the concept of private property, according to Petrov. Burke and Smith discuss how the history of government interactions with indigenous peoples continues to play a significant role in how preservation laws are constructed. Deacon describes how the South African Heritage Resources Agency was established in 2000 to address past inequities created by colonialism and apartheid. In the United States, as discussed by Davis, private ownership of land and individual rights generally trump all else.

Authors discuss how the study and management of heritage developed in their countries and how heritage work is organized. Twentieth-century political upheavals and regime changes have greatly affected policies, for example, in South Africa (see Deacon), Russia (see Petrov), and Poland (see Kobyliński). In Mexico, according to Robles García and Corbett, a fierce nationalism created a strong national archaeology program, but it also tends to place blinders on established institutions, impeding their ability to change with the times. The formation of regional alliances, such as the European Union, has an impact on heritage policies and practices, according to Willems, as does the dismantling of political entities, such as the Soviet Union, as described by Petrov and Kobyliński.

Authors discuss the impact of economic conditions on the development and sustainability of heritage studies and management. Infrastructure development and economic growth can both support and outpace preservation policies and practices. In China, for example, the development of the Three Gorges Dam and the South-North Water Project threaten to destroy both known and unknown heritage sites faster than mandated practices can study or protect them, according to Shen and Chen. Recession can turn the heritage sector upside down. Okamura and Matsuda consider the case of Japan, whose well-developed archaeological heritage management infrastructure was severely challenged by the bursting of the economic bubble in the 1990s, offering important insights for the heritage sector in the first decades of the twenty-first century, as the effects of the current global economic crisis manifest themselves at all levels of the cultural heritage sector.

Preservation philosophies are influenced by religious beliefs, as well as politics. In Thailand, according to Lertcharnrit, the country's Buddhist practices are carried out seamlessly at ancient sites where Buddha images are re-dressed, renewed, and rebuilt as needed. And of course, the practices and beliefs of indigenous cultures, and how they are acknowledged and accounted for in heritage management policies, continue to have a major impact in many countries, including Argentina, Australia, Brazil, Canada, Mexico, Peru, and the United States.

Authors also address policies and issues that influence the management of cultural heritage not only within the borders of individual countries but within the broader global community. For this volume, policy is defined as actions undertaken by governments (national, subnational or local), organizations (public or private, multinational, national or local), and private sector entities or civic groups. Policies can exist at different levels or realms of influence in reference to heritage. For example, some grand policies may set goals or ideals and define what should be done, while others may state how those goals should be attained. The existence or absence of either level of policy can affect how well cultural heritage management activities unfold.

Several authors focus on how existing policies of governments and large multinational funding organizations affect resource allocation related to cultural heritage issues. Jansen discusses how organizations such as the World Bank and USAID contribute to cultural heritage protection through programs focused on economic growth and poverty reduction. Fleming and Campbell make a plea for those responsible for cultural heritage to evolve from custodians of the past to become an integral part of the modern construct for socioeconomic development and environmental management, especially by making full use of the environmental impact assessment tools already in place in the policies of the World Bank and the International Finance Corporation.

In the legal arena, O'Keefe discusses the various international conventions and resolutions related to cultural property and urges that their content be incorporated into national and international public policies. Brodie discusses the relationships affecting economic value and cultural heritage in a global economy, while Thapa addresses issues of funding for World Heritage sites in lesser developed countries.

Several authors address archaeologists' and heritage managers' evolving roles in accountability to various publics. Endere discusses the impact of Latin American state formation on indigenous access to and control over their sacred places. Morgan addresses the difficulties faced by legislators, practitioners, and communities in honoring indigenous concepts of culture and heritage within a national framework.

Willems's discussion of the status of archaeology and heritage management in Europe presents a contrasting story of long traditions of highly developed management practices, each influenced by different languages, laws, and academic traditions. While the European Union intentionally does not have a common policy on cultural heritage, it does provide financing for the inclusion of archaeological concerns in environmental impact assessments, consistent with the practices of international funding agencies as discussed by Fleming and Campbell. Some current developments in management practices in Europe reflect similarities with discussions of national practices described by other authors and suggest both opportunities and concerns for defining and managing cultural heritage in countries with less well-developed histories of concern for heritage. In Europe today there is a movement toward contextualizing sites and monuments as part of a larger whole, that is, studying and managing the historic environment in terms of history and present-day relevance (see also Morgan's discussion of National Heritage Areas in the United States).

What the authors in this volume make clear is that, regardless of geography, economics, or politics, connecting to our past through material remains and the stories they represent is a powerful and important human experience. The language and actions we use to describe cultural heritage and to represent its relationship to stakeholders are important in an era of emerging postcolonial nations, growing regional identities, and globalization. Countries, regions, and institutions with more advanced heritage management practices are aiding those in need of assistance. International laws and agreements are providing increased safeguarding of heritage sites and are allowing for repatriation of cultural objects. Nevertheless, regional conflicts often are fraught with ethnic and cultural conflicts, and symbols of cultural heritage are targeted for eradication or reinvention. Renowned museums and world-class sites can still fall victim to armed conflict, dictatorial regimes, or the wrecking ball of development. Even in a democratic society, cultural heritage will be protected and managed only if there are laws, public policies, well-trained professionals, and sufficient public interest to do so.

References Cited

Ahmad, Yahaya
2006 The Scope and Definitions of Heritage: From Tangible to Intangible. *International Journal of Heritage Studies* 12(3):292–300.

Carman, John
2000 "Theorising a Realm of Practice": Introducing Archaeological Heritage Management as a Research Field. *International Journal of Heritage Studies* 6(4):303–308.
2005 *Against Cultural Property: Archaeology, Heritage and Ownership*. Duckworth and Company, London.

Cleere, Henry L.
1989 *Archaeological Heritage Management in the Modern World*. Unwin Hyman Ltd., London.

Cleere, Henry L. (editor)
1984 *Approaches to the Archaeological Heritage: A Comparative Study of World Cultural Resource Management Systems*. Cambridge University Press, Cambridge.

Council of Europe
2005 Faro Framework Convention on the Value of Cultural Heritage for Society. Electronic document, http://conventions.coe.int/Treaty/EN/Treaties/Html/199.htm, accessed April 18, 2009.

Fairclough, Graham
2008 New Heritage, an Introductory Essay—People, Landscape and Change. In *The Heritage Reader*, edited by Graham Fairclough, Rodney Harrison, John H. Jameson, Jr., and John Schofield, pp. 297–312. Routledge, London.

Fairclough, Graham, Rodney Harrison, John H. Jameson, Jr., and John Schofield (editors)
2008 *The Heritage Reader*. Routledge, London.

Green, Ernestene L.
1984 *Ethics and Values in Archaeology*. Free Press, New York.

Harvey, David C.
2001 Heritage Pasts and Heritage Presents: Temporality, Meaning and the Scope of Heritage Studies. *Journal of Heritage Studies* 7(4):319–38.

Hoffman, Barbara
2006 Introduction: Exploring and Establishing Links for a Balanced Art and Cultural Heritage Policy. In *Art and Cultural Heritage: Law, Policy and Practice*, edited by Barbara Hoffman, pp. 1–18. Cambridge University Press, Cambridge.

International Council on Monuments and Sites (ICOMOS)
1964 *International Charter for the Conservation and Restoration of Monuments and Sites (The Venice Charter)*. ICOMOS.

Johnson, Ronald W., and Michael G. Schene
1987 *Cultural Resources Management*. Robert E. Krieger Publishing Company, Malabar, Fla.

King, Thomas R., Patricia Parker Hickman, and Gary Berg
1977 *Anthropology in Historic Preservation: Caring for Culture's Clutter*. Academic
    Press, New York.
Layton, Robert (editor)
1989a *Conflicts in the Archaeology of Living Traditions*. Routledge, London.
1989b *Who Needs the Past: Indigenous Values and Archaeology*. Routledge, London.
Lipe, William D., and Alexander J. Lindsay, Jr. (editors)
1974 *Proceedings of the 1974 Cultural Resource Management Conference, Federal Center,
    Denver, Colorado*. Northern Arizona Society of Science and Art, Flagstaff.
McGimsey, Charles R., III.
1972 *Public Archaeology*. Seminar Press, New York.
McManamon, Francis P., and Alf Hatton
2000 *Cultural Resource Management in Contemporary Society: Perspectives on
    Managing and Presenting the Past*. Routledge: London.
Messenger, Phyllis Mauch (editor)
1999 *The Ethics of Collecting Cultural Property: Whose Culture? Whose Property?* 2nd
    ed. University of New Mexico Press, Albuquerque.
Meyer, Karl E.
1973 *The Plundered Past*. Atheneum, New York.
Schiffer, Michael B., and George J. Gumerman
1977 *Conservation Archaeology: A Guide for Cultural Resource Management Studies*.
    Academic Press, New York.
Schofield, John
2008 Heritage Management, Theory and Practice. In *The Heritage Reader*, edited by
    Graham Fairclough, Rodney Harrison, John H. Jameson, Jr., and John Scho-
    field, pp. 16–30. Routledge, London.
Smith, George S., and Francis P. McManamon
1988 *Archeology and the Federal Government*. CRM Bulletin 11, special issue.
Smith, Laurajane
2000 "Doing Archaeology": Cultural Heritage Management and Its Role in Identifying
    the Link Between Archaeological Practice and Theory. *International Journal of
    Heritage Studies* 6(4):309–16.
2008 Towards a Theoretical Framework for Archaeological Heritage Management. In
    The Heritage Reader, edited by Graham Fairclough, Rodney Harrison, John H.
    Jameson, Jr., and John Schofield, pp. 62–74. Routledge, London.
United Nations Educational, Scientific and Cultural Organization (UNESCO)
1972 Convention Concerning the Protection of the World Cultural and Natural Heri-
    tage. Electronic document, http://whc.unesco.org/archive/convention-en.pdf,
    accessed May 30, 2008.
U.S. House of Representatives, One Hundredth Congress
1988 *The Destruction of America's Archaeological Heritage: Looting and Vandalism of
    Indian Archaeological Sites in the Four Corners States of the Southwest*. U.S.
    Government Printing Office, Washington, D.C.

1

The Challenge of Protecting
Archaeological Heritage in Argentina

MARÍA LUZ ENDERE

Argentina is a federal republic divided into 23 provinces and the autonomous government of Buenos Aires. According to its National Constitution, natural and cultural resources, including cultural heritage, are part of the provincial domain, although they are also under national jurisdiction. This means that they should be ruled by national and provincial legislation and controlled by both national and provincial authorities.

This chapter presents a brief review of the extant legislation applied to archaeological cultural heritage and to indigenous communities regarding heritage issues in Argentina. Problems and contested situations generated by the application of these laws in everyday life are also discussed. Concluding comments address the next steps that Argentina should take in order to put into practice its constitutional obligations, as well as those deriving from the international conventions ratified by the country.[1]

The Legal and Administrative Framework
of Cultural Heritage Protection

In 1913, Law 9080 (no longer enforced) placed archaeological and palaeontological resources under federal jurisdiction. In 1968, the Argentinean National Civil Code established that archaeological heritage of scientific value belongs to the public domain of the nation (Civil Code, article 2340, clause 9), regardless of whether the resources are located on public or private lands. This means that the national government had assumed the legal authority and responsibility for their protection.

In 1994, an amendment of the National Constitution solved the conflicts between federal and provincial laws with respect to ownership and jurisdiction over archaeological resources. The new constitution recognized provincial ownership over archaeological heritage and stated that the national government has the duty to develop policies for the management and protection of this heritage in coordination with provinces (article 41).

In 1999, the Register of the National Cultural Heritage was created by Federal Law 25.197, which established the need to carry out an inventory of cultural property, including "the materials recovered through terrestrial and underwater archaeological and palaeontological surveys and excavations" (article 2). Finally in 2003, a new law concerning the protection of archaeological and palaeontological resources was passed (Law 25.743).

This law, which replaced the antiquated Law 9080, stipulates that the preservation, protection, and control over archaeological and palaeontological resources is part of the national cultural heritage in order to enable their scientific and cultural exploitation. Law 25.743 created new national authorities to protect these resources in federal lands (that is, the Instituto Nacional de Antropología y Pensamiento Latinoamericano [National Institute of Anthropology and Latin American Thought] is in charge of the protection of archaeological resources and the Bernardino Rivadavia National Natural Sciences Museum is responsible for palaeontological remains). It has also distributed responsibilities between the national government and the provinces and has created a register of sites and collections as well as one for law offenders.

At the subnational level, legal protection of cultural heritage is quite variable. Only some provinces have updated their cultural heritage legislation in the last few years (for example, the provinces of Mendoza, Law 6034/93; Chubut, Law 3559, Decree 1387/98; Tierra del Fuego, Law 370/97; and Santa Cruz, Law 2472/97). However, some of these laws are not being applied because the necessary decrees have not yet been enacted (for example, Tierra del Fuego and Santa Cruz). This is complicated by the fact that most of them were enacted before Federal Law 25.743 (an exception is the new Law 7500/05 of Tucumán Province). However, many provinces have already signed agreements with national authorities in order to update and coordinate their policies and actions according to the new federal law. To complicate the complex Argentinean legal structure for cultural resources protection even more, local (municipal) governments have also enacted their own rules (called "*ordenanzas*") to preserve archaeological sites located in their territories (Endere 2000).

As a consequence, the legal framework of archaeological heritage protection in Argentina is the result of a mosaic of local, provincial, and national laws that create separate governing bodies. This makes it necessary to carry out a case-by-case study in order to determine the legislation applicable at each particular site. The lack of a clear national heritage management policy—to be applied throughout the territory in accordance with provincial authorities—results in preservation actions without coordination between different governmental levels or continuity through time. Thus, accomplishments depend exclusively on decisions of the particular authority in charge.

Furthermore, natural and cultural heritage is artificially divided into different governing bodies ruled by diverse legislation (see also Burke and Smith, this volume). As a result, despite the statements of Law 25.743, archaeological resources may be under the jurisdiction of other authorities. For example, if these sites have been declared "national monuments," they are also governed by the National Monument Commission, or if sites are located in national parks or natural reserves, they must be protected by the National Park Service. Thus, cultural and natural heritage is frequently managed by cultural, environmental, or tourist authorities, which seldom act in coordination. This division is often reproduced at provincial and local levels, making it extremely difficult to put into practice comprehensive protection programs for cultural and natural resources.

Argentina has ratified several conventions of the United Nations Educational, Scientific and Cultural Organization (UNESCO), including the Convention for the Protection of Cultural Property in the Event of Armed Conflict (The Hague, 1954) and the First and Second Protocols (1954 and 1999) by Federal Laws 19.943/72 and 25.478/99; the Convention on the Means of Prohibiting and Preventing the Illicit Import, Export and Transfer of Ownership of Cultural Property (Paris, 1970) by Federal Law 19.943/72; the Convention Concerning the Protection of the World Cultural and Natural Heritage (Paris, 1972) by Federal Law 21.836/78; and the Convention for the Safeguarding of the Intangible Cultural Heritage (Paris, 2003) by Federal Law 26.118/06. Furthermore, Argentina has voted in favor of the adoption of the Convention on the Protection of the Underwater Cultural Heritage (Paris, 2001), although it has not yet been ratified by law. Argentina also ratified the International Institute for the Unification of Private Law (UNIDROIT) Convention on Stolen or Illegally Exported Cultural Objects (Rome, 1995) by Federal Law 25.257/2000 and the Convention on the Protection of the Archaeological, Historical and Artistic Heritage of the American Nations (San Salvador, 1976) by Federal Law 25.568/02. However, Argentina still needs to improve its legislation by enacting a new set of policies to make them agree with these conventions.

The ratification of the UNIDROIT Convention had a significant impact on the struggle against illegal trafficking in Argentina. In 2000, a federal judge, using this convention and the outdated Law 9080, ordered two police raids on offices of antique dealers in Buenos Aires. As a result, 15,000 archaeological specimens were confiscated, some of them brought from Peru and Colombia. For decades, looting and robbery, together with the increasing value of archaeological pieces in international trade, have threatened the preservation of archaeological sites and collections in Argentina (Schávelzon 2002). However, until the year 2000 there had not been any record of court proceedings in cases of illegal trafficking despite the fact that Argentina had not only developed an important internal trade network, but had also become the place from which archaeological specimens from all over South America were taken out of the continent.[2] In 2003, the national government organized a special committee to deal with the illicit traffic of cultural objects. The aim of this committee is to coordinate actions between different national and international agencies, including the secretary of culture, security forces, and International Council on Monuments and Sites (ICOMOS).

It is worth noting that the process of gradual integration between Argentina and the neighboring countries of Brazil, Uruguay, and Paraguay, known as Mercosur, has focused not only on economic policies, but also on cultural matters. In the context of the so-called Mercosur cultural (Alvarez and Reyes 1999), a number of general policies have been adopted, although Mercosur has not yet had any significant impact on heritage issues.

Indigenous Claims and Legal Recognition

The existence of indigenous peoples has been historically neglected in Argentina (Serbín 1981; Slavsky 1992). However, a census of the indigenous population carried out between 2004 and 2005 has demonstrated the existence of descendants of 21 different native groups (Ava Guaraní, Chané, Charrúa, Chorote, Chulupí, Comechingón, Diaguita/Diaguita calchaquí, Guaraní, Huarpe, Kolla, Mapuche, Mbya Guaraní, Mocoví, Ona, Pillagá, Rankulche, Tapiete, Tehuelche, Toba, Tupí Guaraní, and Wichi). More than 485,000 inhabitants identified themselves as belonging to an indigenous community or as direct descendants of indigenous peoples. This means that at least 1.34 percent of the total Argentinean population consider themselves to belong to an indigenous group (see Encuesta complementaria de Pueblos Indígenas 2004; Población por pueblo indígena y región muestral, años 2004–2005).

The return to democracy in 1983, after several decades of dictatorship, marked a turning point in official ideology toward the acknowledgment of indigenous peoples. The idea of being a "multicultural society" was emphasized both in political speeches and educational curricula (Podgorny 1999). The new legislation of indigenous communities (Law 23.515/85) and, later, the amendments to the National Constitution (article 75, clause 17) have resulted in the recognition of a new set of civil rights regarding indigenous communities, thus generating new responsibilities for the nation-state (Carrasco 2000).

Constitutional rights include respect for the indigenous identity and indigenous peoples' right "to participate in the matters of their interests," which may include issues related to their cultural heritage (Endere 2000:56). Moreover, in 2000 Argentina ratified the 169 International Labor Organization (ILO) Convention Concerning Indigenous and Tribal Peoples in Independent Countries, which states that "governments shall consult the peoples concerned, whenever consideration is being given to legislative or administrative measures which may affect them directly" and shall also "establish means by which these peoples can freely participate at all levels of decision-making in elective institutions and administrative and other bodies responsible for policies and programs which concern them" (article 6, clauses a and b) (Hualpa 2003).

These changes have considerably improved the legal situation of indigenous peoples in Argentina although they are not always perceived in their everyday life. Many of them hardly enjoy minimal standards of food and health, particularly those living in rural areas or in the rainforest of provinces such as Salta, Chaco, and Formosa. Some provincial governments are especially reticent to give property rights for land with mineral or farming potential to the indigenous communities that have traditionally inhabited them, even when these communities have the constitutional right to claim them.

Regarding their cultural heritage, several indigenous groups have been campaigning in the last few decades for the repatriation of indigenous human remains of famous chiefs held in museums (Podgorny and Miotti 1994; Podgorny and Politis 1992). However, since these remains are part of national archaeological collections, their restitution must be mandated by law. As a consequence, only two chiefs have been successfully returned to their communities. In 1991, the first law of repatriation ordered that the remains of the Tehuelche chief Inakayal be returned to his homeland in Tecka, Chubut Province (Federal Law 23.940). The restitution was not carried out until 1994, as many bureaucratic problems had to be overcome, along with political and academic resistance. The second law authorized the return of the remains of the Rankulche chief Panquitruz Güor—better known by his Christian name Mariano Rosas—from the La Plata Museum to the Rankulche community in La Pampa Province (Federal Law 25.276/2000). His remains were delivered in an official ceremony of reparation to the Rankulche people in 2001 (Endere 2002, 2005a).

In 2001, a general law concerning repatriation was passed. It states that the human remains held in museums must be delivered to the indigenous peoples or communities that have claimed them (Federal Law 25.517/01, article 1). The law also declares that those human remains that have not been claimed may continue to be under the custody of the museums and institutions that have kept them, although they must be treated with respect according to their condition (article 2). It finally states that any scientific activity that involves indigenous communities, including their historic and cultural heritage, should previously be agreed upon with those communities (article 3). This law has not come into force because the necessary decree has not yet been enacted.

Finally the new Federal Law 25.743 concerning archaeological and palaeontological heritage has not made any provision on indigenous peoples' rights to their own cultural heritage, thus generating a deep sense of unease among several indigenous leaders who have claimed that this law contradicts constitutional rules.

The Role of Archaeologists Regarding Heritage Issues and Their Relationship with Indigenous Peoples

Argentinean archaeologists have traditionally been concerned with academic research and teaching in universities. There are not many archaeologists working in contract archaeology due to the scarce number of archaeological impact assessments requested by authorities, with the exception of those demanded before performing mining activities. As a result, not many professionals work as private consultants or develop permanent activities related to public archaeology. Not surprisingly, these issues have not attracted much attention in the archaeological debate.

In the last few years, attention has focused on legal weaknesses and administrative obstacles that affect not only the protection of sites but also the sustainability of the archaeological work (for example, Berberián 1992, 2000; Endere and Politis 2001; Molinari 1998). Several critical reports of the situation have been produced (for example, González 1982, 1991; Pérez Gollán 1991; Tarragó and Piñeiro 1995), some of them discussing how to implement mechanisms to control the quality of archaeological impact studies (Aschero 1998; Endere and Politis 2001; Ratto 1998). More general topics, such as the relationship between politics and archaeology in Argentina (Madrazo 1985; Politis 1992, 1995, 2006), as well as cultural policies and uses of the past, were also explored, but these studies tend to discuss what happened in the past more than what is going on in the present (Cortegoso and Chiavazza 2003; Manasse and Rabey 1989; Podgorny 2000; Podgorny and Miotti 1994). As a result, relatively few researchers have discussed the theoretical framework of the archaeological heritage management system in Argentina in order to develop alternative models (Delfino and Rodríguez 1992; Endere 2007; Haber 2005a; Politis 2006).

Concerning the relationship between archaeologists and indigenous communities, two contested situations have attracted the attention of both groups and encouraged the debate on indigenous rights to cultural heritage. The first was the exhibition of the Llullaillaco's Inca mummies (see Reinhard 1999) at a museum in Salta Province, a project planned by the provincial authorities without regard for the strong criticism that it generated among indigenous groups, many archaeologists, and even national cultural authorities, who expressed the need to respect the feelings of those who believe in the sacredness of these mummies (Endere 2005a; Politis 2001). The second case was motivated by the apparently disastrous consequences that the nomination of the Quebrada de Humahuaca as a World Heritage site has brought to the local people, as well as to cultural and natural resources. Many local people have complained to the authorities, alleging that they failed to implement the necessary measures to prevent the transfer of lands traditionally occupied by local people to the hands of private investors and to mitigate the impact of massive tourism. The debate also attracted the attention of anthropologists and archaeologists who discussed not only the facts but also their own role as social scientists (see Belli and Slavutsky 2005; Endere 2005b; Haber 2005b).

Nevertheless, some improvements have occurred in the relationship between archaeologists and indigenous peoples, at least in some areas of the country. Examples of mutual collaboration include archaeologists and historians working with the Rankulche people in La Pampa (Endere and Curtoni 2006); joint projects such as the In Situ Museum of Añelo in Neuquén Province, which is under the custody of the Painemil Mapuche community (Biset 1989; Cúneo 2004); and joint management of a sacred site at the Lanín National Park by the park's authorities and the Ñorquinco Mapuche Community (Molinari 2000).

Moreover, a first national meeting among archaeologists and indigenous peoples to discuss common concerns was held in Río Cuarto, Córdoba, in May 2005, and an agreement of mutual understanding was reached (see Canuhé 2005; Pérez Gollán 2005). At present, some indigenous leaders are actively participating in scientific meetings and getting involved in discussions about the legal and intellectual ownership of indigenous cultural heritage.

The Qhapac Ñan Project and the Agenda for the Next Few Years

In 2003 representatives of the governments of Argentina, Bolivia, Colombia, Chile, Ecuador, and Peru met in Lima to advance the initiative to nominate the Qhapac Ñan—Camino Principal Andino (the pre-Hispanic Andean road system)[3] for inscription on the World Heritage List. Today, the Qhapac Ñan has become a multidisciplinary and long-term project that involves part of the most significant natural, cultural, tangible, and intangible heritage of those countries. It has also required the participation of almost 300 researchers from different disciplines and the celebration of a number of agreements among governments, including issues related to the legal protection of their cultural, natural, and intangible heritage. Some countries have also enacted specific laws to regulate and protect the Andean road system and associated values in their own countries.

Argentina seems to be actively and enthusiastically involved in this project. However, its particular legal system represents the major weakness for the protection of the Andean road system since it is in the hands of each of the provinces affected by the project to enact their own separate laws to protect this heritage in their territories. In this sense, the nomination of the Qhapac Ñan means a new challenge for the Argentinean national authorities, who will have to overcome a number of legal and political obstacles between provinces, as well as between natural heritage and cultural heritage authorities. They will need to build a dialogue among all of them, as well as with the involved communities.

Conclusion

The inability of heritage legislation and policymakers to achieve their goals is not exclusively the consequence of financial problems, as is often suggested. Most current laws are not the result of a clear policy on heritage matters but are the product of sporadic inclusion of archaeology on some legislators' agendas, often promoted by archaeologists' lobbying ability, or by a spectacular discovery.

The success or failure of the heritage system, however, must be analyzed in the context of a wider scenario in which authorities must face multiple political and economic crises. In this context, not only are indigenous groups starting to challenge the national state, but the whole civil society is questioning the way that democratic authorities have conducted public affairs in the last few decades.

From 1913, when the first heritage law was passed, until today, national and provincial states have proved to be inefficient and bureaucratic in the protection of archaeological heritage. A new set of laws that integrates natural, cultural, tangible, and intangible heritage and coordinates legal and administrative systems between national and provincial authorities is, without hesitation, the most urgent need. It also seems clear that changes in legal and administrative heritage systems should enable and encourage social participation to guarantee their long-term success. The empowerment of the institutions that represent different sectors of the population (that is, nongovernmental organizations, such as professional associations, indigenous groups, and community organizations) to participate in heritage issues in collaboration with local, provincial, and national governments should be necessary in order to create new commitments and responsibilities as well as new opportunities for dialogues about the protection of cultural heritage. This seems to be the only reasonable way to turn the "public heritage" into a matter of public concern and to give heritage "a function in the life of the communities" (as stated in 1972 by the UNESCO Convention, article 5, clause a).

Notes

1. This research has been funded by the Programme PATRIMONIA-INCUAPA (Núcleo de Investigaciones Arqueológicas y Paleontológicas del Cuarternario Pampeano) and Project PICT 2007–01563 (Agencia Nacional de Promoción de Científica y Tecnológia [ANPCyT] and the Universidad Nacional del Centro de la Provincia de Buenos Aires [UNICEN]).

2. See Mayor Fontana, Policía Aeronáutica, *Clarín*, July 29, 2001.

3. "The Qhapac Ñan or Camino Principal Andino is the denomination of the extensive communication networks of roads that in pre-Hispanic times connected the

territories of present day Colombia, Ecuador, Peru, Bolivia, Chile, and Argentina and that found culmination, as one integrated system, under the Inca rule. The system was composed of the roads themselves and associated architectural and engineering structures (lodging houses, storage facilities, bridges, etc.). It connected human settlements, administrative centres, agricultural and mining areas and religious and sacred places. Up to the present day, the road system passes through areas of high cultural value and natural bio-diversity" (Nomination of the Qhapac Ñan—Camino Inca).

References Cited

Alvarez, Marcelo, and Patricio Reyes
1999   El Patrimonio según el Mercosur (Heritage according to Mercosur). In *Temas de Patrimonio Cultural II* (Themes of cultural heritage II), edited by the Comisión para la preservación del Patrimonio Histórico-cultural de la Ciudad de Buenos Aires, pp. 95–107. EUDEBA, Buenos Aires.

Aschero, Carlos
1998   Arqueología y situaciones de impacto: Reflexiones sobre el Caso Tafí (Archaeology and impact situations: Reflections regarding the Tafi Case). *Mundo de Antes* 1:15–19.

Belli, Elena, and Ricardo Slavutsky
2005   Patrimonio: Territorio, objetos, símbolos, personas. ¿Cuál es la disputa? (Heritage: Territories, objects, symbols, people. Which is the dispute?) *Mundo de Antes* 4:13–17.

Berberián, Eduardo
1992   *La protección jurídica del patrimonio arqueológico en la República Argentina* (The legal protection of archaeological heritage in the Argentine Republic). Comechingonia, Córdoba.
2000   El patrimonio arqueológico nacional (The national archaeological heritage). *Investigaciones y ensayos* 50:547–60. Academia Nacional de la Historia, Buenos Aires.

Biset, Ana
1989   El Museo de Sitio de Añelo (The Añelo Site Museum). *Actas, Jornadas sobre el uso del pasado, Symposium Administración de Recursos y Manejo de Bienes Culturales Arqueológicos*, pp. 8–14. Universidad Nacional de La Plata, La Plata, Argentina.

Canuhé, Germán
2005   Comentario. Declaración de Río Cuarto. Primer Foro Pueblos Originarios—Arqueólogos. Río Cuarto, Argentina, May 2005 (Comments. Declaration of Rio Cuarto. First Forum, Original Peoples—archaeologists). *Revista de Arqueología Suramericana* 1(2): 288–89.

Carrasco, Morita
2000   *Los derechos de los pueblos indígenas en Argentina* (The rights of indigenous peoples in Argentina). Vinciguerra-IWGIA, Buenos Aires.

Cortegoso, Valeria, and Horacio Chiavazza

2003   Teoría y práctica arqueológica: Concepciones del pasado y sociedad en Mendoza, República Argentina (Archaeological theory and practice: Perceptions about past and society in Mendoza, Argentine Republic). In *Análisis, interpretación y gestión en la arqueología en Sudamérica* (Analysis, interpretation and management of archaeology in South America), edited by Rafael Curtoni and María Endere, 251–276. Serie de Teoría Arqueológica 2. INCUAPA, Universidad Nacional del Centro de la Provincia de Buenos Aires (UNCPBA), Olavarría.

Cúneo, Estela

2004   Huellas del pasado, miradas del presente: La construcción social del patrimonio arqueológico del Neuquén (Tracks from the past, views from the present: The social construction of archaeological heritage in Neuquén). *Intersecciones en Antropología* 5:81–94.

Delfino, Daniel, and Pablo Rodríguez

1992   La recreación del pasado y la invención del patrimonio arqueológico (The recreation of the past and the invention of archaeological heritage). *Publicar en Antropología y Ciencias Sociales* 2:29–68.

Encuesta complementaria de Pueblos Indígenas (Complementary survey of indigenous peoples)

2004   Electronic document, http://www.indec.gov.ar/encampo/indigenas.asp, accessed April 21, 2009.

Endere, María

2000   *Arqueología y legislación en Argentina: Cómo preservar el patrimonio arqueológico* (Archaeology and law in Argentina: How to preserve the archaeological heritage). Serie Monográfica INCUAPA Vol. 1. Departamento de Publicaciones de la UNCPBA, Tandil.

2002   The Reburial Issue in Argentina: A Growing Conflict. In *The Dead and Their Possessions: Repatriation in Principle, Policy and Practice*, edited by Cressida Forde, Jane Hubert, and Paul Turnbull, pp. 266–83. Routledge, London.

2005a   Talking about Others: Archaeologists, Indigenous Peoples and Heritage in Argentina. *Public Archaeology* 4:155–62. James and James, London.

2005b   Discusión del Ensayo de Opinión de Elena Belli y Ricardo Slavutsky, "Patrimonio: Territorio, objetos, símbolos, personas. ¿Cuál es la disputa?" (Comments on the essay written by Elena Belli and Ricardo Slavutsky, "Heritage: Territories, objects, symbols, people. Which is the dispute?") *Mundo de Antes* 4:18–20.

2007   *Management of Archaeological Sites and the Public in Argentina*. British Archaeological Research (BAR) Series, International Series 1708. Archaeopress, Oxford.

Endere, María, and Rafael Curtoni

2006   Entre lonkos y "archaeólogos": La participación de la comunidad indígena Rankülche de Argentina en la investigación arqueológica (Among indigenous chiefs and archaeologists: The participation of the indigenous community Rankülche of Argentina in archaeological research). *Revista de Arqueología Suramericana* 2(1):72–92.

Endere, María, and Gustavo Politis

2001   Cultural Resource Protection and Archaeological Research in Argentina: Between Bureaucracy and Inefficiency. In *Archaeological Research and Heritage Preservation in the Americas*, edited by Robert Drennan and Santiago Mora, pp. 69–75. Society for American Archaeology, Washington, D.C.

González, Alberto

1982   Arqueología de rescate en Sudamérica: Sumario de proyectos que se llevan a cabo (Rescue archaeology in South America: A review of current projects). In *Arqueología de Rescate* (Rescue archaeology), edited by Rex Wilson and Gloria Loyola, pp. 103–9. The Preservation Press, Washington, D.C.

1991   En el país del Nomeacuerdo: La situación del patrimonio cultural en la Argentina; El Testimonio de Rex González (In the country of no memory: The situation of cultural heritage in Argentina; The testimony of Rex González). *Ciencia Hoy* 3(16):33.

Haber, Alejandro (editor)

2005a   *Hacia una arqueología de las arqueologías sudamericanas* (Toward an archaeology of the South American archaeologies). Universidad de Los Andes, Facultad de Ciencias Sociales, Centro de Estudios Socioculturales e Internacionales (CESO), Bogotá.

2005b   Discusión del ensayo de Elena Belli y Ricardo Slavutsky, "Patrimonio: Territorio, objetos, símbolos, personas. ¿Cuál es la disputa?" (Comments on the essay written by Elena Belli and Ricardo Slavutsky, "Heritage: Territories, objects, symbols, people. Which is the dispute?") *Mundo de Antes* 4:21–22.

Hualpa, Eduardo

2003   *Sin despojos: Derecho a la participación mapuche-tehuelche* (Without remains: Mapuche-Tehuelche indigenous peoples' right to participation). Cuadernos de ENDEPA, Trelew.

Madrazo, Guillermo

1985   Determinantes y orientaciones de la antropología Argentina (Tendencies and approaches in Argentinean anthropology). *Boletín del Instituto Interdisciplinario Tilcara*, 13–56.

Manasse, Bárbara, and Mario Rabey

1989   El pasado en el conocimiento andino (The past in the Andean consciousness). *Actas, Jornadas sobre el Uso del Pasado, Simposio Administración de Recursos Arqueológicos y Manejo de Bienes Culturales Arqueológicos*, pp. 8–14. Universidad Nacional de La Plata, La Plata, Argentina.

Molinari, Roberto

1998   Orientaciones para la gestión y supervivencia de los recursos culturales: Proyecto de reglamento para la preservación del patrimonio cultural en areas protegidas de la administración de parques nacionales (Guidelines for cultural resource management and survival: Project for the preservation of cultural heritage in protected areas under the custody of the National Park Service). Paper presented in El Primer Congreso Virtual de Antropología y Arqueología, Facultad de Filosofía y Letras, Universidad de Buenos Aires (UBA), 1998. Electronic document, http://www.naya.org.ar/congreso/ponencia3–8.htm, accessed April 21, 2009.

2000   ¿Posesión o participación? El caso del Rewe de la comunidad Mapuche Ñorquinco (Parque Nacional Lanín, Provincia de Neuquén, Argentina) (Possession or participation? The case of the Rewe [sacred place] of the indigenous community Ñorquinco, National Park Lanín, Neuquén Province, Argentina). Paper presented at the Segundo Congreso Virtual de Antropología y Arqueología, Facultad de Filosofía y Letras, Universidad de Buenos Aires (UBA), October 2000. Electronic document, http://www.naya.org.ar/congreso 2000/, accessed April 21, 2009.

Nomination of the Qhapac Ñan—Camino Inca

2003   WHC-03/27.COM/INF.13:18. Electronic document, http://whc.unesco.org/archive/2003/whc03–27com-inf13e.rtf, accessed January 2, 2007.

Pérez Gollán, José

1991   En el país del Nomeacuerdo: La situación del patrimonio cultural en la Argentina; Mesa Redonda (In the country of I don't remember: The situation of cultural heritage in Argentina; Round table). *Ciencia Hoy* 3(16):32.

2005   Comentario. Declaración de Río Cuarto, 2005. Primer Foro Pueblos Originarios—Arqueólogos. Río Cuarto, Argentina, May 2005 (Comments to the Declaration of Rio Cuarto. First native peoples—archaeologists' forum). *Revista de Arqueología Suramericana* 1(2):290–303.

Población por pueblo indígena y región muestral, años 2004–2005 (Population by indigenous town and region sample, years 2004–2005).

2006   Electronic document, http://www.indec.mecon.gov.ar/webcenso/ECPI/pueblos/datos/W020601.xls, accessed April 21, 2009.

Podgorny, Irina

1999   *Arqueología de la Educación: Textos, indicios, monumentos; La imagen de los indios en el mundo escolar* (Archaeology of education: Texts, signs, monuments; The image of the Indians in the world of education). Sociedad Argentina de Antropología, Buenos Aires.

2000   *El Argentino despertar de las faunas y de las gentes prehistóricas: Coleccionistas, museos, estudiosos y universidad en la Argentina, 1875–1913* (Argentinean awakening to prehistoric fauna and peoples: Collections, museums, scholars and university in Argentina, 1875–1913). Editorial Universitaria de Buenos Aires (EUDEBA), Buenos Aires.

Podgorny, Irina, and Laura Miotti

1994   El pasado como campo de batalla (The past as a battlefield). *Ciencia Hoy* 5(5):16–19.

Podgorny, Irina, and Gustavo Politis
1992   ¿Qué sucedió en la historia? Los esqueletos araucanos del Museo de La Plata y la Conquista del Desierto (What happened in history? The Araucanian skeletons of the La Plata Museum and the Conquest of the Desert). *Arqueología Contemporánea* 3:73–79.

Politis, Gustavo
1995   The Socio-Politics of the Development of Archaeology in Hispanic South America. In *Theory in Archaeology: A World Perspective*, edited by Peter Ucko, pp. 197–228. Routledge, London and New York.
2001   On Archaeological Praxis, Gender Bias and Indigenous Peoples in South America. *Journal of Social Archaeology* 1(1):90–107.
2006   Theoretical and Ethical Issues of Archaeology in South America. In *A Future for Archaeology: The Past in the Present*, edited by Robert Layton, Stephen Shennan, and Peter Stone, pp. 173–86. University College London Press, London.

Politis, Gustavo (editor)
1992   *Arqueología en América Latina Hoy* (Archaeology in Latin America Today). Biblioteca Banco Popular, Bogotá.

Ratto, Norma
1998   Arqueología y situaciones de impacto (Archaeology and impact situations). Debate 2. *Mundo de Antes* 1:23–27.

Reinhard, Johan
1999   A 6,700 metros niños incas sacrificados quedaron congelados en el tiempo (At 22,000 feet children of Inca sacrifice found frozen in time). *National Geographic* 5(5):36–55.

Schávelzon, Daniel
2002   What's Going on Around the Corner? Illegal Trade of Art and Antiquities in Argentina. In *Illicit Antiquities: The Theft of Culture and the Extinction of Archaeology*, edited by Neil Brodie and Kathy Tubb, pp. 228–34. Routledge, London.

Serbín, Andrés
1981   Las organizaciones indígenas en la Argentina (The indigenous organizations in Argentina). *América Indígena* XLI(3):407–34.

Slavsky, Leonor
1992   Los indígenas y la sociedad nacional: Apuntes sobre políticas indigenistas en la Argentina (Indigenous people and the national society: Comments on indigenous policies in Argentina). In *La problemática indígena: Estudios antropológicos sobre Pueblos Indígenas en Argentina*, edited by Alejandro Balazote and Juan Radovich, pp. 67–79. Centro Editor de América Latina, Buenos Aires.

Tarragó, Miriam, and Mónica Piñeiro
1995   La práctica de la arqueología en Argentina (The practice of archaeology in Argentina). *Revista de Arqueología Americana* 9:167–188.

2

Vestiges of Colonialism

Manifestations of the Culture/Nature Divide in Australian Heritage Management

HEATHER BURKE AND CLAIRE SMITH

These natives were coloured with iron-ochre, and had a few feathers of the white cockatoo, in the black hair of their foreheads and beards. These simple decorations gave them a splendid holiday appearance, as savages. The trio who had visited us some days before, were all thoughtful observation; these were merry as larks, and their white teeth, constantly visible, shone whiter than even the cockatoo's feathers on their brows and chins. Contrasted with our woollen-jacketed, straw-hatted, great-coated race, full of work and care, it seemed as if nature was pleased to join in the laugh, at the expense of the sons of art. Sun never shone upon a merrier group of mortals than these children of nature appeared to be.

Thomas Mitchell, *Journal of an Expedition into the Interior of Tropical Australia*, 1848

When Thomas Mitchell and others of his ilk described their encounters with Indigenous peoples,[1] they did so within a social framework that placed the colonizers at the apex of progressive "civilized" society. In contrast, Indigenous peoples, lacking any appreciable European understandings of "culture," were placed in a state of nature—the simple, innocent inhabitants of a far away past or geographically distant present (Griffiths 1996:9–27). The "children of nature" syndrome was predicated upon a fundamental dichotomy between culture and nature that underlay the philosophy of the age of progress and its resulting imperial impulse. Nature was a resource to be encompassed, developed, and profited from—civilized society's role was to observe it, classify it, and collect it (Griffiths 1996). As post-Enlightenment western European society increasingly distanced itself from nature, the culture/nature divide became the filter for many aspects of ethnological, anthropological, and archaeological enquiry throughout the nineteenth and twentieth centuries. In relatively raw settler societies, in particular, this dichotomy had important ramifications, first for the conservation movement, and second for the subsequent shift to the recognition and management of cultural heritage.

Lacking the ancient monuments and works of high art (European "culture") encompassed by the Venice Charter of 1957 (International Council on Monuments and Sites [ICOMOS] 1964), settler nations had to look to other facets of their new worlds in the process of inscribing their identity. Australian settler culture thought itself bereft of visible signs of culture or history: "I miss the picture galleries, Statues, and fine buildings of England, there are no fine churches, or cathedrals, no antiquities here, except the sea and the hills" (Snell [1850] quoted in Griffiths 1996:152).

It is perhaps not surprising, then, that the first attempts to protect any asset for an appreciative public applied to the natural features of these new lands. In Australia, a process of reserving public lands to protect their scenic values began in the early 1860s. Influenced by British ideas of conservation and concepts such as the "garden city movement"—the provision of public space and "green belts" as antidotes to the pollution and crowding of industrial cities (Lennon 2003)—the conservation movement was initially closely linked to recreation and the potential for public lands to provide a wide variety of entertainments.

By the early twentieth century, however, a significant shift had taken place, from nature as a leisure resource to nature as a reserve of pristine and edifying wilderness. Framed by older European romantic sensibilities, the idea of wilderness sought to evoke an emotional connection with the natural environment, at the same time creating a sense of temporal depth through the physical aspects of the landscape itself: "wilderness was appreciated as a source of national identity, a reservoir of images that were unique and awe-inspiring, and a match for Old World cultural grandeur" (Griffiths 1996:261). Moreover, in line with notions derived from landscape painting, naturalness and primitiveness went hand in hand: to qualify as wilderness a place needed to appear ancient, pristine, and timeless (Griffiths 1996:260).

There was a time lag between recognition that the natural environment had important civic, emotional, and amenity-providing qualities, however, and recognition of the existence of anything approaching cultural heritage. Moreover, when this did occur, it remained an outgrowth of the long-standing European desire to appreciate nature in its pure and pristine state, and the culture/nature divide this was predicated upon. Just as the "children of nature" syndrome structured many European interactions with Indigenous people, so, too, did it provide the foundation for an understanding of cultural heritage. In essence, eliding Indigenous people and nature consistently positioned Indigenous people as a facet of natural history, and allowed Europeans to view both as primitive and wild: the opposite of themselves. The tension created from over 200 years of fashioning this divide is evident in several key areas of cultural heritage management: the choice of language used to describe Indigenous heritage; the way legislation has been structured and worded; the differing emphases placed on Indigenous and non-Indigenous (settler European) heritage; and the different regimes that still separate Indigenous heritage from settler European heritage today. More importantly, a clash between Indigenous and European worldviews resulting from this tension is evident in the changing attitudes to the management of Aboriginal sites and has helped to push Australian cultural heritage management in new and creative directions.

Relics, Pristineness, and the Notion of Antiquity

There was a significant perception during the early to mid-twentieth century that researchers working with Aboriginal peoples were dealing with a "fossilized" past (Smith 2004:146). At a time when Aboriginal people and traditions were assumed to be dying out, the idea was to identify and protect relict material remains as tangible "monuments" to past Aboriginal achievement. Throughout the nineteenth century and the early twentieth, settler European people saw the destiny of Aboriginal Australians as one of enforced integration into European society. Their past was therefore something to be excised and frozen in the glass cabinets of collectors.

The first legislation in Australia to protect heritage places and objects was the Northern Territory's Native and Historical Objects Preservation Ordinance of 1955. The ordinance was specifically designed to protect Aboriginal material— "relics"—as the remains of a vanishing and endangered way of life. It was soon joined by other similar acts with equally antiquarian names, such as the Aboriginal and Historic Relics Preservation Act of 1965 in South Australia, or the Aboriginal Relics Preservation Act of 1967 in Queensland. The nature/culture divide is implicit in the formation and wording of this legislation. While the recognition that Aboriginal places and sites were significant was a huge step forward, the protection of Aboriginal culture was still shaped by the concept of "primitiveness": Aboriginal sites were the "record" of a fast receding past, and "relics" were the material remains of an antique and severed way of life.

The passage of time did little to diminish this idea: the strong identification of Aboriginal culture with nature was epitomized with the inclusion of Aboriginal heritage as a logical component of the National Parks and Wildlife Act of 1967 in New South Wales (NSW). While the act was designed to protect natural values as well as a limited suite of cultural values, it constructed national parks as "primitive areas"—along with all of the features, whether natural or cultural, contained within them. At the time, archaeologists explicitly argued that the intent of such legislation was largely social: it would be useful for Aboriginal people in renewing cultural ties and gaining knowledge of lost traditions, as well as bringing non-Indigenous people to an understanding and appreciation of Aboriginal culture (Sutcliffe 1979:56).

Three things are apparent from the way this legislation functioned. First, only objects or areas that were incontrovertibly recognizable as deriving from

Aboriginal culture could constitute the record; in other words, they had to be "authentic" (Sutcliffe 1979:56). Unmodified places—lacking any of the obvious (read "European") attributes of "achievement"—were not indisputable and therefore could not be protected by relics legislation. The legal definition of a relic as connoting something no longer a part of the contemporary world, and therefore disconnected from present values and interests, has since been successfully challenged by Indigenous and other researchers (for example, Fourmile 1989; Smith 2004) who have had the term removed from the many state Indigenous heritage acts. The only place where this term has been retained is in the historic heritage legislation of some states, although this is not as ironic as it may seem. Linked to the European notion of linear time, which places objects in a past increasingly and inevitably distant from the present, non-Indigenous objects are relics in the classic sense: regardless of whether they are 30, 50, or 150 years old, they are constantly moving away from us into a quickly vanishing past.

Second, the idea of "the record as monument" linked directly to nineteenth-century ideas of the changelessness and timelessness of Aboriginal culture. The classic definition of primitiveness (a social wilderness) mandated that these sites be preserved as they were, without alteration, for future generations.

Third, these systems of classification were developed in terms of European understandings of how nature and culture were constituted, and failed to recognize Aboriginal worldviews that elided the two. A divide that placed Aboriginal peoples in natural landscapes and European Australians in cultural landscapes remained consistent through the development of Australia's heritage legislation in the 1970s. As a facet of the natural, taxonomic environment, there was no recognition that heritage management could be informed by the worldviews of Australia's Indigenous population (Sullivan et al. 2003:1).

This complex history has had several implications for Aboriginal people when dealing with their own heritage and has led to some crucial conflicts over alternative ways to manage and care for Aboriginal sites. It has also led to widely variant histories in the management of Indigenous and European heritage that only highlight the tenacity of the divide and its prevalence still in the frameworks with which we understand both the past and the present.

Giving Australia a Sense of History: Historic versus Indigenous Management Regimes

Apart from the limited provisions of the original National Parks and Wildlife Act in New South Wales, there was no legislation in Australia to protect non-Indigenous (often referred to as "historic") heritage until the 1970s. Victoria became the first state to enact such legislation with the passage of the Historic Buildings Preservation Act (HBP) in 1974. Such an act was a response to thirty or so years of agitation by various committees of the National Trust, a body that later became notable throughout the 1960s and 1970s for devoting itself largely to the protection of stately homes, reflecting its predominantly Anglophile and upper middle-class tastes (Simpson 1994:161). In 1975, Victoria's HBP Act was followed by the first federal legislation aimed at heritage issues: the Australian Heritage Commission Act. This act created the Australian Heritage Commission (AHC), whose task was to identify and conserve the National Estate, which was defined as "those places, being components of the natural environment of Australia, or the cultural environment of Australia that have aesthetic, historic, scientific or social significance or other special value for future generations as well as for the present community" (AHC Act, section 4[1], 1975).

In terms of the recognition of European-based heritage places, the AHC Act was important for creating Australia's first national register of heritage places: the Register of the National Estate (RNE). The first site to be listed on the RNE in 1977 was, however, a natural one: Fraser Island in Queensland, now on the World Heritage List. Of the final 13,129 places listed on the register before its termination in 2003, 76 percent of these were historic sites, while less than 1 percent were Indigenous. As is the case in other settler countries, such as the United States, much of the effort devoted to listing places on such a register was part of crafting and legitimating Australia's sense of history (see Davis, this volume), and therefore involved many patrimonial icons thought important to the creation of the nation. European places were clearly seen as being cultural in a way that Indigenous places were not. A more pernicious outcome of such a Eurocentric approach was that historic sites legislation was customarily created and administered through designated heritage departments, while responsibility for Indigenous heritage legislation remained with various departments of natural resources, mines, environment, or conservation. As of 2009, all Australian states still have separate legislation and administrative systems to deal with Aboriginal and historic heritage, a legacy of over 220 years of the culture/nature divide.

A recent development in Australia's cultural heritage management regime has been the addition in 2003 of a heritage component to the Federal Environment Protection and Biodiversity Conservation Act of 1999. Among other things, this created two new lists for heritage places to replace the original RNE: the national and commonwealth heritage lists. The National Heritage List records places deemed to be of value to the nation, whereas the Commonwealth Heritage List only includes sites owned or managed by the federal government or its agencies. Neither includes sites that are deemed to be of state or local significance, responsibility for which rests with state or local government authorities. While the lists can include natural, Indigenous, and historic sites, nomination is a relatively new process and subject to the same limitation: an assumed separation of European from Indigenous heritage. Only 23 of the 101 places on the National Heritage List are entered because they possess Indigenous cultural heritage value; the remainder are all European-based places. Furthermore, 16 of the listings with Indigenous values are actually for national parks or wilderness areas: only 5 sites merit inclusion on the basis of their Indigenous cultural heritage value alone.

A larger scale manifestation of the separation of natural heritage from cultural heritage can be seen in the ascription of places to the World Heritage List. The first Australian site to be included on the list (the Great Barrier Reef) was recognized for its outstanding and universal natural values, the second and third (Kakadu National Park and the Willandra Lakes) for their combination of natural values and cultural values associated with extreme Indigenous antiquity and consequent high archaeological or scientific potential. While it could be argued that this was a clear recognition of cultural heritage as encompassing Aboriginal behaviors and activities, we would argue that it was also an extension of the long-standing association of Aboriginal peoples with nature. These places were not listed because cultural value *per se* was accepted as a central part of universal value (if they had been, then one could expect more European places to be listed). Rather, they reflect the cultural cringe that can exist within settler nations, in which great antiquity is assumed to be one of the central defining features of value. Another element of this process relates to the construction of national identities in settler societies. In a sense, settler nations were construed primarily in relation to their natural environments and identified as such in the mythological status given to the American Wild West, the Australian outback, or the colonial frontier. Note that we are not arguing here that such listings are a denigration of Indigenous heritage, more the reverse: such listings elevate the antiquity of Indigenous heritage and make it a central facet of universal value. There is a clear parallel with the heritage lists in other settler countries.

This bias toward Indigenous heritage in settler nations is in sharp contrast to an overall bias toward European sites in the World Heritage List: the list for any European nation abounds in palaces, historic cities, cathedrals, churches, and gardens; the lists for settler societies are still focused almost exclusively on natural and Indigenous places (World Heritage Committee 1994). It was only in July 2004 that Australia's first non-Indigenous cultural heritage place was inscribed on the World Heritage List: the Royal Exhibition Building of 1880 and the corresponding Carlton Gardens, both in Melbourne.

These issues are receiving increased attention in light of the approaching fortieth anniversary of the World Heritage Convention in 2012 and the inscription of the one thousandth property to the World Heritage List. Australia has taken a proactive role in these discussions and in 2007 was elected to its fourth (nonsequential) four-year term on the World Heritage Committee. One of Australia's first actions in its current term was to propose a workshop on the future of the World Heritage Convention (see World Heritage Committee 2009), which was held in Paris in February 2009. A major focus of this meeting was strengthening the credibility of the convention to ensure its ongoing success and viability. One key challenge identified at an international level was the long-standing bias toward European sites and consequent pressure to counter this bias through inscribing low-value sites for representational reasons, and the importance of ensuring that the World Heritage List remains an inventory of properties of outstanding universal value.

The Language of Heritage Management

The colonial divide between culture and nature is also apparent in the language of heritage management. People constitute their worlds and the people around them through language (Butler 1997). In heritage management, language tends to reinforce the authority of archaeology as a discipline and to position Indigenous peoples in particular, often non-empowering, ways. The effects of colonial discourse are particularly apparent in the change from the term "cultural resources management" to "cultural heritage management" as the description for the heritage process in Australia. In order initially to identify the range and variety of archaeological sites and evaluate their significance, Australia consciously adopted the American model of cultural resources management, which was developed in the mid-1970s (Sharon Sullivan, personal communication, October 19, 2006). Variously referred to as "contract archaeology" (for example, Sullivan and Hughes 1979), "archaeological resource management" (for example, McKinlay and Jones 1979), or "public archaeology" (for example, Sullivan 1984:v; Witter 1979), "cultural resource management" (CRM) as a key term can be identified in the Australian literature as early as 1978 (for example, Stockton and Cane 1978).

The North American literature on cultural significance had a crucial impact on the development of Australian cultural resource management (see, for example, Sullivan and Bowdler 1984), although a key divergence was a deliberate focus by Australians on conserving sites rather than salvaging them. The overseas literature on archaeological resources management was perceived as overemphasizing salvage work, with the associated implication that the sole value of a site lay in its resource value for science, and that the main object of CRM, therefore, was to rescue as much as possible (Sullivan 1986; Sharon Sullivan personal communication, September 22, 2006). During the 1980s, a drive to engage with Aboriginal notions of a living heritage began to inform the archaeological literature (for example, McBryde 1985; Sullivan 1985). Speaking at the XV Pan Pacific Science Congress, in Dunedin, New Zealand, in February 1983, Sandra Bowdler urged: "Let us have a living archaeology in the fullest sense of the term . . . not sterile stamp collecting, crossword puzzling of interest only to ourselves. Let us come to terms with the living Aboriginal presence, and in so doing, help the general public also to do so."

The conjunction of these two developments was the catalyst for slow but profound change in Australian heritage management, perhaps most clearly evident in a gradual terminological change from cultural resource management to "cultural heritage management" (CHM). During the late 1980s and 1990s CHM gradually became the preferred term. This move was a direct response to criticisms by Indigenous people within such institutions as the Australian Heritage Commission and the NSW National Parks and Wildlife Service that a "resource" implied a universal reserve for everyone (and, at the extreme, something to be exploited), while "heritage" recognized a group's particular and special relationship, and implied conservation (Smith 2004:6). At the same time, the green conservation movement reached a similar conclusion and began referring to natural heritage rather than natural resources (Sharon Sullivan, personal communication, October 19, 2006).

The shift from cultural resources to cultural heritage was more than just a change in terminology; it encapsulated a shift in attitude about the purposes of management and the outcomes of managing a system largely composed of someone else's heritage. This change can be seen as the response to the incorporation of Aboriginal worldviews into the practice of heritage management, but it was also a means to redress those manifestations of colonialism identified as the core of this chapter—a system that continues, often unwittingly, and as a result of embedded modes of unreflective thought, to associate Indigenous people more closely with nature. What is to be done when Indigenous people disagree? The core Western system of understanding itself changes only superficially, leaving the cultural heritage management sector to develop novel and nuanced ways of dealing with this ever-present tension.

Living Landscapes

It is almost a truism that the first heritage management legislation and policies in Australia failed to recognize Indigenous worldviews. Legislation, like history, is made by the victors. From a European perspective, culture is clearly made by humans. For Indigenous peoples, however, culture can be nature, or an outcome of human interactions with nature. In fact, the landscape itself is a cultural artifact, not just in terms of human changes to the environment (for example, regular burning by Aboriginal Australians) but also because ancestral beings and the spirits of those who have died in the recent past inhabit the landscape and continue to monitor the management of their country in the present.

Many of these places cannot be identified by traditional archaeological methods, and knowledge concerning them is held in the hands of old people. While elements of these traditions have been subjected to transformation as part of colonialism, others are directly linked to the ancestors of contemporary Indigenous peoples. For Indigenous peoples, cultural heritage is a living and evolving tradition, its continuity vital to their identity and cultural survival (Janke 1999:7). As a living tradition, Indigenous cultural heritage is closely tied to oral histories and the process of re-creating those traditions: "For a living culture based on spirit of place, the major part of maintaining culture and therefore caring for place is the continuation of the oral tradition that tells a story. The process of re-creation, rather than reproduction is essential to the reality of Indigenous people. To them, reproduction is unreal, while re-creation is real. The [European] fixation on the written word has implications for the practice of cultural heritage" (Department of Aboriginal Affairs, NSW, cited in Janke 1999:8).

This Aboriginal notion of a living legacy is very different from the European Australian notion of a pristine or unchanging heritage, a situation that has clear implications for heritage management philosophies. The European philosophy of conserving the past and maintaining original authenticity is based on a notion of linear time. In contrast, the Indigenous notion of time, in which the past continues to exist in the present, underwrites a cultural heritage management philosophy in which the past is kept strong and active through appropriate and recurrent use of the land and sites in the present.

For Aboriginal people, natural features can be the tangible expression of a wide range of cultural concepts. Moreover, keeping the past strong in the present often requires material expression. Some of the complexities inherent in opposing notions of heritage conservation can be seen in the debate over the repainting of Wandjina sites in the Gibb River area of the Kimberley region in Western Australia. In 1987, funded under the Community Employment Project, young Aboriginal people repainted several major rock art galleries under the supervision of senior custodians (Mowaljarlai et al. 1988). However, the repainting of these sites caused an outcry when the media picked up criticisms by non-Aboriginal people (for example, Walsh 1992), on the grounds that young people would not have undertaken repainting in a "traditional" context, and that the artistic standard of the painted images was low. Mowaljarlai and Peck's (1987) description of the motivations behind this program, however, drew upon the notion of a living heritage: "At a big meeting we decided that we would only re-paint sites that were faded and needed re-painting. Photographs were taken at each site before any re-painting took place. We talked to the senior traditional owners who are responsible for the sites and they agreed that the re-painting should be done. An elder was present at each site when it was re-painted and told the stories about the place and showed the young people how to re-paint the sites . . . Our language and our art must be shared and given to the next generation—this is how it has always been. It is not just nice to re-paint the site, it's got to be done. You see Wandjinas have power and we must look after them so the power is used properly" (Mowaljarlai and Peck 1987:71, 72).

The repainting debate can be better understood when considered in terms of core facets of the nature/culture divide: in particular, a European imperative that "authentic" Aboriginal cultures be changeless and timeless, and associated definitions of primitiveness that mandate that Aboriginal sites be preserved without amendment. Predicated on differing notions of time, Aboriginal and European Australians have different ideas of aesthetics in rock art, and whether or not rock paintings should be renewed. In contrast, the European notion of linear time underpins a museum approach to preserving the past, which focuses on the preservation of art works in their original condition as treasured objects from a distant past. Such objects need conservation, rather than renewal.

In a similar fashion, and again contrary to entrenched European notions of authenticity, Aboriginal people tend to value the contemporary or very recent past as highly as they do the distant past; without the linear construction of European time all parts of the past are equally important. In the Barunga-Wugullar area of the Northern Territory, when Aboriginal people visit sites, they tend to show little interest in the stone or bone artifacts archaeologists are most concerned with. Instead, they are more interested in the contemporary "rubbish" that denotes recent visitation to the site by others. The senior traditional owners, who serve as custodians, continually stop to consider who might have left these remains, when they might have been here, and what they might have been doing. These physical materials reaffirm the continuing importance of the place, but, because they are linked to direct memory and living people, they do this in a way that older physical materials do not. For the same reason senior traditional custodians regularly and deliberately discard their own rubbish—a drink can, a chip packet, an empty tobacco tin—at the sites they visit. While to a European sensibility this is "rubbish" and should be removed as something that interferes with the pristineness of the site, to Indigenous people this is a reaffirming facet of their custodianship of that place, and a tangible sign to others that the place is still being visited and cared for.

Place-Based Approaches to Recording Heritage: Mapping Intangibles

While in some ways it is obvious that Australian attitudes to culture and its management still owe many of their implicit assumptions to modes of thinking about nature, time, and Aboriginal people that were prevalent in the nineteenth century and earlier, there are also many ways in which being forced to deal with such conflicts over heritage can create new ideas and forms of cultural heritage management. One such development is place-based approaches to recording heritage, in which emphasis is placed on mapping intangibles. While the importance of intangible heritage was recognized in the 1970s by a number of archaeologists, most notably Harry Creamer and Ray Kelly (see Kijas 2005), it was only in the 1990s that it became part of the mainstream of cultural heritage management practice. Truscott (2003) argues that an increasing focus on intangible heritage values may provide a potential unifying force in reconciling practical and meaningful management with the needs and desires of diverse communities. In particular, for Indigenous people, such revision recognizes that heritage values change through time and are part of the living connection between past, present, and future. While acknowledging the importance of intangible heritage "manifest as place, object, stories (written or oral) and in values, uses, traditions and customs" (Australia ICOMOS 1999) and its central importance in recognizing how living communities invest meaning in places and objects, this does not mean that access to, and control over, the mechanisms of transmitting this knowledge will be straightforward. As Truscott (2003) points out, such issues have vexed Australia's Indigenous peoples in their revitalization of traditional culture. Early recordings of sacred ceremonies allow communities to reconnect with past customs, but tension can occur regarding who has rights in such ceremony, or which version is "correct." Tension also arises in terms of who has rights to knowledge generally, and discussion over the control of Indigenous cultural and intellectual property is a matter of current debate.

In recent years, place-based approaches have emerged from a growing recognition that Aboriginal cultural heritage exists within a wider cultural landscape not just composed of the places themselves, but also the web of connections between them (for example, Byrne et al. 2001; Byrne and Nugent 2004). Denis Byrne and Maria Nugent, using the concept of "geo-biographies"—the geographical mapping of intangible heritage (travel pathways, daily rounds, memories), documented through a variety of means, particularly oral histories—describe the importance of this work in terms of an enrichment of archaeological data: "Geo-biographies . . . illustrate how autobiographical memory can be used to identify and record Aboriginal post-contact heritage. They show that biographies and geographies, lives and landscapes, are interconnected: that all lives have a landscape. As such, most, if not all, oral history interviews will have embedded in them a network of places significant to the narrator. This is what makes autobiographical memory such a rich resource . . . It provides information about places that most likely have not been recorded in government and other archives, or in written form at all. Indeed, a person's memory might be the only repository for [such] information" (Byrne and Nugent 2004:179).

The geo-biographical approach has two aims:

- To recognize that Aboriginal heritage is intrinsically connected to the landscape—not so much to the event, the activity, or the individual site, but to the total landscape that gives meaning and form to these events.

- To create a more culturally-responsible framework from which to understand sites. By moving away from an idea of sites as discrete and bounded entities, it is possible to trace the interconnections between places and the many intangible aspects of heritage that are still imprinted on the landscape through people's experiences, emotions and memories. "It is the landscapes themselves that ought to be considered heritage, rather than discrete and dispersed 'sites' within them." (Byrne and Nugent 2004:73)

Shared Landscapes, Heritage Landscapes

The increased emphasis on place-based approaches to recording Aboriginal heritage has also led to a greater concern with shared landscapes (for example, Byrne et al. 2001; Harrison 2004) and, to some extent, on social interpretations of the past (see David et al. 2006). Shared landscapes are much more than the sum of their physical places. Of equal interest are the spaces between places and how these are given meaning by different groups of people, as well as how memories are woven around both. The different, but interlocking, understandings of this shared heritage have the potential to form a basis for reconciliation between Aboriginal and settler Australians.

A related development is something we characterize as heritage landscapes. Recent directions outlined by one of Australia's leading bodies for managing cultural landscape values, the New South Wales National Parks and Wildlife Service (now the Department of Environment and Climate Change), specify that cultural heritage assessment work should follow "an integrated, or whole-of-landscape, approach with regard to the identification and assessment of all cultural (both historic and pre-contact Aboriginal) and natural values; and a cultural landscape approach to understanding the values of the item within its wider environmental/biogeographic, historic and social setting" (New South Wales National Parks and Wildlife Service 2002).

However, this is still more easily conceptualized for Indigenous (read "natural") landscapes rather than for historical/European ones. The exception to this is the National Heritage listing in 2003 of the Castlemaine Diggings National Heritage Park, a palimpsest of over 100 years of European activity: "The Castlemaine Diggings are significant at an Australian scale, in the extent to which their goldfields landscapes have been preserved. The importance of the Castlemaine Diggings is not just in the considerable significance of the individual relics and sites themselves but in the cultural landscapes formed where large numbers of sites and relics persist in their original settings and demonstrate a range of cultural themes over several phases of human occupation" (Lennon 2005:n.p.).

The listing of the Castlemaine Diggings created a new category of heritage place similar to a national park but recognized primarily for its cultural values rather than its natural ones. This is congruent with contemporary developments in Europe that focus on historic environments rather than individual monuments or sites (see Willems, this volume), or that seek alliances with "green" environmental interests (MacInnes and Wickham-Jones 1992), both of which can be interpreted as postmodern dimensions to heritage management.

Conclusion

This chapter has explored the manner in which a colonial division between culture and nature has informed developments in Australian heritage management. While we have moved a long way from Thomas Mitchell's Eurocentric myopia, we have retained some core prejudices that have shaped our attitudes to the heritage of Australian settler society, as well as our attitudes and relationships to other forms and ideas of heritage. Our systems of heritage management continue to perpetuate a Western divide between culture and nature, and its associated constructions of authenticity, monuments, pristineness, and extreme antiquity as key factors in cultural significance (see Lowenthal 2005 for a wider discussion of this issue). We have teased out some of the strands to the culture/nature division in Australian heritage management, in particular in the language of heritage management, legislation, and the practical application of heritage policies. The history of cultural heritage management regimes in a settler nation such as Australia is embedded within the complex interactions between Indigenous people and a European colonial system. This history is complicated by the conflicts inherent in settler and Indigenous notions of heritage, the past, and its purpose. We are not suggesting that Indigenous and settler worldviews are irreconcilable, but we recognize that it is in these places of tension that we learn most about our society and ourselves.

Acknowledgments

We would like to thank Sharon Sullivan, Laurajane Smith, and Val Attenbrow for answering our many questions about the history of CRM versus CHM and for sharing their personal experiences of both transitions with us.

Note

1. The convention we have adopted here is to use "Indigenous" when we write of issues, such as cultural and intellectual property rights, that have an impact on all Aboriginal and Torres Strait Islander people. Following the increasing practice of Indigenous authors (for example, Craven 1999; Smith 1999; various essays in Smith and

Wobst 2005), we use the term "Indigenous peoples." The capital "I" emphasizes the nationhood of individual groups, while use of the plural "peoples" internationalizes Indigenous experiences, issues, and struggles (Smith 1999:114–15). We use the term "Aboriginal" to refer to Aboriginal people from mainland Australia, and "Torres Strait Islander" to refer to people from the Torres Strait Islands.

References Cited

Australia ICOMOS
1999   *The Burra Charter: The Australia ICOMOS Charter for Places of Cultural Significance.* Australia ICOMOS, Melbourne.
Bowdler, Sandra
1983   Aborigines and Archaeologists: Fear and Loathing or Mutual Benefit? Paper presented at the XV Pan Pacific Science Congress, Dunedin, New Zealand.
Butler, Judith
1997   *Excitable Speech: A Politics of the Performance.* Routledge, London.
Byrne, Denis, Helen Brayshaw, and Tracey Ireland
2001   Social Significance: A Discussion Paper. Department of Environment and Conservation (NSW), Sydney.
Byrne, Denis, and Maria Nugent
2004   *Mapping Attachment: A Spatial Approach to Aboriginal Post-Contact Heritage.* Department of Environment and Conservation (NSW), Sydney.
Craven, Rhonda
1999   *Teaching Aboriginal Studies.* Allen and Unwin, Sydney.
David, Bruno, Bryce Barker, and Ian McNiven (editors)
2006   *The Social Archaeology of Australian Indigenous Societies.* Aboriginal Studies Press, Canberra.
David, Bruno, and Meredith Wilson
2002   *Inscribed Landscapes: Marking and Making Place.* University of Hawaii Press, Honolulu.
Fourmile, Henrietta
1989   Aboriginal Heritage Legislation and Self-Determination. *Australian-Canadian Studies* 7(1–2):45–61.
Griffiths, Tom
1996   *Hunters and Collectors: The Antiquarian Imagination in Australia.* Cambridge University Press, Cambridge.
Harrison, Rodney
2004   *Shared Landscapes: Archaeologies of Attachment and the Pastoral Industry in New South Wales.* University of New South Wales Press, Sydney.
International Council on Monuments and Sites (ICOMOS)
1964   *International Charter for the Conservation and Restoration of Monuments and Sites (The Venice Charter).*

Janke, Terri
1999   *Our Culture, Our Future: Proposals for the Recognition of Indigenous Cultural and Intellectual Property*. Australian Institute of Aboriginal Studies and the Aboriginal and Torres Strait Islander Commission, Canberra.

Kijas, Joanna
2005   *Revival, Renewal and Return: Ray Kelly and the NSW Sites of Significance Survey*. Department of Environment and Conservation, Sydney.

Lennon, Jane L.
2003   Re-engaging with the Land: Designed Cultural Landscapes. *Australian Garden History* 15(5):9–20.
2005   The Evolution of Landscape Conservation in Australia: Reflections on the Relationship of Nature and Culture. In *Linking Nature, Culture and Community*, edited by Jessica Brown, Nora Mitchell, and Michael Beresford, pp. 205–217. IUCN—The World Conservation Union, Gland, Switzerland and Cambridge, United Kingdom. Electronic document, http://data.iucn.org/dbtw-wpd/edocs/2005-006.pdf, accessed April 2, 2009.

Lowenthal, David
2005   Natural and Cultural Heritage. *International Journal of Heritage Studies* 11(1):81–92.

MacInnes, Lesley, and Caroline Wickham-Jones
1992   *All Natural Things: Archaeology and the Green Debate*. Oxbow, Oxford.

McBryde, Isabel
1985   *Who Owns the Past? Papers from the Annual Symposium of the Australian Academy of the Humanities*. Oxford University Press, Melbourne.

McKinlay, James Royce, and Kevin Lewis Jones (editors)
1979   *Archaeological Resource Management in Australia and Oceania*. New Zealand Historic Places Trust, Wellington.

Mowaljarlai, David, and Cyril Peck
1987   Ngarinyin Cultural Continuity: A Project to Teach the Young People the Culture Including the Re-Painting of Wandjina Rock Art Sites. *Australian Aboriginal Studies* 2:71–78.

Mowaljarlai, David, Patricia Vinnicombe, Graeme K. Ward, and Christopher Chippindale
1988   Repainting Images on Rock in Australia and the Maintenance of Aboriginal Culture. *Antiquity* 62:690–96.

New South Wales National Parks and Wildlife Service
2002   *Cultural Heritage Conservation Policy*. NSW National Parks and Wildlife Service, Hurstville.

Simpson, Cheryl
1994   Heritage, What's in a Name? *Alternative Law Journal* 19(4):161–64.

Smith, Laurajane
2004   *Archaeological Theory and the Politics of Cultural Heritage*. Routledge, London.

Smith, Linda T.

1999   *Decolonizing Methodologies: Research and Indigenous Peoples.* 2nd ed. Zed
        Books, London.

Smith, Claire, and H. Martin Wobst (editors)

2005   *Indigenous Archaeologies: Decolonizing Theory and Practice.* Routledge, Lon-
        don.

Stockton, Jim, and Scott Cane

1978   Cultural Resources Information for Eaglehawk Neck, South East Tasmania.
        Unpublished report to the National Parks and Wildlife Service, Tasmania.

Sullivan, Marjorie, and Philip J. Hughes

1979   Contract Archaeology: A Consultant's Viewpoint. In *Archaeological Resource
        Management in Australia and Oceania*, edited by James Royce McKinlay and
        Kevin Lewis Jones, pp. 48–51. New Zealand Historic Places Trust, Welling-
        ton.

Sullivan, Sharon

1984   Introduction. In *Site Surveys and Significance Assessment in Australian
        Archaeology*, edited by Sharon Sullivan and Sandra Bowdler, pp. v–x. Depart-
        ment of Prehistory, Research School of Pacific Studies, Australian National
        University, Canberra.

1985   The Custodianship of Aboriginal Sites in Southeastern Australia. In *Who
        Owns the Past?*, edited by Isabel McBryde, pp. 139–56. Oxford University
        Press, Melbourne.

1986   The "Management" in Cultural Resource Management: Training for Public
        Archaeologists and Other Cultural Resource Managers. In *Archaeology at
        ANZAAS 1984*, edited by Graeme K. Ward, pp. 236–40. Canberra Archaeo-
        logical Society, Canberra.

Sullivan, Sharon, and Sandra Bowdler (editors)

1984   *Site Surveys and Significance Assessment in Australian Archaeology.* Depart-
        ment of Prehistory, Research School of Pacific Studies, Australian National
        University, Canberra.

Sullivan, Sharon, Nicholas Hall, and Shelley Greer

2003   Learning to Walk Together and Work Together: Providing a Formative Teach-
        ing Experience for Indigenous and Non-Indigenous Heritage Managers. Pa-
        per presented at the Fifth World Archaeological Congress, Washington, D.C.

Sutcliffe, Kate A.

1979   Cultural Resource Management in Queensland. In *Archaeological Resource
        Management in Australia and Oceania*, edited by James Royce McKinlay and
        Kevin Lewis Jones, pp. 56–66. New Zealand Historic Places Trust, Welling-
        ton.

Truscott, Marilyn

2003   Intangible Values as Heritage in Australia: Proceedings of the International
        Scientific Symposium "Place, Memory, Meaning: Preserving Intangible Val-

ues in Monuments and Sites." Electronic document, http://www.international. icomos.org/victoriafalls2003/papers.htm, accessed April 2, 2009.

Walsh, Grahame

1992   Rock Art Retouch: Can a Claim of Aboriginal Descent Establish Curation Rights over Humanity's Cultural Heritage? In *Rock Art and Ethnography*, edited by Michael Morwood and Doug Hobbs, pp. 46–59. Australian Rock Art Research Association, Melbourne.

Witter, Dan

1979   Predictive Theory and Public Archaeology. In *Archaeological Resource Management in Australia and Oceania*, edited by James Royce McKinlay and Kevin Lewis Jones, pp. 44–48. New Zealand Historic Places Trust, Wellington.

World Heritage Committee

1994   *Global Strategy*. United Nations, UNESCO World Heritage Centre. Electronic document, http://whc.unesco.org/en/globalstrategy, accessed April 2, 2009.

2009   *32COM 10—Future of the World Heritage Convention*. United Nations, UNESCO World Heritage Centre. Electronic document, http://whc.unesco.org/en/decisions/1565, accessed April 2, 2009.

3

Twenty Years of Heritage Resource Management in Brazil

A Brief Evaluation (1986–2006)

PAULO DEBLASIS

Cultural heritage resource management, including archaeology, heritage-based education, and decision making in the public sphere, is a very recent concern in Brazil. Legal specifications for evaluating environmental and cultural impact before implementation of large development enterprises have been in place for 20 years, thus promoting the emergence of environmental and sociocultural studies and related mitigation programs. Nevertheless, the overwhelming rates of economic growth and the "development at any cost" mentality still prevailing at all levels of government make it a very important political matter in Brazil today. Losses related to archaeological heritage are immense, but surely losses regarding regional traditional culture, whether indigenous or just "local" (what sometimes has been called "intangible cultural resources"), are even more severe, not only because the cultural and social characteristics of indigenous or "local" peoples are usually ignored but, more important, they are systematically estranged from decision-making processes regarding their own land and life (see Endere; Burke and Smith, this volume). These people are frequently displaced and relocated to new areas in circumstances completely adverse to their own cultural and economic habits and uses, thus in time reinforcing not only deculturation and social degradation, but also rural exodus and inflation of underdeveloped suburban peripheral areas around major towns like São Paulo, Rio de Janeiro, and Brasília. This chapter will review the historical and legal background of cultural resource management (CRM) development in this country, as well as some recent achievements and perspectives.

The first archaeological rescue programs in Brazil began in the early 1970s, mostly as a result of the hydroelectric industry initiative and large damming projects conducted by militaristic governments of the period with funding from international agencies. These programs drew attention to the impacts on the natural environment and cultural resources therein, including archaeology. To meet the need for scientific research, these enterprises turned to university-based archaeologists, who have been involved since then. At that time, archaeology as a regular academic discipline in Brazil was only ten years old, and archaeologists were trying to consolidate it as a scientific branch. Following European tradition, archaeology was in most cases related to historical and natural sciences, only rarely linked to anthropological perspectives. This first generation of professionals, attached to museums and universities, was the one to define and develop these early archaeological salvage programs, typically reproducing the operational research-praxis of a still immature academic discipline.

Archaeological research in Brazil through the 1960s and 1970s alternated between two very different, and frequently opposed, research orientations, deeply influenced by the French archaeological palaeoethnographical tradition on the one hand, and the regional approach of the cultural-historical American branch on the other. During this time, archaeological survey projects were developed throughout the country, creating the first regional- and continental-scale models for interpreting the archaeological evidence of the pre-Columbian past on the eastern side of South America, as well as the first essays relating it to ethnographically known societies such as the Tupi-speaking peoples. These pioneering research programs have been heavily criticized in recent years, on both methodological and political grounds, but they produced the first macro-regional perspectives for Brazilian archaeology. Much of this research, including the establishment of archaeological cultural traditions, is still in use.[1]

Although extensive and previously unknown portions of the country were investigated by the first contract projects, these studies resulted in rather descriptive reports involving sites' cultural affiliations and some chronological sequencing. Some of these investigations focused on the study of only some site categories, reflecting the researchers' interests and expertise. Results were usually self-contained, meaningless in terms of regional sampling and contextualization, and rarely presented in a broader context.[2]

Since 1986, when laws concerning the need for cultural resources studies and management were promulgated in Brazil, "contract" or "rescue" archaeological projects have become increasingly common throughout the country. Large-scale projects such as dams, pipelines, big hotels, and a variety of other enterprises are obliged to report on environmental impact, as well as to produce some kind of mitigation plan. This has generated a demand for archaeological expertise too great for universities to provide. As a consequence, many private companies were created, with a professional profile geared toward meeting the customers' needs without losing the legal, ethical, and scientific perspectives of the discipline. Some companies have their own installations with laboratories and other research facilities, and administrative and legal support, allowing them to face the ever growing and diversifying needs of this expanding market. At the same time, due to the lack of legal professional support and ethical principles, many small companies and individuals started to explore this open market without providing minimal quality in terms of scientific standards, a situation that has become a matter of great concern today.

Legal and Normative Background

The first bill protecting Brazilian archaeological legacy dates back to 1937 and, although the law in itself might be very clear, the privileging of material legacy from historical times by heritage professionals has helped to support the exclusion of native peoples from national history.[3] This created a tradition at public agencies where historians and architects, rather than archaeologists, became the professionals responsible for the preservation and management of Brazilian heritage (see Endere, this volume). This bill protected Brazilian historical, archaeological, and artistic legacy, but it was restricted to properties that had been registered as historic sites by the federal government. These sites were often architectural or easily visible and patriotically manipulated as evidence for the "origins of the Brazilian nation." In 1961, another federal law (no. 3924) extended legal protection to all archaeological sites and monuments in the country. The law furthermore prohibits economic exploitation, destruction, or mutilation of this legacy before archaeological analysis is conducted. This legal posture has been reiterated by the Federal Constitution of 1988, which considers archaeological sites to be part of Brazilian cultural legacy, therefore under the custody and protection of the federal government. In 1998, the Law of Environmental Crimes (9.605) was promulgated, imposing criminal and administrative sanctions to behavior and activities considered harmful to the environment; it also stipulated penalties for the destruction of, or aggression to, properties or landscape features (such as archaeological sites) protected by law, establishing fines and enforcing convictions to repair any damages already produced against the environment.

Environmental impact evaluation in Brazil started with Law 6938, passed in 1981, which rules on the National Environmental Policy, regulated in 1986, establishing standards and criteria for licensing activities that affect the environment. Only then did archaeology become part of environmental assessment projects, included in the so-called Environmental Impact Study and the Environmental Impact Report (whose acronyms in Portuguese are, respectively, EIA and RIMA). Since 2002, studies have been required before construction, in order to allow the entrepreneur to get an installation license (*Coletânea* 2006). The reports generated by these studies, which in most cases imply field research, must include: 1) diagnosis of the site or area in question, including an assessment of the nature of affected heritage and its importance; 2) analysis of the environmental impacts; 3) definition of mitigation measures and expected effects due to its application; and 4) presentation of environmental control programs, including the monitoring of the most relevant recommendations. Since 2002, heritage education programs must be included in the rescue project and, since 2003, marginal areas from previously existing dams also must be included in periodic reevaluations of the operation license.

It is important to point out that a federal resolution from 1988 specifies type and size of the enterprises that must undergo environmental impact studies (for example, hydroelectric power plants that generate above 10 megawatts). However, some Brazilian states and municipalities are in the forefront of preserving their cultural legacies, demanding evaluations for smaller enterprises or even for any commercial enterprise, such as land divisions, cemeteries, or gas stations, to be implemented. The municipal action became even stronger with the passage of Law 10.257 in 2001, establishing the creation and definition of community responsibilities for cultural legacy management. Underwater heritage (such as shipwrecks and, in the case of damming or river banks, any other archaeological feature) is under the custody of the Brazilian navy, which allows for their commercial exploitation. This has alarming consequences for sunken ships all along the very large Brazilian coast. Efforts to remedy this situation have so far come to nothing.

The National Historic and Artistic Heritage Institute (whose acronym in Portuguese is IPHAN), which is linked to the Ministry of Culture, is in charge of the oversight of Brazilian heritage resources at the federal level. Any intervening measure or action related to this legacy requires a specific authorization for implementing archaeological research, issued according to the terms established in governmental decree 07/1988. The IPHAN is also responsible for evaluating the results of these studies, as well as for the destination and final use of the documents and artifact collections generated by research. As public heritage, archaeological artifacts may be curated at the private companies' laboratories, but they must be delivered to a public institution, such as a museum, as a final destination. Because of the expansion of private CRM projects throughout the country, many traditional museums have expanded their scope and infrastructure to maintain these sometimes large new collections. Many new small museums have emerged outside the main cities, where most of the larger and more traditional museums can be found.[4] Nevertheless, storage of collections is an ever growing and unsolved problem throughout the country.

It might be said that Brazilian legislation regarding the protection of the environment, including cultural resources, is among the most advanced in the world, but things do not always run smoothly when it comes to practice. Inspection or supervision conducted by the IPHAN and other public agencies have not kept up with the overwhelming expansion of CRM projects throughout the country in the last decades, and some projects are still implemented without proper evaluation and/or archaeological research. The IPHAN keeps the National Register of Archaeological Sites (CNSA in Portuguese), a necessary and useful service that, unfortunately, is still technically inefficient and difficult to use, making long-term control and supervision of heritage almost negligible.

Developments and Problems since 1986

To understand the current situation in Brazil, let us first examine some positive consequences of the multiplication of CRM studies, turning then to the problems archaeologists face in dealing with heritage management today.

Most traditional archaeological research developed in Brazil since the 1950s has taken place in the coastal and southern parts of the country. Archaeological rescue programs, in contrast, tend to occur throughout the vast central and northern Brazilian hinterland, where most large development projects, including damming, electrical grids, and roads, are taking place, most never covered by previous research. These are archaeologically unknown areas and contract archaeological projects turn out to be, thus, decisive opportunities to shed light on the prehistory of these vast areas, with results that might bring important contributions to the understanding of the prehistory of South America as a whole.[5] Unfortunately, the majority of these studies remain unpublished.

In addition, until some years ago, archaeological research in large areas did not employ regional methods of systematic survey, paying little attention to the representativeness of sites and/or areas covered. In this same sense, efforts toward defining regional occupation sequences on the basis of careful analysis of selected sites were rare. Even when native or traditional communities are still in, or near, the area, little effort has been made to investigate the possible relationships between the archaeological contexts recovered and the ethnological record of the societies known to have long inhabited the same area. However, recent CRM projects are taking a different approach, mostly based on systematic sampling and landscape history, allowing for an interpretive scope where both past and present cultures and perspectives might be taken into account.

During the last decades, interest in cultural resources is growing at a fast pace, both in the so-called third sector and at the universities. In fact, the beginning of the twenty-first century has seen the multiplication of graduate courses directed to environmental sciences and management of natural and cultural resources. But archaeological training is still insufficient, particularly regarding methodological strategies. An examination of most CRM reports shows a clear tendency for descriptive reports, almost always lacking theoretical approaches or a more daring interpretive modeling. Whenever present, interpretation is still rooted almost exclusively in cultural-historical perspectives, derived from the description of the material culture traits and the ecological setting.

In the last few years, government agencies have also acquired a deeper concern for the nature of impacts on nonrenewable cultural resources, and mitigation plans tend to be discussed in a much deeper and wider scope than before.

This is particularly true of large projects that often reach the public media, including newspapers, TV, and weekly magazines. At the local or community level, advances can also be seen, and "no dam" movements sometimes get large audiences capable of delaying or even stopping projects.

Due to the fast growth of this emergent market for commercial archaeology, the lack of enough institutionalized archaeological teaching and education has become a major problem, aggravated by the feeble legal background for the professional practice of archaeology in Brazil. In fact, there are no clear rules to establish who is allowed to practice archaeology and who is not; the regular status of the profession has not been formalized, making legal control of archaeological practice rather difficult. Thus, the market has been filled with offers of "servicing archaeology," small companies conducted by people with little technical training or scientific background. This situation has led to a generalized impoverishment of quality standards on technical practice and scientific results, a major concern of the archaeological community today.

Besides these difficulties, public outreach of archaeological heritage studies, whether based in academia or in CRM firms, is slowly growing, and, in fact, archaeologists themselves have become more attentive to it. Cultural sections of the most important newspapers run full-page stories on brand-new discoveries, ecological TV shows occasionally air archaeological reports, and books for the general public have been published. Public education has become more common in recent archaeological research projects, and since 2002, it has been mandatory in CRM projects. Archaeologists now go to local schools and community centers to speak about the past, the environment, the things they find, history, and material culture. It also has become common to see groups of school children visiting archaeological excavations, usually conducted by trained guides.

Challenges

Some challenges are ahead if archaeologists are to face the enormous threats to heritage resources that the fast development of the country brings at a more intense pace every day. One of the first is to make an intensive movement in education: we need not just more archaeologists, but ones trained to undertake archaeology in all its diverse applications, in order to prevent the tremendous losses in information we are facing right now with every new soybean plantation, every new dam or road, or even the rapid expansion of urban areas. Brazilian archaeology is still young, without well-developed regional data and theoretical background. These new, well-trained professionals must be equipped with a variety of methodological tools and the ability to adapt them to difficult situations, such as pristine tropical forest environments (for example, Araujo-Costa et al. 1988). They must be able to apply well thought-out research designs to different areas and situations, to think archaeologically, and to create or transform interpretive models for areas as distinct and poorly known as southwestern Amazonia, the northern Central Plateau, the Pantanal (Chaco) area, or even large portions of the central Atlantic coast. In addition, considerable investments must be made to publish the reports being produced by CRM studies. Much information is available only at a few libraries or at the IPHAN's offices, and most researchers and students have no access to it, let alone the general public. The decree of 1988 established the need to disseminate results, but this is rarely accomplished. It must become more widely accepted that publication is an essential part of archaeological research.

Another challenge is the considerable effort that must be dedicated to the regulation of the archaeological profession. It has an enormous impact on the lack of quality standards for archaeological practice throughout the country. This legal issue is on the desk of politicians, who must take action soon for the sake of Brazilian heritage.

But perhaps the biggest challenge faced by Brazilian archaeologists involved with CRM today is related to the political role archaeology might assume in the very process of generating these reports and its evaluation. Taking control of this process might result not only in an immense advance toward a more comprehensive scientific approach, but also toward environmental context preservation, and the decentralization of decision making and social inclusion, with results that could be shared by all players involved. This potential role for archaeology derives from a new mentality, where archaeologists must act not just to clear up the area to fill the dam or for the road to go through; on the contrary, by making use of holistic and encompassing historical landscape approaches, they can integrate a large spectrum of information and take the lead in the impact evaluation processes. The lengthy reports required to obtain a license for a development project are still technically oriented with lists and descriptions attached. Archaeological and anthropological reports are often appended together with little or no connection to the body of the report. Archaeologists and other specialists are overseen by engineers or other managers with a technical perspective, rather than a human-oriented one. In this context, local communities and other players, particularly those with different perspectives, can hardly be heard. Traditional societies and long-standing landscape perceptions are often wiped out by dominant political and economic postures.

Some changes in this scenario are occurring and more holistic perspectives are taking over the CRM scene in Brazil. Archaeology is now in a position to take the lead in this process, as it is the discipline best suited to integrate it all from a sociological/historical perspective, which is sensitive to the traditional communities, their historical inception, and the ecological and cultural meaning of the environmental setting, as well as to the need to develop transportation infrastructure and energy sources.

Anthropologists have always been important defenders of native peoples in Brazil, but they have not successfully linked defense of these peoples with environmental laws. Archaeology, on the other side, having had a rather technical approach for quite a while (reports based mostly on lists of sites, dates, descriptions, and typologies), now begins to find itself as a privileged discipline able to integrate all other research areas, whether natural or cultural, in a broader culturally and sociologically contextualized landscape approach where the impacts of any enterprise can be seen in an integrative and encompassing perspective. This brings into the political arena the decision spheres, and into the public domain the voices and points of view of all parties, including native peoples.

Archaeology in Brazil today is poised to be the leading intellectual discipline to stand against economic exploitation without environmental concern and to voice the rights of traditional communities to assert their historically based right to a specific heritage. In this sense, archaeology is able to bring to the decision-making scene players that, until now, have been outside the sphere of political decisions, thus exercising its potential to act as a democratic, socially inclusive discipline, and an academic and scientific bastion against savage and socially excluding capitalism for the emerging societies of the third world. This situation brings an enormous responsibility to the archaeologists working in the market as resource managers and, in fact, many of them are still not aware of it. Even the public agencies dealing with the evaluation of these studies have a poor understanding of the range of the problems and perspectives that can be potentially involved in each large-scale development project. But a truly democratic approach to these polemic questions involves creating a real sphere of debate where all parties can make themselves heard, thus opening a space for negotiations where even the most affected local minorities might not be ignored anymore.

Acknowledgments

I would like to thank Emilio González and André Penin for the long enlightening conversations. Of course, responsibility for this chapter is my own.

Notes

1. About the history and evolution of Brazilian archaeology, see Mendonça de Souza 1991; Prous 1992; Funari 1989 and 1995; and Barreto 1998 and 2000. Earlier evaluations of CRM studies in Brazil appear in Bezerra de Meneses 1988 and 1996; Araujo-Costa et al. 1988; and Caldarelli and Santos 2000.

2. An exception is the Itaipu Project, a large dam on the Paraná River between Brazil and Paraguay, developed by both governments. Although the whole project has been heavily criticized on environmental grounds, the archaeological rescue nevertheless produced some interesting results, and a local museum was established.

3. This is according to mainstream historical perspectives prevailing in those days, whose origins date back to the nineteenth century when, like many other flourishing countries, a nationalistic Brazilian thought had emerged (Miceli 1986; Ortiz 1985).

4. The most traditional archaeological museums in Brazil are the Museu Nacional (today related to the Federal University of Rio de Janeiro) and the Museu de Arqueologia e Etnologia, related to the University of São Paulo. Their stories have much in common, with collections that date back to the nineteenth century (Bruno 2000).

5. See, for example, the Lajeado Dam Archaeological Project results at the threshold of the southern border of Amazonia and the Brazilian Central Plateau (DeBlasis and Robrahn-González 2003).

References Cited

Araujo-Costa, Fernanda, Walter A. Neves, and Solange Caldarelli
1988   Rescue Archaeology in Brazilian Amazon: Retrospect and Perspectives. In *Archaeology and Society: Large Scale Rescue Operations; Their Possibilities and Problems*. ICOMOS-ICAHM Report no. 1, edited by G. Trotzig and G. Vahline, 277–85. Stockholm.

Barreto, Cristiana N. G. B.
1998   Brazilian Archaeology from a Brazilian Perspective. *Antiquity* 72:573–81.
2000   A construção de um passado pré-colonial: Uma breve história da arqueologia no Brasil (The building-up of a precolonial past: A short history of archaeology in Brazil). In *Antes de Cabral: Arqueologia brasileira* (Before Cabral: Brazilian archaeology), edited by Walter A. Neves. *Revista USP* 44:32–51. University of São Paulo.

Bezerra de Meneses, Ulpiano T.
1988   Arqueologia de Salvamento no Brasil: Uma avaliação crítica (Rescue archaeology in Brazil: A critical evaluation). Paper presented at the symposium S.O.S. Preservação do Patrimônio Arqueológico (Archaeological heritage preservation), September 5–9, Pontifical Catholic University, Rio de Janeiro.
1996   A pesquisa fora da Universidade: Patrimônio cultural, arqueologia e museus (Research outside the university: Cultural heritage, archaeology and museums). In *Humanidades, pesquisa, universidade* (Humanities, research, university). Seminários de Pesquisa (Research seminars), Istvan Jancsó (org.) 1:91–103. Comissão de Pesquisa da Faculdade de Filosofia, Letras e Ciências Humanas da Universidade de São Paulo (Research commission of the philosophy, letters, and human sciences faculty, University of São Paulo).

Bruno, Maria Cristina
2000   Museologia: A luta pela perseguição ao abandono (Museology: The fight against the abandonment). Ph.D. dissertation, University of São Paulo.

Caldarelli, Solange B., and Maria do Carmo M. Monteiro dos Santos
2000   Arqueologia de contrato no Brasil (Contract archaeology in Brazil). In *Antes de Cabral: Arqueologia brasileira* (Before Cabral: Brazilian archaeology), edited by Walter A. Neves. *Revista USP* 44:52–73. University of São Paulo.

Coletânea de Leis sobre Preservação do Patrimônio (Recollection of heritage preservation laws).

2006   IPHAN, Edições do Patrimônio, Rio de Janeiro.

DeBlasis, Paulo, and Erika M. Robrahn-González

2003   *Programa de resgate arqueológico da UHE Lajeado, Estado do Tocantins* (Lajeado power plant archaeological rescue program, Tocantins state). Final Report. Museum of Archaeology and Ethnology, University of São Paulo.

Funari, Pedro Paulo A.

1989   Brazilian Archaeology and World Archaeology: Some Remarks. *World Archaeology Bulletin* 3:60–68.

1995   Mixed Features of Archaeological Theory in Brazil. In *Theory in Archaeology, a World Perspective*, edited by J. J. Ucko, pp. 236–50. Routledge, London.

Kipnis, Renato, Irmhild Wust, Tom Dillehay, and Christopher Chippindale (editors)

1998   Issues in Brazilian archaeology. *Antiquity* 72:573–721.

Mendonça de Souza, Alfredo

1991   *História da arqueologia brasileira* (History of Brazilian archaeology). Pesquisas (Antropologia) 46. Instituto Anchietano de Pesquisas, São Leopoldo.

Miceli, Sérgio

1986   *Estado e cultura no Brasil* (State and culture in Brazil). Difel, São Paulo.

Ortiz, Renato

1985   *Cultura brasileira e identidade nacional* (Brazilian culture and national identity). Brasiliense, São Paulo.

Prous, André

1992   *Arqueologia brasileira* (Brazilian archaeology). University of Brasília, Brasília.

4

Archaeological Heritage Resource Protection in Canada

The Legislative Basis

DAVID POKOTYLO AND ANDREW R. MASON

Canada, the second largest country in the world by area with a population of 33 million, is a constitutional monarchy with a colonial past, and a confederation of 10 provinces and 3 northern territories. The Constitution Act of 1867 splits legislative powers between federal and provincial governments. This division is reflected in legislation to protect and manage archaeological heritage in Canada. Provinces are responsible for property, civil rights, and management of provincially owned public ("Crown") lands. The federal government is responsible for federally owned public lands, including lands reserved for Canada's Aboriginal people (Lee 2002).[1] Until recently, most land in the 3 territories (Yukon, Northwest Territories, and Nunavut) was under federal control, but this is changing with the resolution of Aboriginal land claims. In southern Canada, only a minor amount of land is under federal jurisdiction, and provincial statutes dominate.

While government protection and management of Canadian archaeological heritage resources can be traced back prior to confederation of the country in 1867, substantial developments started in the 1970s. Archaeological heritage resource management underwent unprecedented growth in the 1980s and 1990s and continues today. Presently, there is some legislative protection for archaeological heritage resources on most public and private lands in Canada, although significant gaps remain in federal legislation. In this chapter, we review the historical development and current legislative framework of archaeological heritage resource protection in Canada.

The Early Development of Archaeological Heritage Resource Protection

The roots of archaeological heritage resource protection in Canada extend to late seventeenth-century antiquarian interests in the colony of Canada, New France, in a report of 1696 on Aboriginal implements found during farming activities at Québec City (Martijn 1978:12). Stone artifacts unearthed in 1700 by workmen at Bécancour, Québec, and curated in a museum in Trois-Rivières, represent the oldest surviving archaeological collection in Canada (Trigger 1981:70). Little other antiquarian activity was recorded until the 1830s, when relic hunters dug Iroquoian burial sites in Ontario (Dade 1852:6).

The shift in Canada to a more intellectual interest in archaeology, and concern with preservation issues, started in the 1850s, mainly through the efforts of Sir Daniel Wilson and Sir John W. Dawson, who played major roles in natural history societies such as the Canadian Institute (later the Royal Canadian Institute) (Killan 1998; Trigger 1966a, 1966b). Prompted by increasing discoveries of archaeological sites during agricultural settlement and railway construction, the institute circulated a questionnaire in 1852 to collect information on mounds, artifacts, and Aboriginal place names, which encouraged collectors to donate artifacts to the institute's planned museum (Killan 1998:16–17). In reaction to increasing relic hunting, Daniel Wilson (1855, 1856) advocated the careful excavation and recording of archaeological sites. In 1860, John Dawson collected artifacts from a Montréal site exposed by construction and tried to relate the material to the Huron Iroquoian village visited by the French explorer Jacques Cartier in 1535 (Dawson 1860; Trigger 1966b). Dawson's work is considered to mark the birth of Canadian archaeology (Gibbon 1998:199; Trigger 1966b), and it is the earliest recorded case of "salvage" archaeology in Canada.

The earliest legislation to protect archaeological material in Canada dates prior to confederation. The Colony of British Columbia enacted the Indian Graves Ordinance in 1865, which made it an offense to "steal, . . . cut, break, destroy, damage or remove any image, bones, article or thing deposited on, in, or near any Indian Grave in this Colony, or induce, or incite any other persons to do so, or purchase any such article or thing . . . knowing the same to have been so acquired or dealt with" (Isaac 1993:6–7), and asserted that all items noted are the property of the Crown. The penalty was a fine of up to 100 pounds and/or imprisonment up to 6 months (12 months maximum for repeat offenders).

A provincial antiquities act, modeled after Sir John Lubbock's Ancient Monuments Act of 1812 in England, was proposed when the Ontario Provincial Museum (now the Royal Ontario Museum) opened in 1887 (Noble 1972:5). Also in 1887, the Canadian Institute hired David Boyle as a full-time archaeologist, who urged the provincial government to pass legislation to protect archaeological sites (Killan 1998). However, these early initiatives did not result in legislation.

The Geological Survey of Canada's Anthropological Division was established in 1910, with a mandate to preserve information on Aboriginal societies in Canada (Sapir 1911). Most of its resources were allocated to ethnography, as archaeological sites were not considered endangered. In 1911, Harlan I. Smith became the survey's first archaeologist. Over the next three decades, Smith conducted archaeological work throughout Canada and raised public interest in archaeology through his lecture series at the Victoria Memorial Museum in Ottawa—now the Canadian Museum of Civilization (Dyck 1998:123–24). Concerned about the preservation of archaeological sites, in 1913 Smith convinced the Canadian Parks Branch to mark housepit sites in Banff National Park, Alberta with a warning of penalties if disturbed (Smith 1914).

In 1885, the Canadian federal government moved toward environmental and heritage protection by creating national parks—the first at Banff, Alberta. In 1919, James B. Harkin, Canada's first national parks commissioner, persuaded the federal government to establish an advisory board to focus specifically on historic site protection. This Historic Sites and Monuments Board was to advise government on commemoration of heritage sites of national importance; however, it had no formal authority for designation, conservation, or public ownership of such properties.

Except for a small provision in the amendments of 1927 to the Indian Act (see below), Canada's Parliament took no formal legislative action on heritage sites until the National Parks Act of 1930 (amended in 1988) that mandated Parks Canada (also now known as the Parks Canada Agency) to protect and develop areas of national significance to Canada's natural and cultural heritage. Also in 1930, the Ordinance Respecting the Protection and Care of Eskimo Ruins was passed, giving protection to archaeological sites in the Northwest Territories and providing the basis for current regulations there (Arnold and Stenton 2002:35).

In British Columbia, the Historic Objects Preservation Act of 1925 provided some legal protection to archaeological sites—primarily rock art sites (pictographs and petroglyphs). The act allowed the government to declare "any primitive figure or legend cut in or painted upon rock, or any group of such figures or legends, or any structure, or any natural object existing within the Province to be an 'historic object'" and erect signage in the vicinity of a designated historic object to warn against its disturbance or removal without a government-issued permit. Convicted violators could be fined up to C$500.

The Manitoba provincial government passed An Act Respecting Historic Sites and Ethnological Objects in 1946, but it only protected designated properties (Gonsalves et al. 1965). Ontario established legislation similar to that existing in British Columbia, to "sign" select sites in the Archaeological and Historic Sites Protection Act of 1953. Protection was restricted to well-known sites that had received "professional" investigation (Neal Ferris, personal communication, 2007). Designation under this act protected sites from untrained individuals and tried to ensure that landowners did not inadvertently destroy sites through development.

In the late 1940s, Charles E. Borden began excavating archaeological sites in British Columbia. Through the 1950s, Borden and the anthropologist Wilson Duff lobbied government and private developers to take responsibility for archaeological heritage resource protection, and promoted public awareness of the need for legislation. This resulted in the Archaeological and Historic Sites Protection Act of 1960, which was a model for other provinces developing similar legislation in the 1970s. The most salient aspects of the act were acknowledgment of the financial responsibility of developers to conduct salvage work on threatened sites and the protection (through a permit process) for archaeological sites on both designated and provincial Crown land.

Also in 1960, Saskatchewan passed The Provincial Parks, Protected Areas, Recreation Sites, and Antiquities Act. While not as strong as British Columbia's legislation, it allowed for creation of "protected areas" that could contain burials, pictographs, or other kinds of archaeological sites.

Archaeologists in Canada in the 1960s faced the critical task of establishing a baseline understanding of the country's archaeological record (Kelley and Williamson 1996; Wright 1985) at a time of substantial growth and development affecting archaeological heritage resources across the country. With the few exceptions noted above, Canadian legislation to protect archaeological heritage resources was woefully inadequate prior to the 1960s, and archaeologists urgently needed to find ways to protect and preserve the diminishing record.

A significant event was the founding of the Western Canadian Archaeological Council in 1960, which passed a set of resolutions recommending that 1) federal and provincial governments enact legislation similar to that in British Columbia; 2) the federal government pass legislation adopting international principles pertaining to archaeological excavations formulated by the United Nations Educational, Scientific and Cultural Organization (UNESCO) in 1956 (see O'Keefe, this volume); and 3) the federal government amend the Indian Act to protect archaeological sites on reserve lands (Western Canadian Archaeological Council 1960:9). Another important outcome was the identification of archaeological sites, and the material they contain, as resources—"essentially like fishery or timber resources; no persons are legally or morally justified in squandering any part of the public heritage" (Western Canadian Archaeological Council 1960:9). Efforts like these continued through the 1960s (see Burley 1994:59; Turnbull 1977:122), resulting in the founding of the Canadian Archaeological Association (CAA) in 1968 to represent concerns of the Canadian professional archaeological community. In the 1970s, legislation, mainly at the provincial level, was passed to protect archaeological heritage.

International Obligations after 1970

One of the mandates of UNESCO is preservation of world cultural heritage. The organization has advanced conventions and recommendations regarding cultural heritage to be observed by states within their own land, as well as that of other states. Canada has played a central role in the development of, and response to, a number of these conventions, but at the expense of enacting legislation to protect the country's own archaeological resources.

In 1976, Canada ratified UNESCO's Convention Concerning the Protection of the World Cultural and Natural Heritage of 1972, commonly referred to as the World Heritage Convention. The World Heritage Committee, struck under this convention, has recognized the universal heritage significance of 15 properties in Canada, placing them on the World Heritage List. Of these, 9 are parks and natural areas, and 3 of the 6 historic sites have archaeological components (L'Anse aux Meadows National Historic Site, Head-Smashed-In Buffalo Jump, and SGang Gwaay).

In 1978, Canada became a signatory to UNESCO's Convention on the Means of Prohibiting and Preventing the Illicit Import, Export and Transfer of Ownership of Cultural Property of 1970, after the introduction of the Cultural Property Export and Import Act as Canada's implementing legislation for the convention in 1977. This convention places the onus on each country to develop its own rules for protecting and preserving its cultural heritage.

Consistent with the UNESCO Convention of 1970, Canada and the United States signed a bilateral agreement in 1997 to protect archaeological and ethnological material of cultural significance. Under this agreement, the United States, under the authority of the Convention on Cultural Property Implementation Act, placed import restrictions on certain classes of objects, allowing Canada to recover and repatriate cultural material that may have been illegally exported to the United States. This agreement lapsed in 2002 and, despite the Canadian government's request for renewal, the United States has not responded positively.

The Convention for the Protection of Cultural Property in the Event of Armed Conflict, known as the Hague Convention (1954, 1999), addressed concerns over the destruction of cultural property during the Second World War (see O'Keefe, this volume, for details); in 1999, Canada became a state party to the convention. Following the passage of Bill S-37 (An Act to Amend the Criminal Code and Cultural Property Export and Import Act), Canada deposited its instruments of accession to the First (1954) and Second (1999) Protocols of the Hague Convention with UNESCO, which subsequently came into force in March 2006. The amendments to the Cultural Property Export and Import Act allow for prosecution of persons residing in Canada who illegally export cultural property from an occupied territory of a state party to the Second Protocol of the Hague Convention.

The Federal Context after 1970

Despite the contributions of the Canadian federal government on the international stage, presently there is no comprehensive federal statute directing how (or whether) a given department is supposed to treat archaeological resources on federal Crown land (Department of Communications 1988; see also Canadian Archaeological Association [CAA] 1986). Canada has the dubious distinction of being the only member of the G8 nations lacking comprehensive federal cultural resource management legislation (see Burley 1994 for a detailed discussion of why this has not occurred; see also Lee 2002; Wiebe 2006). In the absence of such legislation, federal land managers rely on general agency policies or departmental directives, if they exist (Canadian Environmental Assessment Agency [CEAA] 1996; Denhez 2000; Parks Canada 1993, 1994; Yellowhorn 1999).

Canada's Indian Act is the primary federal statute pertaining to Aboriginal people and management of reserve lands and finances. The Indian Act was enacted in 1876; the modern version of the act was passed into law in 1951 and amended in 1985. With respect to archaeological heritage, the Indian Act is largely silent, although section 91(3), "Trading with Indians," provides limited protection for some classes of objects located on Indian reserves: grave houses, grave poles, totem poles, carved house posts, and rock art. This provision, present since 1927, provides a minimal penalty for contravention—C$200 or imprisonment for a term up to three months. Yellowhorn (1999) notes that section 81, "Powers of the Council," of the act enables bands to develop local bylaws consistent with the Indian Act; this could include management of archaeological resources on Indian reserve lands. While this avenue of protection has not been explored, First Nations are now developing their own legally nonbinding instruments, which are discussed later in this chapter.

Currently, questions pertaining to federal archaeological policy and legislation fall to the Parks Canada Agency to "provide advice, tools and information to other federal land managers on archaeology and environmental assessment to help implement the Government of Canada's Archaeological Heritage Policy Framework (1990)" (Parks Canada 2005).

Beyond Parks Canada policy and guidelines, federal legislation relevant to archaeological resources include the Historic Sites and Monuments Act, the Canadian Environmental Assessment Act, the Canada Shipping Act, and the Cultural Property Export and Import Act.

In 1953, the Historic Sites and Monuments Act formally recognized the Historic Sites and Monuments Board of Canada (HSMBC) by statute and expanded its mandate. The HSMBC reviews requests for commemoration of significant places, people, and events in Canadian history. There are presently over 1,500 designated National Historic Sites in Canada. Relatively few relate to Aboriginal history, and over the past decade, the National Historic Sites Program has improved the representation of sites, including archaeological sites (for example, Xá:ytem—see Pokotylo and Brass 1997), commemorating Aboriginal history. Commemoration as a National Historic Site, however, does not carry any special protection; the act has no penalty for damage or destruction to such sites, although a charge of mischief could be laid under the Criminal Code (Ward 1988:68).

The Canadian Environmental Assessment Act (CEAA) was passed in 1992 to ensure that projects in which federal authorities have an interest do not have "significant adverse environmental effects" (CEAA section 4[1][a]). The CEAA makes specific reference to archaeological resources and traditional use sites of Aboriginal people in the definition of "environmental effect." Under the CEAA, a federal authority must assess the effects of any change resulting from alteration to the environment caused by a project (CEAA section 2[1][b]). The act also requires all studies and assessments of a project to consider the significance of these environmental effects, as well as "technically and economically feasible" restitution or mitigation measures (CEAA section 16[1]).

The CEAA Reference Guide (CEAA 1996) presents a framework for assessing and mitigating the potential environmental effects of a project on cultural heritage resources. Conspicuously absent are statutory directives regarding how these resources and features are to be "considered" (that is, managed). Although the CEAA explicitly states that archaeological concerns must "receive careful consideration," how this is to be done is not clear given the absence of comprehensive heritage resource management legislation at the federal level.

The Canadian Shipping Act,[2] implemented in 2001, protects heritage wrecks in all navigable waters, including those on provincial land, but not submerged cultural resources (for example, archaeological sites). Given that heritage wreck regulations are not yet in place, these sites remain at risk (see Grenier 2006). Archaeological resources in Canadian waters would receive further protection if Canada ratifies the UNESCO Convention on the Protection of Underwater Cultural Heritage (2001).[3]

In 1975, the Cultural Property Export and Import Act was implemented to regulate export and import of moveable cultural property. It requires permits to transport items out of the country, and it provides incentives to encourage the donation or sale of important objects to public institutions in Canada. Archaeological material is one category of objects on the Canadian Cultural Property Export Control List. When an object on the control list is considered of national cultural significance, the Canadian Cultural Property Review Board may deny an export permit. If denial is followed by an unsuccessful appeal, then the applicant must wait two to six months, during which time approved Canadian institutions may purchase the item at fair market value. Partial funding is available from the board to assist with purchases. If a Canadian institution does not acquire the item by the end of the waiting period, an export permit is granted—thus, initial denial of an export permit does not guarantee that significant objects remain in Canada. The act also has provisions prohibiting the import into Canada of cultural property illegally exported from foreign states, and includes procedures for recovery and return of foreign cultural property illegally exported from its country of origin.

Soon after enactment, the Canadian archaeological community criticized the Cultural Property Export and Import Act, particularly 1) the legal assumption that archaeological objects are private property to be bought and sold, and the assignment of monetary value to archaeological objects to establish fair market value—in effect, sanctioning a legitimate market system for Canadian archaeological antiquities; 2) the inability of the legislation to stop the export of significant Canadian heritage objects if not acquired by a Canadian institution; and 3) lack of consideration for provincial restrictions on the movement or disposition of artifacts.

In 1979, the CAA passed a set of resolutions objecting to the act (Loy 1979). The most contentious one instructed members of the CAA who were serving as expert examiners to express opposition by approving all export permit applications referred to them, declaring archaeological objects to have no market value, and alerting the public of the imminent export of these objects. This strategy was ineffective, resulting in the export of two seated human figurine stone bowls from British Columbia (see Bernick 1983, 1984a, 1985). The resulting media attention was not positive toward the CAA's position, and the federal government threatened to ban the CAA's members as expert examiners. In 1984, the CAA's official position changed, and members were not bound to approve export permits for archaeological artifacts (Bernick 1984b; Burley 1984).

In 1993, a seated human figurine stone bowl was purchased under provisions of the act by the Simon Fraser University Museum of Ethnology and Archaeology, in trust for the Saanich Native Heritage Society, as the only legal recourse to prevent its export from Canada (Winter 1995). This highlighted the fact that archaeological objects have special significance to First Nations communities, and their interests are not represented in the export review process (Winter and Henry 1997).

This controversy prompted major lobbying efforts by regional and national organizations to prohibit permanent export of all archaeological objects, as well as to enact legislation to protect and manage archaeological heritage under federal jurisdiction (CAA 1986). The federal government commissioned a report on Canadian archaeological resource management (Department of Communications 1988) and proposed legislation in 1990 (Haunton 1992). This bill never became law for many reasons, including opposition by Aboriginal peoples to federal assertion of ownership of Aboriginal archaeological resources (see Dunn 1991a, 1991b; Lee 2002). The federal government reviewed the Cultural Property Export and Import Act in 1997 to address the problems with it. Although some changes were passed in 2005 (An Act to Amend the Criminal Code and the Cultural Property Export and Import Act), the above issues have yet to be resolved and permits to export archaeological objects continue to be approved.

The Historic Places Initiative

In 1999, recognizing that Canada was lagging behind other nations in the protection of heritage sites on federal lands, the federal government initiated the Historic Places Initiative. This created the Canadian Register of Historic Places, developed the Standards and Guidelines for the Conservation of Historic Places in Canada, and renewed the process of creating comprehensive legislation to protect federally owned historic places, including archaeological sites. The Canadian Register of Historic Places, a collaborative initiative between the federal government and the provinces and territories, consists of a searchable database of significant historic places compiled from all jurisdictions within Canada.

The Standards and Guidelines for the Conservation of Historic Places in Canada (Parks Canada 2003) were developed to guide interventions on federal historic places and assess projects where proponents seek to access financial incentives under the proposed legislation. These currently focus on the conservation of known archaeological sites but remain largely silent on archaeological investigations (for example, how to test and evaluate sites).

The third component of the Historic Places Initiative is a proposed "historic places act" that will finally put the federal house in order. Under this proposed legislation, the Historic Sites and Monuments Act, the Treasury Board Heritage Buildings Policy, and the Canadian Register of Historic Places will formally address archaeological site protection on federal land, including land under water. For the first time in Canada's history, statutory protection would exist for archaeological sites on all federal lands, with the exception of lands already covered under territorial regulations, heritage wrecks protected under the Canadian Shipping Act, and possibly, Indian reserves.

The possible exemption for Indian reserves is based on feedback from Aboriginal groups on the proposed act (Canadian Heritage 2002). This position contrasts with Resolution no. 2004(20) of the Assembly of First Nations (Canada's largest national Aboriginal political body), which directs its leadership to initiate development of national heritage legislation with the federal government and the CAA (Assembly of First Nations 2004). Given the substance of this resolution, it may be possible to review the proposed exemption for Indian reserves prior to finalizing the scope of the act.

The preceding discussion has summarized federal archaeological heritage protection in Canada, identified some of the current shortcomings, and described the future potential to finally realize comprehensive federal heritage legislation. Clouding this optimism is the uncertain state of Canadian federal politics, in which discretionary legislation remains in a state of flux as governments, particularly those in a minority position, focus on retaining power. Given the change in government in 2006 and the consequences of the re-election in 2008 of this minority government, the proposed historic places act is stalled until it again becomes a priority of the government. There is growing trepidation among heritage professionals that, should this proposed legislation fail to be passed into law, as occurred in the early 1990s, it may take a generation before another attempt is made. It seems unlikely that there will be the appetite among the present generation of heritage professionals to try again. In the meantime, Canada will continue with its patchwork of laws, guidelines, policies, and protocols until it gets its federal act together.

The Provincial-Territorial Context

Space does not allow a detailed review of legislation protecting archaeological heritage in each province and territory in Canada. Recent detailed reviews of the development of archaeological resource protection measures are available for British Columbia (Apland 1993; Ward 1988), Ontario (Ferris 1998, 2002; MacLeod 1975; Pearce 1989), the Northwest Territories (Arnold and Stenton 2002), and western Canada in general (Spurling 1986). The major statutes are listed in Table 4.1; most have been enacted since the 1970s, and many have since undergone revision. Although there is regional variation to address specifics of the archaeological record in each jurisdiction, these laws share common aspects with respect to the nature and kind of archaeological resources protected, provisions for special protection, control over permits and licenses to conduct archaeology, ownership and stewardship, approaches to the management of impacts to the record, and civil remedies for contravention.

Table 4.1. Major Provincial-Territorial Statutory Laws Affecting Archaeological Heritage in Canada

Jurisdiction	Statute	Date[a]
British Columbia	Heritage Conservation Act	1996
Alberta	Historic Resources Act	2006
Saskatchewan	Heritage Property Act	2005
Manitoba	Heritage Resources Act	1986
Ontario	Ontario Heritage Act	2006
Québec	Cultural Property Act	2004
New Brunswick	Historic Site Protection Act	2000
Nova Scotia	Special Places Protection Act	1995
Prince Edward Island	Archaeological Sites Protection Act	2000
Newfoundland-Labrador	Historic Resources Act	2005
Yukon	Historic Resources Act	2002
Northwest Territories	Archaeological Sites Regulations	2001
Nunavut	Archaeological and Palaeontological Sites Regulations	2001

Source: Data drawn from publicly available Canadian provincial and territorial government websites.

a. Date refers to the most recent amendment of the statute, which may not be the initial date of enactment.

While these acts and regulations define archaeological resources as evidence of human occupation found in the ground or underwater, some (British Columbia and Ontario) include items above the ground, such as culturally modified trees (see Klimko et al. 1998), petroglyphs, and pictographs. Most are unspecific about how old a site or object must be to be considered "archaeological." In the Northwest Territories and Nunavut, 50 years old is the minimum age for archaeological objects where an unbroken chain of possession cannot be demonstrated. British Columbia provides blanket protection to all sites and artifacts dating prior to 1846. Many of the statutes pertain to "heritage," "cultural," or "historic" interests; this may explicitly or implicitly include palaeontology, although British Columbia and Québec specifically exclude it.

A complex series of federal and provincial laws come into effect upon discovery of human remains, and most provinces and territories recognize the need for the involvement of First Nations with Aboriginal human burial discoveries. All jurisdictions have developed protocols for managing discovered "historical" (that is, non-crime scene) buried human remains, and liaisons between authorities and interested groups. However, policies for burials already in institutional collections vary considerably across the country (Hanna 2003).

Each province and territory has an administrative unit to implement archaeological heritage legislation, and its placement in each government varies considerably. For example, British Columbia's Archaeology Branch is in the Ministry of Tourism, Culture and the Arts, while Ontario's Heritage Division is in the Ministry of Culture. These units maintain site inventories, authorize archaeological work, and identify projects that potentially affect archaeological heritage resources. The nature of archaeological work requiring authorization varies across jurisdictions. In western Canada, a permit is not required for archaeological investigations that do not disturb the ground, but in other provinces and territories, all archaeological investigations, invasive or not, require authorization. Permits are issued for specific archaeological projects in all provinces but Ontario, where archaeologists can obtain an annual license to carry out investigations. Penalties vary considerably across the country (see Table 4.2). For example, in Prince Edward Island, the maximum individual fine is C$2,000, while in Newfoundland, Alberta, Ontario, and Québec, the fine is C$50,000 or more, and up to one year in prison. Penalties for corporate violations can be larger than those for individuals, with British Columbia allowing fines of up to C$1 million.

The Municipal Context

Archaeological site protection at the local level (for example, municipalities or regional districts) is weak or nonexistent, with the exception of Ontario, where recent legislation requires local planning decisions to be consistent with provin-

Table 4.2. Penalties for Contravention of Provincial-Territorial Statutes on Archaeological Heritage in Canada

Jurisdiction	Penalty
British Columbia	- If a resource is altered or damaged without a permit: individual fine up to C$50,000 or up to 2 years in prison or both, corporate fine up to C$1,000,000. - All other infractions: fine up to C$2,000 or no more than 6 months in prison or both.
Alberta	- Fine no more than C$50,000 or up to one year in prison, or both.
Saskatchewan	- Individual: penalty maximum fine of C$5,000 and a maximum 6 months in prison or both; corporate maximum fine is C$250,000. - For all violations, cost of restoration due to damage is the responsibility of the perpetrator.
Manitoba	- Individual is fined no more than C$5,000 for every day the offense continues; corporation is fined no more than C$50,000 for every day the offense continues. - Perpetrator may also incur costs of damage restoration or repair in addition to fine.
Ontario	- Individual maximum fine of C$50,000 or imprisonment for up to one year or both; corporate maximum fine of C$250,000. - Penalties can also include the costs of restoration as a result of damages.
Québec	- Individual who contravenes the act in relation to alteration restrictions can be fined a minimum of C$625 and a maximum of C$60,700. - Offenses against proper time periods for notification or permit submission can be fined a minimum of C$75 and a maximum of C$625.
New Brunswick	- Fine of no less than C$140 and no more than C$300 for each day of violation.
Nova Scotia	- Individual maximum fine of C$10,000; corporate maximum fine of C$100,000.
Prince Edward Island	- Maximum fine of C$2,000.
Newfoundland-Labrador	- Maximum fine of C$50,000 or a maximum imprisonment of 1 year, or both; this penalty applies to one conviction, and every day or part of a day an offense occurs is considered a separate infraction. - Perpetrator is also responsible for any costs of restoration as a result of the contravention.
Yukon	- Individual maximum fine of C$50,000 or imprisonment up to 6 months, or both; corporate maximum fine of C$1,000,000. - Costs of damage restoration are the responsibility of the perpetrator.
Northwest Territories	- No penalty defined in the legislation; maximum fine of C$1,000 or up to 1 year in prison, or both, under the Northwest Territories Act.
Nunavut	- No penalty stated in the legislation; maximum fine C$5,000 or six months in prison, or both, as a summary offense under the Nunavut Act.

Source: Data drawn from publicly available Canadian provincial and territorial government websites.

cial policy statements. Local governments and approval authorities in Ontario now incorporate detailed archaeological conservation objectives and policies into their planning and development approval processes (Ontario Ministry of Culture 2006). Some municipalities in Ontario have had their own archaeological master plans since the late 1980s. There are almost 20 such plans, led by the 5-year Toronto project (Archaeological Services Inc. 2004), which has among the world's most aggressive protection policies in place, including building permit requirements for areas of archaeological sensitivity (Ron Williamson, personal communication, 2007).

Ontario's leadership role with local municipalities emphasizes the fact that much site destruction in the province results from development on private land, not Crown land. Elsewhere in Canada, local governments fail to adequately protect archaeological resources, leaving the matter to other levels with the legislative mandate to do so, even though municipal officials have considerable influence in determining when, or if, archaeological assessments precede development projects (Mason 2005). This regulatory disconnect has resulted in many otherwise avoidable impacts to archaeological sites across the country (for example, McIntyre and Davis 2005).

Challenges and New Developments

The diversity of legislation has changed the practice of archaeology in Canada over the last three decades. Various government agencies and programs have resulted from this legislation, and a substantial private-sector industry of professional archaeologists has developed to deal with the legal requirements for archaeological resource management. While this legislation and resulting activity has increased protection of the country's archaeological heritage, it has also raised the public profile of archaeology, and the involvement of Aboriginal people in decisions affecting the practice of archaeology. We discuss some of these changes below.

Public Profile and Enforcement

Laws protecting archaeological sites are important, but their successful enforcement is critical. Archaeological heritage protection legislation has a low profile within law enforcement in Canada. In many cases, the public, as well as the police, are unfamiliar with these laws. A recent national survey showed that while 98 percent of Canadians think archaeological sites should be legally protected, nearly 20 percent were uncertain if such laws existed at either the federal or provincial level (Pokotylo 2001:104–8). This lack of familiarity also translates into reluctance by police and Crown prosecutors to investigate and take cases forward, as well as a poor success rate for prosecutions. Thus, with few exceptions (for example, Angelbeck 2007; Apland 1997; Fox 1985, 1986; Jacques Whitford Environment Limited 2001), most acts protecting archaeological heritage in Canada remain untested.

This lack of understanding is acknowledged by professional and avocational archaeological communities throughout the country; there is general recognition that a public that is educated about archaeology as part of Canadian heritage and about the importance of site protection is a critical component of a solution to the problem. The CAA recently identified public understanding, appreciation, and support for the value of archaeological resources—particularly the message that preservation of the archaeological record is central to Canadian identity—as a major objective in its strategic five-year plan (CAA 2008). Public education in archaeology occurs in many formats and venues throughout the country; a review of these programs is beyond the scope of this chapter.

It is critical that education efforts increase awareness of the importance of Canada's archaeological heritage and the existence of heritage protection legislation to those responsible for enforcement of the heritage legislation. Some government agencies administering the acts provide awareness training for other agencies, including the police (Ray Kenny, personal communication, 2009).There also needs to be a strong political commitment at municipal, provincial-territorial, and federal levels of government to enforce existing legislation, as well as reconciliation of Aboriginal rights regarding stewardship of their archaeological heritage. In some parts of the country, there is a growing call for community-based stewardship that would include the recognition and application of conservation efforts by municipal authorities to archaeological sites in their land use plans in the same manner that they treat natural heritage features (see MacLay 2004). It would be useful to reconsider the recruitment of local communities (Aboriginal and non-Aboriginal) as archaeological watchdogs who could contact officials about threats to archaeological sites. Such volunteer archaeological warden programs operated in British Columbia and in Ontario during the 1970s and 1980s until they were terminated in the late 1980s due to the withdrawal of government support.

Working with First Nations

The past two decades have been a period of considerable debate and change for archaeologists studying Aboriginal heritage in Canada (see Nicholas and Andrews 1997). There are increasing demands for control by First Nations, but present heritage acts are not explicit about Native ownership of their archaeological heritage. Given recent Canadian Supreme Court rulings that reaffirm the principle of fiduciary responsibility to protect the interests of Aboriginal people, some archaeologists suggest that there is a fiduciary obligation on the part of the Crown to care for Aboriginal archaeological sites and materials (see Ferris 2000, 2003; Ferris and Leclair 1999).

Two initiatives within the profession have developed principles as a basis for policies and new working relationships between archaeologists and Aboriginal people in Canada. The joint Task Force Report on Museums and First Peoples of the Assembly of First Nations and Canadian Museums Association states that involvement of Aboriginal peoples in museum work is essential in order to improve the representation and interpretation of Aboriginal pre- and post-contact histories and cultures, and equal partnerships need to be forged between museums and Aboriginal peoples (Hill and Nicks 1992). After nationwide consultation with the professional archaeological community and Aboriginal people, the CAA prepared the Statement of Principles for Ethical Conduct Pertaining to Aboriginal Peoples in 1996 (CAA 1997; Nicholson et al. 1996). These principles acknowledge Aboriginal people's interest in the protection and management of the archaeological record, as well as its interpretation and presentation, and encourage partnerships with Aboriginal communities in archaeological research, management, and education, based on respect and mutual sharing of knowledge and expertise. Many institutions and archaeologists in Canada have adopted recommendations from both of these documents as guidelines, and these principles are restructuring the practice of Canadian archaeology.

As Canada's Aboriginal peoples have become increasingly interested in the management of archaeological resources in their traditional territories, there have been some memoranda of understanding (MOUs) or similar agreements between Aboriginal peoples, government, and industry for the management of archaeological resources on traditional lands (for example, Budhwa 2005). Although there is considerable variability across the country, these MOUs tend to outline mutually agreed upon archaeological resource management protocols, including a commitment to consult on a regular basis and to discuss proposed changes to archaeological resource management policy.

Furthermore, many of Canada's Aboriginal groups have been dissatisfied with existing heritage legislation and often narrow legal definitions of archaeological sites (see Nicholas 2006). Wanting to assert influence within their traditional territories, they have developed their own heritage policies and permitting systems. While not legally binding, the archaeological community has largely respected this parallel management regime.

Conclusion

Legislation and regulatory frameworks provide limited latitude in implementation and interpretation and are, by their very nature, prescriptive or rules-based. However, the Aboriginal decision-making process in archaeological heritage resource decisions, particularly those related to human burial sites, may be more values-based than rules-based. This difference in worldviews continues to be a challenge for First Nations, archaeologists, and government regulatory agencies in Canada.

If there is to be effective archaeological heritage preservation legislation at all government levels in Canada, it is crucial that government, archaeologists, and Aboriginal people recognize and respect the validity of each other's values. They must acknowledge the differences and find common ground to achieve what is essentially the same underlying objective for all concerned.

Acknowledgments

We gratefully acknowledge the comments and suggestions from Charles Arnold, Steve Daniel, Neal Ferris, Ben Hjermstad, Julie Hollowell, Ellen Lee, Marty Magne, Andrew Martindale, David Mason, R. G. Matson, Robert Paterson, Sue Rowley, Doug Stenton, Barbara Winter, and Ron Williamson in the preparation and revision of this essay. Thanks are owed to Christopher Ames, who assembled comparative data on provincial and territorial statutes. Any errors of fact or interpretation are solely our own.

Notes

1. Names are a problem and, in the case of Canadian Aboriginal people, have changed with the times. Although the Indian Act remains in force in Canada, the term "Indian" is widely disfavored by those whom the term is used to describe. "Native" (but not "Native Canadian") and "Aboriginal" are occasionally used in self-reference, but "First Nations" and "First Peoples" are more commonly accepted at present. As there is no universally accepted term or definition, these four terms are used interchangeably in this chapter.

2. Heritage wrecks are addressed under the Canadian Shipping Act due to their potential overlap with salvage rights.

3. The UNESCO Convention on the Protection of the Underwater Cultural Heritage (2001) currently requires an additional eight state parties for it to come into force. Canada has yet to ratify this convention.

References Cited

Angelbeck, Bill
2007   The Message of the Poets Cove Sentence. *The Midden* 39(2):2.
Apland, Brian
1993   The Role of the Provincial Government in British Columbia Archaeology. *BC Studies* 99:7–24.
1997   Heritage Conservation Act—Enforcement. *The Midden* 29(4):3–4.

Archaeological Services Inc.

2004   *A Master Plan of Archaeological Resources for the City of Toronto: Interim Report*. Report on file, Heritage Preservation Services, Culture Division, City of Toronto.

Arnold Charles D., and Douglas R. Stenton

2002   New Archaeological Regulations for the Northwest Territories and Nunavut, Canada. *Revista de Arqueologia Americana* (Journal of American Archaeology) 21:33–43.

Assembly of First Nations

2004   Resolution no. 20. Electronic document, http://www.afn.ca/article.asp?id=1128, accessed on September 3, 2007.

Bernick, Kathryn

1983   B.C. Government Signs Permit to Export Artifacts. *The Midden* 15(5):2.

1984a   Protesting Archaeologists Sacrifice Artifacts. *The Midden* 16(1):2–3.

1984b   C.A.A. Balks When Challenged. *The Midden* 16(3):9–10.

1985   How Many Stone Bowls Will It Take? *The Midden* 17(2):4.

Budhwa, Rick

2005   An Alternate Model for First Nations Involvement in Resource Management Archaeology. *Canadian Journal of Archaeology* 29:20–45.

Burley, David V.

1994   A Never Ending Story: Historical Developments in Canadian Archaeology and the Quest for Federal Heritage Legislation. *Canadian Journal of Archaeology* 18:77–98.

Burley, David V. (editor)

1984   Bill C-33 and the Cultural Property Export and Import Act. *Canadian Archaeological Association Newsletter* 4(2):1–3.

Canadian Archaeological Association (CAA)

1986   The Need for Canadian Legislation to Protect and Manage Heritage Resources on Federal Lands. *Canadian Archaeological Association Newsletter* 6(1):1–8.

1997   Canadian Archaeological Association: Statement of Principles for Ethical Conduct Pertaining to Aboriginal Peoples. *Canadian Journal of Archaeology* 21:5–6.

2008   Canadian Archaeological Association Five-Year Strategic Plan 2008–2013. Electronic document, http://www.canadianarchaeology.com/documents.lasso, accessed on September 17, 2009.

Canadian Environmental Assessment Agency (CEAA)

1996   *A Reference Guide for the Canadian Environmental Assessment Act: Assessing Environmental Effects on Physical and Cultural Heritage Resources*. Minister of Supply and Services Canada, Hull.

Canadian Heritage

2002   *Historic Places and Aboriginal People: A Discussion Document*. Public Works and Government Services Canada, Ottawa.

Dade, Rev. C.
1852   Indian Remains—Being a Description of an Indian Burial Ground in Beverly
        Township, Ten Miles from Dundas. *Canadian Journal* 1:6.
Dawson, John W.
1860   Notes on the Aboriginal Antiquities Found at Montreal. *Canadian Naturalist
        and Geologist* 5:430–49.
Denhez, Marc
2000   *Unearthing the Law: Archaeological Legislation on Lands in Canada.* Archaeo-
        logical Services Branch, Parks Canada Agency, Ottawa.
Department of Communications
1988   *Federal Archaeological Heritage Protection and Management: A Discussion
        Paper.* Ottawa.
Dunn, Martin
1991a   *A National Overview of the Department of Communications Consultation with
        Aboriginal Peoples on Canadian Archaeological Heritage.* Report submitted to
        Department of Communication, Ottawa.
1991b   *My Grandfather Is Not an Artifact: A Report on the Aboriginal Archaeological
        Heritage Symposium, February 17–18, 1991, Hull, Québec.* Report submitted to
        Department of Communication, Ottawa.
Dyck, Ian
1998   Toward a History of Archaeology in the National Museum of Canada: The
        Contributions of Harlan Smith and Douglas Leechman, 1911–1950. In *Bringing
        Back the Past: Historical Perspectives on Canadian Archaeology,* edited by Pa-
        mela J. Smith and Donald Mitchell, pp. 115–33. Archaeological Survey of Can-
        ada Mercury Series Paper 158, Canadian Museum of Civilization, Hull.
Ferris, Neal
1998   I Don't Think We Are in Kansas Anymore: The Rise of the Archaeological Con-
        sulting Industry in Ontario. In *Bringing Back the Past: Historical Perspectives
        on Canadian Archaeology,* edited by Pamela J. Smith and Donald Mitchell, pp.
        225–47. Archaeological Survey of Canada Mercury Series Paper 158, Cana-
        dian Museum of Civilization, Hull.
2000   Current Issues in the Governance of Archaeology in Canada. *Canadian
        Journal of Archaeology* 24:164–70.
2002   When the Air Thins: The Rapid Rise of the Archaeological Consulting In-
        dustry in Ontario. *Revista de Arqueologia Americana* (Journal of American
        Archaeology) 21:53–88.
2003   Between Colonial and Indigenous Archaeologies: Legal and Extra-legal Own-
        ership of the Archaeological Past in North America. *Canadian Journal of
        Archaeology* 27:154–90.
Ferris, Neal, and Laurie Leclair
1999   Archaeology as Possession: Who Owns the Past in Ontario? Paper presented
        at the 1999 Chacmool Conference, University of Calgary, Calgary.

Fox, William A.

1985   The Freelton/Misner Site Looting and Prosecution. *Kewa* 85(5):4–13.

1986   Epilogue to a Prosecution. *Kewa* 86(1):10–11.

Gibbon, Guy

1998   Dawson, John W. (1820–1899). In *Archaeology of Prehistoric North America: An Encyclopedia*, edited by Guy Gibbon, p. 199. Garland, New York.

Gonsalves, C. T., W. J. Mayer-Oakes, and J. Robertson

1965   Report of Committee on Manitoba Historic Sites Act. *Manitoba Archaeological Society Newsletter II*(4):7–8.

Grenier, Robert

2006   Introduction. In *Heritage at Risk Special Edition, Underwater Cultural Heritage at Risk: Managing Natural and Human Impacts*, edited by Robert Grenier, David Nutley, and Ian Cochran, pp. x–xi. International Council on Monuments and Sites, Paris.

Hanna, Margaret G.

2003   Old Bones, New Reality: A Review of Issues and Guidelines Pertaining to Repatriation. *Canadian Journal of Archaeology* 27:234–57.

Haunton, Marion

1992   Canada's Proposed Archaeological Protection Act. *International Journal of Cultural Property* 1:395–396.

Hill, Tom, and Trudy Nicks

1992   *Turning the Page: Forging New Partnerships between Museums and First Peoples*. Task Force Report on Museums and First Peoples Assembly of First Nations and the Canadian Museums Association, Ottawa.

Isaac, Thomas

1993   *Pre-1868 Legislation Concerning Indians: A Selected and Indexed Collection.* Native Law Centre, University of Saskatchewan, Saskatoon.

Jacques Whitford Environment Limited

2001   *Research on Looting of Canada's Archaeological Heritage.* Report submitted to Canadian Heritage Movable Cultural Heritage Program, Hull.

Kelley, Jane H., and Ronald F. Williamson

1996   The Positioning of Archaeology within Anthropology: A Canadian Historical Perspective. *American Antiquity* 61:5–20.

Killan, Gerald

1998   Toward a Scientific Archaeology: Daniel Wilson, David Boyle and the Canadian Institute 1852–96. In *Bringing Back the Past: Historical Perspectives on Canadian Archaeology*, edited by Pamela J. Smith and Donald Mitchell, pp. 15–24. Archaeological Survey of Canada Mercury Series Paper 158, Canadian Museum of Civilization, Hull.

Klimko, Olga, Heather Moon, and Doug Glaum

1998   Archaeological Resource Management and Forestry in British Columbia. *Canadian Journal of Archaeology* 22:31–42.

Lee, Ellen
2002   Archaeology and the Public Cultural Conscience in Canada—The Federal Story. *Revista de Arqueologia Americana* (Journal of American Archaeology) 21:45–51.

Loy, Thomas H. (editor)
1979   C.R.M. News. *Newsletter of the Canadian Archaeological Association* 1(1):9–10.

MacLay, Eric
2004   Archaeological Heritage of the Southern Gulf Islands. *The Midden* 36(3–4): 12–17.

MacLeod, Donald G.
1975   Peddle or Perish: Archaeological Marketing from Concept to Product Delivery. In *Canadian Archaeological Association—Collected Papers March 1975*. Ministry of Natural Resources, Historic Sites Branch, Research Report 6:57–67.

Martijn, Charles A.
1978   Historique de la Recherche Archéologique au Québec. In *Images de la Préhistoire du Québec*, edited by C. Chapdelaine, pp.11–18. Rechereches Ameriniennes au Québec, Montréal.

Mason, Andrew R.
2004–2005   Urban Archaeological Sites at Risk. *ICOMOS Canada Momentum* 11(1):44–48.

McIntyre, A. D., and Stephen A. Davis
2005   The Central Trust Affair. In *Underground Halifax: Stories of Archaeology in the City*, edited by Paul Erickson, pp. 18–24. Nimbus Publishing, Halifax.

Nicholas, George
2006   Decolonizing the Archaeological Landscape: The Practice and Politics of Archaeology in British Columbia. *American Indian Quarterly* 30:350–80.

Nicholas, George, and Tom Andrews (editors)
1997   *At a Crossroads: Archaeology and First Peoples in Canada*. Simon Fraser University Archaeology Press 24, Burnaby, British Columbia.

Nicholson, Bev, David Pokotylo, and Ronald Williamson (editors)
1996   *Statement of Principles for Ethical Conduct Pertaining to Aboriginal Peoples: A Report from the Aboriginal Heritage Committee*. Canadian Archaeological Association. Electronic document, http://www.canadianarchaeology.com/aboriginal.lasso, accessed September 15, 2009.

Noble, William C.
1972   One Hundred and Twenty-five Years of Archaeology in the Canadian Provinces. *Canadian Archaeological Association Bulletin* 4:1–78.

Ontario Ministry of Culture
2006   Archaeological Resources and Areas of Archaeological Potential. *Provincial Policy Statement (PPS, 2005)*, Information Sheet Serie—Infosheet no. 3. Ontario Ministry of Culture, Toronto.

Parks Canada

1993   *Guidelines for the Management of Archaeological Resources in the Canadian Parks Service*. Parks Canada Agency, Ottawa.

1994   *Parks Canada Guiding Principles and Operational Policies*. Minister of Supply and Service Canada, Ottawa.

2003   *Standards and Guidelines for the Conservation of Historic Places in Canada*. Parks Canada Agency, Ottawa.

2005   *Parks Canada Guidelines for the Management of Archaeological Resources*. Parks Canada, Ottawa.

Pearce, Robert J.

1989   Cultural Resource Management at the Federal, Provincial, Municipal and Corporate Levels in Southern Ontario. In *Archaeological Heritage Management in the Modern World*, edited by Henry Cleere, pp.146–51. Unwin Hyman, London.

Pokotylo, David

2001   Public Opinion and Canadian Archaeological Heritage: A National Perspective. *Canadian Journal of Archaeology* 26:88–129.

Pokotylo, David, and Gregory Brass

1997   Interpreting Cultural Resources: Hatzic Site. In *Presenting Archaeology to the Public: Digging for Truths*, edited by John H. Jameson, Jr. and John E. Ehrenhard, pp. 156–65. AltaMira Press, Walnut Creek, Calif.

Sapir, Edward

1911   An Anthropological Survey of Canada. *Science* 4:789–91.

Smith, Harlan I.

1914   Archaeology. In *Summary Report for the Geological Survey, Department of Mines, for the Calendar Year 1913*, pp. 380–84. Ottawa.

Spurling, Brian E.

1986   Archaeological Resource Management in Western Canada: A Policy Science Approach. Unpublished Ph.D. dissertation, Department of Archaeology, Simon Fraser University, Burnaby, British Columbia.

Trigger, Bruce G.

1966a   Sir John William Dawson: A Faithful Anthropologist. *Anthropologia* 8:351–59.

1966b   Sir Daniel Wilson: Canada's First Anthropologist. *Anthropologia* 8:3–28.

1981   Giants and Pygmies: The Professionalization of Canadian Archaeology. In *Towards a History of Archaeology*, edited by G. Daniel, pp. 69–84. Thames and Hudson, London.

Turnbull, Christopher

1977   Of Backdirt and Bureaucracy: The Role of Government in Canadian Archaeology. In *New Perspectives in Canadian Archaeology*, edited by A. McKay, pp. 119–35. Royal Society of Canada, Ottawa.

Ward, Philip R.

1988   Heritage Conservation in British Columbia. *University of British Columbia Law Review* 22:61–106.

Western Canadian Archaeological Council

1960   The Present State of Archaeology in Western Canada. Western Canadian Archaeological Council Proceedings 1. Glenbow Foundation, Calgary.

Wiebe, Christopher

2006   Historic Places Act: Canada Needs a Binding Law! *Heritage* IX(3):4–9.

Wilson, Daniel

1855   Hints for the Formation of a Canadian Collection of Ancient Crania. *Canadian Journal* 3:345–47.

1856   Discovery of Indian Remains, County Norfolk, Canada West. *Canadian Journal n.s.* 1:511–19.

Winter, Barbara J.

1995   New Futures for the Past: Cooperation between First Nations and Museums in Canada. In Material Culture in Flux: Law and Policy of Repatriation of Cultural Property (Special Issue), *UBC Law Review*, 29–36.

Winter, Barbara J., and Diana Henry

1997   The Sddlnewhala Bowl: Cooperation or Compromise? In *At a Crossroads: Archaeology and First Peoples in Canada*, edited by G. P. Nicholas and T. D. Andrews, pp. 214–23. Simon Fraser University, Archaeology Press, Burnaby, British Columbia.

Wright, James V.

1985   Development of Prehistory in Canada 1935–1985. *American Antiquity* 50: 421–33.

Yellowhorn, Eldon

1999   Heritage Protection on Indian Reserve Lands in Canada. *Plains Anthropologist* 44(170), Memoir issue 31:107–16.

5

Cultural Heritage Management in China

Current Practices and Problems

CHEN SHEN AND HONG CHEN

Cultural heritage management in China has undergone several decades of intensive development, with many key events taking place in 2006. In April of that year, the Wuxi Proposal detailing the preservation of industrial heritage was adopted at the first forum for the preservation of industrial heritage in Wuxi, Jiangsu Province. In May, the State Council of the Government of China announced the Sixth List of National Major Cultural Heritage Protection Units, which named 1,080 new cultural heritage sites. On June 10, China celebrated its first Cultural Heritage Day. In July, the United Nations Educational, Scientific and Cultural Organization (UNESCO) designated Yin Xu, the 3,000-year old archaeological ruin of the Bronze Age Shang Dynasty as a World Heritage site. In October, the international scientific symposium hosted by the International Council on Monuments and Sites (ICOMOS) in Xi'an, Shaanxi Province, commemorated the first anniversary of the Xi'an Declaration. In November, the Ministry of Culture executed the Acts of World Heritage Site Protection and Management, which provides the first ever guidelines and regulations for managing the 38 World Heritage sites in China (as of 2009), along with those being considered for future application for World Heritage designation. At the end of 2006, the State Administration of Cultural Heritage (SACH), the top agency of central government authority, announced plans to carry out the Third National Cultural Heritage Survey and Registration as part of its next strategic five-year plan.

China has a rich and diverse cultural heritage representing the foundation of Chinese civilizations and cultural traditions. In addition, through thousands of years of historic interactions and cultural exchanges with other areas, China is now recognized as having played an important part in the cultural heritage of other parts of the world. In the past two decades, China has demonstrated stunning economic development, providing unprecedented opportunities for implementing managerial measures for cultural heritage conservation. At the same time, it has produced unforeseen preservation challenges that management authorities and professionals share.

While it is impossible to fully address the magnitude of cultural heritage management (CHM) in China within these limited pages, we will discuss the practices of CHM in relation to current economic development in the nation, and the problems arising from the challenges commonly seen during the development stage. We focus on the existing system of CHM in China, evaluating common policies and practices, and then on problems of CHM for the ongoing South-to-North Water Transfer Project that exemplifies the current problems of CHM practices in China.

The Establishment of the Yin Xu Museum

We begin by sharing an example that illustrates the excitement, as well as the problems, of CHM in China. In the summer of 2005, Chen Shen, the senior author of this essay, received an urgent call from Dr. Tang Jigen, the director of the Anyang Archaeological Station of the Institute of Archaeology, Chinese Academy of Social Sciences, who had been asked by the local government to design and install a permanent gallery of Shang civilization in the new Yin Xu Museum in the city of Anyang (population 700,000) in northern Henan Province. The government gave just two months to finish the task, from concept designs to complete installation of about 500 artifacts in 2,400 square meters of exhibition space. The mission was straightforward and nonnegotiable because, at the time of the museum's construction, Yin Xu was being considered as one of the candidates in the competition of 2006 for World Heritage designation. The museum had to be completed, with the gallery in place, by the time the representative from the UNESCO World Heritage Committee visited Anyang to inspect the site.

Shen spent the first week of July at Anyang with Tang's team working on the concept design. He left with strong misgivings as to how they could finish the task for the targeted opening date in September, particularly as construction of the building was still in progress.

The opening of the Yin Xu museum to the public in October 2005 was as amazing as any other recent economic development event in China. The speed with which the museum was established, and the beauty and quality of the spectacular Shang gallery, probably set a new record for any country in today's world of museum development. During the museum's first ten days of operation, the attendance reached approximately 2,000 to 3,000 per day. When Yin Xu was designated as a World Heritage site in July 2006, attendance reached its peak with 63,000 visitors in the first month (Tang, personal communication, 2006).

This event has multiple implications. First, direct involvement and support of local government are effective driving forces for quickly establishing and organizing cultural heritage preservation projects. Second, the benefits from championing local cultural heritage for national or international titles are recognized by local authorities who are aware of the potential value of cultural heritage to the local economy through the tourism business. Third, public engagement in cultural appreciation through museum collections and visiting archaeological sites has raised public awareness for the preservation of cultural heritage at large. The case of the Yin Xu Museum is only one of hundreds, or maybe thousands, of similar establishments in the cultural sector today in China, which are the direct result of the growth of local economic development. At the same time, these same factors of economic development and public awareness are also contributing to the destruction of archaeological and historic sites by bulldozers and the loss of cultural relics through looting and smuggling at an unprecedented rate.

Cultural Heritage in China: Ongoing Surveys

It is difficult to have accurate numbers of heritage sites and collections in China, although endless efforts have been made over two or three generations to survey cultural relics in this vast land. In a press conference at the Ministry of Culture held on May 25, 2006 in association with the opening event of the first national Cultural Heritage Day in China, Shan Jixiang, the general director of the SACH, announced to the media that the nation has about 400,000 immovable heritage sites, and 20 million objects in museums and research institutes (the State Council Information Office 2006). Although these figures are probably drawn from the information registered at the SACH's database, it is unlikely that they represent the real quantity of Chinese heritage; the actual numbers are certainly much higher.

Chinese cultural heritage is managed in two general categories: immovable and movable cultural relics. The immovable cultural relics are divided into six classes: (1) ancient cultural/archaeological sites, (2) ancient tombs, (3) ancient architectural structures, (4) cave temples, (5) stone carvings and murals, and (6) important modern and contemporary historic sites and memorable buildings. In general, these immovable sites are preserved by local governments; some important relics are selected as national or provincial preservation sites. Since 1961, the state has established a sophisticated system of evaluating heritage sites for the three levels of managerial responsibility—national, provincial, and municipal or county.

By 2006, a total of 2,351 sites were listed as National Major Heritage Protection Units (for the complete list of these sites, see State Administration of Cultural Heritage [SACH] 2007a), 9,300 sites were named as Provincial Major

Heritage Protection Units, and over 58,000 sites were designated as Municipal/ County Major Heritage Presentation Units. Together, these sites, accounting for a small percentage (17.5 percent) of the registered immovable sites, are the true beneficiaries of preservation supported by three levels of governments, while most of the unlisted ones are simply ignored if they are not in immediate danger. Compared to other heritage-rich nations like Egypt and India, the number of heritage sites under the watch list of the central government is considerably lower in China (2,351) than in Egypt (more than 20,000) and in India (more than 5,000). Even in Vietnam, heritage sites under central government management are about 500 more than in China (Cai 2006; also see Ota, this volume).

In the category of movable cultural relics, artifacts are classified into four grades: Grade 1 (the most rare and valuable), Grade 2, Grade 3, and Ordinary. It is our understanding that the nationwide inventorying of collections, in association with class evaluations, was carried out at museums and research institutes recently, and a sophisticated database system cataloging the roughly 20 million museum artifacts is being established. The disorderly nature of collection management practices and ignorance of the value of cultural treasures inherent at most state-owned museums has become a thing of the past, although there are still many areas to be improved.

In 1982, as a preservation measure to control speedy expansion and development in urban areas, the state authority designated a new category of immovable cultural heritage: "cultural city/town/village with important historic and cultural values." By 2006, the State Council had verified a total of 96 such cultural heritage cities, 44 heritage towns, and 36 heritage villages (see the SACH website for the complete list: SACH 2007b). Heritage preservation measures for the places on the list are now being implemented in conjunction with the new regulations from the Ministry of Construction of the Central Government in dealing with rapid urbanization in these places.

The current understanding of cultural properties in China is based on the second National Cultural Heritage Survey and Registration that was carried out in the 1980s (the first was done in the 1950s). The survey included identification and registration of archaeological and cultural sites and inventories of museum collections all over the nation. However, due to some difficulties and conditions, the survey could not be conducted in 320 (or 12.1 percent) of the 2,650 county establishments of the nation at that time (Shan 2006). Moreover, during the past two decades, with an annual double-digit rate increase in the GDP, the scale of construction, land development, highway building, and urbanization has reached an unprecedented level, which in turn has generated a large number of new discoveries of previously unknown cultural remains. For example, a new wave of CHM investigations in the 1990s in the middle of the Yangtze River, triggered by the construction of the controversial Three Gorges Dam, discovered 465 archaeological and historic sites not documented in the heritage census of the 1980s in this relatively isolated region, about 632 square kilometers in reservoir area (Shen 2003, 2010). In the Inner-Mongol Autonomous Region, 64 of the 2,068 immovable heritage objects listed in the census list of the 1980s have been lost due to development. Therefore, the need for reinvestigation of cultural property is being cited, and a state-backed Third National Cultural Heritage Survey and Registration began in 2007. The results of this survey and registration of cultural properties will provide data for more feasible and durable policies and practices for long-term CHM activities in China.

Organizations, Policies, and Practices

The principal policy of cultural heritage management, stated in article 4 of the Law of the People's Republic of China on Protection of Cultural Relics, is that, "in the work concerning cultural relics, the principle of giving priority to the protection of cultural relics, attaching primary importance to their rescue, making rational use of them, and tightening control over them shall be carried out" (SACH 2007c). Today, all aspects of cultural heritage management are governed; and related activities, including archaeological excavation, foreign collaboration, traveling exhibition, and conservation, are regulated, under this single law in China. The first version of the law was inaugurated in 1982, with partial revision in 1991. A completely revised new edition was approved in 2002. It took just 20 years for China to start implementing scientific measures and professional management in CHM. It is fair to say that Chinese CHM has undergone a painstaking process to reach a point close to the expectations of international CHM communities, but at the expense of the loss of many national treasures and the grief of a whole generation of CHM professionals.

For half a century, the establishment of a hierarchical administrative system has been effective for managing state affairs of heritage management, especially in regard to enforcing the implementation of acts and bylaws derived from the Law on the Protection of Cultural Relics after 1982. At the top of the administrative pyramid is the SACH, a powerful and independent bureau under the Ministry of Culture. This bureau also owns a research institute (the Institute of Cultural Relics Research), a cultural heritage information center, a newspaper, a magazine company, and a giant publishing house. This multilayered and comprehensive structure suggests a highly centralized organization of management, from policymaking to research dissemination, all under one roof.

The SACH directly administers 31 provincial-level bureaus of cultural heritage, one in each province, autonomous region, or municipality directly under the central government (like Beijing, Shanghai, Tianjing, and Chongqing). The provincial bureaus act with similar functions on behalf of the provincial governments on affairs of cultural heritage preservation. In particular, each provincial bureau governs a provincial museum and a research institute of archaeology and/or cultural relics; the latter operate all of the salvage archaeological projects within its province. Archaeologists from these institutions, as government employees, work in the field just like most contract archaeologists in North America on CHM field projects. Under the provincial bureaus, authorities in the cultural division of local government at the county and municipal levels are responsible for reporting and assisting CHM activities in their respective administrative districts. At the bottom of this hierarchical system are the offices of representatives in villages where heritage sites were given priority.

Undoubtedly this type of administration, typical within political systems in countries like China, is the most effective means for setting priorities for needed CHM projects and to best coordinate their implementation from top to bottom. State funding for preservation projects alone, not including operating budgets, was 534 million renminbi (RMB, U.S.$68.4 million) in 2005. These funds are allocated to provinces by the SACH based on the reports and budget proposals from the provincial bureaus, which in turn give the SACH bureaucratic power.

However, bureaucratic problems with preservation increase when local governments set their own standards and priorities for the best interests of the region. For example, in some regions, including the city of Shanghai and Guangdong Province, where economic growth is well established and where heritage sites are relatively fewer, the support for CHM is substantial and consistent. In other areas, such as Henan and Shanxi provinces, where local economies are underdeveloped and where cultural heritage sites are numerous, the works of CHM are merely at a satisfactory level.

When the first version of the Law on the Protection of Cultural Relics was adopted in 1982, the lawmakers did not expect that complicated scales of CHM were soon to come. With the reform and open-door policy of the post-Mao era, the country stepped quickly into a period of socioeconomic transformation. Resumption of private ownership, market exchange, urban development, labor mobilization, and booming tourism all became new human threats that endangered sites and objects; there was no time to implement preservative plans before many were lost to these forces. Facing this new challenge, cultural authorities turned to international communities for help, with great success. In 1985, China became a signatory to UNESCO's Convention Concerning the Protection of the World Cultural and Natural Heritage. Two years later, China's first six heritage sites—the Peking hominid site at Zhoukoudian, the Great Wall, the Forbidden City, the Mausoleum of the First Qin Emperor, the Mogao Caves, and Mount Taishan—were designated as World Heritage sites (see Thapa, this volume). In 1997, UNESCO and the SACH jointly held China's first training session on the management of world heritage preservations. In 2005, the Fifteenth General Assembly and Scientific Symposium of ICOMOS was held in Xi'an, China, where the Xi'an Declaration on the Conservation of the Setting of Heritage Structures, Sites and Areas was adopted (International Council on Monuments and Sites [ICOMOS] 2005).

In the 20-year period between 1982 and 2002, painful lessons were learned from preservation projects such as the Three Gorges Dam project, before China reached the international standards of preservation for cultural heritage practiced elsewhere in the world. The proactive role assumed by the Chinese government led to the production of a new edition of the Law on the Protection of Cultural Relics in 2002. The revised policy and regulations are set to close many of the loopholes identified during the practice of the previous version of the law. For example, Dinghai, an ancient city with over 1,000 years of history, is filled with hundreds of traditional architectural buildings and streets belonging to the Yuan, Ming, and Qing Dynasties (1271–1911). The province of Zhejiang listed the city as a Historic and Culture City in 1991, and had preservation plans for the old downtown, an area famous for its ancient street layout. In June 2000, the newly amalgamated city, Zhoushan municipality, decided to revive its city by tearing down ancient architectural buildings in the old town, and turning this area into a modern landmark plaza. Within weeks, a heritage town that had survived more than a thousand years disappeared from the earth, but the officials who were responsible for such destruction walked away from the court because there was no clear bylaw for how to punish the officials working on the government projects (Qu 2000). With the new law in place, similar incidents will result in charges against the chief administrators of the municipality for misconduct and may even result in their prosecution according to the law (see Appendix 5.1).

Problems in Cultural Heritage Management Related to Economic Development

Like many other countries with a rich heritage, China also experiences the inevitable loss of heritage by human looting and natural weathering. Such loss can be minimized as long as law enforcement is strengthened and conservation technology is advanced. However, today in China, the biggest loss of cultural heritage is due to economic development, which often occurs before adequate documentation of the loss can take place. This is the case for the largest hydraulic project in history—the Three Gorges Dam. According to Shen, the CHM work in association with the dam project was a "mission impossible" (Shen 2003, 2010). Unfortunately, another even greater loss of heritage is occurring because of the ongoing South-to-North Water Transfer Project.

Over the past five decades, the Chinese government had investigated the possibility of moving millions of tons of water from the frequently flooded regions of the Yangtze River network to the water-starved northern areas centered around Beijing. In 2002, the central government gave the go-ahead for the official launch of the South-to-North Water Transfer Project. The project will have three routes (east route, middle route, and west route) of interconnected canals and reservoirs. The planning of this project had, in part, an obvious political mandate: that water would reach Beijing by 2008 before the Olympic Games began, with the areas beyond receiving water by 2010.

The debates on the socioeconomic and environmental impacts of this project repeat exactly what was stated for the Three Gorges Dam project (Li 2005). And again, CHM was the weakest voice in the discussion. But the danger to cultural heritage is greater because a larger number of sites will be lost, and that cannot be ignored (Liu et al. 2005; Shan and Wang 2004). The construction will occur in five provinces (Hubei, Henan, Shandong, Hebei, and Jiangsu) and two municipalities (Beijing and Tianjin), which comprise the heartland of Chinese civilization. In 2005, the SACH reported in a news conference, "Cultural departments investigated the construction area of the east route and middle route and determined that nearly 800 cultural heritage sites will be affected, including some with the most important historic and cultural value, like the Yuzhengong Palace World Heritage site, Xing Kiln site, and a cemetery site of the North Dynasty" (Gui et al. 2005). Cultural authorities also predicted that many more would be identified once the salvage work started, but the scale of archaeological sites would not be known until then.

The real problem with the CHM work in infrastructure projects is the failure of the CHM strategic planning at the beginning of the projects. This leads to the loss of hundreds of immovable heritage sites, hundreds of thousands of movable cultural relics, and, especially, scientific information of the human past. This failure cannot be blamed on the CHM authorities and professionals; it is because engineering departments consciously or unconsciously fail to include the CHM process at the planning stage, or in some cases to consider the needs of the CHM process at all. For example, the engineering departments did not establish a mediation committee to coordinate with CHM representatives to discuss the preservation plan until two years after the launch of the South-to-North Water Transfer Project. In September 2005, when a high-level discussion panel was held to evaluate the feasibility of the final construction plan, no CHM representatives were invited to participate except a low-ranking SACH official who attended the meeting as a nonvoting member.

Unacceptable ignorance on the importance of CHM by engineering departments, which are probably under pressure from politically driven deadlines, resulted in a radical change of the CHM plan and reduction of funding for the benefit of the construction of the South-to-North Water Transfer Project. The philosophy is clear; the project cannot be held up for preservation works. The cultural authorities proposed 1.3 billion RMB (U.S.$180 million) for CHM preservation activities, but the engineering departments only agreed to 300 million RMB (U.S.$37 million) as they excluded many preservation projects in favor of their construction schedules. For example, in November 2004, the Hubei provincial bureau submitted a report on the preservation plan for the inundated areas of the Danjiangkou Reservoir under construction, proposing 241 preservation projects for a total of 560,000 square meters of excavation area. In April 2005, the engineering department approved only 192 preservation projects for a total of 340,000 square meters of excavation area. Engineering bureaucrats suspected that cultural authorities had overestimated the expense for the benefit of the cultural sector, while cultural administrators argued that they had not even considered the follow-up financial impacts after the salvage excavations. The truth is that there is no governing law to justify the arguments between the two sides, so that even officials from the engineering side suggest that the current law on heritage preservation is vague. "Yes, maybe our plan is not making sense [to CHM], but we did not break the Law" (Li 2005:25).

As with the Three Gorges Dam Project, CHM works in the South-to-North Water Transfer Project have the same shortage of money and time to complete the mission. Archaeologists had to start working in the field while their administrators were still negotiating the preservation plans. For example, the 461 km long Hebei section of the middle route cuts across the area whose sites represent 7,000 years of history on the central plain. Starting in July 2002, the Hebei Provincial Institute of Archaeology sent out five teams for reconnaissance surveys, and it repeated the process again in 2003. Their well-researched report proposed 155 preservation projects, including excavation of 23,000 square meters. However, the construction in the Hebei Province section was scheduled to be completed by the end of 2006. With no available time and money, this CHM work became another "mission impossible."

The Future of Yin Xu: Conclusion

In some of the public debates on cultural heritage preservation, people ask, "What is the big deal if we lose a few sites here or there, given that our country has so many of such treasures?" And, "Why is this issue given priority over improving the subsistence needs of people in economically underdeveloped areas?" Unfortunately, many people share this mind-set, and worse is that many of these people are in administrative positions. It is because of this questioning of priorities that similar incidents involving the loss of cultural heritage happen repeatedly. The CHM works in China are not concerned solely with the problem of a lack of preservation professionals and managers, nor with the lack of policies and regulated procedures, but are also concerned with the problem of public awareness in this nation of 1.3 billion people.

Although it took two decades to systemize CHM, it is a sign that today Chinese cultural authorities can play an important role with international communities in this field. Until recently, international exchanges were limited to high-level administrations. Holding the ICOMOS general assembly and symposium in China in 2005 was a good start to having international scholars participate directly in the front-line practice of Chinese heritage preservation. We also anticipate that international policymaking on CHM would benefit from a greater understanding of the Chinese experience, which offers widely diversified case studies. We welcome every opportunity to discuss Chinese CHM from a global perspective.

As we finish this chapter, our colleagues in China are still celebrating the designation of Yin Xu as a World Heritage site in China. Yin Xu was identified as the capital of the Late Shang Dynasty (1300–1046 B.C.) in 1899 when a Qing Dynasty (1644–1911) scholar recognized the inscriptions from oracle bones. The ruin, first excavated in 1929 and still being investigated today, represents a complex ancient urban society that produced masterpieces of exquisite bronze and jade artwork (Li 1977; Shen 2002). Treasures from Yin Xu are appreciated by millions of people outside China at museums, including the Metropolitan Museum of Art, the Asian Art Museum of San Francisco, the British Museum, and the Royal Ontario Museum. Cultural management at Yin Xu over nearly a century has been a successful example of Chinese CHM. Over these years, archaeologists and conservators from the Institute of Archaeology, at the Chinese Academy of Social Sciences, have been working very closely with the city authorities who gave a higher priority to heritage management than the recent economic development and business expansion. They successfully persuaded the commissioner of the South-to-North Water Transfer Project to change the middle route around the site; of course, Yin Xu's application for World Heritage designation was the political pressure used by the Anyang authorities for this detour. Consequently, we now have faith that this heritage site will receive better preservation management than any other heritage site in China, particularly in light of the diligence of archaeologists and cultural heritage managers and the substantial efforts made by both the state and local governments to preserve Yin Xu for future generations.

Appendix 5.1. A Case Study: Who Pays for the Renovation?

One day in 2003, in Zhangguying, a remote village in Hunan Province with approximately 2,000 people, an ordinary farmer, Zhang Zaifa, repaired a wall in his courtyard because he saw it was in danger of collapse. But doing such a do-it-yourself home repair resulted in his being sent to jail.

The village of Zhangguying retained the integrity of its entire ancient formation, including 62 lanes and 206 courtyard complexes, for 500 years, and is so far the most complete village complex built in the traditional southern Chinese architectural style. In 2001, the village was listed by the State Administration of Cultural Heritage (SACH) as one of the National Major Cultural Heritage Protection Units, and in 2003, it was listed by the SACH as one of the Famous Villages with Important Historic and Cultural Value. Therefore, all of the houses in the village, including Zhang's, have become immovable cultural relics. That also means that after June 2001 Zhang had lost his right to do any renovations by himself at his own house.

According to article 26 of the Law on the Protection of Cultural Relics: "The principle of keeping the immovable cultural relics in their original state shall be adhered to in their use, and the users shall be responsible for the safety of the structures and the cultural relics attached to them, see to it that the immovable cultural relics are not damaged, rebuilt, or dismantled and that no additional structures are built on the site."

Village administrators warned Zhang that if he needed to repair the home, he had to talk to the representatives of the local cultural authority about obtaining permission, and he would need to hire certified designers and contactors— an option that he could not afford.

Wishing to comply with the law, he initially asked for financial assistance from the local cultural department, to which he thought he was entitled, according to article 21 of the law. But Zhang's request for a financial subsidy was turned down because no one could identify which departments of the local government should be responsible: either the village council, which has revenues generated from tourism of the heritage village, to which Zhang made his contribution, or the cultural offices that received annual conservation budgets. But both bureaus refused Zhang simply because they believed that Zhang, as the owner, should pay for his own repairs. The real problem here was that the individuals in the administrative positions were not willing to use their budget funds on Zhang's repairs, even though helping with conservation and heritage preservation was a perfectly justifiable expense. Many bureaucrats in the front line have little sense of the importance of cultural heritage management (CHM) works. Moreover, their misconduct in these matters is sometimes well protected for the best interests of the local bureaucracy.

References Cited

Cai, Xiaoming
2006   A New Important Achievement on Cultural Heritage Conservation (in Chinese). *Chinese Cultural Heritage* 13(3):8–9.
Gui, Juan, Chang Liu, and Xueqing Dong
2005   The Backward Situation for Rescuing Cultural Heritage during the South-to-North Water Transfer Project (in Chinese). *Perspectives* (Oct. 24)43:10.
International Council on Monuments and Sites (ICOMOS)
2005   Xi'an Declaration on the Conservation on the Setting of Heritage Structures, Sites and Areas. Electronic document, http://www.international.icomos.org/xian2005/xian-declaration.htm, accessed March 15, 2007.

Li, Ji

1977   *Anyang.* University of Washington Press, Seattle.

Li, Yang

2005   The South-to-North Water Transfer Project: Repeating the Pitfall of Cultural Heritage Management in the Three Gorges Dam Project (in Chinese). *Chinese Newsweek.* Nov. 14, 2005. pp. 23–27. Beijing.

Liu, Chang, Juan Gui, and Xueqing Dong

2005   The South-to-North Water Transfer Project and Fates of Cultural Heritage (in Chinese). *Xingxi Daokan* 45:24–27.

Qu, Guanjie

2000   Who Is Responsible for the Disappearance of Dinghai Ancient City? (in Chinese). *Guangming Daily.* July 19, 2000, Beijing.

Shan, Chungang, and Wenhua Wang

2004   The South-to-North Water Transfer Project Forces a Big Rescue of Cultural Heritage (in Chinese). *Perspectives* (July 5, 2005)(27):10.

Shan, Jixiang

2006   Campaigning for the Preparation for the Third Survey and Registration of Cultural Relics in China (in Chinese). Public speech on Dec. 18, 2006. Full text at http://www.sach.gov.cn/publishcenter%5Csach%5Cspeech/11517.aspx, accessed August 31, 2007.

Shen, Chen

2002   *Anyang and Sanxingdui: Unveiling the Mysteries of Ancient Chinese Civilizations.* Royal Ontario Museum, Toronto.

2003   The Great Rescue Project of China. *Rotunda* 35(3):20–31.

2010   Mission Impossible: Current Archaeological Practices in the Three Gorges Reservoir, China. In *Damming the Past: Dams and Cultural Heritage Management,* edited by S. A. Brandt and F. A. Hassan. Lexington Books, Lanham, Md. In press.

State Administration of Cultural Heritage (SACH)

2007a   The List of the National Cultural Protection Units. Full list of six announcements at http://www.sach.gov.cn/sachwindow/centerchina/first/, accessed August 31, 2007.

2007b   The List of Cultural City/Town/Village with Important Historic and Cultural Values. Full lists of three announcements at http://www.sach.gov.cn/sachwindow/historycity/historycity001/, accessed August 31, 2007.

2007c   The Law of the People's Republic of China on Protection of Cultural Relics. Full text in English at http://law.sach.gov.cn/law/detail1.asp?id=1057, accessed August 31, 2007.

State Council Information Office, People's Republic of China

2006   The State News Conference Reporting on the Current Situation of Cultural Heritage Preservation in China, May 25, 2006. Full text in Chinese at http://www.gov.cn/xwfb/2006–05/25/content_292272.htm> accessed August 31, 2007.

6

Archaeological Heritage Resource Management in India

The roots of archaeological heritage management in India can be traced to the beginning of the nineteenth century with antiquarian investigations alongside sporadic concern about the preservation of heritage by the government. To understand the present state of heritage policy, legislation, organization, and archaeological research in India, it is essential to look into the beginning and subsequent development from a historical perspective.

For some of the earliest and finest comprehensive accounts of archaeological resource management in India, see *Revealing India's Past* (Cumming 1939; see also Chakrabarti 1988; Ghosh 1953; Roy 1953, 1996; Sarkar 1981). This chapter provides an overview of the development of archaeological policy, organization, and legislation, and discusses the present scenario in the country.

The History of Archaeology in India

Archaeological research in India had its beginning with the pioneering efforts made by Sir William Jones, an associate judge of the Calcutta Supreme Court, who in 1784 founded the Asiatic Society for enquiring into the history, antiquities, arts, sciences, and literature of Asia. Following the formation of the Asiatic Society, the first serious attempt at antiquarian studies was made by Francis Buchanan in the early nineteenth century. He described the history and documentation of antiquarian remains of Mysore State and eastern India as part of a topographical and statistical survey of the area. Government policy toward cultural property depended upon the interest and caprice of the governor general. Thus, while Lord Minto (1807–1813) appointed a committee to look after the maintenance of the Taj Mahal, the administration of Lord William Bentinck (1828–1835) entertained a move to demolish the Taj Mahal for the value of its marble (Thapar 1984:63).

When James Prinsep took over as secretary of the Asiatic Society in 1832, a new phase in Indian archaeology began. Prinsep was responsible for deciphering both the Brahmi and the Kharoshti scripts that paved the way for understanding the early history of the country.

In 1844, following a suggestion from the Royal Asiatic Society of the United Kingdom, the Indian government authorized repairs to the caves at Ellora and Ajanta, and a commission was formed to collect data relating to the nature and state of existing monuments (Thapar 1984:64). This was the first conscious effort by the government to save the cultural heritage of the country from further decay.

When Alexander Cunningham was appointed as the archaeological surveyor in 1861, he initiated a five-year survey project of antiquarian remains, following in the footsteps of the Chinese traveler Huien-Tsang, covering northern India from Gaya in the east to the Indus in the west. However, the conservation of monuments remained outside the scope of his program. In 1873, the central government entrusted the work of preservation of buildings of historical and architectural interest to the local governments. This responsibility bounced back and forth for another 30 years with little progress on the listing of monuments and little support or encouragement of archaeology (Brown 1905:91, as taken from the *Journal of the Society of Arts* XXXIV, p. 562).

Finally in 1900, a proposal to revive the post of director general, with power to exercise a centralized general supervision of all archaeological work in the country, led to the appointment of John Marshall as the director general in 1902. While conservation remained in the hands of provincial governments, Marshall carried out a program of conservation and excavation and was responsible for the first conservation manual in 1923—a guideline for heritage maintenance and conservation in India (Marshall 1990). The Archaeological Survey of India (ASI) finally became a permanent establishment in 1906. The organizational structure was then patterned as proposed by Marshall, combining various functions such as conservation, excavation, epigraphy, museums, and publications within the survey. Meanwhile, the Ancient Monuments Preservation Act of 1904 was enacted for the protection of ancient monuments and antiquities in the country.

"Archaeology" was classified as a central subject for the first time following the Devolution Rules of 1921. As a result, all monuments protected under the act of 1904 came under the control of the central government. Subsequently, the Government of India Act of 1935 included ancient and historical monuments, archaeological sites, and remains in the Federal List without any corresponding entry in the Provincial List. Thus, the government of India assumed all the powers vested in the provincial governments under the act of 1904.

In 1944, when Mortimer Wheeler joined the ASI as the director general, he took over the conservation work from the Provincial Public Works Departments and gave it to the ASI, thus ensuring a proper and uniform standard of repairs.

The History of Antiquarian Laws in India

In India, legislation is promulgated at both the national and the state levels. Legislation has been formulated at both levels for protection of archaeological heritage of the country. The focus here is on national legislation and policy; in general, the extensive body of state-level legislation follows the pattern of the national legislation.

Toward the end of the eighteenth century, large-scale public awareness of the need to preserve the cultural heritage of India developed as a result of the work of antiquarians and dilettanti. With expectations of stopping the continued pillage and destruction of ancient buildings, the first ever antiquarian legislation in India was enacted—the Bengal Regulation XIX of 1810 and its counterpart, the Madras Regulation VII of 1817. These empowered the respective governments to intervene whenever any historical building was threatened with misuse by private individuals. However, both laws were silent on buildings under private ownership, nor did they apply to government officials (Thapar 1984:65). The initiation and formulation of heritage legislation in India can be better understood with a global perspective, particularly in Europe in the nineteenth century, which has been beautifully described by G. Baldwin Brown (1905).

Nearly half a century later, during the period of Cunningham's first tenure as the director general of the Archaeological Survey, the government passed Act XX in 1863, investing itself with the authority to prevent injury and to preserve buildings remarkable for their antiquity for their historical or architectural value. Following this, the Indian Treasure Trove Act of 1878 was promulgated; it invested the government with powers to claim possession of any unearthed treasure that exceeded 10 rupees in value. As a follow-up action in 1886, the government issued two directives at the insistence of James Burgess, then the director general of the Archaeological Survey, one debarring public officials from disposing of antiquities found or acquired by them without official approval, and the other making the digging up of ancient remains of any kind without the consent of the Archaeological Survey unlawful. Burgess also wanted to amend the Indian Treasure Trove Act to make the export of antiquities without an official permit illegal, but he did not succeed in his endeavors (Thapar 1984:66).

Toward the end of the nineteenth century, the government of India drafted a bill, based on the existing English Acts and embodying some relevant provisions of corresponding legislation in Greece and Italy. This resulted in the Ancient Monuments Preservation Act of 1904, "to provide for the preservation of ancient monuments, for the exercise of control over traffic in antiquities and over excavation in certain places and for the protection and acquisition in certain cases of ancient monuments and of objects of archaeological, historical or artistic interest" (Government of India 1904). This act provided effective preservation and authority over monuments, particularly those in the custody of individual or private ownership.

The government, hoping to make "better provision for controlling the export of objects of antiquarian or historical interest or significance," passed the Antiquities (Export Control) Act of 1947 (Act no. XXXI of 1947), thus realizing, in some measure, the objectives of James Burgess's proposal to amend the Indian Treasure Trove Act. Under this act, no antiquity (comprehensively defined as an object of human workmanship that has been in existence for not less than 100 years) may be exported except under the authority of a license granted by the central government.

As mentioned earlier, the Indian Constitution divided responsibility for archaeology between the central government and the states. In fulfillment of the provisions made in the constitution, Parliament passed the Ancient and Historical Monuments and Archaeological Sites and Remains (Declaration of National Importance) Act (no. LXXI of 1951), by which all monuments previously protected under the Ancient Monuments Preservation Act of 1904 were designated as monuments and sites of national importance. In addition, over 450 monuments and sites in the former princely states were included in this list. Subsequently, through section 126 of the State Reorganization Act of 1956, some additional monuments and archaeological sites were designated as of national importance.

The Present Situation in Legislation

Considering the changed scenario in archaeological resources and management, a comprehensive statute entitled the Ancient Monuments and Archaeological Sites and Remains (AMASR) Act of 1958 (no. 24 of 1958) was enacted "to provide for the preservation of ancient and historical monuments and archaeological sites and remains of national importance, for the regulation of archaeological excavations, and for the protection of sculptures, carvings and other like objects" (Parliament of the Republic of India 1958). This act defines ancient monuments and antiquities as those that have been in existence for no less than 100 years. Subsequently, the Ancient Monuments and Archaeological Sites and Remains Rules were framed, and both act and rules came into force in 1959. The act repealed the Ancient Historical Monuments and Archaeological Sites and Remains (Declaration of National Importance) Act of 1951, but not the Ancient Monuments Preservation Act of 1904, which remains in force.

Like that of the AMASR Act of 1958, the illicit traffic in antiquities required the amendment of the Antiquities (Export Control) Act of 1947 for effective control over moveable cultural property. A new act called the Antiquities and Art Treasures Act (no. 52 of 1972) was enacted "to regulate the export trade in antiquities and art treasures, to provide for the prevention of smuggling of, and fraudulent dealings in antiquities, to provide for the compulsory acquisition of antiquities and art treasures for preservation in public places, and to provide for certain other matters connected therewith or incidental or ancillary thereto" (Parliament of the Republic of India 1972). Under this act, the term "antiquity" was defined so as to include objects of human craftsmanship that have been in existence for no less than 100 years, and manuscripts and records, and the like that have been in existence for no less than 75 years. The act inter alia required persons possessing antiquities to register specified categories of those antiquities before the registering officer. This act was also supplemented by the Antiquities and Art Treasures Rules (1973), and both act and rules have been in force since 1976, repealing the earlier Antiquities (Export Control) Act (Act no. XXXI of 1947).

To summarize, the acts still in force for management of archaeological resources include the Ancient Monuments Preservation Act (1904), the Ancient Monuments and Archaeological Sites and Remains Act (1958), the Treasure Trove Act (1878), and the Antiquities and Art Treasures Act (1972) (Biswas 1999).

The Limitations of Existing Legislation

Since the implementation of the Antiquities and Art Treasures Act (AAT) in 1972, certain gaps have been noticed that have diluted the effectiveness of the act. With the growth of the international market for art and cultural artifacts, the global problem of the smuggling of antiquities has increased over the years. Consequently, the task of the law-enforcing agencies has become more difficult and complex. Therefore, the government has proposed amendments to give the act more teeth and bring it up to date in the changed circumstances. Further, an extension of the limits of the area for bringing antiquities discovered in marine archaeological investigation within the purview of the act is needed.

The Ancient Monuments and Archaeological Sites and Remains Act of 1958 has been periodically amended to address the contemporary situation. Recognizing that urban growth was threatening to obliterate monuments and sites, the government amended the act in 1992 by introducing a perimeter of up to 100 meters around the protected monument as prohibited area, and an additional 200 meters as regulated area, for the purposes of mining operations or construction or both. Implementation of this regulation rests with local authorities and is often violated. Clearly, dialogue between planning authorities and the ASI is a necessity that must not be driven by crisis, but as a matter of course (Baig 2003:247). However, due to the rapid growth of cities in recent years and the complex nature of village settlement, it is now thought that certain amendments need to be made. In addition, this act is completely silent about rescue archaeology activities.

In India where various development schemes are in progress, the ASI and the various state departments of archaeology face challenges of a complex nature calling for special efforts in regard to the preservation of the cultural heritage (Thapar 1989a:167). The impact of tourism on heritage is another issue that needs to be examined from a different perspective (Guzder 1989; Thapar 1989a:167). These issues in heritage management were certainly not envisaged while framing the Ancient Monuments and Archaeological Sites and Remains Act of 1958. Therefore this act falls short of addressing developments, suggesting the need for a thorough amendment to the existing act in the future.

State Legislations

In pursuance of their constitutional obligations, the federating states are required to care for monuments other than those of national importance (see List II of the Seventh Schedule of the Constitution) that are looked after by the ASI. Almost all the states have their own Department of Archaeology and have enacted legislation largely patterned on the Ancient Monuments and Archaeological Sites and Remains Act of 1958. Under their respective legislations, the states have protected about 3,500 monuments and sites through their respective Departments of Archaeology.

Besides the initiatives taken both by the central and state governments to preserve the archaeological monuments, sites, and remains through legislation, efforts are underway to protect historic cities. For the last 25 years, the preservation of the urban historic fabric has become an important issue in India. Through the constant effort and pioneering work of the Bombay Environment Action Group, the first such regulation, the Heritage Regulations for Greater Bombay of 1995, was passed as part of Maharashtra Regional and Town Planning Act of 1966.

In fact, specific heritage-related legislation was not required, as laws under the Town and Country Planning Act were enabled with bylaws, regulations, and mechanisms such as the transfer of development rights. Inclusion of a property in the heritage list implies that changes to the property need the prior approval of a multidisciplinary expert group appointed by the government (Chainani 2002a:16–17).

Following the Heritage Regulations for Greater Bombay of 1995, other cities have introduced similar regulations. Efforts also are being made to extend such regulations to other major cities with historic fabric in the country.

Other Relevant Legislation and Regulations

At the international level, India has ratified the UNESCO Conventions on the Protection of Cultural Property in the Event of Armed Conflict (1959), the Means of Prohibiting and Preventing the Illicit Import, Export and Transfer of Ownership of Cultural Property (1970), and the Protection of the World Cultural and National Heritage (1972). In 2001, the United Nations Educational, Scientific and Cultural Organization (UNESCO) adopted the International Convention for the Protection of the Under Water Cultural Heritage. India is initiating actions to ratify this convention.

In addition to the international legislation, there are several related laws and regulations that can be utilized to protect the interest of management of cultural heritage in the country (Chainani 2002a, 2002b). Unfortunately, these are rarely applied because of lack of awareness by those who are responsible for preservation of the country's cultural heritage.

Administrative and Organizational Structure within the Department of Culture

The Constitution of India says, "It shall be the duty of every citizen of India to value and preserve the rich heritage of our composite culture" (Constitution of India 1949, p. 20). Based on this vision and the allocation of functions related to archaeology in the Constitution, the government of India established the Department of Culture in the 1980s to protect, preserve, and promote the rich and diverse cultural heritage of India. It became the responsibility of the department to implement heritage-related legislation, in particular the Ancient Monuments and Archaeological Sites and Remains Act of 1958, and the Antiquity and Art Treasure Act of 1972, through the ASI.

In 1950, the Constitution of Free India came into effect. Under it (see the Seventh Schedule, article 246), functions relating to archaeology were divided between the union and state governments.

The union was given responsibility for ancient and historical monuments and records and archaeological sites and remains declared by Parliament to be of national importance. The state was responsible for other ancient and historical monuments and records. The union and states share responsibility for other archaeological sites and remains.

Responsibility for the preservation of archaeological heritage in India rests with the ASI and the respective state departments of archaeology. The ASI is one of 43 institutions within the Department of Culture, which is under the control of the Ministry of Tourism and Culture.

The mandate of the Department of Culture is to preserve and promote all forms of art and culture from tangible to intangible cultural heritage, both in time and space (Department of Culture 2006). In addition to generating cultural awareness at the grass roots, the department also provides financial assistance and scholarships to encourage research activities, and organizes training programs in the field. It develops cultural contact and relations with other countries through cultural exchange programs.

The Archaeological Survey of India (ASI)

Today the ASI protects 3,675 monuments and sites of national importance under the provisions of the AMASR Act of 1958. Of 22 World Heritage cultural properties in the country, 19 are being maintained by the ASI. The directorate office of the ASI is located in New Delhi and is headed by a director general. To better manage these protected monuments, museums, cultural properties, and archaeological investigations throughout the country, the ASI has field offices known as circles and branches, which are directly responsible for implementation of the legislation and other related activities.

In addition to the protected monuments and sites, there is extensive architectural heritage less than 100 years old that is architecturally and aesthetically very important. For conservation of such buildings, the ASI gives financial assistance under grants-in-aid.

At the field office level, circle offices are headed by a superintending archaeologist, assisted by archaeologists and conservation and administrative staff. Their responsibilities include structural conservation and maintenance of monuments, maintenance of site museums, archaeological research, heritage awareness programs, liaison with concerned state authorities, and implementation of the AMASR Act of 1958 and the Antiquities and Art Treasures Act (AAT) of 1972. The ASI includes 24 circles covering the country. Specialized types of branches include one prehistory branch, six excavation branches, two temple survey projects, one building survey project, two epigraphy branches, one science branch, and one garden branch.

A data bank of registered antiquities in the country is also maintained by the ASI. In addition to the antiquity collections at site museums and site repositories, the ASI has one of the largest collections of antiquities, called the Central Antiquity Collection, in its repository at Delhi. This collection includes priceless antiquities from Stone Age times to the Mughal period from across the country. It has accumulated antiquities over time from various excavated sites, donated and seized antiquities, and so on. The collection has catered to the needs of students and scholars over the years.

The National Research Laboratory for Conservation of Cultural Property

The National Research Laboratory for Conservation of Cultural Property (NRLC), a subordinate office of the Department of Culture, is located at Lucknow. The objectives of the NRLC are to develop the capabilities of different cultural institutions of the country in the conservation of cultural property and provide conservation services to museums, archives, archaeology departments, and other similar institutions. To meet these objectives, the NRLC provides conservation training and library services to conservators throughout the country.

The Indira Gandhi National Centre for the Arts

The Indira Gandhi National Centre for the Arts (IGNCA) was established in 1987 as an autonomous institution under the Department of Culture. It is a center for research, academic pursuit, and dissemination in the field of arts in a wide spectrum that also includes archaeological heritage.

The National Mission on Monuments and Antiquities

India is extraordinarily rich with a vast and diverse cultural heritage in the form of monuments, sites, and antiquities spread across the country. This finite and nonrenewable resource of the country is fast disappearing. In recent years, there has been an increasing trend in illicit trafficking of India's cultural heritage. This is mostly due to the lack of public awareness, ignorance of the law, and the lack of a comprehensive national-level data bank of the total built heritage and antiquarian wealth.

It is now realized that if we want to understand our history and also ensure and preserve our heritage for posterity, we must have a proper management plan of our highly fragile cultural resources (Ota 2005:77–80). The government of India has launched the National Mission on Monuments and Antiquities (NMMA) with a mandate to create a national database on built heritage, sites, and antiquities as part of the tangible heritage management of the country; to initiate a sense of heritage preservation among the masses through community participation, awareness, and capacity building; and to develop synergy between institutions, including both governmental and nongovernmental organizations committed to the preservation of the country's tangible heritage. The ASI is the nodal agency for the implementation of this mission (ASI 2007).

The National Mission for Manuscripts

India is known for its ancient knowledge system belonging to the different periods of history. Most of the knowledge that constitutes religion, philosophy, systems of science, arts, and literature is preserved in the form of manuscripts. These manuscripts are on different materials, such as birch bark, palm leaf, cloth, paper, wood, and stone, and are composed in different Indian languages and scripts. India has the largest collection of manuscripts in the world. In order to save one of the most valuable but less visible of the country's cultural assets, the National Mission for Manuscripts was launched in 2003 by the Ministry of Culture.

An ambitious five-year project, the mission seeks not merely to locate, catalogue, and preserve India's manuscripts, but also to enhance access, spread awareness, and encourage their use for educational purposes. The Indira Gandhi National Centre for Arts (IGNCA) is the national nodal agency for the implementation of the mission, and it will house the National Manuscripts Library in the form of a central repository for microfilms and digital copies of all Indian manuscripts.

The National Cultural Fund

The National Cultural Fund (NCF) was launched in 1997 by the government of India. It was created with the aim of mobilizing extra resources by inviting the participation of the corporate sector, NGOs, state governments, the private/public sector, and individuals in the task of promoting, protecting, and preserving India's cultural heritage, both tangible and intangible. To encourage the corporate sector to contribute funds for heritage conservation and maintenance, there is a tax benefit for all donations to the NCF.

The Proposed National Commission for Heritage Sites

The union government has recently proposed to create the National Commission for Heritage Sites, realizing that the present legal and institutional framework is not adequate to address the documentation, inventory, and conservation of the enormous built heritage of the country. The commission would develop broad cultural policy guidelines and take steps to ensure that such guidelines are observed. The proposed commission would advise the government on heritage matters, frame guidelines for the conservation of archaeological heritage, and suggest appropriate amendments to the existing heritage legislations.

Nongovernmental Initiatives

India is a land of extraordinary heritage. While government agencies are able to protect a few thousand monuments, there are literally thousands of beautiful heritage sites that remain unprotected. The first heritage trust to be set up in India more than 30 years ago was the Indian Heritage Society, which is located in several major cities of the country. In recognition of the need to establish a national agenda to protect and conserve the natural and cultural heritage of the country, the Indian National Trust for Art and Cultural Heritage (INTACH) was set up in 1984.[1] As an NGO, INTACH has grown several fold with a nationwide network. It has successfully acted as a vehicle for civil action by moving judicial courts to save heritage, as well as engaging and educating the public in heritage awareness through a campaign called "fighting to preserve what is rightfully ours."

In recent years, due to growing awareness about heritage, a large number of

NGOs have started functioning all over the country, lobbying for the conservation and preservation of India's natural and cultural heritage. Professionals and activists are engaged in understanding the cultural compulsions and aspirations of communities whose futures are as fragile as their heritage. The sustained efforts of these NGOs, along with those of the government, emphasize the importance of designating new cultural resources and moving beyond conservation and legislation to management challenges (Baig 2004:171).

As mentioned earlier in the discussion of existing legislation, 3,675 monuments and sites are looked after by the central government and about 3,500 monuments and sites by the states. For a country of the size of India with its cultural wealth, this admittedly is not a big number. There are still a large number of monuments and sites that fall outside the purview of either the central government or the states. Taking this in consideration, INTACH adopted the Charter for Conservation of Unprotected Architectural Heritage and Sites in India in 2004 (Indian National Trust for Art and Cultural Heritage [INTACH] 2005:231–59). The main objective of this charter is to value the unprotected architectural heritage and sites in India and formulate appropriate guidelines for conservation sympathetic to the contexts in which they are found.

Education

The ASI, under the control of the union government, is the principal organization in the country for archaeological field work and for maintaining standards in archaeological excavation, heritage conservation, and maintenance. In addition, some of the state departments of archaeology and nearly a dozen or more universities undertake field surveys and excavations, which also serve as training in archaeological investigation by the staff and students.

The 1940s and 1950s

Based on Leonard Woolley's review report of 1939 of the archaeological work of the country, it was realized that specialized training and comprehensive planning were needed for a better future for archaeology and archaeological activities in the country. Following Woolley's report, Mortimer Wheeler was appointed as the director general of the Archaeological Survey in 1944. Wheeler's first task was to convert the activities of the survey to professional archaeological activities, with the establishment of a training camp for archaeology at Taxila in 1944, which came to be known as the Taxila School of Archaeology. This was the first organized phase of archaeological training in the country. During the four years of his stay in India, Wheeler trained over 100 students (Thapar 1989b: 288).

In the 1950s, field research projects in archaeology were initially set up in six universities where some trained staff was already available. More universities have subsequently established composite departments of ancient Indian history, culture, and archaeology, and over two dozen universities now offer courses in archaeology. But today only a few of these universities have fully equipped departments and trained staff to undertake field research. More fully trained professionals are needed.

1959 to the Present

Realizing the need for integrated training in archaeology, the Central Advisory Board of Archaeology passed a resolution urging the government to open a school of archaeology under the Archaeological Survey. The school was opened in 1959 (Thapar 1989b:289), offering courses in theoretical and field archaeology, as well as refresher courses on conservation. This diploma course also attracts foreign students from neighboring countries.

In 1983, an expert group appointed by the government to review the functioning of archaeology in India recommended that the diploma course be extended from one year to two so that students could receive more intensive field training. The two-year course was put into operation in 1986. The group also recommended that the School of Archaeology be upgraded to an Institute of Archaeology with expanded functions (ASI 1997).

In addition to archaeological research, archaeological heritage conservation and management are the key issues that are essential for effective heritage resource management of any country. It is now realized that heritage conservation and management should form a core discipline. Unfortunately, there is hardly any professional course on archaeological heritage management in India today. Furthermore, the archaeological heritage conservation that forms a part of a course in the Institute of Archaeology should form a full-fledged course in itself in light of the demand on heritage conservation in the country. In addition to the ASI's courses, the School of Planning and Architecture in New Delhi, an institute of the government of India, also offers a specialized course in structural conservation to the students of architecture. But this course is based more on theory than on practical measures.

Additional specialized training is offered by the INTACH U.K. Trust, which was set up with funds bequeathed by Charles Wallace, a British businessman in India, who died in 1916. In his will he held the view that "all possessions great and small being acquired from or through the people as mine should return to the people" (About the Charles Wallace Trusts 1981). The INTACH U.K. Trust exists to foster closer ties in the field of art and cultural heritage between the United Kingdom and India. As part of its activities, the INTACH U.K. Trust through the Charles Wallace India Trust offers fellowships to professionals from India in the fields of architecture, civil engineering, and archaeology to visit Britain to obtain professional experience in heritage conservation and management.

The INTACH U.K. Trust has supported the York Scholars' program since 1985. This program has assisted several professionals to acquire best practices and skills in conservation through long- and short-term conservation courses under the Charles Wallace Scholarship program. So far, more than 75 professionals have been trained under this program, providing a boost to the field of heritage conservation in the country. Today, one can see that many of these trained professionals have their practices in the field catering to the fast growing needs of heritage conservation in the country.

Employment

The employment potential for archaeologists in the country is very limited and is confined to the requirements of the ASI, the state departments of archaeology, and, to some extent, the universities. Among these, the ASI is the largest employer.

It is unfortunate that there is no opportunity for archaeologists to be self-employed by undertaking activities such as rescue archaeology or heritage resource management. This situation is due to the lack of public awareness and an indifferent attitude toward rescue archaeology investigations in the country. However, in recent years there has been a growing interest in heritage management and conservation, and this perhaps may lead some to take up archaeology, heritage conservation, and management as a profession.

Public Attitude and Archaeological Heritage

For the last two decades, there has been growing interest among the public toward heritage. It is mainly because of the activities of various heritage-related NGOs and the electronic media. This awareness has mobilized public opinion to such an extent that when any part of the cultural and natural heritage is threatened with imminent danger of damage or destruction, the threat also creates an awareness among the public for the need to preserve the cultural heritage of the country. One can understand the present attitude of the public toward heritage from the growing amount of public interest litigation in the courts for heritage preservation and the increasing number of NGOs acting as pressure groups for heritage preservation in the country.

In addition, the growing incidence of thefts and vandalism of archaeological property in recent years has created awareness among the public for its safety and protection. Therefore, tracking of illicit trafficking of antiquities has become a major assignment among concerned law enforcement agencies in the country.

Recognizing that a paradigm shift in heritage conservation was urgently needed, a group of professionals met in February 2004 to develop guidelines for heritage protection. The resulting document is known as the Marwar Initiative (2004:56). To succeed, there must be a recasting of policies, legislation, management systems, and existing approaches to conservation in the Indian context. The group concluded, "We must respect and acknowledge the history, collective memory and living traditions of our diverse culture. There is an emergent need to forge a close collaboration between multiple stakeholders, which recognizes the advances in conservation tools and techniques and achieves a broader definition of the heritage that we seek to protect" (Marwar Initiative 2004:56). Further, "The existing structures within which we seek to preserve our heritage and culture have proved to be inadequate for this purpose and must be reevaluated" (Marwar Initiative 2004:56).

Conclusion

In recent years, there have been discussions on cultural resource management and public archaeology (Khandwalla 2004). There has been a growing realization, both within the government and throughout the country, that cultural heritage is the country's identity and has relevance to contemporary society. Therefore, it needs to be preserved for posterity and it is the responsibility of every citizen to respect the heritage. In fact, it is only through the active and collective participation of government, voluntary groups, and individuals that the preservation and management of cultural resources is possible. It has been realized that public participation through community involvement in heritage preservation is the only way to achieve better management of India's vast archaeological resources.

Note

1. The main mission of INTACH is to sensitize the public about the pluralistic cultural legacy of the country; to protect and conserve the natural, built, and living heritage by undertaking necessary actions and measures; to document cultural resources and unprotected buildings of archaeological, architectural, historical, and aesthetic significance to develop heritage policy and regulations, and make legal interventions to protect our heritage, when necessary; to provide expertise in the field of conservation, restoration, and preservation of specific works of art and to encourage capacity building by developing skill through training programs; to undertake emergency response measures during natural or man-made disasters, and to support local administration wherever heritage is threatened; and to foster collaborations, memoranda of understanding (MOUs), and partnerships with government and other national and international agencies.

References Cited

About the Charles Wallace Trusts
1981   Electronic document, http://www.wallace-trusts.org.uk/, accessed December 5, 2007.
Archaeological Survey of India (ASI)
1997   *Report of the Expert Group on Archaeology (Mirdha Committee)*. Archaeological Survey of India, New Delhi.
2007   *National Mission on Monuments and Antiquities*. Published on the occasion of the launching of the National Mission on Monuments and Antiquities on March 19, 2007. Archaeological Survey of India, New Delhi.
Baig, Amita
2003   Cultural Policies in India and the Opportunities for the 21st Century. In *Proceedings of the Tenth Seminar of the Conservation of Asian Cultural Heritage*, edited by Shinwasha, pp. 241–64. National Research Institute for Cultural Properties, Tokyo.
2004   Country Report of India: Cultural Heritage Management in India. In *Public Systems for the Protection of Cultural Heritage: Organization, Human Resources and Financial Resources (Proceedings of Eleventh Seminar on the Conservation of Asian Cultural Heritage)*, edited by Shinwasha, pp. 167–87. National Research Institute for Cultural Properties, Tokyo.
Biswas, S. S.
1999   *Protecting the Cultural Heritage (National Legislations and International Conventions)*. Aryan Books International, New Delhi.
Brown, G. Baldwin
1905   *The Care of Ancient Monuments*. Cambridge University Press, Cambridge.
Chainani, Shyam
2002a   Heritage Legislation and Conservation in Bombay: An NGO Effort (Revised). Paper presented at the International Workshop "Training Workshop for Asia and the Pacific—Management and Conservation of World Heritage Sites Law, Policy and Administrative Aspects," Hiroshima, Japan, October 1–6, 2001, organized by UNESCO, UNITAR, and the Hiroshima Prefectural Government.
2002b   Heritage Policy for India. In *A Case for National Policy for Heritage Conservation and Management*, edited by Rajeshwari Tandon, pp. 25–36. INTACH, New Delhi.
Chakrabarti, Dilip K.
1988   *A History of Indian Archaeology: From the Beginning to 1947*. Munshiram Manoharlal Publishers Pvt. Ltd., New Delhi.
The Constitution of India
1949   Part IVA, 51A(f), p. 20. Available as a paginated MS Word document at http://aptel.gov.in/pdf/constitutionof%20india%20acts.pdf, accessed March 14, 2010.
Cumming, Sir John
1939   *Revealing India's Past*. The India Society, London.

Department of Culture
2006   *Annual Report 2005–06: Ministry of Tourism and Culture.* Government of India, Delhi.

Ghosh, A.
1953   Fifty Years of the Archaeological Survey of India. *Ancient India* 9:29–52.

Government of India
1904   The Ancient Monuments Preservation Act (An Act to Provide for the Preservation of Ancient Monuments and Objects of Archaeological, Historical, or Artistic Interest), Act No. VII of 1904 [March 18, 1904].

Guzder, Cyrus
1989   Tourism and Conservation in India—Problems and Opportunities. In *Conservation of the Indian Heritage*, edited by B. Allchin, F. R. Allchin, and B. K. Thapar, pp. 173–82. Cosmo Publications, New Delhi.

Indian National Trust for Art and Cultural Heritage (INTACH)
2005   Charter for the Conservation of Unprotected Architectural Heritage and Sites in India. In *INTACH Vision 2020*, edited by Rajeshwari Tandon, pp. 231–59. INTACH, New Delhi.

Khandwalla, K. P.
2004   Preservation of India's Archaeological Heritage Through Archaeologists—Public Interaction: Issues and Strategies. In *Archaeology as History in Early South Asia*, edited by H. P. Ray and C. M. Sinopoli, pp. 118–52. Indian Council of Historical Research, New Delhi.

Marshall, John
1990   *Conservation Manual.* Reprinted. Asian Educational Services, New Delhi.

The Marwar Initiative
2004   *Seminar* 542:56.

Ota, S. B.
2005   National Missions for Built Heritage, Sites and Antiquities: A Step Towards Heritage Resource Management. In *INTACH Vision 2020*, edited by Rajeshwari Tandon, pp. 77–80. INTACH, New Delhi.

Parliament of the Republic of India
1958   The Ancient Monuments and Archaeological Sites and Remains Act. Act no. 24 of 1958 [August 28, 1958].
1972   The Antiquities and Art Treasures Act. Act no. 52 of 1972 [September 9, 1972].

Roy, Sourindranath
1953   Indian Archaeology from Jones to Marshall. *Ancient India* 9:4–28.
1996   *The Story of Indian Archaeology 1784–1947.* Archaeological Survey of India, New Delhi.

Sarkar, H.
1981   *Museums and Protection of Monuments and Antiquities in India.* Sundeep Prakashan, Delhi.

Thapar, B. K.

1984   India. In *Approaches to the Archaeological Heritage*, edited by Henry Cleere, pp. 63–72. Cambridge University Press, Cambridge.

1989a   Agencies for the Preservation of Cultural Heritage of India. In *Conservation of the Indian Heritage*, edited by B. Allchin, F. R. Allchin, and B. K. Thapar, pp. 163–68. Cosmo Publications, New Delhi.

1989b   Policies for the Training and Recruitment of Archaeologists in India. In *Archaeological Heritage Management in the Modern World*, edited by Henry Cleere, pp. 285–91. Unwin Hyman, London.

7

Archaeological Heritage Management in Japan

KATSUYUKI OKAMURA AND AKIRA MATSUDA

At present, Japan, a country inhabited by 127 million people, has over 440,000 registered archaeological sites (Agency for Cultural Affairs 2001b:36). Wherever people live today, human activities have some effect on the land. The greatest effects are caused by development projects, which may have an impact on archaeological sites and require on-site archaeological investigation through rescue excavation in advance of the projects. The number of rescue excavations in Japan increased exponentially from the 1970s to the mid-1990s, reflecting the rapid growth of the nation's economy in that period. Since the mid-1990s, there has been a gradual decline in the amount of archaeological investigation. During 2006, approximately 3,000 proposals were made for development and construction works to be implemented in areas including registered archaeological sites. These proposals resulted in more than 900 rescue excavations, which were carried out after preliminary site assessments. Today, rescue excavations account for approximately 95 percent of all archaeological excavations in Japan (Watanabe 2008:39).

Historically speaking, archaeological heritage management (AHM) in Japan began in the second half of the nineteenth century, when several national laws were established to protect cultural heritage, including archaeological heritage, across the country (Nakamura 1999:13–19; Watanabe 2006:74–76). In contrast, the current national system of AHM, whose principal component is rescue investigation of archaeological sites, has developed in the period since World War II, especially since the mid-1960s (Agency for Cultural Affairs 2001a:263). The current system has developed particularly at boards of education (*kyouiku iinkai*) of local government, on both the prefectural and municipal levels, under the national government's supervision. These boards of education have not only been responsible for implementing rescue excavations; they have also been in charge of the protection and restoration of archaeological sites in each prefecture or municipality, as well as the dissemination and publication of information gained from archaeological investigations for educational purposes. They have thus contributed to the establishment of a comprehensive system of AHM in Japan (Tanaka 1984:84–86; Tsuboi 1992). This system, which has been in operation since the 1960s, is today faced with a new challenge posed by the growing pressure for privatizing rescue excavations (Inada 2006).

With these issues in mind, this chapter will first outline the development of AHM in Japan after World War II; second, it will illustrate several characteristics of the relationship between archaeology and the Japanese public; third, it will explain current challenges facing it; and finally, it will discuss its prospects in the near future.

Archaeological Heritage Management: The Development of AHM in Japan after World War II

In Japan, it is conventionally accepted that the cost of archaeological investigation prior to construction of private homes is borne by the state. However, when rescue excavation takes place as a result of construction work for commercial purposes, the cost is paid by the "polluter," namely the developer, be it a public or private body. This cost includes the expenses for excavating the site, processing the finds, and publishing the excavation report.

The Law for the Protection of Cultural Properties does not clearly stipulate the principle of "the polluter pays" (Tanaka 1984:84). Its clause 93–2 states that when there is a "particular need" to protect the "buried cultural properties" (*maizo bunkazai*, a term officially used in Japan to indicate "underground archaeological remains") that are going to be affected by development works, the commissioner of the Agency for Cultural Affairs can specify "necessary measures to be taken." It is generally accepted that these "measures" include asking the developer to pay the expenses of rescue excavations. However, there is no specific obligation for the developer to pay the expenses, as these "measures" constitute merely administrative direction. This issue, recurrently raised by developers, is one of the major problems of the Law for Protection of Cultural Properties.

The principle of "the polluter pays" was first adopted in 1958, when rescue excavation required in advance of construction of the Meishin Expressway was financed by the developer, the Japan Highway Public Corporation (Agency for Cultural Affairs 2001a:268–69). The same principle was repeated in protocols that the Agency for Cultural Affairs exchanged with other bodies in charge of public works, such as the Japan Housing Corporation and the Japan Railway Construction Public Corporation (Tsuboi 1992:3). Thereafter, the principle came to be applied, conventionally, to private development companies as well.

In the 1960s, the Japanese government implemented the Comprehensive National Development Plan (Zenkoku Sougou Kaihatsu Seichou Keikaku). This resulted in a considerable amount of infrastructural development, including highways networks, industrial estates, new industrial towns, new towns, high-speed railways, and airports. This in turn created an urgent need to undertake rescue excavations throughout the country.

Archaeological bodies, such as national research institutes, local museums, and universities, conducted excavations during the first two decades of the postwar period. However, since the 1960s, it has been mainly archaeologists working for local governments' boards of education that were in charge of rescue archaeology operations. In 1965, there were only 8 experienced field archaeologists employed in boards of education, but by 1968, this number had risen to 35 (Tsuboi 1992:3). As archaeologists were increasingly employed and positioned at the local government level, the administrative system for managing buried cultural properties and conducting rescue excavations was gradually established, first at prefectural and then municipal levels, under the national government's supervision.

The Plan for Remodeling the Japanese Archipelago (Nihon Rettou Kaizou Ron), proposed in 1972 by Kakuei Tanaka, then the prime minister, further accelerated nationwide development. Local authorities began setting up their own units for looking after cultural properties, and in some cases they instituted "semi-public" self-governing foundations specializing in archaeological investigation. The reason for the latter was partly economic. The local authorities could avoid the financial burden of hiring archaeologists as direct employees by incorporating the salaries of archaeologists into the budgets to be presented to the developers for funding (Tanaka 1984:83). Thus, the employment of archaeologists increased. Some prefectures, municipalities, and foundations even established within themselves "centers for buried cultural properties," which were in charge of excavation, analysis and storage of archaeological finds, and dissemination of archaeological knowledge and information in a systematic manner (Agency for Cultural Affairs 2001a:272–73; Tsuboi 1992:10).

The revision of the Law for the Protection of Cultural Properties in 1975 clarified local governments' responsibilities in archaeological investigation. It stipulated that the local authority, when undertaking rescue excavation, is entitled to ask for cooperation of the developer (clause 99–3 in the current law). This stipulation indicated some grounds for supporting the principle of "the polluter pays." However, just like the aforementioned "necessary measures" to be specified by the commissioner of the Agency for Cultural Affairs, it does not legally oblige the developer to pay the cost of archaeological investigation entailed as a result of development work. The unclear nature of this stipulation has from time to time become a central issue in legal disputes pursued by developers.

The so-called Resort Law, enacted in 1987, helped extend the reach of development projects beyond urban areas. Now the countryside and seaside became subject to development projects, and natural environment and archaeological sites were in danger. There were even more rescue excavations.

Boosted by Japan's steady economic growth after the 1960s, the Japanese AHM was incrementally established as the national system of rescue excavation and continued to develop until the 1990s, when the nation's economic growth declined rapidly. Thanks to the stable operation of this system, the number of archaeological sites destroyed without being investigated and recorded prior to development work has decreased considerably. It should be remembered, however, that recorded sites have seldom been preserved following rescue excavation (Tsuboi 1992:5).

Because of their entire, or at best partial, dependence on the developer to fund rescue excavations, archaeologists rarely broach the subject of site preservation in situ. Only archaeological sites of outstanding importance are physically preserved through the amendment of development plans, or their designation as national "historic sites" (*shiseki*), which often requires purchase of the land by the national or local government (Tanaka 1984:83; Tsuboi 1992:5–8). Except for these rare cases, the majority of sites are preserved only "by record," and thus transformed into over 2,000 excavation reports annually (Agency for Cultural Affairs 2001a:284).

Archaeology and the Japanese Public

It is not just archaeologists and developers who have played a key role in the establishment of AHM in Japan. Public opinion and movements have also significantly contributed to its development. For example, civic movements for the preservation of archaeological sites have been influential in the formation of heritage management on the local level (Japanese Association for Preservation of Cultural Properties 2006; Tsuboi 1992:3).

In 1962, the movement to protect the Heijo Palace site (a World Heritage site since 1998) in Nara, which was threatened by railway construction, was supported by many citizens, scholars, historians, and archaeologists. The effort to save the Heijo Palace evolved into a nationwide movement. The successful preservation of the Heijo site had a great impact on later preservation movements. In the late 1960s and at the beginning of the 1970s, when public concern for the conservation of nature and against pollution was increasing, people acted to protect archaeological sites in proposed development areas and to conserve nature. In such movements, it was often the local people, rather than historians and archaeologists, who played the major role. In 1970, with the development of these movements, the Japanese Association for Preservation of Cultural Properties (Bunkazai Hozon Zenkoku Kyougikai, a nongovernmental organization) was set up as a center for the exchange of information related to site protection. This initiative has enhanced communication among many Japanese site protection groups and continues to the present day.

Sensational archaeological discoveries have also raised public awareness of the importance of archaeological heritage (Agency for Cultural Affairs 2001a:275; Okamura 2000:57). For example, the discovery of the wall paintings in the Takamatsuzuka Tomb (Nara Prefecture) in 1972 encouraged a nationwide public interest in archaeology. This interest increased with the discovery of an iron sword from the Sakitama-Inariyama Tomb (Saitama Prefecture) in 1978. The inscription on this sword refers to the fifth-century emperor Yuryaku, his career, and early state formation in Japan. Both discoveries initiated a boom in archaeology in Japan. Since that time, the mass media has been broadcasting and publishing an increasing variety of information on archaeology (Okamura 2000:62; Tanaka 1984:83). As a result, "archaeology" has become more visible to the public and has developed an increasing body of interest and enthusiasm in the wider public.

Site protection movements, coupled with the enhanced public interest in archaeology, brought about successful preservation of several archaeological sites in the late 1980s and early 1990s, notable among which are the Yoshinogari site (a late Yayoi period large settlement enclosed with a ditch and palisades) in Saga Prefecture (Okamura and Condon 1999:66–67) and the Sannai-Maruyama site (Jomon period settlement) in Aomori Prefecture. Both sites were conserved as nationally designated "historic sites," partially reconstructed, and presented to the public. They are now very famous archaeological sites in Japan, attracting hundreds of thousands of visitors every year, and they are featured in most Japanese school textbooks.

At the same time, archaeologists working at local government and semi-public archaeological foundations have made efforts to raise public awareness of archaeological resources through a variety of educational activities under the supervision of boards of education. A good example of such activities is the "public site explanation" (*genchi setsumei kai*, or simply *gensetsu*), during which the results of the excavation are presented to the public at the site. The *gensetsu* was first held in 1956 at the excavation of Asuka Temple in Nara, and has been widespread throughout the country since the mid-1970s (Agency for Cultural Affairs 2001a:290). Today, *gensetsu*, usually held on weekends, are announced in newspapers and on television prior to the selected date. Sometimes *gensetsu* draw thousands of visitors, not only archaeological enthusiasts, but also local lay people (Okamura 2000:62). In addition to *gensetsu*, public lectures and symposia on archaeological subjects are frequently held, and interested people can often read reports on recent archaeological discoveries and listen to professional archaeologists.

Usually archaeologists working for local government and semi-public archaeological foundations are in charge of presenting the results of archaeological excavations to the public. They attempt to communicate clearly to a normally non-specialist audience the results of their work and its significance. In this sense, these archaeologists are responsible not only for studying and managing archaeological resources, but also for utilizing them for social and educational purposes.

Current Challenges to Japanese AHM

Effects of the Depression

The 40-year-old Japanese AHM has been driven and strongly characterized by the incremental establishment of the national-level system for dealing with rescue excavation of buried cultural properties. It was the nation's economic growth, rather than relevant legislation, that has allowed this system to be developed.

Japan's development was seriously affected by the severe economic downturn in the second half of the 1990s, when public works projects started to dwindle considerably. Until then, the annual national expenditure related to buried cultural property had constantly increased since 1989. It reached its peak in 1997 at 132 billion yen (U.S.$1.14 billion, based on the exchange rates of September 2007). However, by 2006 it had diminished to 75 billion yen (Watanabe 2008:40). In Osaka City, where development work is the most intense and extensive in Japan, development projects decreased to one-third of their peak in 2004. The decrease of development projects in itself should be welcomed, as it implies fewer rescue excavations and, hence, less destruction of archaeological heritage. However, the situation is far more complex in reality, because the current system of AHM exists and functions on the basis of certain supposed amounts of development works.

The recession has affected semi-public archaeological foundations the most, where approximately 30 percent of AHM archaeologists are employed. In 2007, there were approximately 6,300 archaeologists working at local government and semi-public archaeological foundations in Japan (see Watanabe 2008:36). Unlike "public" archaeological units belonging directly to local governments' boards of education, the "semi-public" foundations are more loosely attached to local government and more fiscally independent. As such, they cannot maintain themselves without undertaking archaeological excavations. These foundations have been in charge of not only rescue excavations, but in effect also every aspect of AHM. Their weakening and abolition would lead to the impoverishment of AHM in several areas.

Public archaeological units have their own problems. The reduction of development works has already caused some units to suspend new employment for over ten years, and, in worse cases, their demotion or abolishment. The so-called 2007 problem (the year when the majority of baby boomers were expected to enter mandatory retirement) is likely to create an irregular age structure in the unit labor force (Agency for Cultural Affairs 2001a:287). Because of these problems, the transmission of AHM professional skills to younger generations may well be hindered.

The Impact of "Privatization"

The biggest challenge the current AHM system is faced with is the growth and expansion of private archaeological units (see Inada 2006). Private archaeological units have already been in operation for a few decades, particularly in the Kanto region (including Tokyo and Yokohama), but most of them were small in size and led by professional archaeologists. In contrast, newly emergent private units are established at the initiative of, and more significantly "within," building or engineering companies, and they are now mainly large enterprises.

These units gained momentum for expansion particularly under the Koizumi cabinet (2001–2006), which pursued privatization and budget cuts in various aspects of public works under slogans such as "From public, to private" and "What the private can do must be entrusted to the private." Private units waged lobbying campaigns for privatization of rescue excavations, and, to further pursue this objective, established in 2005 their own business association, Nihon Bunkazaihogo Kyoukai, in which about 70 units participate. They have been successful in increasing the number of excavations they undertake and are today aiming to further expand their areas of activity.

It should be noted that major construction companies such as Obayashi Corporation, Kajima Corporation, and Shimizu Corporation are "supporting members" of Nihon Bunkazaihogo Kyoukai. This means that, for these construction companies—private developers—rescue excavations present a new attractive business market for profit, particularly to counteract the effect of the recent recession of the construction industry. There is concern that the developer is likely to be less interested in the quality of excavation than in the effective management of the process. It is feared that the partnership between developers and private archaeological units might lead to the deterioration of the quality of excavation and publication of its results.

In 1996, the Agency for Cultural Affairs announced its basic policy concerning the privatization of rescue excavations in the Notice Regarding the Preservation of Buried Cultural Properties and the Facilitation of Rescue Excavation (Maizou Bunkazai No Hogo To Hakkutsu Chousa No Enkatsuka Tou Ni Tsuite, Agency for Cultural Affairs 2001a:280, 289). According to this notice, private units are permitted to undertake rescue excavation only when the archaeological unit of the local authority concerned cannot execute the excavation, either by itself or with help from other local authorities. Even when a private unit is to carry out rescue excavation, the notice further states, the excavation needs to be incorporated into an existing archaeological investigation program of the local government. Thus, in effect, the Agency for Cultural Affairs is attempting to restrict the privatization of rescue excavations.

Despite this effort, privatization of the nation's public services as a whole has made further progress. For example, the passage of the Bill Regarding the Reform of Public Services via the Introduction of Competition, also known as the Market Testing Law, in May 2006 brought the Agency for Cultural Affairs under stronger pressure for privatization from other governmental departments in charge of development. Kanagawa Prefecture, which has highlighted the large amount of rescue excavation it undertakes, recently announced that it would seek to abolish its archaeological foundation and introduce a competitive tendering system for rescue excavation by 2010. Such a system would establish, as it were, an open market of rescue excavation, into which private archaeological units could freely enter for profit. The announcement of Kanagawa Prefecture has swayed the policy of other prefectures and municipalities and remains a threat to the current Japanese system of AHM, which has thus far been run predominantly by public institutions.

Privatization has other implications, too. Currently, the Agency for Cultural Affairs has made efforts, with some success, to narrow the regional and geographical gaps in the practice of AHM through its supervision and instruction. The Decentralization Act (1999), however, encouraged the devolution of power from the national government to local government. As a result, the geographical gaps in AHM are likely to expand. Privatization of rescue excavations would only contribute to further widening of these gaps, as larger private archaeological units, usually based in big cities in economically powerful prefectures, would be able to undertake rescue excavation in other prefectures and regions. At worst, it is feared that archaeology might come to be dominated by a limited number of large private units, thus weakening the activity of smaller and more locally based archaeological units.

With privatization in progress across the country, Japanese AHM is now entering a new phase. In terms of practice, rescue excavations are increasingly standardized, and the control over archaeological investigation by local authorities, which must follow the instruction of the Agency for Cultural Affairs, is being gradually tightened. In terms of theory, there are increasing discussions on the public benefit of archaeology and heritage.

Prospects for the Future

For the great majority of archaeologists based in Japan, the nationwide stagnation over the last ten years of archaeological investigations has been a new experience. Feeling a sense of crisis, archaeologists have started considering issues such as the problem of the current system of Japanese AHM, the role of archaeology in contemporary society, and the meaning of archaeological heritage to the general public (see Fawcett 1996). In other words, many archaeologists have become conscious, for the first time, of issues related to the social, economic, and political complexity of contemporary Japan.

Looking back on the 40-year history of Japanese AHM, one should recognize several successes it has achieved, despite the destruction of many archaeological sites. It has effectively built a nationwide consensus on the need to examine and record archaeological sites before they are destroyed. It has also established a reasonably efficient system with which to publish and disseminate the results of archaeological investigations (Okamura 2000:55).

Given the general decrease of archaeological operations across the country, some reduction of public archaeological units is inevitable. However, one should not expect further improvement of Japanese AHM unless the current AHM system, based on local government units, maintains at least the present quality of rescue excavation, public benefit through dissemination of the results of rescue excavations, and impartial provision of opportunity to access archaeological heritage.

Sooner or later, the recent steady decrease in the number of rescue excavations undertaken will likely come to a halt. Before this happens, Japanese AHM will still need to be more informed of the broader scope of heritage management, with which to hold a dialogue with the public, making effective use of knowledge gained from and accumulated through archaeological investigation.

Contemporary Japan demands "value for money" in every aspect of social life. Unfortunately, archaeological heritage, which should be priceless per se, is no exception (Klamer and Throsby 2000). As a result, people are increasingly interested in the "present value" of archaeological heritage. In other words, the utilization of archaeological heritage as a cultural resource is at stake.

In the coming years, those who work with AHM will need to recognize and assess various values attached to the "silent" archaeological heritage by diverse social groups and individuals, namely stakeholders (about this method, see De la Torre 2002; Pearson and Sullivan 1995:126–86). The values, although occasionally conflicting with each other (Darvill 1995), will need to be fully explored and digested, and then orchestrated in the most balanced and effective manner, according to each social context. This should happen primarily by practicing archaeological education on more diverse levels—such as school and adult education (Okamura 2000:63–64). Regrettably, archaeology and heritage are not taught as much as "history" in the present Japanese education system. This is partially because archaeology is considered one of the subfields of history. Consequently, archaeology is predominantly dealt with in the context of historical education (see Fawcett and Habu 1990) despite its potential use for interdisciplinary crossover, with, for example, geology, architecture, art, mathematics, and chemistry, and above all an evidence-based learning.

Given the interdisciplinary nature of archaeology, archaeological education could be effective particularly in elementary education. Collaboration between archaeologists and educators would be essential in developing the theory and methodology of teaching archaeology in primary schools. Professional archaeologists need to discuss and explore its possibilities more fully in conferences and workshops.

Since archaeological sites are, by definition, immovable, they should also be more closely linked to town and country planning. It is encouraging that in 2004 the Law for the Protection of Cultural Properties adopted "cultural landscape" as one of the categories of cultural properties to be protected. Planners have become more interested in utilizing archaeological sites—instead of freezing them for all-out protection—as part of a wider landscape and townscape. Heritage managers should seek collaboration with planners to achieve more archaeologically informed town and country planning.

Universities are expected to train and foster new types of archaeologists who can comprehend the basic principles of AHM and public archaeology (Merriman 2004; Schadla-Hall 1999, 2006), and have an insight into the social context in which archaeological heritage exists and functions, including the knowledge of tourism and cultural landscape. These new archaeologists should be able to understand the significance and values of archaeological heritage, and further "add" new values to it.

In a rapidly changing contemporary society like Japan, the archaeologist should not be satisfied with being just an excellent researcher of "the past" (Ascherson 2000:2). She or he needs to be an ethically and socially responsible educator, a mediator between archaeological heritage and the public, and a manager of archaeological resources who can carefully and insightfully look at "the present" as well. Archaeological heritage management in Japan is in need of "sturdy" archaeologists who can respond to such difficult demands of the times.

References Cited

Agency for Cultural Affairs
2001a   *Bunkazaihogohou Gojyunenshi* (Fifty years of history of the Law for the Protection of Cultural Properties). Gyousei, Tokyo.
2001b   Maizou Bunkazai Hogo Taisei Ni Kansuru Chousakenkyuu Kekka No Houkoku Ni Tsuite (Report of results of the research on the system for the protection of buried cultural properties). *Gekkan Bunkazai* 459:20–44.
Ascherson, Neal
2000   Editorial. *Public Archaeology* 1(1):1–4.
Darvill, Timothy
1995   Value Systems in Archaeology. In *Managing Archaeology*, edited by M. A.

Cooper, A. Firth, J. Carman, and D. Wheatley, pp. 40–50. Routledge, London and New York.

De la Torre, Marta (editor)
2002   *Assessing the Values of Cultural Heritage.* The Getty Conservation Institute, Los Angeles.

Fawcett, Clare
1996   Archaeology and Japanese Identity. In *Multicultural Japan, Palaeolithic to Postmodern*, edited by D. Donald, M. Hudson, G. Macormack, and T. Morris-Suzuki, pp. 60–77. Cambridge University Press, Cambridge.

Fawcett, Clare, and Junko Habu
1990   Education and Archaeology in Japan. In *The Excluded Past: Archaeology in Education*, edited by P. G. Stone and R. MacKenzie, pp. 217–32. Unwin Hyman, London.

Inada, Takashi
2006   Archaeological Heritage Management and Administrative Reform. *Koukogaku Kenkyuu (Quarterly of Archaeological Studies)* 53(2):73–93.

Japanese Association for Preservation of Cultural Properties
2006   *Encyclopedia of Preservation of Archaeological Heritage.* Heibonsha, Tokyo.

Klamer, Arjo, and David Throsby
2000   Paying for the Past: The Economics of Cultural Heritage. In *World Culture Report 2000: Cultural Diversity, Conflict and Pluralism*, edited by UNESCO, pp. 130–45. UNESCO, Paris.

Merriman, Nick
2004   Introduction: Diversity and Dissonance in Public Archaeology. In *Public Archaeology*, edited by N. Merriman, pp. 1–17. Routledge, London and New York.

Nakamura, Kenjiro
1999   *Bunkazaihogoseido Gaisetsu* (Outline of the system for the protection of cultural properties). Gyousei, Tokyo.

Okamura, Katsuyuki
2000   Conflict between Preservation and Development in Japan: The Challenges for Rescue Archaeologists. In *Cultural Resource Management in Contemporary Society: Perspectives on Managing and Presenting the Past*, edited by F. P. McManamon and A. Hatton, pp. 55–65. Routledge, London.

Okamura, Katsuyuki, and Robert Condon
1999   Reconstruction Sites and Education in Japan: A Case Study from the Kansai Region. In *The Constructed Past: Experimental Archaeology, Education and the Public*, edited by P. G. Stone and P. Planel, pp. 63–75. Routledge, London.

Pearson, Michael, and Sharon Sullivan
1995   *Looking after Heritage Places: The Basics of Heritage Planning for Managers, Landowners and Administrators.* Melbourne University Press, Carlton.

Schadla-Hall, Tim
1999   Editorial: Public Archaeology. *European Journal of Archaeology* 2:147–58.

2006   Public Archaeology in the Twenty-First Century. In *A Future for Archaeology*, edited by R. Layton, S. Shennan, and P. G. Stone, pp. 75–82. UCL Press, London.

Tanaka, Migaku
1984   Japan. In *Approaches to the Archaeological Heritage: A Comparative Study of World Cultural Resource Management Systems*, edited by H. Cleere, pp. 82–88. Cambridge University Press, Cambridge.

Tsuboi, Kiyotari
1992   Issues in Japanese Archaeology. In *Acta Asiatica 63*, edited by K. Tsuboi, pp. 1–19. Toho Gakkai, Tokyo.

Watanabe, Akiyoshi
2006   The Japanese System for Safeguarding Cultural Heritage. In *Proceedings of the International Conference on the Safeguarding of Tangible and Intangible Cultural Heritage: Towards an Integrated Approach*, edited by UNESCO, pp. 74–97. UNESCO, Paris.

Watanabe, Takehiko
2008   Maizou Bunkazai Kankei Toukei Shiryou No Kaisetsu To Bunseki: Heisei 19 Nendo Ban (Statistical data on buried cultural properties in 2007: Commentary and Analysis). *Gekkan Bunkazai* 535:36–42.

8

Heritage Resource Management in Mexico

NELLY M. ROBLES GARCÍA AND JACK CORBETT

To talk of heritage resource management in Mexico is to address a topic that today constitutes one of the most interesting academic challenges in a country widely recognized for its cultural complexity and which historically has led Latin America in the conservation of cultural heritage. At the same time, such discussion has become part of a tension between traditional academic approaches to and characterizations of cultural heritage and the contemporary effort to develop new perspectives, an effort influenced by theory and practice at the international level. These tensions play out against a backdrop of social contradictions and conflicts that define the operational setting for heritage professionals.

The core of these tensions over heritage management manifests itself in a series of disagreements about how to conceptualize new perspectives and the implications of such conceptualization in shaping academic discourse. For example, there are the debates over the domains of archaeology and archaeological resource management, or anthropology and grass-roots development, debates that shape how these domains are to be applied to society at large. To date, the principal response has been a timid result labeled "cultural management" by some of the institutions undertaking the creation of academic programs supporting new approaches.

Background

In Mexico, cultural resource management emerged as a concept applied to archaeological resources at the end of the 1990s (Robles García 1996, 1998), differentiating it clearly from the practice of archaeology as an academic discipline. This approach to cultural resource management followed that of Henry Cleere in the United Kingdom (1984, 1989), which was widely disseminated through projects of the International Council on Monuments and Sites (ICOMOS), the International Centre for the Study of the Preservation and Restoration of Cultural Property (ICCROM), and other advisory bodies of the United Nations Educational, Scientific and Cultural Organization (UNESCO). This first attempt to distinguish between archaeology as a science and the broader management of archaeological resources became a watershed between the traditional institutional arrangements for overseeing archaeological projects, and their subsequent futures in the hands of archaeologists and the Mexican government, and multidisciplinary innovations in archaeological research and management. The critical factor in the multidisciplinary approach is that it goes beyond the traditional emphasis on technical treatment to address the various sectors of society that for whatever reason occupy the same social and physical space as the heritage resource. In effect the multidisciplinary approach treats the context of the archaeological resource as critical in managing the resource itself.

The interdisciplinary nature of archaeological resource management becomes problematic precisely because it challenges the dominance of archaeology as the arbiter of the future of archaeological heritage, and therefore asserts a realignment of power and priorities within the academic and professional communities. The long-standing dominance of archaeologists in allocating resources, defining conservation in terms of restoration practices, and deciding the social use of sites and monuments encounters new voices articulating new paradigms that alter the place of archaeology as a discipline and the status of archaeologists as the sole voice of practice and value.

Historical Context

The array of formal archaeological projects undertaken by Mexicans in the early twentieth century under the control of Leopoldo Batres, and subsequently by scientific archaeologists such as the incomparable Alfonso Caso, bound what has been called the "golden age" of Mexican archaeology, particularly the period between 1930 and 1960. During this period, archaeology had a dual focus. First, its technical and scientific side sought to define the cultural characteristics of the different regions of Mesoamerica. Second, archaeologists sought to complement exploration with architectural restoration. Reconstruction of large monumental sites served the nationalist and nation-building interests of the state, a purpose of particular importance in the consolidation of a post-revolutionary society seeking to establish an independent national identity (Schávelzon 1990; Vázquez León 1996).

It is in this context that in 1939 President Lazaro Cardenas created the National Institute of Anthropology and History (Instituto Nacional de Antropología e Historia, or INAH). Its authorizing legislation defines clearly its purposes: to conserve, study, and disseminate the archeological, historical, and artistic heritage of Mexico. Each of these has a temporal referent: 1) archaeological: from the origins of human occupation until the Spanish Conquest of 1521; 2) historical: from the Conquest until the end of the nineteenth century; and 3) artistic: since the start of the twentieth century.

This had the effect of institutionalizing a permanent link between the science of archaeology and architectural restoration, with both resting on the shoulders of archaeologists within the legal-institutional framework of the INAH. At the same time, however, the formation of the National School of Anthropology and History (in Spanish, ENAH), a university-level institution, gave primacy to a curriculum and intellectual orientation based on the social sciences. In practice this distinction became the first grand contradiction in the management of archaeological resources in Mexico, although the reconstructions carried out in this era became popular public icons: Teotihuacan, Palenque, Monte Albán, Xochicalco, Uxmal, and Chichén Itzá, to name a few.

The place of archaeologists in architectural restoration was roundly criticized by the professional restorers who had emerged within the INAH. Augusto Molina Montes (1975) and other restorers emphasized the level of specialization needed to carry out appropriate restoration, a topic not even covered within the ENAH's curriculum. But in Mexico architectural reconstruction, although prohibited by the Charter of Venice, was and, in many cases, continues to be a practice based on trial-by-error experience and improvisational empiricism.

The INAH's role in managing Mexico's cultural heritage is one of monopoly power, as federal law confers upon it absolute jurisdiction in relation to research and conservation, without the possibility of sharing these responsibilities with other entities (Breglia 2006; Robles García 2000). Paradoxically this burdens the INAH with the need to operate in a complex social environment where heritage protection requires responses to problems of land tenure, social conflict, indigenous rights, and in numerous other areas beyond the INAH's legal mandate. In effect, the law requires it to operate in arenas where it has no legal authority and holds it accountable for outcomes over which it has no control. In addition to the formal structures established by law, for decades the only place in Mexico to study anthropology and archaeology was the ENAH, a circumstance that had the effect of reinforcing the official perspective. With its sister institution, the National School for Conservation, Restoration, and Museography (in Spanish, ENCRyM), education as well as law and practice speaks in support of federal policy, emphasizing a nationalist, centralized perspective and a strong socialization to institutional values. Thus, neither school is in a position to contribute to debates over contending heritage management theories or to challenge doctrine, a fundamental element in any university curriculum.

This is not meant to discredit the INAH's schools; on the contrary, the point is to underscore the narrow theoretical base for the development of the intellectual foundations of archaeology, conservation, and the management of archaeological resources in Mexico. In spite of this narrow base, the INAH's personnel have made a notable difference by pushing beyond the formal limitations of theory and suffocating practices marked by institutional commitments and norms (Vázquez León 1996).

Throughout its history, the INAH has continued the same scientific-conservationist tradition concentrating on monumental sites, leaving an unmistakable imprint on practice through extensive reconstruction. For decades Mexican archaeology and restoration practices enjoyed an exceptional reputation in Latin America because of the impressive imagery associated with the visual impact of reconstructed sites. As a consequence, Mexico has long been regarded in Latin America as in the vanguard of practice, even though such practice has long since fallen out of favor with most of the heritage management community. A lamentable byproduct of this situation is that it reinforced the internal gaze of many in the INAH, weakening further development of archaeological theory. Even today this perspective encourages a resistance to "foreign" influences in the form of international archaeological theories and defensive self-assurance in relation to international contact.

Modern formulations in archaeological conservation developed in an international setting (Cleere 1989), such as ICOMOS, ICCROM, and the International Committee on Archaeological Heritage Management (ICAHM), call into question the institutional logic that had backed conservation through archaeological projects. Additionally, voices such as those of indigenous groups concerned about archaeological vestiges of their past, or groups affected by the formal proclamation of archaeological zones that constrain their use of their land while yielding them little in return, have begun to question traditional approaches to conservation. The rhetoric of heritage and a weak federal law no longer suffice as effective mechanisms for heritage management in dynamic and uncertain settings, but the burden of the past obstructs vigorous debate and institutional innovation.

By the early 1980s, pockets of dissension were beginning to appear in the INAH, driven by unresolved needs or new demands. Community and indigenous voices pressed claims for the right to be consulted about or be active participants in the management of heritage, particularly archaeological sites or materials related to them. And political figures and professionals in institutions related to indigenous affairs and cultural heritage became more assertive about the interests of indigenous populations and grass-roots development as a central concern in policy proposals. Two decades later we have yet to see an inspiring example of a successful fusion of indigenous concerns and heritage management, but the demands for inclusion are greater than ever. The central dilemma, however, is the persistent tendency of the INAH to operate with limited reference to the world beyond its institutional boundaries, a tendency reinforced by its legal base, while external demands and pressures continue to build.

Archaeological Resource Management as an Academic Concern

In 1996, when the term "archaeological resource management" was first used in Mexico, it was important to explain clearly that archaeological resource management is an interdisciplinary field with a social impact beyond just archaeology. Although archaeological resource management places this discipline in a place of importance within the new framework, in a broader sense the contemporary framework implies managing archaeological resources in multiple ways, such as education, moving beyond the traditional foci of protecting, conserving, studying, and conserving elements of heritage in socially defined contexts (Robles García 1998).

The overall concept, enriched by a diversity of currents flowing from Spain and the European Community, the United Kingdom, Canada, and the United States, contributes to the growth and development of a new field in Mexico, a field today recognized as cultural management. As in any other discipline, it is possible to see the difference between theory and practice, and the emergence of a limited but consistent bibliography on diverse aspects of the general theme (Bonfil Castro 2003; Garcia Canclini 1989; Nivón Bolán 2004; Olive Negrete and Cottom 1995; Robles García 1996, 1998; Robles García and Corbett 1995; Viladevall i Guasch 2003;).

In recent years, there have been some important initiatives to institutionalize this focus as part of the INAH. For example, there have been serious efforts by the academic community, such as the Seminar on Management of Cultural Heritage, conducted with the participation of archaeologists and anthropologists organized by the national coordinator for anthropology, that tried to identify some of the most important themes to be found within the new conceptual framework of management. This effort has been, above all, a praiseworthy search for guidelines that can serve to define new concepts of heritage, and through this to identify tasks that can be developed as part of the existing institutional mandate. Nevertheless, as always, what is lacking is the articulation of theory with practice, not for lack of will but because this is where one finds the institutional constraints on facilitating flexibility in traditional styles of thinking and action.

Another major effort, the application of the general principles of UNESCO's Convention on World Heritage, was carried out by decision makers of the INAH. They created the World Heritage Directorate, which in its first years of operation (1999–2005) opened an important space for the discussion of topics with international relevance, facing the complexity at the heart of being the country in the Western Hemisphere with the largest number of sites enrolled on the World Heritage List.

This project was especially successful in the sense that it called attention to central themes under discussion at the international level, such as the determination of authenticity and integrity of heritage, international conventions, the search for management indicators, the importance of international guidelines for heritage classification, and the importance of new categories for levels of protection of heritage sites. These discussions finally opened the possibility of moving beyond traditional categories, such as historic districts and archaeological zones, and utilizing broader categories of cultural resource conservation, such as cultural landscapes, cultural corridors, transfrontier sites, mixed (natural/cultural) sites, and contemporary architecture, among other innovative categories.

Besides its success in overseeing the 26 Mexican sites on the World Heritage List, this office of the INAH fomented academic participation in an array of international meetings, thereby broadening individual perspectives and contact while challenging the INAH's closed environment.[1] Despite massive social change inside and outside Mexico, the INAH has in fact done relatively little to address the enormous gap that has opened between official heritage discourse and claims pressed by various sectors with respect to two factors: 1) the direct advantages that could be generated for populations that share the settings of heritage sites, which such populations may value for their economic potential, and; 2) a desire by indigenous groups to exercise jurisdiction over lands, archaeological sites, sacred places, and other resources that are, in the end, their heritage. In both cases these claims run counter to the tendencies of academics, institutional and agency representatives, and other stakeholders to appropriate the traditions, dances, fiestas, archaeological remains, and crafts of these communities and groups, justifying such appropriations on grounds of national interest, superior knowledge and understanding, legal authority, or greater agility in the marketplace.

The themes of self-management and grass-roots control in relation to cultural and natural heritage remain as laudable but unattainable ideas from the institutional perspective, a situation that appears to be a sharp contradiction given the INAH's original charge to serve an educational mission, a charge reflected by its placement within the office of the Secretary of Public Education. One effort, undoubtedly the most valuable in this respect, has been the Community Museums Program in Oaxaca, one frequently cited by the INAH to demonstrate its grass-roots commitment, but in actuality the product of voluntary and personal convictions among atypical academics. We will return to this topic later.

Institutional Responses

In 1998, faced by increasing pressure to apply several international agreements related to heritage conservation (the World Heritage Convention, the Convention on Archaeological Heritage, and various agreements and documents on authenticity, among others), the INAH took steps to establish institutional mechanisms to respond to the obligations it had acquired. These included the creation of comprehensive management plans for World Heritage sites and the creation of mechanisms to evaluate heritage management. By creating the Directorate for Site Operations and Continuity, the INAH sought to give the appearance of attaching considerable importance to its responsibilities. Strategically, however, it separated the office from the mass of archaeologists and anthropologists who do much of the daily work, instead leaving the apparent innovation in the hands of an isolated group distinguished by a lack of experience. This inexperience and lack of knowledge of heritage management was in sharp contrast to the enthusiasm and expectations generated when the office was announced, and this gap continues to the present.

By creating a high-level office, senior administrators generated something of a fad for the development of management plans and triggered a struggle over "who knows best" and who was qualified to propose and assess management plans. As might be anticipated, what followed was a struggle between those who assert authority based on position and those who assert it based on experience. Suffice it to say that the waste of time and energy in competing for status and authority served the INAH poorly; the wasted time and energy could have been directed toward more valuable undertakings, and soured some personnel on the notion of management planning.

Given the lack of meaningful theory and appropriate methodologies grounded in the Mexican context, the INAH, via the directorate, finally adopted the methodology devised by the National Park Service in the United States as the basis for configuring management plans for heritage sites in Mexico. In doing so, it introduced into its planning process concepts and terminology associated with the American business world (mission, vision, managers) without considering the degree to which these fit a Mexican public bureaucracy. The predictable outcome was rejection by the INAH professionals of a framework that not only used an alien vocabulary, but seemed unsuited for planning heritage conservation. Furthermore, the legal and bureaucratic nature of a Mexican federal agency, lacking budgetary flexibility and subject to an extraordinary level of centralized control, hardly fit an entrepreneurial model emphasizing a very different notion of measuring organizational accomplishments. Finally, notions of public-private partnerships, interagency collaboration, and other institutional arrangements largely taken for granted in the National Park Service are far more problematic in Mexico.

Recently, there have been efforts to resume management planning via the publication of more detailed guidelines and frameworks (see Instituto Nacional de Antropología e Historia [INAH] 2006a, 2006b, and 2006c). All of these suffer from the lack of a solid conceptual framework and demonstrate clearly that the INAH in reality has no expectation of facilitating participatory or self-management of heritage properties. Instead, it continues its traditional nation-alist-authoritarian, top-down management model decades after social change and national development rendered it obsolete.

In spite of the constraints placed on institutional innovation by the conditions we have described, alternative models of cultural heritage management continue to emerge. The common denominator in these models is the commitment by field-level professionals to make them work, often in spite of official structure and process. Two brief case studies illustrate aspects of these alternatives.

Monte Albán as an Alternative inside the INAH

The management plan for Monte Albán, one of the great archaeological sites of Mexico, emerged inside the INAH as a pioneering experiment in the integration of theory and practice in the management of cultural resources, an attempt to integrate central elements of conservation archaeology, archaeological research, and applied natural resource management with ongoing attention to visitor education, site services, and protection of the legal and social integrity of the archaeological zone. What is striking about this model is that it assumes that 1) it is possible to sustain long-term site integration despite the centripetal forces pulling on it; 2) the key to sustaining integration is the development of a self-managing, multidisciplinary team; and 3) effective performance in terms of heritage management depends more on constructing a horizontal network among a complex array of social actors than it does on the vertical relationships within the INAH.

After nearly a decade of pursuing and refining its model, Monte Albán continues to generate a series of strategies intended to facilitate problem solving and resource allocation. For example, categorizing the 5,000-acre archaeological zone according to permitted visitor use rather than archaeological criteria permits a more productive way of managing protection of the site and encourages attention to possible stress points. This in turn helps manage interactions among different actors and enables staff to be proactive. The INAH's response to the integrated management model and strategy development has been to use Monte Albán as a test platform for management techniques and strategies. For a time, it even permitted Monte Albán to manage a certain portion of the income from its ticket sales to provide greater flexibility in addressing local needs, a decision hailed at the time as a great innovation in managing heritage but later abandoned because it reduced the budget leverage of central administrators.

As Mexico's flagship site from the standpoint of on-site planning and management, Monte Albán has received considerable attention from INAH personnel as well as foreign professionals. Its attention to inter-institutional relations has positioned the Monte Albán staff within a dense and fertile network of contacts that enrich their individual and collective experience. These contacts extend to the international arena, a reflection not only of Monte Albán's World Heritage status but of its efforts to maintain permanent relations with heritage organizations and agencies around the globe. All of this requires a commitment of energy and sense of teamwork far in excess of the norm. The Monte Albán experience demonstrates that it is possible, even within the institutional constraints it confronts on a daily basis, to manage archaeological heritage in an innovative and productive fashion. But such management depends heavily on staff capacity to function in an institutional environment that is, at best, passively supportive.

The central dilemma for the INAH, and for the Monte Albán management team, is that the latter's success depends to a substantial degree on how effective it is in distancing itself from the organizational values and processes characterizing the former. While archaeologists typically dominate conceptual thinking about archaeological zone management, at Monte Albán the emphasis is on a multidisciplinary team, which seeks to build relations with local communities and stakeholders using a collaborative, sociological framework.[2]

Heritage Self-Management among Community Museums

Another alternative management approach is the emergence of the community museums movement. Born in Oaxaca with the support of INAH anthropologists, this management approach draws on traditional self-government models in Oaxacan communities and responds to community interest in safeguarding cultural heritage. Traditional community organization serves as the basis for this model, as each community elects in open assembly a committee that serves as an unpaid heritage manager by maintaining and staffing the community's museum. The community itself decides on the museum's focus, and rotation of committee membership within the community assures a broad base of community involvement. In this fashion the community develops not only a museum but additional experience in self-managed institutions. These are linked horizontally in the Association of Community Museums, in which they share experiences and collaborate on projects and training. Participation in the association takes committee members not only to different parts of the state, providing exposure to new places and ideas, but occasionally to national and even international meetings.

After 20 years, this model, although it started with the support of the INAH, has outstripped all expectations and become a serious alternative for community management of cultural heritage. In Mexico the community museums have largely escaped from the INAH's control; instead they have become one mechanism by which communities challenge the INAH's monopoly on heritage management. As the community museums movement has spread to other Latin

American countries, the traditional heritage management institutions find themselves, in some circumstances, relegated to oversight and standard-setting functions as communities take active responsibility for heritage matters.

The INAH's minimal financial support for community museums creates two ongoing problems for the agency and for communities. First, it undermines assertions that the INAH sees the museums as significant partners in heritage management. Rather, they are useful settings for making symbolic statements about shared responsibilities and for pressing communities to absorb burdens associated with routine site maintenance. Second, committees have pushed to generate income for their museums by creating cultural and ecological tours that generate fees and customers for museum shops. This in turn has persuaded some communities that their museums and committees should be seen as adjuncts to economic development efforts, and heritage values subordinated to tourism and commercial concerns. At least one community museum has gone so far as to withdraw from the association to gain more flexibility and control over its resource base. The unanswered question is whether an organizational arrangement originally created to support heritage management might end up threatening it, even inadvertently, as community concerns shift to economic development. Yet the INAH's inability or unwillingness to respond to community interests in treating heritage as a resource, which could contribute to development, undermines its role in protection.

Final Discussion

Undoubtedly in Mexico we are seeing a gradual transition from the dominance of heritage thinking by archaeology to management of archaeological resources, from a nationalistic and bureaucratic discourse to one more sensitive to conservation, problem solving, and flexibility. Nevertheless, as with all new areas of knowledge, this one needs its own shape and process. This form is most likely to emerge through academic experience and professional preparation that becomes increasingly formal and systematic. The INAH must make an enormous effort to facilitate this shift; otherwise it risks losing time and wasting resources in trial-and-error processes reminiscent of the struggle over management plans.

Even if the INAH has the will to pursue cultural resource management, it confronts its own institutional reality. In the current institutional framework, there is no way to apply proposals to link the management of cultural resources with matters of development, social participation, poverty, or other concerns. The INAH's own history of rigid principles and the fact that it is an institution serving the state offers it little space for modernization. In this respect the gamut of economic interests that have grown up around cultural heritage in general and archaeology in particular, interests that appear in forms from hotel managers and real estate speculators to travel agents and street vendors, represent challenges that the INAH as an institution is not prepared to address.

We believe the experience of the Association of Community Museums offers a valuable lesson to Mexico in terms of grass-roots heritage management. Although the INAH publicizes it, the INAH does not support it, in part because the current normative and budget structures do not permit certain actions. These include 1) providing economic incentives to communities (under the current system it is not possible to contemplate options such as tax exemptions or payments for cultural services, and official budgets cannot support the construction or museography of modest museums); 2) delegating jurisdiction over heritage properties (not negotiable, according to the majority of voices in the INAH); and, 3) taking the role of just another actor in the social landscape (Robles García 2006). The INAH was created as a dominating agency and wishes to continue that way in spite of changing conditions. The INAH insists on a central role even when that complicates productive inter-institutional relations with the Secretaría de Medio Ambiente y Recursos Naturales (SEMARNAT, Mexico's natural resource management agency) or other institutions.

There is a long way to go, but the positive experiences in managing heritage in Mexico have left some important marks. One incredibly important task is reducing the gap that the INAH has unconsciously opened between academic expertise and top-level administrative decisions related to cultural resource management. This gap is dangerous, and if not addressed it could signal the beginning of the end of an institution that still has a lot to offer provided it can open itself to opportunities for innovation and adapt its processes to address the new relationship between society and heritage. The critical challenge for the INAH is not simply managing cultural heritage, but somehow finding the will and insight to reform itself.

Notes

1. It also published a newsletter, *Hereditas*, dedicated to discussions of site conservation and various international themes. Unfortunately, as in many other cases, this project was the product of the knowledge and academic focus of a single individual. When for institutional reasons that individual was no longer available to guide the office, there was not sufficient professional depth to maintain the quality and focus hitherto available, nor senior management commitment to sustain it. Thus an effort that at first appeared to signal a change in organizational perspectives toward the larger professional world in the long run succumbed to the dominant organizational culture.

2. In contrast, the INAH and other central government agencies favor standardization of archaeological zone contracting. The central administration defines relationships with other stakeholders primarily in hierarchical and legal terms. Thus the desire to benefit from Monte Albán's success collides with the painful reality that this success is largely attributable to deviating from, rather than embracing, institutional norms.

References Cited

Arizpe, Lourdes

2004   *Los retos culturales de México* (Mexico's cultural challenges). Editorial Angel Porrúa, Universidad Nacional Autónoma de México (UNAM), Cámara de Diputados, México, D.F.

Bonfil Castro, Ramón

2003   Patrimonio cultural, gestión y proyecto de nación (Cultural heritage, management, and national planning). In *Gestión del patrimonio cultural: Realidades y retos* (Management of cultural patrimony: Realities and challenges), edited by Mireia Viladevall i Guasch, pp. 107–20. Benemérita Universidad Autónoma de Puebla, Puebla, México.

Breglia, Lisa

2006   *Monumental Ambivalence: The Politics of Heritage.* University of Texas Press, Austin.

Cleere, Henry F.

1984   *Approaches to the Archaeological Heritage.* Cambridge University Press, Cambridge.

1989   *Archaeological Heritage Management in the Modern World.* One World Archaeology 9. Unwin Hyman, London.

García Canclini, Néstor

1989   *Culturas híbridas: Estrategias para entrar y salir de la modernidad* (Hybrid cultures: Strategies to enter and leave modernity). Grijalbo, México, D.F.

Instituto Nacional de Antropología e Historia (INAH)

1976   *Ley federal sobre monumentos arqueológicos, artísticos e históricos* (The federal law on archaeological, artistic and historical monuments). INAH, México, D.F.

2006a   *La planeación y gestión del patrimonio cultural de la nación manual de políticas* (Planning and management of the nation's cultural heritage). INAH, México, D.F.

2006b   *Reglamento para la apertura de zonas arqueológicas en México* (Regulations for the opening of archaeological zones in Mexico). Propuesta de la Dirección de Operación de Sitios. INAH, México, D.F.

2006c   *Lineamientos para la atención del patrimonio cultural afectado por desastres naturales o antropogénicos* (Manual of policies and guidelines for attending to cultural heritage affected by natural or man-made disasters). INAH, México, D.F.

Molina Montes, Augusto

1975   *La conservación de monumentos arqueológicos en México* (Conservation of archaeological monuments in Mexico). Colección Científica, INAH, México, D.F.

Nalda, Enrique

2004   Patrimonio arqueológico, problemas antiguos, soluciones nuevas (Archaeological heritage, ancient problems, new solutions). In *Los retos culturales de*

México (The cultural challenges of Mexico), edited by Lourdes Arizpe, pp. 301–18. Editorial Ángel Porrúa, México, D.F.

Nivón Bolán, Eduardo

2004   Nuevas formas de gestión cultural. In *Los retos culturales de México*, edited by Lourdes Arizpe, pp. 327–50. Editorial Ángel Porrúa, México, D.F.

Olive Negrete, Julio Cesar, and Bolfy Cottom

1995   *INAH: Una historia* (INAH: A history). Consejo Nacional para la Cultura y las Artes, México, D.F.

Robles García, Nelly M.

1996   *El manejo de los recursos arqueológicos en México: El caso de Oaxaca* (The management of archaeological resources in Mexico: The case of Oaxaca). Unpublished Ph.D. dissertation, University of Georgia, Athens.

1998   *El manejo de los recursos arqueológicos en México: El caso de Oaxaca* (The management of archaeological resources in Mexico: The case of Oaxaca). CONACULTA-INAH, México, D.F.

2000   Archaeological Resources Management in Mexico: The Case of Oaxaca. Translated by Jack Corbett. Electronic document, http://www.saa.org/publications/oaxaca/TOC.html, accessed September 8, 2007.

2003   Arqueología y manejo de recursos arqueológicos en México (Archaeology and archaeological resource management in Mexico). In *Gestión del patrimonio cultural: Realidades y retos* (Management of cultural resources: Realities and challenges), edited by Mireia Viladevall i Guasch, pp. 139–58. Benemérita Universidad Autónoma de Puebla, Puebla, México.

2006   Social Landscapes and Archaeological Heritage in Latin America. In *Of the Past, for the Future: Integrating Archaeology and Conservation*, edited by Neville Agnew and Janet Bridgland, pp. 113–24. The Getty Conservation Institute, Los Angeles.

Robles García, Nelly M., and Jack Corbett

1995   Land Tenure Systems, Economic Development, and Protected Areas in Mexico. In *8th Conference on Research and Resource Management*. The George Wright Society, Portland, Oregon.

Schávelzon, Daniel

1990   *La conservación del patrimonio cultural en América latina: Restauración de edificios prehispánicos en Mesoamérica 1750–1980* (Conservation of cultural patrimony in Latin America: Restoration of pre-Hispanic structures in Mesoamerica 1750–1980). Universidad de Buenos Aires, Instituto de Arte Americano e Investigaciones Estéticas "Mario J. Buschiazzo," Buenos Aires.

Vázquez León, Luis

1996   *El leviatán arqueológico: Antropología de una tradición científica en México* (The archaeological leviathan: Anthropology from a scientific tradition in Mexico). Editorial Miguel Angel Porrua, México, D.F.

Viladevall i Guasch, Mireia (editor)

2003   *Gestión del patrimonio cultural: Realidades y retos* (Management of cultural resources: Realities and challenges). Benemérita Universidad Autónoma de Puebla, Puebla, México.

9

Heritage Resource Management in Peru

JORGE E. SILVA

As soon as Spaniards reached America in the early fifteenth century, they immediately recognized several societies with strange cultural patterns that were different from them in many ways. They also found empires with high levels of political organization: the Aztec, in what is now Mexico, and the Inca in Peru. The Incas developed as a distinctive society without having a written language, wheeled transport, or other types of vehicles usually associated with Old World civilizations. The Inca Empire, with its capital, Cusco, in the southern highlands of Peru, was part of a long cultural history that evolved independently in South America and achieved a highly centralized political system controlling a large territory from Ecuador to central Chile.

This chapter is intended to provide a preliminary examination of the management of cultural resources in Peru, emphasizing its legal aspects, and the framework of methods and procedures, which have attempted to preserve the Peruvian cultural heritage for future generations.

An interesting analysis of this topic has been published recently by Cortes and Vich (2006). On a global scale, serious efforts have been taken in order to face accelerated destruction of past remains by establishing specific priorities for preservation of cultural heritage (for example, Messenger 1999a). The points discussed below follow a chronological order, outlining the most important legal changes introduced by the Peruvian government concerning heritage management.

Historical Legal Background

After King Carlos V defeated the empire of Tawantinsuyu in the early sixteenth century, he established his right over the property of the entire territory, including relics and monuments. As a result of this land claim, Viceroy F. de Toledo, in 1574, defined a number of conditions in order to control the looting of "Indian treasures" (Avalos de Matos and Ravines 1974:364). At the same time, the Spanish royalty undertook a strong campaign against native religious cults that was referred to as the "extirpation of idolatries." As a result, royal property rights over antiquities were designed to preserve relics and monuments that were considered valuable.

The spirit of preserving past remains is also clearly expressed by the Supreme Decree 89 of April 2, 1822, promulgated during the protectorship of José de San Martin. This decree not only created the National Museum, but also attested to the state's commitment regarding conservation and protection of past remains and the nation's sovereignty over them. Also, this decree prohibited extraction or excavation of old buildings or *huacas* without government permission and established a fine of "mil pesos" (1,000 pesos in the official currency at the time), which was used for public education.

By 1836, President Luis José Orbegoso promulgated Supreme Decree 433, which organized the National Museum to incorporate a section regarding native plants and animals and prohibiting citizens from looting and selling antiquities. In September 1837, the Peruvian government amended this decree with the establishment of a number of measures to avoid their illegal exportation. In 1841, President Agustín Gamarra signed Supreme Decree 556, which reinforced previous legal provisions and included colonial paintings in the list of government-protected cultural patrimony. Almost a century and a half later, in 1971, the military government signed Law 18780, which prohibited the exportation of pre-Hispanic or colonial relics.

But the above-mentioned laws could not eliminate the looting and collecting of antiquities due to the commercial value placed on Peruvian antiquities. According to Avalos de Matos and Ravines (1974:366), looting and trafficking of archaeological artifacts were intense during the construction of the Lima-Ancón railroad line in the 1870s (Ancón being a small town located about 40 km north of Lima). In fact, this has been a widespread activity from the nineteenth century until today.

In order to prevent more looting and demolishing of *huacas* and ancient cemeteries, in 1893 the Peruvian government enacted other legal provisions concerning protection of past remains. First, the government called for the conservation of the past, without which the reconstruction of Peruvian history would be impossible. Second, a special antiquities conservation committee was created in order to assess monuments through an archaeological excavation permitting process. However, permits did not indicate the professional skills required to conduct an excavation. Third, the government allowed an excavator to keep all of the excavated objects, though an inventory was required to be submitted to the committee.

Preserving the Past in Twentieth-Century Peru

Substantial steps toward the protection and study of antiquities were achieved early in the twentieth century. In 1911, Supreme Decree 2612 introduced specific modifications to the law of 1893 stipulating that excavations be supervised by government inspectors, and that the rights to all excavated objects belong to the state. A decade later, the supreme decree of June 11, 1921 marked a valuable change regarding the historical meaning of past remains and the direct responsibility of the state in order to preserve them. As part of this change this law specified that excavations could only be conducted by archaeologists with advanced degrees.

In June 1929, Law 6634 enabled the creation of the Patronage of National Archaeology, which later evolved into the Casa de la Cultura del Perú (House of Peruvian Culture), in the Instituto Nacional de Cultura (INC, National Institute of Culture), at the start of the 1970s. Notably, such patronage was developed by the Ministry of Education, the president of San Marcos University, delegates from minor universities, the director of the Museum of National History, and the president of the Geographic Society of Lima. A similar agency was also created in Cusco, with the possibility of creating other similar agencies across the country. This law also extended to municipalities and central government representatives.

Differing from previous laws, Law 6634 proposed a number of goals, such as the development of an archaeological map of Peru and the inventory of all the past remains, to promote the creation of Peruvian archaeology, to finance protection of these remains, and to finance the study of these past remains. In addition, it must be mentioned that Law 6634 declared the sites of Sacsahuaman, Ollantaytambo, Machu Picchu, Vitcos, Atun Ccolla, Nazca, Pachacamac, the Fort of Chimú, the Castillo de Chavín, Huánuco Viejo, and the Ruins of Chan Chan as national monuments.

In the early 1970s, the military government created the INC as part of a state project designed to deal with Peruvian culture from a different perspective. In fact, even though the INC is dependent upon the Ministry of Education, it has autonomy at the decision-making level, especially regarding problem solving requiring the professional advice of experts. Therefore, technical departments with specific functions devoted to the pre-Hispanic period were organized in the Department of Archaeology, and to the colonial and republican periods in the Department of Historic Monuments.

The INC's efforts on cultural heritage preservation were divided by Lumbreras (2006) into four phases. However, for the purposes of this essay I will consider three main phases. During the first period, between 1970 and the early 1980s, significant steps were taken to conduct conservation projects of large archaeological sites and colonial buildings (for example, churches, government buildings, mural paintings). The second phase is associated with the Peruvian economic bankruptcy, which began in the late 1980s and continued in the 1990s. During this period the INC lost most of its personnel, and the technical departments were almost closed down. The third phase began in the late 1990s and continues today. This last phase marks a renewed effort toward preservation of past Peruvian remains. A number of motivations related to this phase include the development of tourism, the reinforcement of a sense of nationality, and obtaining the support of world organizations for the conservation of cultural and natural patrimony.

Archaeological Heritage Resource Management in Peru

Heritage resource management in Peru is understood differently by archaeologists, the mass media, politicians, and the general public. There are several reasons that may help to explain the diversity of opinions on this issue. For some people cultural resource management is not productive; others think that past remains interfere with progress; and still others think that only impressive monuments must be preserved.

In fact, initially, Peruvian cultural heritage referred mainly to monumental constructions of the pre-Hispanic, colonial, or republican periods, and, with exception, only some specific pieces of gold, fabrics, and pottery showing exquisite decorated designs, and colonial period paintings. Attention was devoted to pre-Hispanic remains according to their size and content (for example, royal tombs), impressive features (such as frieze reliefs), and sculptures (made of clay, stone, or wood).

Such cultural heritage parameters have had negative impacts on the preservation of cultural remains lacking the conditions described above, such as middens, small settlements, quarry shops, single component sites, and site camps. Also, such ideas have resulted in the division of cultural heritage into important and unimportant categories. This division is problematic because of its dependence mostly on personal judgment rather than the intrinsic message that the remains themselves hold. This misconception tends to assume that the unimportant remains do not deserve attention for management purposes at all.

"Cultural patrimony," or cultural heritage as described by Messenger (1999b:xxiii), is hereby understood as the past and the present material and nonmaterial cultural legacy of the entire Peruvian history. Therefore, the term "heritage" refers to both the past remains and the symbolic meaning of them for people of all times and places. This is to say that collective attitudes form a common thread that is expressed through shared behavior, objects, places, and constructions. It is my impression that this way of thinking, including the remains, represents a cultural unit that should be understood and studied together without considering only monumental attributes.

In the 1960s, there were various points of view regarding the types of Peruvian legacy that deserved to be protected. Nevertheless the Casa de la Cultura del Perú conducted a number of conservation programs of large archaeological sites such as Chan Chan (in La Libertad), Pachacamac, Cajamarquilla, Puruchuco, and Huallamarca (all in Lima), and Cuelap (in Amazonas), among others. Although these projects were severely criticized for their strong emphasis on ruin reconstruction (for example, the sites of Puruchuco and Huallamarca) and tourism promotion, they also contributed to the development of local site museums in Peru.

This type of museum was implemented in order to keep excavated ancient belongings and materials, looted from the archaeological sites, close to their original locations. But they also hope to achieve educational goals through the exhibition of these collections. Disregarding the low budget assigned for its appropriate functioning, I think the site museum experience has had a positive impact in Peru thus far; not only has it encouraged work positions in the fields of archaeological tourism, research, and museography, but it also has helped to preserve the adjacent sites. Of course only certain sites received the benefits of this development, particularly Pachacamac and Puruchuco.

In the 1980s and 1990s other site museums were established, at such sites as Túcume and Chan Chan in northern Peru. Construction of these site museums is thought to help prevent looting and destruction of these ancient settlements, as these museums require permanent personnel at the site. In this respect, and considering only sites in the area of Lima, the destruction of the Archaic period (2200 B.C.) domestic and ceremonial settlements of Chilca and El Paraíso, south and north of Lima respectively, could have been avoided by constructing either museums or long-term research centers at the sites.

In the 1960s, the Casa de la Cultura del Perú also sponsored several programs related to the Peruvian cultural patrimony in different fields such as literature, ethnography, and archaeology. Notable was *Cultura y Pueblo* (Culture and People) magazine, published twice a year in Lima. The legal status of this institution was reorganized in 1969 through Supreme Decree 013–69–EP after the military government enacted the Law of Education 17522.

Although it continued under the autonomy gained by the Ministry of Education, a new structure, called Cultural Promotion, Research and Conservation of the Nation's Cultural Patrimony, which included the chairmanship and the Central Administration, was established. It should be pointed out that item 20 of this decree established not only protective measures of the Peruvian cultural heritage, but also acceptance and respect of the diverse regional cultural expressions.

It was with this spirit that, in 1969, J. Cornejo Polar, the director of the House of Peruvian Culture, stated that the existence of this institution is only explained "as long as it fulfills a broad, intense, and systematic cultural promotion, achieving effective participation of cultural possessions and values through it" (Cornejo Polar 1969:3; author's translation). Cornejo Polar added four more points that I believe are still significant today. First, cultural values should be in the hands of marginalized people; second, cultural promotion should allow us to hear the voices of those who have been displaced for many years; third, cultural patrimony has become commercial; and fourth, the problem of cultural promotion will only be solved when cultural values of marginal people are accepted and respected. Based on these principles the House of Peruvian Culture designed several projects, including the Map of Peruvian Folklore, the Experimental Program of Cultural Promotion in the lower-class districts of Lima, the remodeling of the National Museum of History (Lima) based on recommendations of the Organization of American States, and the construction of the first phase of the new Regional Museum of Ica.

In 1970, as part of the reconstruction program that followed the earthquake of that year, the Peruvian government sponsored research and protection projects in the large monumental sites of Chan Chan (in La Libertad), and Sechín and Chavín de Huántar (both in Ancash). The project for research and conservation at Cuelap, which began in 1966 under the direction of the National Museum of Anthropology and Archaeology, also continued in order to protect its buildings from the growing vegetation of the zone.

In 1971, the House of Peruvian Culture changed its structure entirely, incorporating with the INC. Under this new organization, the INC began an impressive program of cultural diffusion, research, and protection of the Peruvian legacy from pre-Hispanic to republican times under a nationalistic orientation (Lumbreras 2006). Archaeology was an important field of interest for the INC administration from the beginning. As a result, a new regulation on explorations and excavations was passed (Reglamento de Exploraciones y Excavaciones). This bylaw established a number of obligations that both Peruvians and non-Peruvians (university graduates in archaeology only) were supposed to fulfill before receiving an archaeological permit either to explore or to excavate in Peru.

In order to obtain a research permit, archaeologists have to complete an application form explaining the scientific reasons as to why a given site was selected for study, which in turn is evaluated by a technical commission of archaeologists appointed by the INC. A particular point in this regard has been the obligation to submit scientific reports to the INC upon completion of fieldwork based on specific report forms developed by the INC.

On January 24, 2000, the INC enacted new regulations (Supreme Resolution 004–2000–ED) about archaeological research named Reglamento de Investigaciones Arqueológicas (RIA, or Rules on Archaeological Investigations). This new law divides archaeological investigation into three areas: research only, archaeological assessment, and emergency archaeology. Each establishes specific obligations for archaeologists, including co-directorship for non-Peruvian projects.

An important goal pursued by the INC has been to have a complete inventory of the cultural patrimony of Peru, from pre-Hispanic to present times.

The main purpose of this work was to further develop the archaeological map of Peru which could be used not only to increase and improve our knowledge about Peruvian history, but also to design future development projects without endangering and destroying archaeological resources. Such projects included several archaeological survey projects conducted along the coast and the highlands during the 1970s and 1980s.

The INC Centro de Investigación y Restauración de Bienes Monumentales (Center for Research and Restoration of Monumental Relics) carried out several conservation and protection projects during the 1970s and 1980s. According to information published by its *Annual Bulletin* (no. 17), the Department of Historical and Artistic Monuments conducted several activities on colonial monuments and relics. For example, the technical committee of architectural projects signed 160 technical recommendations for the protection of colonial buildings and relics.

Additionally, colonial buildings of Lima, Ica, and Puno were studied in order to preserve them. As part of this work the INC declared the churches of Arcata (in Caylloma, Arequipa), Chuquinga (in Aymaraes, Apurímac), Amotape (in Paita, Piura), and Sicuani (in Canchis, Cusco) to be national patrimony. Also, the INC sponsored the restoration of the Palace of Osambela or Oquendo House, the Monastery of Las Trinitarias, the Convent of La Buena Muerte, the Paseo de Aguas, and other colonial period buildings in downtown Lima. In addition, excavation and restoration programs were conducted at colonial buildings of Osambela, Quinta de Presa, the Convent of San Francisco or el Milagro Church (Lima).

The INC Centro de Investigación y Restauración de Bienes Monumentales also carried out other programs, such as registering private collections of pre-Hispanic or colonial periods, and creating a specialized library, which by 1981 included 6,000 reports and projects about Peruvian archaeology, as well as 2,100 maps of Peruvian monuments. Today, the National Museum of Archaeology, Anthropology, and History plays such a role, comprising more than 20,000 reports about Peruvian archaeological projects.

In addition, it should be pointed out that the INC sponsored several archaeological projects oriented to cultural promotion and research purposes. Notably, the La Juliana project (district of Miraflores, Lima) began in 1981 with the economic support of the Municipality of Miraflores.

The INC also conducted several archaeological projects across the country to help develop a countrywide inventory of archaeological sites. In order to achieve this goal, Peruvian central and southern coastal valleys, from Supe to Ica, were entirely surveyed between 1974 and 1979. Presumably, these areas of the coast were first selected due to the progressive urbanization and growth of the areas that was affecting the integrity of past remains. This program also attempted to recover data useful for the development of the archaeological map of Peru. Unfortunately, this program was canceled in the 1980s because of the collapse of the Peruvian economy.

In 1985, Supreme Resolution 16–85–ED was enacted; it confirmed pre-Hispanic remains as part of the Peruvian cultural patrimony. In 1986, Law 24513 established that no title deed could be extended unless settlements were located outside of archaeological zones. In 1990, Law 611 on Environment and Natural Resources established that protection of cultural remains also includes its natural surrounding since they are part of a large unit.

In the 1990s, the Peruvian government established new rules regarding the management and protection of cultural patrimony through Legislative Decree 635, articles 226–31, of 1991. For example, treasure hunting and clandestine excavations, destruction of archaeological remains, and trafficking in illicit cultural patrimony would result in a penalty of three to six years of imprisonment. In 2005, Law 28567 ratified such penalties. It was established that any activity resulting in the removal of soil (road constructions, mining works, habitation complexes, and so forth) must first undertake archaeological studies comprising surveying and excavations in order to verify the existence of ancient remains in the area that may be affected. Once these requisites have been fulfilled, and based on the recovered data, the INC may perform systematic rescue of the identified remains.

With regard to the points already mentioned in the present decade, other reinforcing laws were enacted, including Supreme Decree 022 in 2000 from the Minister of Education declaring as archaeological reserves a series of archaeological and colonial sites in the departments of Amazonas, San Martín, and La Libertad. In 2001, Law 27580 resolved that building, modifications, and repairs in places already declared cultural patrimony require the approval of the INC.

In 2002, two relevant laws were enacted. Legislative Decree 109, the Ley General de Minería (General Law of Mining), established that core drilling is not allowed in archaeological zones unless there exists a specific permit from the INC. Supreme Decree 022 of the Minister of Education specifies that the Certificado de Inexistencia de Restos Arqueológicos (CIRA, Nonexistence of Archaeological Remains Certificate) is the only official document declaring whether or not a given zone or place contains archaeological remains. In 2004, the Peruvian government enacted the Ley General del Patrimonio Cultural de la Nación (General Law of the Cultural Patrimony of the Nation).

The Peruvian government has also established a department within the Ministry of Agriculture called Proyecto Especial de Titulación de Tierras (Special Project of Land Title Deeds), which has been developed to locate, register, and define in situ archaeological sites. To date, this department has recorded a large number of these sites.

Before finishing this section, let me make two final points. First, Yale University and Peruvian representatives are having conversations in order to prepare an agreement about not only repatriation of the collections of Machu Pic-chu, but also scientific cooperation designed to establish a museum in Cusco, and to pursue archaeological research. Second, in December 2007, Law 29164 about Promoción del Desarrollo Sostenible de Servicios Turísticos en los Bienes Inmuebles, integrantes del Patrimonio Cultural de la Nacion (Promotion of Sustainable Development of Touristic Services in Buildings Declared Cultural Patrimony of Peru) caused massive demonstrations and picket lines in Cusco, even in the site of Sacsahuaman, and visits to Machu Picchu were briefly can-celled. In fact, this law grants 30-year concessions for touristic purposes solely for large monuments. Although this law seems to be helpful for preservation, it neither encourages research nor sets specific considerations about alleviating areas adjacent to ancient monuments.

Apart from that, this law creates an advising commission in which archaeolo-gists from academic institutions are absent. Given the strong protests in Cusco, the Peruvian government enacted Law 2902 in February 2008, establishing in article 3 that regional governments will determine what monuments may be considered for concessions while still allowing for tourist services.

Conclusions and Recommendations

Cultural resource management in Peru has been a topic of interest not only for scholars studying the past but also for politicians and governments. How-ever, this topic has had different motivations and goals. Archaeologists expect all aspects of past remains, monumental or not, to be preserved for posterity. In contrast, most politicians and the state administration are more concerned about the so-called relics and large monuments based on the fact that these remains give the best representation of our cultural heritage. In any event, Peru has developed several laws for the protection of the remains of the past. In ad-dition, as a member of the United Nations Educational, Scientific and Cultural Organization (UNESCO), Peru has signed legal conservation measures, which comply with international cultural resources management.

Management of the Peruvian legacy has been a topic of interest for many years. The Peruvian constitution determines that the cultural patrimony of Peru, including archaeological remains and documentary records, is under the protection of the state. As discussed earlier, Peru has established several provisory laws protecting its material and nonmaterial cultural patrimony. In addition, Peru has signed a large number of international commitments, rec-ommendations, letters of understanding, and agreements concerning the legacy of the past.

Why is Peruvian patrimony stolen, looted, or destroyed? Certainly, a large part of the remains of Peru's past has disappeared or has been seriously dam-aged during the last century. Several explanations have tried to identify the reason for this phenomenon. However, it is believed that the removal and/or destruction of these remains is a result of economic motivations (for example, low incomes, lack of permanent jobs).

I believe that it is important to identify remedies to this problem, and, as a result, it is relevant to propose programs that may help to resolve the issue of the progressive disappearance of Peruvian patrimony. Law enforcement is only part of this proposal. In fact, fines and penalties for the destruction or trafficking of patrimony are not dissuasive enough. Except for some isolated cases, no effective imprisonment has been applied to looters and traffickers. Therefore, the enforcement of these penalties or the penalties themselves must be changed.

In addition, as stated by Messenger (1999c:236), it is extremely necessary to pursue educational plans on the significance of the understanding and appraisal of cultural and natural resources. This point is based on the principle that the more we know about our heritage, the more interested we are in it. With regard to this point, international cooperation is helpful. For example, in 1995 Peru and the United States signed a five-year memorandum of understanding regarding the return of stolen archaeological and colonial objects. In 1999, the United States Information Service (USIS) of the U.S. embassy in Peru organized an international symposium of archaeology devoted to discussing research and protection of the Peruvian cultural heritage.

Protective legal measures should work in association with enhancing cultural institutions, not only for the INC, but through economic support and long-term programs oriented to developing better attitudes of people toward the systematic study of Peruvian patrimony as well as its conservation. These measures will help us know ourselves better and share our heritage with the world.

The concept of site museums needs to be encouraged and established as part of a cultural policy. However, the implementation of this policy should take into consideration that it is virtually impossible to build site museums at every archaeological or historical site in the country. Perhaps this policy may be integrated into the management of regional areas comprising projects of different cultural and natural resources. Through this procedure an archaeologically oriented site museum may expose the entire patrimony of a given valley or region to a larger number of people.

Peru encourages investment in programs relating to landscape changes such as irrigation, dams, roads, mining, energy, and long-term resources; natural and cultural management projects should be proposed for those zones of eventual impact. Their implementation should be part of a cooperative effort involving various agencies in which management of patrimony plays an integral role in the development of these programs.

Acknowledgments

I wish to thank several friends and colleagues, including Cecilia Jaime Tello, who made important comments on the manuscript; Mr. Saldaña, Chris Strachotta, and Jeffrey Parsons, who corrected the version in English; and Aldo Brignetti, for all his help.

References Cited

Avalos de Matos, R., and R. Ravines
1974   Las antiguedades peruanas y su protección legal (Peruvian antiquities and their legal protection). *Revista del Museo Nacional* XL:365–458. Instituto Nacional de Cultura, Lima.
Bákula, C. (editor)
1996   *El patrimonio cultural en sus textos* (Cultural patrimony in its texts). Ausonia S.A., Lima.
Congreso del Perú (editor)
2000   *Patrimonio cultural del Perú* (Cultural patrimony of Peru), vols. I and II. Quebecor Perú S.A., Lima.
Cornejo Polar, J.
1969   Casa de la cultura peruana: Cultura y sociedad (House of the Peruvian culture: Culture and society). *Cultura y Pueblo* V(13–14):3. Casa de la Cultura del Peru Ediciones, Lima.
Cortes, Guillermo, and Victor Vich (editors)
2006   *Políticas culturales: Ensayos críticos* (Cultural politics: Critical essays). IEP Ediciones, Lima.
Instituto Nacional de Cultura (INC)
2000   *Reglamento de investigaciones arqueológicas* (Regulations of archaeological investigations). Instituto Nacional de Cultura, Lima.
Lumbreras, L.
2006   El papel del estado en el campo de la cultura (The role of the state in the field of culture). In *Políticas culturales: Ensayos críticos* (Cultural politics: Critical essays), edited by G. Cortes and V. Vich, pp. 71–111. IEP Ediciones, Lima.
Messenger, Phyllis Mauch (editor)
1999a   *The Ethics of Collecting Cultural Property: Whose Property? Whose Culture?* 2nd ed. University of New Mexico Press, Albuquerque.
1999b   Preface to the First Edition. In *The Ethics of Collecting Cultural Property*, 2nd ed., edited by Phyllis Mauch Messenger, pp. xxi–xxiv. University of New Mexico Press, Albuquerque.
1999c   Highlights of a Round Table Discussion and Some Recent Developments in the Cultural Heritage Arena. In *The Ethics of Collecting Cultural Property*, 2nd ed., edited by Phyllis Mauch Messenger, pp. 217–41. University of New Mexico Press, Albuquerque.

Ossio, Juan, Luis Millones, Ramiro Matos, José Lloréns, Félix Oliva, Rafael Varon, Carlos Williams, Francisco Stastny
1986   *Patrimonio cultural del Perú: Balance y perspectivas* (Cultural patrimony of Peru: Balance and perspectives). FOMCIENCIAS, Lima.

10

Management of Archaeological Resources in Poland at the Beginning of the Twenty-first Century

ZBIGNIEW KOBYLIŃSKI

Poland is a large country situated in the center of Europe, and due to this location, most of the main processes and events of European prehistory and history left material traces on Polish soil. The archaeological heritage of this region is therefore both rich and diverse, representing various cultural traditions and various ethnic and national groups. At the same time, Poland has been subject to various forms of external pressure and changes in its frontiers, and at times it has even ceased to exist as an independent state. The repeated threats to the Polish national identity have heightened public awareness and appreciation for the need to preserve and protect the past, which has influenced the development of archaeological resource management. However, in the last 60 years, the historically justified focus on Polish national heritage as the main factor allowing the nation to survive despite all the external threats has caused some difficulties in achieving objectivity regarding interpretation of the country's multiethnic heritage. This has also affected the development of programs dealing with protecting and managing the past that are free from ideological determinants that favor the heritage of the majority over the present-day population.

Historical Development: Polish Traditions in Archaeological Heritage Protection

As a result of political events at the end of the eighteenth century, Poland lost its independence and was divided among the three partitioning empires: Russia, Prussia, and Austria. After the Congress of Vienna in 1815, the nominally autonomous Kingdom of Poland was created on a small part of its former territory. However, it was dependent on the Russian Empire; the Russian emperor was Poland's sovereign. The beginning of Polish archaeology as a scholarly and academic discipline is therefore directly connected with archaeologies of the partitioning states. The university chairs in archaeology were founded in the territory gained by Austria in 1866, where Polish autonomy was the greatest. In the German and Russian parts, there were no universities until independence was regained in 1919. As a result, interests in prehistory were carried out through amateur activity, organized within learned societies (Lech 1997–1998; Kobyliński 2006a).

The beginnings of archaeological resource management and conservation in Poland appeared in the early nineteenth century (see Wysocki 1997–1998) in connection with the activities of the Warsaw Society of the Friends of the Sciences and particularly with the activities of one of the most famous of its members, Zorian Dołęga Chodakowski. He initiated the study of ancient strongholds, not only through written descriptions, but also by preparing contour plans. In the middle of the nineteenth century, Eustachy Tyszkiewicz was the first to suggest that part of a site should remain unexcavated for verification of the investigator's discoveries by future archaeologists. At the end of that century, inspectorates of monuments had been established on the territory of all three of the partitioning powers. The most active inspectorates of monuments were in the Russian zone, where in 1905 Erazm Majewski formulated the first ethical code for archaeologists, and principles of archaeological site protection, which in many ways are still applicable. After the recovery of independence in 1920, the State Assembly of Conservators of Prehistoric Monuments was created to establish a centralized state institution and administration with legal authority. The Statute of the Assembly, apart from rescue excavations, included physical safeguarding, inventorying, documenting, and legally protecting sites.

The activities of the assembly were terminated in 1928, when the president of the republic decreed that the State Archaeological Museum should take over its functions. In 1929, Roman Jakimowicz, the director of the museum, reformulated the philosophical basis for archaeological resource management and conservation, stating that the total excavation of archaeological sites and their complete transformation into documentation and museum materials was to be the appropriate method of management and conservation. Unfortunately, this idea has strongly influenced the subsequent development of Polish archaeology, conflicting with earlier suggestions that portions of the site should remain unexcavated for future verification.

It is difficult to assess the management and conservation of archaeological sites and ancient monuments during the Communist rule. Although a great deal was achieved during this time, much was also irredeemably lost. However, during this period Polish archaeology established a relatively high level of competence and gained a good deal of international prestige (cf. Kobyliński 1991; Lech 1997–1998). New methods of investigation and documentation were developed, and a legion of archaeologists were educated and trained. This would be critical in rebuilding Poland's connection to its past after World War II.

During the Warsaw Uprising in August 1944, more than 85 percent of Warsaw's historic center was destroyed by the Nazis. After the war, a five-year reconstruction campaign resulted in meticulous restoration of the Old Town. In

1980, the Old Town in Warsaw was added to the World Heritage List as an "outstanding example of a near-total reconstruction of a span of history covering the thirteenth to the twentieth century." Historical centers of other towns, such as Gdańsk, Poznán, and Wrocław, have also been reconstructed. In many of these cases, construction preceded archaeological excavations.

Behind this facade, however, there were also great and irreplaceable losses to archaeological resources. In the historic centers of many historic towns, new buildings were erected in line with official policy, in a homogeneous modern style, deliberately departing from the ancient characters of the towns. The designers of these townscapes turned their backs on the medieval and later past, especially in the so-called Regained Territories—areas taken into the Polish state from Germany after 1944. The reason for such an approach was that, in the initial postwar decades, archaeology and history fulfilled an important social and political role in developing a new national consciousness among people who, to a large extent, had been uprooted from their historical lands and shifted several hundred kilometers to the west by the decree of the Three Powers (Kobyliński and Rutkowska 2005). The emphasis was therefore on studies on the early Slavs and the roots of the Polish early medieval state. That which was considered "foreign" was not acknowledged as heritage during this period.

In the period between 1962 and 2003, the legal basis for protection of historical monuments was the Act on Protection of Cultural Goods, which was amended several times due to the changing political situation. The act was generally favorable for archaeology, with the exception of the problem of financing rescue excavations, which was left open without any decision about who should cover the costs in case of industrial and communal development. Despite this gap in the legal system, in Communist Poland, many large-scale industrial developments were preceded by large-scale rescue excavations, but very rarely were there adequate means for processing and disseminating the material thus generated. Only in a very few cases, such as the excavations preceding the building of the steelworks in Cracow, has this material been published. In other cases, material from other large projects of this nature still lies unprocessed in various storerooms. Beginning in the 1960s, the number of excavations increased rapidly, and by the late 1980s, there were over 300 excavations being conducted annually. Most of these were small-scale excavations, and the majority were undertaken for research purposes.

The Endangered Past: Threats to Archaeological Resources

Evidence from the past can be damaged by many different forces, both natural and human, accidental and intentional.

Natural Threats

Forces of nature, including erosion, shifting of sand dunes, animal burrowing, and floods, can do great damage to archaeological evidence. For example, the disastrous flood in July 1997 caused extensive damage to historical buildings, as well as erosion of archaeological sites. Unfortunately, because of the focus of the whole Polish archaeological milieu on rescue excavation preceding large-scale developments, there are almost no activities to prevent this kind of destruction.

Accidental Human Threats

Since about 62 percent of the territory of Poland is agricultural land, much of it is systematically plowed. The most insidious threat affecting most archaeological sites in Poland is the intensification of deep plowing. In many areas of the country, the horse was the main means of plowing until relatively recently. Today, deep plowing is affecting a large proportion of Polish sites, especially where it is accompanied by soil erosion, with many sites being irreparably damaged. In the previous social context, the large state-owned farms could afford to leave earthworks under grass, but changes in the property systems toward intensive profit-orientated individual land use led to serious damage in many cases.

More destruction comes from the draining of wetlands and the regulation of rivers, uncontrolled digging of sand and gravel for building purposes, open-cast mining, and industrial and domestic construction. Urban renewal in historic towns, or in the vicinity of archaeological sites, may lead to the destruction of the historical character and planning of the town, as well as archaeological and architectural remains. The renovation of ancient monuments, such as castles, palaces, and churches, may lead to the destruction of the original fabric. Tourism can be a means of educating the public about archaeology and the past; it can also be a threat to monuments because of uncontrolled trampling and improper use of sites.

Intentional Human Threats

Destruction can result from both legal and illegal excavation. A new threat that has appeared in the last 10 years is the extensive digging of holes in archaeological sites by people seeking buried treasure. The ready accessibility of metal detectors (an estimated 30,000 in Poland) has dramatically increased the extent of this damage. There are two groups of the so-called detectorists. One declares an interest in archaeology but demands the right to excavate sites and to keep the finds. The other may be analogous to the Italian *tombaroli* or Latin American *huaqueros* (described as "subsistence diggers"). These are poor farmers digging archaeological sites for profit by selling Roman period *fibulae*, or brooches, and other spectacular finds. In many cases, this activity is actually a result of irresponsible behavior by archaeologists who have informed the public about their spectacular discoveries but are not interested in the fates of the sites after the excavations. The main problem seems to be the rather antiquarian way in which Polish scholars have presented archaeology to the mass media more as a hunt for buried treasures or works of art rather than for contextual information. This "Indiana Jones" syndrome leads to the imitation of the "archaeological investigations" by amateurs.

In addition, overexcavation is a problem. Many Polish archaeologists, especially those based in universities, still view academic education as providing the right to excavate archaeological sites as they see fit, and do not respect the priority of in-situ preservation. As a result, many unthreatened archaeological sites were extensively excavated for purely research purposes, without taking conservation into account.

Some of these threats existed in the different political and social climate of the period before 1989, and were much more difficult to deal with. In other cases, the problems are new, or result from changing economic and social conditions. The paradox lies in the fact that, while the changes themselves may have sociopolitical benefits, they often have a negative effect on the preservation of Poland's archaeological resources. It is the archaeological heritage itself, often almost invisible until the moment of its destruction, that is especially threatened by these processes.

The Legal Framework for Archaeological Resource Management

The legal basis for archaeological resource management in Poland is the Act on the Protection and Care of Historical Monuments of 2003, which replaced the act of 1962. Following the German philosophy of heritage preservation, the act divides the activities concerning historical monuments into "protection," which is the duty of the state (article 4), and "care," which is the duty of owners and users of the monuments (article 5). At the same time, however, the important principle of the act of 1962, in which "cultural property is part of the wealth of the nation and should be defended by all citizens" (article 1), disappeared from the present text, making the public's responsibility for preserving heritage under the act of 2003 unclear.

With respect to protection of archaeological resources, the act of 2003 must be acknowledged as an important contribution to effective preservation because it not only maintains the principles laid down by the previous legal regulations but also fills gaps and amends errors existing in the act of 1962. All of the provisions of the Malta Convention (European Convention on the Protection of the Archaeological Heritage, which Poland ratified in 1996) are contained in the act of 2003. The most important difference between the act of 2003 and the act of 1962 is the clear formulation of the "polluter pays" principle. All costs for rescue excavations must now be covered by the developer, both in cases of previously known sites as well as sites discovered during preconstruction surveys or located during the construction phase of the project.

For example, in the case of an accidental discovery of archaeological finds, any work that potentially could damage the site must be halted, the place safeguarded, and the respective authorities (provincial inspector of historical heritage, or the head of a village) immediately informed. Within five days of obtaining the information, the provincial inspector must make a decision either to allow the work to continue or to stop the work and undertake rescue excavation paid for by the person or institution financing the development project. According to the decree of the Minister of Culture of 2004, archaeological excavation may include post-excavation activities such as conservation, analysis, and report preparation, all of which must be completed within one month. In the case of an exceptional discovery, the time can be extended to six months. It is worth noting that the "polluter pays" principle has been used in Poland since the early 1990s, but lacking a clear statement in the law, it has been difficult to justify this principle and to convince developers that they should cover costs associated with archaeological excavation.

Unfortunately, in 2007, the ombudsman called in question the "polluter pays" principle, stating that it is contradictory to the constitutional rights of property ownership, and that—especially in the case of smaller-scale developments, such as individual family houses—the state should cover the costs of the excavation. Moreover, in the interpretation of the ombudsman, if a developer pays for the rescue excavation, the records become his or her property, which means that whoever requested protection of the site would have to purchase these records in order to have them in the national archives. As result, despite strong opposition from the side of archaeologists, the law was changed in 2009 in such a way that the developer is obliged now to cover only the costs of the necessary archaeological work to the limit of 2 percent of the cost of the whole development. The remaining costs will be covered by the state budget. Such a solution, especially in a time of crisis in the public budget, may result in destruction of sites without excavation.

The act of 2003 maintains the rule of state ownership of archaeological finds. This rule prevents dispersion of collections, prohibits trade in antiquities, and makes illegal any creation of a private archaeological collection. It also prohibits unqualified people from removing artifacts from archaeological sites either for commercial or personal use. However, the rule has been aggressively attacked as a relic of Communism (though this regulation has been present in Polish law since at least 1928). If the law is liberalized to allow amateurs to metal detect and/or dig and collect artifacts, it will have a disastrous impact on the state's ability to manage and protect the past in the public interest. Fortunately, the National Center for the Study and Documentation of Monuments in Warsaw recently undertook energetic activities to combat crimes against archaeological heritage. This institution controls the antiquities market (especially transactions via the Internet) and organizes training for policemen to allow them to recognize archaeological sites and archaeological finds.

Every activity directed at archaeological sites requires permission from the respective provincial inspector. Authorization to undertake archaeological activities includes not only the spatial extent of excavation, but also the excavation methods allowed and the type of recording required by the inspector. In addition, the compulsory standards for archaeological field documentation have been presented in a decree issued by the minister of culture. This assures that archaeological excavations in Poland are fully controlled by competent authorities. According to the law, only a person having a university degree in archaeology and at least 12 months of field experience after studies may be given permission to lead archaeological excavations.

While artifacts belong to the state, the ownership of archaeological sites and their contents on private land is problematic. Although the act of 2003 places responsibility for care of archaeological sites on land owners, it prohibits any activities that could affect the archaeological heritage in the ground and provides for the seizure of the property in case of threats of destruction by the owner. While theoretically possible, this right has never been used by the authorities.

The main method for protecting archaeological sites and monuments in Poland, according to the act, is listing them on a register of protected sites. The Register of Monuments is administered at the provincial level, but with a central record at the National Center for the Study and Documentation of Monuments in Warsaw (abbreviated in Polish as KOBiDZ). Ownership of the land containing an archaeological site implies certain obligations but also allows privileges, such as tax rebates.[1]

Apart from the scheduled designation as a monument, the other main way that archaeological sites can be protected is by their inclusion in local planning documents as conservation zones. The legal basis for this procedure is the Act on Spatial Planning and Development of 2003. This act obligates all communities to prepare planning documents in consultation with archaeologists and other interested parties early in the planning process. Once approved, these documents have legal status and require that changes in land use must be made in consultation with the provincial inspector, who may impose conditions on future land use to mitigate potential threats, or demand full excavation of the site with costs for such excavations being provided by the investor. This method of archaeological resource management works well when archaeologists are able to provide the necessary information regarding the location of known sites and areas where archaeological sites may occur. This requires systematic reconnaissance programs to be undertaken by archaeologists in order to prepare reliable maps of archaeological resources in the area. In Poland, this was resolved in the late 1970s by creating the so-called Polish Archaeological Record (abbreviated in Polish as AZP). This is based on controlled field walking the entire country and correlating this with archival research and excavation results (Barford et al. 2000). This database, about 90 percent complete, is now being computerized.[2]

The Polish Archaeological Record, apart from its use by provincial inspectors for desktop assessments of developmental impacts on archaeological resources, has enormous scientific potential. Although the AZP program was reduced in the beginning of the 1990s due to a reduction in government funding of what was then seen primarily as scientific research, in the late 1990s it saw a resurgence due to the need for the conservation of archaeological sites and monuments threatened by increased development.

One area where Poland has fallen behind other countries in recent years is the registration of new sites discovered through photographic analysis. This has been due in part to past political issues revolving around the intense secrecy of the state, as well as economic issues. Aerial photography has, in the past, been used by archaeologists in Poland only for recording earthwork sites and those with standing walls. However, since 1996, this method has been used more frequently in association with archaeological surveys.

The Act on Protection and Care of Historical Monuments provides fines or jail sentences for destruction of monuments. The fine, however, will not be higher than 20 times the average annual salary, which means that, in some cases, developers find it more economical to pay the fine than to finance the necessary rescue excavation. Fines can also be levied against landowners who do not safeguard archaeological sites on their property (that is, if they allow people to metal detect and collect artifacts or allow archaeological excavations without permission). Landowners who do not inform the Conservation Service of factors having a negative impact on archaeological sites and monuments, or do not report changes in ownership, are also subject to similar penalties.

As specified by the Minister of Culture Decree of 2004, awards may be provided for protecting the archaeological sites and monuments. In addition, any person who discovers an archaeological site, safeguards it, and notifies the appropriate authorities may be offered a certificate or, in cases where the site has significant scientific or economic value, may be eligible for a financial prize as high as 30 times the average annual salary.

In addition to the Act on Spatial Planning and Development of 2003, other laws provide protection of archaeological sites and monuments. The Building Law of 1994 requires the permission of the provincial inspector when building activities could affect archaeological sites. The Act on Immovable Properties of 1997 regulates changes of ownership of scheduled sites. The Act on Paid Motorways of 1997 mandates that prior to the construction of any motorway there must be an assessment of impact on archaeological sites and monuments. The Environment Protection Law of 2001 extends the same requirements to all developments planned on the provincial and national levels.

The Organization of Archaeological Resource Management

The framework for the modern system of archaeological resource management in Poland was established during the Communist period (cf. Kobyliński 1998). However, it was not until the collapse of the Communist system in 1990 that the State Service for the Protection of Ancient Monuments (abbreviated in Polish as PSOZ) was established as directed by the conservator general, acting under the authority of the minister of culture and arts.

But decentralization and politicization of policymaking and oversight have led to the effective dismantling of state protection of archaeological sites and monuments in Poland in the last decade. Currently, each of Poland's 16 provinces has its own office responsible for the protection of sites and monuments, headed by a monuments curator who is employed by authorities of the province and oversees all matters concerning all types of monuments. Each province also has an inspector for archaeological monuments; however, there is no uniform policy for archaeological heritage management and no central office that would be able to carry out such policy on a national scale. Thus, the burden for archaeological resource management gradually becomes the responsibility of local self governments and nongovernmental organizations.

Archaeological Resource Management and the Archaeological Milieu

One of the most serious problems facing archaeological resource management in Poland is the archaeological community's lack of interest (Kobyliński 2001a, 2002). While Polish archaeology has reached high levels of academic competence and gained international acknowledgment, very few Polish archaeologists are conscious of the importance of archaeological resource protection and management for the future of the discipline. In addition, few archaeologists have accepted public accountability for their archaeological activities. Sometime in the 1970s, Polish archaeology gradually lost its close relationship with the public.

During the period between the two world wars, archaeology was a subject of national pride, especially after the discovery in 1933 of the famous Bronze Age and Early Iron Age fortified settlement at Biskupin (cf. Piotrowska 1997–1998). After World War II, archaeology was extremely important, both for politicians and for the public, because of its role in legitimizing Polish rights to its western and northern territories (cf. Kobyliński and Rutkowska 2005). When the state-sponsored program of archaeological research associated with the millennial anniversary of the Polish state ended soon after 1966, the public seemed to lose interest in archaeology. Archaeologists carried out detailed studies of chronological and typological questions and published jargon-filled books intended for increasingly narrow groups of experts in particular subjects. They seemed to forget about the importance of making their discoveries available and interesting to the taxpayers. At the same time, archaeologists lost interest in the protection of archaeological sites, treating them only as their "hunting grounds," which they could freely exploit according to their research interests. Unthreatened sites were excavated, and in most cases, archaeologists were not interested in their fates after excavation. Until the late 1990s very few publications devoted to the protection of archaeological resources were available in Polish, with the important exception of the book by Konrad Jażdżewski (1966) on the history of protecting archaeological heritage. There were almost no popular books on the archaeology of Poland, and schoolchildren received very limited information about archaeology. The public broadcasting companies, despite their educational mission, did not see archaeology as relevant for the public. As a result, archaeological sites were seen merely as obstacles for economic development of the country.

Training and education in archaeological resource management is almost nonexistent in Poland. Only one university, Cardinal Stefan Wyszyński University in Warsaw, currently offers a specialization in archaeological resource management. In the last decade, about ten books devoted to field conservation of archaeological finds, methods of archaeological excavation, international law and recommendations concerning archaeological resource management, and archaeological resource management in European countries have been published. The first textbook on the theory and practice of archaeological resource management and conservation was published in 2001 (Kobyliński 2001b).

Rescue Excavations and the Effects of Commercialization of Archaeology

In the early 1990s, when the previous system of the state-sponsored scientific research suddenly collapsed, archaeologists had to adjust to the new situation by engaging in rescue excavations preceding development. In the mid-1990s archaeologists in Poland suddenly became deeply interested in archaeological resource management, not because of any theoretical revolution, but simply because of the new economic situation related to large-scale investments and development programs, which, after the collapse of Communism, were financed mostly by private companies.

The most important task in the preservation of archaeological resources in

Poland came from adapting to democratic structures and the principles of a market economy. This involved moving away from reliance upon the state, instead toward the mobilization of social and private resources for the investigation, documentation, and preservation of archaeological resources and monuments. In general, the investor pays for site excavation; however, before 2003, the problem was complicated by the lack of a clear statement of this principle in the existing laws. It was also necessary to introduce legal and financial mechanisms that not only obliged owners of archaeological sites and monuments to maintain the sites, but also motivated them by providing tax reductions and refunds. However, to date, progress in this area has been insufficient.

The requirement for the developer to cover the cost of archaeological mitigation and rescue activities (the rule explicitly included in the Lausanne Charter in 1990 and in the Malta Convention in 1992, followed by the adequate EU directives) has radically changed the character of archaeology in Poland. Research scholars who could previously freely undertake studies according to their personal interests had to transform themselves into "salvers," ready to work on the full range of site types and under various environmental and fiscal conditions. They also had to be ready to excavate in the shadow of bulldozers whose work would begin at the conclusion of their field studies. This phenomenon has both positive and negative results. On the one hand, the legislation presently guarantees that no development, a least a major one, may be carried out without the necessary archaeological studies and protective measures. As a result, there has been an intensification of archaeological excavations resulting in many spectacular discoveries. Also, employment opportunities in archaeology radically improved; in the pre-Malta period archaeology had been a rather elite academic activity. On the other hand, however, the aftermath of the Malta Convention has resulted in archaeological research conducted as a profit-making economic activity resulting in commercialization of the discipline. The emergence of private archaeological firms, active in the business of rescue excavation, and the growing mass of unanalyzed and unpublished data obtained during such commercial excavations, are other concerns. Also, the competition for archaeology contracts has led, in some cases, to a lowering of standards and quality of work in order to provide the lowest contract bid.

Archaeologists involved in rescue archaeological activities continuously find themselves facing ethical dilemmas revolving around those who do commercial archaeology and those officers of deregulated archaeological resource management services that are weak, decentralized, and dependent on local political authorities. Erosion of ethical norms in archaeology has reached epidemic proportions, touching even the highest academic authorities.

In 1997, the first excavations connected with the modernization of the Polish road system got underway. These were financed by both the government (pre-construction) and private investors (sites encountered once work had begun).

Financing and merging the rescue archaeology program with construction time schedules produced complex organizational problems. To address this, the Center for Archaeological Rescue Excavations (abbreviated in Polish as ORBA) was set up in 1995 within the Ministry of Culture and Arts to coordinate with the government. Theoretically, the administration of rescue excavations was to be controlled by the provincial curators for archaeological heritage. Unfortunately, ORBA was situated outside of the control and leadership of the conservator general. This resulted in the Conservation Service losing control over the project, while ORBA's power grew. In 2002, ORBA changed its name to the Center for Protection of the Archaeological Heritage (abbreviated in Polish as OODA). As a result, OODA appointed institutions and private firms for rescue excavations on motorways and pipelines, allowing them to determine excavation costs and quality. In 2006, after archaeologists confessed to having had to pay bribes for rescue contracts, OODA's director was arrested and the entire institution disbanded in January 2007. The whole process of socioeconomic transformation, which occurred after the collapse of Communism in Poland, clearly brought with it conflicts between economic development and conservation ethics.

Challenges

It is clear from the discussion presented that there are numerous challenges facing archaeological resource management in Poland. The most crucial, in my opinion, are implementing the preventive conservation philosophy, adapting the holistic approach to management of historical landscapes, and engaging the public in the processes of archaeological resource management.

Preventive Conservation: The Proactive Approach

Out of the realization that archaeological resources are a nonrenewable public trust came the idea of preventive conservation involving nondestructive research, in situ preservation, and minimal disturbance of original context (Kobyliński 2003). It is a continuous process to slow the deterioration of, or prevent damage to, archaeological materials without interfering with their context. This need for preventive conservation is reflected in numerous archaeological and conservation organizations' codes of ethics, as well as in the charters of the International Council on Monuments and Sites (ICOMOS).

With respect to the archaeological resources, the philosophy of preventive conservation should consist of the following principles: 1) to create optimal conditions for the site's long-term endurance; 2) to leave undisturbed the original context of the site; 3) to monitor the state of the site environment; and 4) to intervene only in cases of emerging threats.

The key element of such a strategy must include designing a program for long-term preventive site conservation as part of the planning process, an evaluation of the present condition, and an analysis of potential threats. Ecological, landscape, and social and economic factors must be taken into account, and research, managerial, legal, administrative, and educational actions necessary for long-term preservation must be defined. To date, only at Biskupin has such a program been implemented in Poland (Piotrowski and Zajączkowski 1993). Adopting a preventive conservation philosophy and designing programs for the long-term conservation of archaeological sites is one of the main challenges for the future.

Adapting the Holistic Approach to the Management
of Historical Landscapes

One of the most important changes in the archaeological resource management and conservation philosophy in the second half of the twentieth century is the shift from protection of isolated "pearls" of history to preservation of entire landscapes, therefore joining nature and culture in a meaningful way and presenting historic continuity. In Poland, the concept of landscape is not a new one. It has been present for some 50 years. In the beginning, the term "landscape" was mostly used in relation to natural environmental forms, then gradually its meaning was extended to cover works of humanity. However, initially only those that were connected with man-made green areas, such as gardens, parks, and cemeteries, were considered.

In 1990, a special institution, the Center for Protection of Historical Landscape, was established within the Ministry of Culture, dealing mostly with historical parks. By the early 1990s cultural heritage was understood and protected in a holistic way in Poland, without fragmenting it into separate architectural, archaeological, or any other types of heritage. Since that time, the concept of landscape has been used more and more frequently. Still, it is mostly considered as the domain for the protection of nature rather than cultural heritage. This can be clearly seen in the gradual process of adapting the concept in various legal documents in Poland. The concept of landscape appears in the Act on the Protection of Nature (1991), in the Environment Protection Law (2001), and in the Act on the Protection and Care of Historical Monuments (2003).

When the European Landscape Convention was opened for signatures in 2000, Poland was ready to subscribe to it relatively quickly, thanks to the previous development of theory and practice already underway. In 2001, Poland signed the convention. In 2004, the convention was ratified by the Polish parliament, and in 2005 the text was officially published in Polish and became a part of the Polish legal system. No changes were made in previous national legal acts, since it was believed that previous Polish laws and acts fulfilled all of the requirements of the convention. The Ministry of Nature Protection is responsible for overseeing the provisions of this convention.

To summarize the legal matters, it is necessary to stress that questions of protection and creation of landscapes are present in four acts: the Act on the Protection of Nature (1991), the Environment Protection Law (2001); the Act on Spatial Planning and Development (2003); and the Act on the Protection and Care of Historical Monuments (2003). Of these, the most important are the Act on the Protection of Nature (1991) and the Act on the Protection and Care of Historical Monuments (2003) because they offer possibilities to create protected landscapes.

The Act on the Protection of Nature defines "cultural park" as an area created to protect a cultural landscape, which is defined as "historically created space, containing both the creations of human civilization, as well as the natural forms" (article 3). It is important that possibilities to create these forms of protection are in the hands of the provincial political government, as well as the local democratically elected self-government. The initiative to create a cultural park lies in the hands of local inhabitants. This is a democratic approach, but within the context of a country experiencing political and social transformation this can be dangerous for some landscapes, especially for those that are not spectacular and not easily understandable by the general public, such as rural and archaeological landscapes.

Important provisions are also contained in the Environment Protection Law and in the Act on Spatial Planning and Development. These acts require that at every stage of planning for spatial development, landscape protection must be taken into account, and that every environmental impact assessment must consider the impact of the planned development on landscape values.

The concept of cultural parks as a form of protection of cultural landscapes is a very important new tool for protecting archaeological resources because it allows the process to go from the protection of isolated sites toward the management of entire historical landscapes (Szpanowski 2002; Kobyliński 2006b). Also, the idea that the public should participate in protecting and managing historical landscapes is concordant with the European Landscape Convention.

In practice, however, many questions arise. Because all of the costs for creating such parks have to be covered by the local community, we can only hope that local authorities would be willing to do this, especially when they have to cope with the many difficult problems resulting from socioeconomic transformations. To date, no cultural park has been organized in Poland. Although the mechanisms and tools are in place to establish such parks, there appears to be little will to begin the real conservation work.

Public Participation in the Conservation Processes

Democratization means a much greater public role in the protection and maintenance of archaeological resources and monuments (partly as a result of the transfer of state property to territorial self-governments and private persons).

Another important aspect of democratization is the necessity to take the opinions and assessments of the general public, and particularly local inhabitants, into account in the conservation process. With all of the positive aspects of this process, it must be noted that in some cases conflicts between conservation decisions based on expert opinions and public evaluations can arise. Such a conflict can take two different forms. In the one case, conservation services can protect areas or sites that, according to the local community, have no value, and therefore conservation measures can be perceived as an action against the local interests and quality of life of local citizens. In the other case, local communities can value buildings, sites, or landscapes that, according to experts, are not worth conservation measures.

There is also another aspect of democratization with respect to the protection of archaeological resources. Protecting the past is a common good, but this also means that various sectors and groups may wish to use heritage resources in various, sometimes contradictory ways. Democratization means that we can no longer argue that, for example, the interests of archaeologists are more important than the interests of farmers, developers, tourists, or local inhabitants. The concept of the multiple use of archaeological resources, based on democratic principles, can lead to attempts to justify even such extreme activities as treasure hunting. We must therefore be prepared to engage in discussions with all of the stakeholders regarding the preservation of authentic historical values.

At this stage of deregulation, the best hope for effective protection and preservation of archaeological resources is to increase public awareness of, and appreciation for, heritage resources and values. However, many Polish archaeologists are still not interested in this sort of "missionary" activity. It appears that the most crucial challenge may actually come from within the archaeological community itself. The need to educate and train Polish archaeologists to work effectively with the public, and regional and local authorities, is critical if the Polish people are to have a meaningful connection to their past, and if places representing the past are to be available for future generations.

Notes

1. Listing an archaeological site as a scheduled monument is a complex and time-consuming process. The practical problem is that to protect a site this way it is necessary to prove, in a court of law, that the site exists, as well as precisely define its boundaries, and indicate how the landowner can identify its location on his or her property. In addition, every stage of the procedure, such as field walking, eventual drilling, or test excavation, must be undertaken in the presence of the owner, since the decision will strongly affect his or her ownership rights. Unfortunately, this means that the owner can actually hinder and/or delay the process and, in the meantime, destruction

of the site may proceed. The process is particularly difficult in the case of large sites situated on land owned by many different people and/or institutions, which is the case, for example, with historic towns. This is the reason that, of the estimated half a million archaeological sites in Poland, only about 9,000 are included in the register. Increasing the number and representation of site types protected is an urgent priority.

2. It should be noted that, at present, this "completion" is based on just one reconnaissance level survey that was dependent on many changeable factors, such as land use, vegetation and weather. Because plowing partially disturbs or destroys the uppermost layers of archaeological sites, field walking must be repeated cyclically in order to maintain a current database.

References Cited

Barford, Paul M., Wojciech Brzeziński, and Zbigniew Kobyliński
2000   The Past, Present and Future of the Polish Archaeological Record Project. In *The Future of Surface Artefact Survey in Europe*, edited by John Bintliff, Martin Kuna, and Natalie Venclova, pp. 73–92. Sheffield Academic Press, Sheffield.

Barford, Paul M., and Zbigniew Kobyliński
1998   Protecting the Archaeological Heritage in Poland at the End of the 1990s. In *Theory and Practice of Archaeological Research*, vol. 3, edited by S. Tabaczyński and P. Urbańczyk, pp. 461–82. Institute of Archaeology and Ethnology, Polish Academy of Sciences, Warsaw.

Jażdżewski, Konrad
1966   *Ochrona zabytków archeologicznych: Zarys historyczny* (Protection of archaeological monuments: A historical outline). PWN, Warsaw.

Kobyliński, Zbigniew
1991   Theory in Polish Archaeology 1960–1990: Searching for Paradigms. In *Archaeological Theory in Europe: The Last Three Decades*, edited by I. Hodder, pp. 223–47. Routledge, London.
1998   Archäologischer Denkmalschutz in Polen am Ende des 20. Jahrhunderts (Archaeological heritage protection in Poland in the end of the twentieth century). *Archäologisches Nachrichtenblatt* 2:133–44.
2001a   Archaeological Sources and Archaeological Heritage: New Vision of the Subject Matter of Archaeology. In *Quo vadis archaeologia? Whither European Archaeology in the Twenty-first Century?*, edited by Z. Kobyliński, pp. 76–82. Institute of Archaeology and Ethnology, Polish Academy of Sciences, Warsaw.
2001b   *Teoretyczne podstawy konserwacji dziedzictwa archeologicznego* (Theoretical foundations of the archaeological heritage conservation). Institute of Archaeology and Ethnology, Warsaw.
2002   Archaeology on the Ruins of Ivory Towers: What Sort of Theory Do We Need? In *Archäologien Europas/Archaeologies of Europe: Geschichte, Methoden und Theorien/History, Methods and Theories*, edited by P. F. Biehl, A. Gramsch, and

A. Marciniak, pp. 421–24. Tübinger Archäologische Taschenbücher 2. Waxmann Verlag, Münster.

2003   Wet Archaeological Sites: Problems of Research and Conservation. In *Peatlands: Archaeological Sites—Archives of Nature—Nature Conservation—Wise Use*, edited by A. Bauerochse and H. Hassman, pp. 132–42. Verlag Marie Leidorf, Rahden/Westf.

2006a   Beginnings of the Academic Archaeology in Poland. In *Die Anfänge der ur- und frühgeschichtlichen Archäologie als akademisches Fach (1890-1930) im europäischen Vergleich*, edited by J. Callmer et al., pp. 209–219. Berliner Archäologische Forschungen 2. Verlag Marie Leidorf, Rahden/Westf.

2006b   Protection, Maintenance and Enhancement of Cultural Landscapes in Changing Social, Political and Economical Reality in Poland. In *Landscapes under Pressure: Theory and Practice of Cultural Heritage Research and Preservation*, edited by L. R. Lozny, pp. 207–36. Springer, New York.

Kobyliński, Zbigniew, and Grażyna Rutkowska

2005   Propagandist Use of History and Archaeology in Justification of Polish Rights to the "Recovered Territories" after World War II. *Archaeologia Polona* 43:51–124.

Lech, Jacek

1997–1998   Between Captivity and Freedom: Polish Archaeology in the Twentieth Century. *Archaeologia Polona* 35–36:25–222.

Piotrowska, Danuta

1997–1998   Biskupin 1933–1996: Archaeology, Politics and Nationalism. *Archaeologia Polona* 35–36:255–85.

Piotrowski, W., and Wiesław Zajączkowski

1993   Protecting Biskupin by an Artificial Barrier. *NewsWARP* 14:7–11.

Szpanowski, P.

2002   Before and After the Change: The Social-economic Transition Period and Its Impact on the Agriculture and Cultural Landscape in Poland. In *Europe's Cultural Landscape: Archaeologists and the Management of the Change*, edited by G. Fairclough and S. Rippon, pp. 125–132. Europæ Archaeologæ Consilium Occasional Papers 2. Brussels.

Wysocki, J.

1997–1998   The Protection of the Archaeological Heritage in Poland in the Twentieth Century: Concepts and Practices. *Archaeologia Polona* 35–36:427–52.

11

Cultural Heritage Management in Russia

NICK PETROV

The English term "cultural heritage" corresponds in Russian to the word combination *pamyatniki istorii i kul'turi*, meaning "objects of history and culture." At the same time, there are important semantic differences. The primary meaning of the Russian word *pamyatnik* goes back to the word *pamyat*, meaning "memory." So the best direct translation of *pamyatnik* would be "memorial." As such, the word combination *pamyatniki istorii i kul'turi* covers the full range of cultural heritage, including buildings, monuments, pieces of art, archaeological sites, and any other non-natural sites. At the same time, *pamyatnik istorii i kul'turi* (singular) means "some particular material object." The term "cultural heritage" was borrowed from English and is currently in use in Russian. For example, the relevant state department of the Ministry of Culture and Mass Communications of the Russian Federation is called the Federal Service on Supervision under the Observance of Legislation in the Sphere of Mass Communications and Protection of Cultural Heritage. "Cultural heritage" is used most commonly as a formal substitute for the words *pamyatniki istorii i kul'turi*. That is the reason, for example, that Federal Law 73–F3, the Russian law of 2002 dealing with cultural heritage is entitled On the Objects of Cultural Heritage (Historical and Cultural Sites) of the Peoples of the Russian Federation.

The main feature of modern Russian history, which has affected heritage management, is the absence of political and developmental continuity. This can be traced to heritage management's swift development during the nineteenth century, which was then interrupted by the political events of 1917. The formation of heritage management during the Soviet period of Russian history took place, but it was developed within the context of specific political and economic conditions of the Soviet state. For example, the absence of private property on the lands in Russia at that time significantly influenced the development of heritage management. The history of heritage management in Soviet Russia can be considered the history of good intentions. In spite of various laws and rules, actions were taken, with the approval of Soviet authorities, that were not in the best interest of heritage management. Extensive international sales of pieces of art from Russian museums took place during the 1920s and there was mass destruction of medieval Orthodox churches during the 1960s (Formozov 2004:272–78, 293–99). Although developers have been required to bear the expenses of archaeological research in the Soviet Union since 1934, in most cases excavation was the result of individual archaeologists' efforts and not implementation of the law (Smirnov 2006). Disintegration of the Soviet Union and the fast formation of new political and economical conditions during the 1990s necessitated essential changes in heritage resource management.

New federal laws dealing with "objects of cultural heritage" began to appear in the 1990s. Without this legislative base, Russian cultural heritage management would be in serious peril. Currently, these laws are working within the context of very complicated public and legal issues and opinions. Current heritage management in Russia, with its fresh legislative backbone, forms the legal basis for heritage management within the context of appropriate state institutions. With additional supporting documents and instructions regarding heritage resource management, the legal process will become more effective and efficient in its application.

Historical Background

The protection of cultural heritage in Russia can be traced to the early eighteenth century. Before the eighteenth century there were isolated instances of efforts to protect the past, such as the reconstruction in 1471 of St. George's Cathedral, built in 1234 in the town of Yuriev-Polskoy (Formozov 1990:12; Yermolinskaya Letopis' 1910:159). Systematic research and protection of cultural heritage started during the period of Peter the Great's reforms, as part of his efforts to integrate Russia into Europe. There are three events that stand out with respect to the development of cultural heritage management in Russia: 1) the decree of 1718 that founded Kunstkammer, the first Russian museum (this decree mandated that all "old and unusual" finds, found in the ground or water, be handed over to this museum; see Laws of the Russian Empire 1830:541–42, no. 3159); 2) the Russian research expedition to Siberia in 1719, which was led by the German doctor and biologist Daniel Gothlib Messerschmidt (Formozov 1986:20); and 3) the first questionnaire for the collection of geographical and historical information (including archaeological data), which was prepared by the historian Vasiliy Tatishchev in 1737. While the questionnaire appeared after Peter the Great's death in 1725, it can be considered to be directly related to his reforms (Tatishchev 1950:87–88).

Additional events that contributed to the development of heritage management in the Russian Empire include the prohibition of 1826, by Czar Nicholas I, of the destruction of ancient buildings; the protection of cultural heritage in the provinces being delegated to the regional "building and road committees" in 1854; and the establishment in 1859 of the Imperial Archaeological Committee (which was subordinated to the Ministry of the Imperial Court; Smolin 1917:136–46). This committee included archaeological supervision as part of prominent building projects. However, this authority was extremely modest in dealing with archaeological discoveries.

Following 1889, all permits for archaeological excavations were granted by the Imperial Archaeological Committee. At first, this rule applied only to state lands, but after 1910 permits were required for excavations on private lands as well. In 1893, similar authority was given to the Imperial Academy of Arts. After that, restoration of "the monumental objects of antiquity" was done in coordination with both the Imperial Archaeological Committee and the Imperial Academy of Arts.

By the end of the nineteenth century, Russian researchers and officials realized the need for a unified law that would regulate societies' needs with cultural heritage needs. A draft of such a law was prepared and discussed at the first and second Russian Archaeological Congresses (1869 and 1871), but was not passed. In 1911 another draft of the law dealing with the protection of cultural heritage was prepared for submission to the Russian Parliament, or Duma, but further development of this legislation was interrupted by the beginning of the First World War in 1914 and the political events of 1917.

After the October Revolution in 1917, the Council of the National Commissars, the new supreme executive institution in Russia, decreed the importance of the registration and protection of objects of art and antiquity in 1918, which was augmented on January 7, 1924 by another decree concerning the registration and protection of objects of art, antiquity, and nature (Sovetskaya Rossiya 1973:14, 22–24, 38–40, 42–53). In 1919, the Archaeological Committee was reorganized into the Academy of the History of Material Culture (the predecessor of the modern Institute of Archaeology in the Russian Academy of Sciences),[1] which also had the responsibility for providing permission for archaeological field research (Formozov 2004:304).

Transition of the objects of cultural heritage from the previous owners to the new Russian authorities was considered to be in the spirit of the Marxist doctrine of social justice. Thus, heritage management obtained not only practical and juridical significance, but also ideological and political significance. The addendum to the decree of 1924 lists the objects of cultural heritage as "architectural objects," "archaeological sites," "museum collections," "parks and gardens," and "sites of nature." Architectural objects were subdivided into the following groups: (a) the demonstrative objects that cannot be used for practical purposes in principle; (b) the demonstrative objects that can be used just for research or museum purposes; and (c) the objects that can be used without any prejudice by organizations or persons. During the 1930s, owners of historical buildings were required to bear the expenses for their protection and repair. At the same time, the users of archaeological sites were required to bear expenses for their research (Sovetskaya Rossiya 1973:60–62).

After the Second World War, The Regulations on the Protection of the Objects of Culture (October 14, 1948) added to the definition of cultural heritage "architectural objects," "objects of art," "archaeological sites," and "historical sites" described as places connected with the most important historical events in the life of the peoples of the Soviet Union. As a result of this revised listing, Russian legislators began to consider historical landscapes as part of the protected cultural heritage. The use of architectural objects stated during the 1920s (see above) was "extended" to the other groups of the heritage objects in the late 1940s (Sovetskaya Rossiya 1973:65–82).

The main law for heritage management in Soviet Russia was the Law of the USSR on the Protection and Use of the Objects of History and Culture (no. 4692–IX, October 29, 1976). The objects of history and culture were listed in the law as 1) "the objects of history, the buildings, constructions, memorable sites, which are connected with the most important historical events in the life of people"; 2) "the archaeological sites"; 3) "the objects of town-planning and architecture, architectural ensembles and complexes . . . , and also connected with them . . . artificial and natural landscapes"; 4) "the objects of arts"; and 5) "the documentary objects." This law stated once more that the users of objects of history and culture should bear the expense for their protection, and developers should coordinate their activities with the state institutions on heritage protection and should provide safety for heritage objects. An important point of this law was the authority to stop building and similar works in the event of a threat to heritage objects. This authority was given to the state institutions on heritage protection. The last important event in the development of heritage management in Soviet Russia was the ratification of UNESCO's Convention Concerning the Protection of the World Cultural and Natural Heritage in 1988.

Current Law and Practices

The first attempt to pass a new law for cultural heritage in post-Soviet Russia was made in the early 1990s, when a draft law was prepared by the Institute of Archaeology (Russian Academy of Sciences) and delivered to the Supreme Council (the Russian Parliament of that time). But it was not considered. In 1993, the Supreme Council was dissolved by the president and the draft of this law was burned in the Russian Parliament building during a tank bombardment (Formozov 2004:304).

Currently, cultural heritage is regulated by Federal Law 73–F3, On the Objects of Cultural Heritage (Historical and Cultural Sites) of the Peoples of the Russian Federation (see Land Code of the Russian Federation). It addresses the following groups of objects as outlined in article 3:

1) Separate buildings, monuments, memorials, and archaeological sites (in Russian law this enumeration discloses the meaning of the term *pamyatniki*). Archaeological sites are defined as "the traces of human existence, which are concealed in the ground or under water, partly or completely (including all movable objects related to these traces) and for which archaeological excavations and finds are the main source of information." This definition elaborates on the definition of archaeological sites and is more useful than just the list of the main types of archaeological sites, such as hill forts and barrows, in the law of 1976.

2) Ensembles. The groups of buildings and monuments (in the Russian text just one word, *pamyatniki*, is used instead of "buildings and monuments").

3) Objects of landscape architecture, including gardens, parks, avenues, and necropolises.

4) Sites. This group is a new one in Russian legislation dealing with cultural heritage such as:
   - Places where folk artistic crafts exist;
   - Centers of historical settlement;
   - Memorable places;
   - Cultural and natural landscapes connected with the history of ethnic groups, historical events, or the life of outstanding historical persons;
   - Cultural stratigraphy, remains of buildings at ancient town, hill fort, and settlement sites; and
   - Places where religious rituals were practiced.

The inclusion of such a detailed definition of cultural or historical landscapes in the list of the sites included as protected objects of cultural heritage was very important for its management (compare with the regulations of 1948, see above). In contrast, consideration of cultural stratigraphy as sites brings confusion in the law because they are not considered as the archaeological objects. According to this law, heritage objects should be included in The United State Register of the Objects of Cultural Heritage (article 15).

Preservation of an object of cultural heritage is interpreted in the law as "repair and restoration works . . . directed at providing for the physical safety of an object" (article 40). Rescue archaeology is treated as an "extraordinary case" for preserving heritage objects. The law establishes that archaeological objects are the property of the Russian Federation and that archaeological objects and their settings are important (article 49). The current Land Code, which went into effect in 2001 and established the concept of private property, considers a place where archaeological or any other heritage objects are located as "a land of historical and cultural destination" and changing special designation is prohibited (article 99 of the Land Code; see also articles 27 and 56).

Prior to development, the area should be examined by experts to identify historical and cultural objects, the cost of which will be covered by the developer (article 31). Financing of the work associated with the protection of heritage objects that are located in development areas is the responsibility of the developer, including archaeological excavations (article 36). As in the law of 1976, development can be stopped in the event of threats to heritage objects (article 37).

With respect to archaeological excavations, these works should be allowed (article 37). Permission to excavate is authorized by the Institute of Archaeology (Russian Academy of Sciences) for a particular archaeological site for a period not to exceed one year. According to the Regulations on Making of Archaeological Field Works (approved by the Academic Council of the Institute of Archaeology, Russian Academy of Sciences, March 30, 2007), when excavations are finished, archaeologists must send a detailed research report to the Institute of Archaeology. Acceptance of the report means that the same archaeologist can apply for permission for another year's research. Archaeological artifacts and supporting documentation must be handed over for permanent storage to a federal museum within three years after the fieldwork is completed.

The law also introduces the concept of "a historical settlement" (article 59), which is defined as a settlement within which the objects of cultural heritage (having "important significance for the preservation of originality of peoples of the Russian Federation") are located. The special feature of a historical settlement is that all of the important historical settlement-forming objects (such as planning, composition, landscape, correlation between the different settlement spaces, and the different functions of a historical settlement acquired during its development) are protected.

An example of the application of current heritage legislation took place in St. Petersburg in August 2006. A private company worked on the area around the Kazan Cathedral in the historical center of St. Petersburg. In spite of the fact that this company was directed not to dig deeper than 30 cm, it did, thus not only removing modern asphalt, but also damaging the cobblestone square, which dates to the early nineteenth century. This was in direct violation of local regulations specifying how construction projects in the historic center of St. Petersburg should be conducted, and clearly stating that ground disturbance should not exceed 30 cm below surface (see About Ascertainment of Temporary Boundaries, Procedure of Maintenance and Use of the Areas of Historical Cultural Layer at St. Petersburg of December 24, 2001). As a result of this violation, the work was stopped, and the company was fined and required to restore and conserve the cobblestone square. In this example, the most important thing is not the violation of current heritage legislation by that company, but the prompt reaction from the public, mass media, and the city and federal authorities. Just a few years ago, it would have been impossible to imagine such meticulous control on building activity in the historical center of St. Petersburg.

It would be incorrect to describe current heritage management in Russia as a succession of positive examples of the application of federal and local heritage legislation. A contradictory situation in the management of cultural heritage was recently reported as having taken place in the town of Staraia Ladoga (Selin 2005:479–89). This town is located some 120 km from St. Petersburg. Pagan monumental barrows, churches with frescos from the twelfth century, a medieval stone fortress, and other historical sites are still present in Staraia Ladoga, making it one of the best-preserved medieval towns in the Russian Northwest. In 860 A.D., Staraia Ladoga was the residence of the first Russian prince, Ryurik, and was considered the first Russian capital. In 2003, coinciding with the 300th anniversary of St. Petersburg's founding, the 1,250th anniversary of Staraia Ladoga was also commemorated. In 2003 and 2004, the Russian president, Vladimir Putin, took part in the archaeological excavations at Staraia Ladoga. Although this might have seemed a favorable political situation for heritage resources in this town, it was overshadowed by a significant violation of current heritage legislation. In 2003, three wooden merchants' houses from the nineteenth century, which were officially protected as architectural heritage, were destroyed by the local authorities. What is truly amazing is that this demolition took place in association with the Varazhskaya (Varangian) Street project, one of the most significant historical town-planning areas in Staraia Ladoga. Russia heritage management is a work in progress. With continued vigilance and public and governmental support, situations like those that occurred in St. Petersburg and Staraia Ladoga will not happen again.

Conclusion

During the last few years, various federal organizations have suggested the idea of privatization of heritage objects. For example, in November 2005, the Minister of Economic Development and Trade stated that he considers privatization of the objects of history and culture a necessary measure: "The state should be the owner of those objects of history and culture that are necessary for the fulfillment of federal functions; other buildings must be privatized and delivered to a private sector; this will allow us to keep them."[2]

This idea received additional support from a statement, in September 2006, by the deputy minister of culture and mass communications. The essence of this statement was that the moratorium on privatization of the cultural heritage (which was introduced by Federal Law 73–F3, On the Objects of Cultural Heritage [Historical and Cultural Sites] of the Peoples of the Russian Federation) would be cancelled very soon in order to provide for the safety of the cultural heritage. The appropriate draft of the law was prepared by the Ministry of Culture and Mass Communications to be sent to the Russian Parliament for consideration. At the same time the deputy stressed that the wide interest of investors in privatization could not be forecast because of the very small amount of heritage objects that have investment potential.

Such a turn in the development of Russian heritage resource management was predictable in general, but not the specifics. How will heritage objects from the state be transferred to private owners? Who will determine the list of the owner's obligations regarding preservation of a heritage object, and who will control the objects? The list of such particular questions could go on; however, it is more important to stress the need for further immediate development of heritage management in Russia. What is needed are ways to integrate Russian cultural heritage into the country's new economic structure.

Notes

1. See the Institute of Archaeology in the Russian Academy of Sciences at http://archaeolog.ru (in Russian).

2. See Novosti (Russian News and Information Agency), formerly available at http://www.rian.ru/culture/20051122/42173704.html (in Russian).

References Cited

About Ascertainment of Temporary Boundaries, Procedure of Maintenance, and Use of the Areas of Historical Cultural Layer at St. Petersburg (in Russian).
2001   Electronic document. December 24. http://gov.spb.ru:3000/law?d&nd=8361781&prevDoc=8361781, accessed September 2007.
Federal Law 73–F3, On the Objects of Cultural Heritage (Historical and Cultural Sites) of the Peoples of the Russian Federation (in Russian)
2002   Electronic document, June 25. http://www.akdi.ru/gd/proekt/083799GD.SHTM, accessed September 2007.
Federal Service on Supervision under the Observance of Legislation in the Sphere of Mass Communications and Protection of Cultural Heritage (in Russian)
2007   Electronic document, http://www.rosohrancult.ru, accessed September 2007.
Formozov, Aleksandr Aleksandrovich
1986   *Stranitzi istorii russkoy arkheologii* (The pages of history of Russian archaeology). Nauka, Moscow.
1990   *Russkoye obshchestvo i okhrana pamyatnikov kul'turi* (Russian society and protection of cultural heritage.) Sovetskaya Rossiya, Moscow.
2004   *Russkiye arkheologi v period totalitarizma: Istoriographicheskiye ocherki* (Russian archaeologists during the period of totalitarianism: Historiographical sketches). Znak, Moscow.

Institute of Archaeology in the Russian Academy of Sciences (in Russian)
2007   Electronic document, http://archaeolog.ru, accessed September 2007.

Land Code of the Russian Federation (in Russian)
2001   Electronic document, http://www.akdi.ru/gd/proekt/086544GD.SHTM, accessed September 2007.

Law of the USSR on the Protection and Use of the Objects of History and Culture (no. 4692–IX) (in Russian)
1976   Electronic document, http://www.zaki.ru/pages.php?id=1851&page=1, accessed September 2007.

Laws of the Russian Empire
1830   *Polnoye sobraniye zakonov Rossiyskoy Imperii s 1649 goda* (Complete set of the laws of the Russian Empire), set 1, vol. 5, 1713–1719. St. Petersburg.

Ministry of Culture and Mass Communications of the Russian Federation (in Russian)
        Electronic document, http://www.mkmk.ru, accessed September 2007.

Regulations on the Making of Archaeological Field Works (in Russian)
        Electronic document, http://archaeolog.ru/index.php?id=36, accessed September 2007.

Selin, Adrian
2005   Staraia Ladoga: A Medieval Russian Town in a Post-Soviet Context. *Russian History* 32(3–4):479–90. Festschrift 2 for Thomas S. Noonan.

Smirnov, Aleksandr Sergeievich
2006   Sokhraneniye arkheologicheskogo naslediya Rossii v sovremennokh usloviyakh (Preservation of Russian archaeological heritage in current conditions). Electronic document, http://www.archaeology-russia.org/link/sohr_smirhov.shtml, accessed September 2007.

Smolin, V. F.
1917   Kratkiy ocherk istorii zakonodatel'nikh mer po okhrane pamyatnikov starini v Rossii (Brief sketch of the history of legislative measures on the protection of the objects of antiquity in Russia). *Izvestiya Arkheologicheskoy Kommissii* 63. Petrograd.

Sovetskaya Rossiya
1973   *Okhrana pamyatnikov istorii i kul'turi: Sbornik documentov* (Protection of the objects of history and culture: Collected documents). Sovetskaya Rossiya, Moscow.

Tatishchev, Vasilii Nikitich
1950   *Pledlozheniye o sochinenii istorii i geografii Rossiyskoy* (Proposal on the writing of Russian history and geography). Tatishchev V. N. Izbranniye trudi po geografii Rossii. Nauka, Moscow.

Yermolinskaya Letopis' (Yermolin's chronicle)
1910   *Polnoye sobraniye russkikh letopisey izdannoye po Visochaishemy poveleniyu Imperatorskoyu Arkheograficheskoyu Kommissiyeyu* (Complete set of Russian chronicles . . .) 23. St. Petersburg.

12

Heritage Resource Management in South Africa

JANETTE DEACON

During the twentieth century, the historical development of heritage resource management in South Africa followed a pattern typical of most of the former British colonies in the region. The type of legislation has been reactive rather than proactive, and for most of the past century identification of significant heritage places has been higher on the agenda than conservation and management. With each new stage in the process, there has been a growth of expectations, staff, budget, and responsibilities. At regular intervals, legislative reform has been driven by public demand and has satisfied changing needs for official recognition of the value of various heritage resources. A troubling factor has been a general lack of capacity and financial resources to implement the legislation. Between 1994 and 2000, a major change took place with the demise of apartheid, the democratic election of a non-racial government, a progressive Constitution, and the inclusion of cultural sites in environmental impact assessments. The National Heritage Resources Act (NHRA) (Act no. 25 of 1999) came into force in April 2000; it was designed to incorporate heritage resources management into broader planning initiatives and to recognize and celebrate the tangible and intangible cultural values of all South Africans. This summary focuses mainly on the ideas that underpin the NHRA and the way in which policies have been implemented.

The Historical Development of Legislation

It is significant that the Bushman-Relics Protection Act (1911), the earliest legislation protecting heritage resources in South Africa (Table 12.1), was one of the first to be passed by the new government of the Union of South Africa, which was formed in 1910 as a self-governing British colony after the end of the South African War of 1899–1901. The new law made it necessary to apply for a permit from the Department of the Interior to destroy, damage, remove, or export rock paintings, rock engravings, and other heritage resources. The need for legislation had been raised by members of the public over the previous decade and was further fueled after the South African National Society was formed in 1905

Table 12.1. Summary of Heritage Resources Legislation in South Africa

Year	Act Number and Name	Body Administering the Act
1911	Act No. 22: Bushman-Relics Protection Act	Permits issued by the Department of the Interior. Surveys undertaken by the South African National Society
1923	Act No. 6: Natural and Historical Monuments Act	Commission for the Preservation of Natural and Historical Monuments of the Union
1934	Act No. 4: Natural and Historical Monuments, Relics and Antiques Act	Historical Monuments Commission (HMC)
1969	Act No. 28: National Monuments Act	National Monuments Council (NMC)
1999	Act No. 25: National Heritage Resources Act	South African Heritage Resources Agency (SAHRA) and provincial heritage resources authorities

Source: Data drawn from Deacon and Pistorius 1996; Scheermeyer 2005

"to foster appreciation of the country's heritage and to make the public aware of the necessity for preserving [its] monuments in the widest sense of the word" (Hall and Lillie 1993). Debates raged against the removal of San (Bushman) rock engravings from their original sites for export to museums in Europe, mainly Germany, and against the proposed demolition of colonial buildings, such as the seventeenth-century "castle" built by the first Dutch settlers in Cape Town, which was targeted to make way for a larger railway station.

There was, however, no mechanism provided to administer the law at this stage, although enthusiastic volunteer members of the South African National Society recorded sites of interest. Activities were not coordinated at the national level, and there was no plan for the development of expertise or skills within government departments. Later, the establishment of the Historic Monuments Board in Britain provided inspiration for a similar body in South Africa, and in 1923 the Commission for the Preservation of Natural and Historical Monuments of the Union was appointed under new legislation with the task of compiling a register of monuments (Deacon and Pistorius 1996). A decade later, perhaps once the scale of the task had been better understood, more comprehensive protection and a higher profile bureaucracy was established under the Natural and Historical Monuments, Relics and Antiques Act of 1934. This enabled the Historical Monuments Commission (HMC) to appoint staff (a secretary and a clerk) and to protect sites declared as historical monuments. Decisions were taken by a commission of experts who were appointed by the minister but were not paid for their services. The secretary of the HMC served simultaneously as the director of the newly created Bureau of Archaeology (Malan 1962). The bureau was disbanded in the early 1960s and incorporated into the new Department of Archaeology at the University of the Witwatersrand. The HMC was replaced by the National Monuments Council (NMC) and the National Monuments Act in 1969.

In drafting the National Monuments Act (Act no. 28 of 1969), those responsible had the benefit of 40 years experience, but they also had to contend with the growing impact of urbanization and inner city development that threatened the loss of older buildings. At this stage archaeological sites could be "saved" only in exceptional circumstances and funds for mitigation seldom came from the developer. The purpose of the new act remained essentially the same as before, but more detailed specifications for the appointment of council members and staff, and legal mechanisms to follow up on transgressions, were added. The range of protected places increased, largely as a result of public pressure from several nongovernmental organizations that lobbied for legal protection of heritage places of the colonial period and made funding available for the conservation of buildings and streetscapes (Hall and Lillie 1993:107–9; Marx 1996). The new option for provisional declaration as a temporary conservation measure was especially useful after an earthquake in the Tulbagh area northeast of Cape Town in September 1969, as it allowed time for original fabric to be rescued and careful reconstruction to take place under the guidance of experts (Deacon and Hofmeyr 1996:17).

Amendments to the act in the late 1970s and 1980s (Pistorius 1996) included provisions to protect war graves and historical shipwrecks and to limit the export of cultural treasures, as well as to give a blanket protection to all structures older than 50 years and to declare conservation areas that would be managed by local authorities. Protection of shipwrecks was necessary to stop commercially motivated looting (Gribble 1996a). Coupled with an exponential growth in the number of staff members at the NMC from 4 in 1970 to 22 in 1990, and linked to the establishment of regional offices in all 4 provinces, the number of declared national monuments over the same period rose from less than 1,000 to nearly 2,000.[1] Of this total, only 38 dated to the precolonial period (Deacon 1993, 1996a).

When the new democratically elected government came into power in 1994, the Department of Arts and Culture created the Arts and Culture Task Group to define a policy for arts, culture, and heritage that was published as a white paper (Department of Arts, Culture, Science and Technology 1996). It undertook to broaden the criteria for assessing the significance of heritage resources in all communities in the country without negating what had gone before. The process took about three years and involved consultation with a wide range of people, both from within Africa and abroad. The National Monuments Act was substantially revised and the new legislation came into force on April 1, 2000.

The Current Legislation (Background and Development)

The National Heritage Resources Act of 1999 established the South African Heritage Resources Agency (SAHRA) to replace the NMC. It currently has a staff of about 50 with offices in all 9 provinces and a head office in Cape Town. A council of 14 members is appointed every 3 years by the national minister of arts and culture to develop policy, appoint and guide the chief executive officer, and oversee the work and financial management of SAHRA. The provinces nominate 9 members and the minister selects the remaining 5 from public nominations.

The new legislation has moved heritage resource management forward in the following six ways:

1. It specifically redresses past inequities created by colonialism and apartheid in order to facilitate healing and symbolic restitution.

    1.1. It promotes previously neglected research into oral traditions and customs with the appointment of a staff member who is responsible for policy formulation and promotion of intangible heritage as an integral part of the national estate (Scheermeyer 2005).

    1.2. It changed the grading of all former national monuments to provincial heritage (Grade II) status so that provinces may reassess them against new criteria and recommend which are of provincial or national significance.

    1.3. It records oral traditions about places nominated as national and provincial heritage sites.

    1.4. It provides a process for the restitution of cultural property to the original owners if held in a public collection.

    1.5. It acknowledges the history of slavery as a key component in the cultural heritage of the country.

2. It introduces a proactive integrated and interactive system for the management of heritage resources designed to link with environmental and planning legislation.

    2.1. It coordinates the identification, documentation, and management of heritage resources through a national database at SAHRA and the formulation of policies and guidelines.

    2.2. It cooperates with other government departments that deal with environmental impact assessments to ensure that heritage resources are included in such assessments.

    2.3. It offers general protection of specified classes of heritage resources (such as archaeological and palaeontological sites, structures older than 60 years, and heritage objects) by requiring that a permit be applied for specified activities such as demolition, destruction, damage, excavation, or export. Applications are assessed by a panel of experts either at regular meetings or by e-mail.

2.4. It specifies further protection and management options for formally protected places, such as provincial or national heritage sites, through conditions attached to permits or by requiring management plans.

2.5. It integrates information about heritage resources into local and provincial planning systems.

3. It uses terminology and internationally accepted principles for best practice from the World Heritage Convention, the Venice Charter, and the Burra Charter (Walker and Marquis-Kyle 2004) for the development of policies, criteria, and guidelines.

3.1. The National Heritage Resources Act (NHRA) is structured to follow the recommended process for nomination and management of World Heritage sites with steps for identification, documentation, assessment of significance, development of conservation management plans, and monitoring.

3.2. The criteria for assessment of significance are based on the Venice and Burra Charters.

3.3. Conservation management plans are required for all national heritage sites and for sites owned by SAHRA.

4. It allows for the establishment of a bottom-up approach for decision making about the significance of heritage places by allowing the lowest competent level of governance to undertake surveys, grade heritage resources, and manage certain permit applications.

4.1. Heritage resources can be managed at all three tiers of government (national, provincial, and local) if the authority is assessed as competent. Competency is judged against several criteria, the most important of which are an adequate budget and qualified staff.

4.2. In order to put the system in place, surveys must be undertaken by local authorities to identify heritage resources of significance to their communities. The local authority can outsource this work to a qualified contractor.

4.3. Those places that are identified as being of local importance (Grade III) should be managed at the local level by municipalities and district municipalities. "Management" means they will be authorized by the provincial heritage resources authority to issue permits for activities such as demolition and alteration of Grade III structures older than 60 years if they are considered to be competent to do so.

4.4. Places of provincial importance (Grade II) are managed by provincial heritage resources authorities who also manage Grade III places where local authorities are not competent.

4.5. Places of national significance (Grade I) are managed by the national body, and SAHRA can also do the work of provincial authorities on an agency basis if the provincial authority is not competent.

4.6. South African Heritage Resources Agency (SAHRA) is also responsible for all shipwrecks (because the great majority lie outside provincial boundaries), for the graves of victims of conflict, and for all export permits.

5. It provides for public participation in decision making.

5.1. Conservation bodies may register their interest with the national or provincial authority and must then be consulted on any matter that lies within their field of interest.

5.2. Members of the public can be appointed as heritage inspectors.

5.3. Members of the public are entitled to attend meetings of the national and provincial authorities. There is also provision for appeals against decisions taken by committees and councils.

5.4 Any person may nominate a heritage resource for declaration as a national or provincial heritage site.

6. It protects a variety of heritage objects by controlling export, managing collections of national significance, and refusing import of certain items without export permits from the country of origin.

Enforcement, Fines, and Penalties

Enforcement of heritage resources legislation requires both monitoring of sites at risk and detective work to follow up on suspects and known offenders. Heritage resources authorities rely heavily on members of the public to report transgressions of the law. Staff members responsible for implementing the NHRA often find it impossible, however, to identify graffiti artists who damage heritage places, and developers who are frustrated at the bureaucracy involved in obtaining permits are known to proceed with illegal demolition in the hopes that the case will not be reported to the police and, if it is, that the fine will not be high.

If a transgression is reported, an affidavit must be lodged with the police, either by the member of the public who reported it or by a staff member of SAHRA or the provincial heritage resources authority. The public prosecutor assesses the affidavit against the provisions of the act and decides whether or not the case will be heard by a magistrate. The magistrate hears the case and, if the offender is convicted, comments on the severity of the offense with a recommendation for a prison sentence or fine. At present, the maximum sentence for a person convicted of damaging a national heritage site without a permit is a prison sentence of up to five years and/or a fine of up to R500,000 (about U.S.$71,500). Since the NHRA came into force, one conviction has resulted from a high-profile case in Johannesburg. A protected building known as Dudley Court was demolished without a permit in 2001. The case was heard in 2005 and a fine of R300,000 was imposed together with a five-year suspended prison sentence. Damaging or excavating an archaeological or palaeontological site without a permit could lead on conviction to a prison sentence of up to three years and/or a maximum fine of R300,000 (about U.S.$43,000).

In addition to penalties imposed by the court, the heritage authority can also demand that damage to a site be made good at the expense of the owner or offender should he or she admit guilt.

The Current Situation and Organization of Heritage Resource Management

The system currently in place for heritage resource management in South Africa is parastatal in the sense that policies and decisions are made (or approved after delegation) by councils and are implemented by staff members who are paid from national or provincial government funds. In terms of the NHRA and the Public Finance Management Act, the councils are also responsible for overseeing budgets and expenditure and may sue and be sued in their corporate name. They are also required to interact with other government departments on heritage issues.

The national or provincial minister responsible for heritage (usually the minister of arts and culture) is required to advertise for nominations of members of the public to serve on the councils of SAHRA and provincial heritage resources authorities respectively. Typically, the nominations will include individuals from universities, the private sector, NGOs, and local organizations. An independent review committee screens the nominations and draws up a short list. The minister then makes a selection from that short list and appoints the council, which has a term of office of three years. In some cases the provincial minister is also responsible for appointing the chairperson. The council is responsible for preparing a strategic plan and budget that is submitted to the minister and the relevant department for an allocation from the national or provincial treasury. In the case of SAHRA, the council appoints the chief executive officer, who in turn appoints staff according to the strategic plan. In some provinces, the department appoints staff to implement the decisions taken by the council. The councils in turn delegate powers to staff and to committees of local experts who deal with the assessment of permit applications.

Heritage conservation bodies can have input into the system by registering their interest either in a specified geographic region or in a specific type of heritage resource. They should then be informed of any activities that will interest them and they are encouraged to inform the authority of issues that require attention. The most active conservation bodies are those interested in the built environment, archaeology, and palaeontology.

Having described the integrated management process set out in the NHRA, it must be admitted that the system is still in its infancy and is not working as well as it should. When the NHRA was drafted, it was intended that the regional offices of SAHRA would be taken over by the provincial heritage resources authorities when the legislation came into force in 2000. For a variety of reasons that are too complex to explain in this chapter, this was not done and SAHRA decided to keep the regional staff and offices to better manage national heritage sites in the provinces. The result was that with a few exceptions (KwaZulu-Natal, Gauteng, and the Western Cape provinces), the provincial departments responsible for heritage were not funded for the expenditure, and did not budget for the establishment of heritage resources authorities. By late 2006, all nine provinces had published regulations and had appointed councils for the provincial authorities, but only four had appointed professional staff, and only two were operating efficiently. The continuing problem of operating a provincial heritage resources authority with what the remaining five provinces regarded as an unfunded mandate came to a head during a national legislative review in 2007. In February 2008, the minister of arts and culture instructed SAHRA to close the SAHRA provincial offices responsible for managing national heritage sites so that the funding could be rerouted to the provincial heritage resources authorities. By March 2009 the process had still not been formally initiated.

In the provinces where budgets are in place and suitable staff members have been appointed, the system is working reasonably well and there is welcome growth in the number of posts and in available expertise. In the seven provinces with limited resources, permit committees have been established only for the assessment of applications for the built environment. For archaeology and palaeontology, the provincial councils have requested SAHRA to act on their behalf on an agency basis for permits and to comment on archaeological and palaeontological impact assessments. This has placed a considerable burden on the SAHRA staff, but it is hoped that the situation will improve in the next five years.

The SAHRA has tightened up on the export of heritage objects by making customs officials aware of the law. Where archaeologists have not been appointed to the staff of provincial heritage resources authorities, the permit system for archaeological and palaeontological excavation, mitigation, collection, and export is well managed by SAHRA (issuing between 160 and 180 permits a year [SAHRA 2007:31]). Where provincial archaeologists have been appointed in KwaZulu-Natal they issue about 10 permits a year, and in the Western Cape they issue about 15 permits a year. Members of the general public who are unaware that a permit is required to collect artifacts and fossils have been given the opportunity to register their collections so that they will not be prosecuted. The SAHRA has registered 164 private collections thus far.

For comparison, about 1,500 permits and records of decision were issued for built environment applications and impact assessments by Heritage Western Cape in the 2005–2006 financial year (Heritage Western Cape 2006), but the number in other provinces was much lower.

The Planning Process and Threats to Heritage Resources

South Africa has a number of challenges to meet in the process of planning for the conservation of heritage resources. The country is experiencing a growth surge and development projects are affecting every level of planning from housing for the poor to urban densification, coastal tourism, and mining. The National Environmental Management Act (NEMA) has established a comprehensive process for scoping, impact assessment, decision making, mitigation, and monitoring that includes consideration of the impact of development on heritage resources. As the bureaucracy for NEMA is situated in a different department from that responsible for heritage resources, there has been some unhappiness about the process of decision making and the time it takes for all records of decision to be coordinated, as well as the lack of adequate monitoring. Discussions have taken place to streamline the process with a "one-stop shop," but the legal ramifications have been problematic.

The threats to heritage resources occur not so much within the planning process as outside of it. There are too few officials to monitor small towns and rural areas and develop capacity among communities so that they become aware of the implications of losing heritage resources. Conservation of old buildings, fossil sites, rock art and other archaeological sites, and graves often falls to interested individuals and NGOs, but there should be greater capacity within the provincial heritage resources authorities to help them to find the best solutions.

Curation of Artifacts and Supporting Documentation

All archaeological artifacts and paleontological fossils belong to the state and may not be bought or sold. All permits issued by SAHRA and provincial heritage resources authorities specify where artifacts recovered from archaeological excavations or fossils recovered by paleontologists will be curated. The applicant is responsible for contacting the museum or university to obtain the signature of the appropriate individual who agrees that the institution will take responsibility for curation. The heritage resources authority will not consider an application without a signature from an acceptable institution. The institution in turn has a policy regarding the size and number of boxes, the marking and packing of artifacts, and the supporting documentation that will be required, and it usually requires a fee if the project is part of mitigation for a development contract.

One of SAHRA's responsibilities is the development of a national database on heritage resources. The national Department of Arts and Culture has allocated substantial funding for this project and it is well under way.

Interpretation

Information collected during research projects and impact assessments provides a broad overview of the types of sites (such as open sites, rock shelters, rock art, shell middens, and stone-walled settlements), their approximate age, and their location and density in the landscape. Thus far, interpretation of the results by archaeologists working as heritage resource managers has been limited, but there is considerable potential for research where the data have been assembled into a geographic information system at the national and provincial level.

All permits require the submission of a report on the excavation or collection of all archaeological and palaeontological material within three years of the end of the project. Interpretation of the significance of the data is invariably included for research projects, but it is less common in reports on mitigation contracts. Where possible, applicants are requested to budget for the post-excavation time required to analyze material. New permits are generally not issued to applicants who are overdue with previous reports. Reports are not required for permits issued for the built environment, but heritage impact assessments often provide valuable information on the status quo of significant buildings and cultural landscapes.

Stakeholders and Public Outreach

The NHRA requires that stakeholders must be consulted for all heritage impact assessments and a record of consultation must be submitted with the report. If graves are encountered, for example, or have to be relocated ahead of development, the developer is required, within 90 days, to make every effort to identify and consult with the descendants or descendant community, who have the right to decide what should be done with the human remains after removal. The SAHRA has the power to suspend development until the matter has been resolved. The costs involved in recovery and reinterment are borne by the developer. In contrast, SAHRA, with the assistance of several stakeholder organizations, has developed a comprehensive database of the names of people who died during the struggle against apartheid. The information has been added to the database of victims of the South African War and the First World War who died in South Africa. In addition, permit applications for archaeology and palaeontology must be signed by the property owner, who agrees to allow access for the excavation and/or collection.

September 24 is Heritage Day in South Africa. Each year the national department, in consultation with provinces, decides on a theme for heritage day, and exhibitions and celebrations are held throughout the month to raise public awareness. The themes over the past few years (music, oral history, food, slavery, and indigenous knowledge) have mirrored the public perception of what heritage is and touch only briefly on the responsibilities of the National Heritage Resources Act. The SAHRA has printed and distributed pamphlets on its activities and legal requirements and public awareness is slowly changing as a result.

The SAHRA and the provincial authorities have had to put most of their energies into establishing an efficient system for the management of heritage resources. They have identified some of the heritage icons, such as Robben Island where Nelson Mandela was imprisoned for nearly 27 years, and 8 sites are on the World Heritage List, but it will take a while to identify and promote more heritage resources that resonate with all sectors of the population.

Training and Education

Several universities in South Africa offer courses in heritage management, but the curricula are focused more on museums and tourism than on building capacity to implement the NHRA. It seems that the skills required to undertake such tasks as preparing or assessing conservation management plans, writing heritage impact assessments, rehabilitating an archaeological excavation, or repairing an eighteenth-century building are not being addressed in sufficient detail, except in specialist courses in rock art and architecture. The University of the Witwatersrand offers a postgraduate degree and diploma in rock art management and aspects of the NHRA are addressed in degree courses at some universities. Short courses on documentation have been held in collaboration with organizations such as the International Centre for the Study of the Preservation and Restoration of Cultural Property (ICCROM), which sponsors the Africa-2009 program, and the Getty Conservation Institute has provided training for rock art tourist guides and rock art site management plans.

As in the United States (see Davis, this volume), professional archaeologists have adapted to the changes, albeit 20 years later. The Association of Southern African Professional Archaeologists (ASAPA) has a committee to assess applications for professional status for contract archaeologists and has developed a code of ethics. Permits are issued only to registered professional archaeologists. Whereas in 1990 there were perhaps 4 contract archaeologists, today there are at least 10 times that number involved in contract work at various levels of survey and mitigation.

Challenges

In hindsight, every new generation of heritage resources legislation has seen a mismatch between what the law aspires to do and what government is prepared to allocate to the councils and their staff for implementation. Since the 1970s, the staff of the NMC/SAHRA has doubled every decade and the funding has increased accordingly, but it requires a major change in corporate vision and public perception to allow the tree to flower.

In comparison with other southern African countries, South Africa has done well, and we face many of the same issues that have been addressed with heritage and environmental impact assessment in countries such as Australia, New Zealand, and Canada. Archaeologists and heritage impact assessors have formed professional associations and have developed codes of conduct, while heritage resources authorities have developed policies and guidelines for best practice and for a variety of activities linked to the NHRA. A particular challenge is to change the mind-set that has led heritage resources authorities to put so much energy into policing and permitting that there is no time for inspiration. The system is in place and now we need experience and expertise to address the bigger picture.

Note

1. In 1996 there were 1,984 declarations that included 4,060 individual structures and places (Gribble 1996b:40).

References Cited

Deacon, Janette
1993   Archaeological Sites as National Monuments in South Africa: A Review of Sites Declared Since 1936. *South African Historical Journal* 29:118–31.
1996a   Case Studies of Conservation Practice at Archaeological and Palaeontological Sites. In *Monuments and Sites South Africa*, edited by Janette Deacon, pp. 53–70. International Council on Monuments and Sites (ICOMOS), Colombo, Sri Lanka.
1996b   Cultural Resources Management in South Africa: Legislation and Practice. In *Aspects of African Archaeology: Papers from the 10th Congress of the PanAfrican Association for Prehistory and Related Studies*, edited by Gilbert Pwiti and Robert Soper, pp. 839–48. University of Zimbabwe Publications, Harare.

Deacon, Janette, and George Hofmeyr

1996   Forms of Protection Provided by the National Monuments Act. In *Monuments and Sites South Africa*, edited by Janette Deacon, pp. 15–23. International Council on Monuments and Sites (ICOMOS), Colombo, Sri Lanka.

Deacon, Janette, and Penny Pistorius

1996   Introduction and Historical Background to the Conservation of Monuments and Sites in South Africa. In *Monuments and Sites South Africa*, edited by Janette Deacon, pp. 1–8. International Council on Monuments and Sites (ICOMOS), Colombo, Sri Lanka.

Department of Arts, Culture, Science and Technology

1996   All Our Legacies, Our Common Future: White Paper on Arts, Culture and Heritage. Government Gazette, June 4. Pretoria.

Gribble, John

1996a   Conservation Practice for Historical Shipwrecks. In *Monuments and Sites South Africa*, edited by Janette Deacon, pp. 81–92. International Council on Monuments and Sites (ICOMOS), Colombo, Sri Lanka.

1996b   National Databases on Monuments and Sites. In *Monuments and Sites South Africa*, edited by Janette Deacon, pp. 33–42. International Council on Monuments and Sites (ICOMOS), Colombo, Sri Lanka.

Hall, Andrew, and Ashley Lillie

1993   The National Monuments Council and a Policy for Providing Protection for the Cultural and Environmental Heritage. *South African Historical Journal* 29:102–17.

Heritage Western Cape

2006   Heritage Western Cape Annual Report 2005/2006. Electronic document, http://www.capegateway.gov.za/culture_sport, accessed May 21, 2007. Heritage Western Cape, Cape Town.

Malan, B. D.

1962   Biographical Sketch: The Contribution of C. van Riet Lowe to Prehistory in Southern Africa. *Supplement to the South African Archaeological Bulletin* 17:38–42.

Marx, Joanna

1996   Non-governmental Organisations in South Africa. In *Monuments and Sites South Africa*, edited by Janette Deacon, pp. 7–8. International Council on Monuments and Sites (ICOMOS), Colombo, Sri Lanka.

Pistorius, Penny

1996   Legislation and the National Monuments Act. In *Monuments and Sites South Africa*, edited by Janette Deacon, pp. 9–14. International Council on Monuments and Sites (ICOMOS), Colombo, Sri Lanka.

Scheermeyer, Collette

2005   A Changing and Challenging Landscape: Heritage Resources Management in South Africa. *South African Archaeological Bulletin* 60:121–23.

South African Heritage Resources Agency (SAHRA)

2007   South African Heritage Resources Agency Annual Report. SAHRA, Cape Town.

Walker, M., and P. Marquis-Kyle

2004   *The Illustrated Burra Charter: Good Practice for Heritage Places.* International Council on Monuments and Sites (ICOMOS), Burwood, Australia.

13

Archaeological Resource Management in Thailand

THANIK LERTCHARNRIT

It is generally accepted that cultural resources, both tangible and intangible, are important, and have potential value and meaning for human beings (for example, see Lipe 1984, 1985). Because a great number of cultural resources, especially archaeological remains and historic sites, have been destroyed and the situation seems to continue, most nations of the world now have some policy of conservation of their cultural resources.

The basic conservation and protection problems most nations have encountered include looting (for example, Bhumadhon 1994; Hutt et al. 1992), smuggling, apathetic public attitudes toward archaeological work, and destructive development activities such as land alteration for agriculture, road construction, and dam building. With increasing concern about the existence and future of cultural resources, many countries in the world have been attempting to mitigate and solve these problems under the rubric of cultural resource management, archaeological heritage management, or archaeological resource management, which is a term commonly used in the United Kingdom, other European countries, Australia, and New Zealand (see Cleere 1989; Hunter and Ralston 1993; McKinlay and Jones 1979).

The term "cultural resource management," or CRM, has been used in the United States for more than two decades. It usually refers to conservation, preservation, protection, and research of archaeological sites and historic buildings (see Fowler 1982; Kerber 1994; Lipe and Lindsay 1974; Smith and Ehrenhard 1991). The concepts and practices of CRM have been developed from concerns over increasing destruction of archaeological sites.

Given that cultural resources yield significance for human society and are nonrenewable, it is reasonable that there should be measures focused primarily on maintaining inventory, evaluating and protecting archaeological resources from destruction by either human or natural phenomenon, or rescuing critical information before destruction. In the following section, I examine the historical background of preservation, administration, legislation, and other aspects of the management of cultural resources in Thailand, with the focus on archaeological resources and current protection problems.

Historical and Administrative Background

Thailand has a long history of cultural development, but the management of cultural resources under a protective framework did not begin until fairly recently. Throughout its history of cultural development, perceptions of the past varied from place to place depending upon influences such as religions, beliefs, and political situations. For example, as Buddhists, Thai people generally perceive the past as something that represents change and the state of becoming. The past may be abandoned quickly and easily. It is expected that new things can be created, invented, or established. Thus, restoration or reconstruction of old pagodas or stupas, pavilions, and other religious buildings is not culturally wrong. Byrne (1995) brilliantly discussed the use of stupa and conservation conflicts in Thailand. Strictly speaking, the past as interpreted by King Rama VI (1910–1925) during his reign was a key tool in building nationalism. He convinced the people to be proud of their culture and past (Vella 1978).

Regarding concern about the destruction of cultural heritage in terms of archaeological resource management in the modern sense, the first protection law, Pra Kaad Khet Rang Wat Poo Rai Khut Wat (Proclamation on Temple Boundary and Temple Looters), was issued in 1851, during the reign of King Rama IV (Fine Arts Department [FAD] 1968). The main objective of the law was to prevent temples from being looted.

It should be noted that during Rama IV's reign (1851–1868), Thailand (or Siam, as it was known at that time) was in an early stage of developing international relations. While the king wanted to open the country to forge relationships with developed countries such as the United States, England, and France (see Syamananda 1993), he was aware of the negative side of colonization. For this reason, he saw the past as a way of supporting nation-building or developing a sense of national unity and pride (Syamananda 1993). During his reign, numerous archaeological research projects, including the preparation of museum displays, were carried out. However, since the works were the result of the king's personal interests, not of government policies, they were conducted only by small elite groups who worked only on royal projects. Nevertheless, the value and meaning of cultural resources were interpreted as important to the nation, deserving protection.

The revival of the past was continued during the reign of King Rama V (1868–1910). King Chulalongkorn, as he was also known, was a reformer and a great scholar. He was interested in a variety of disciplines, such as archaeology, ethnography, and history, and he wrote a number of books concerning archaeology. He set up a museum hall in his palace, solicited the return of stolen objects from the Museum of Ethnology in Berlin, and established the Museum Department as a government agency. In addition, he founded the Antiquity Club, which promoted the study of archaeology, art, and history (Charoenwongsa 1994; FAD 1989; Ketudhat 1995; Sangruchi 1992). The first scientific excavations, conducted by Phraya Boranrajathanin in Ayutthaya, were another important milestone in archaeological resource management.

These efforts greatly increased public awareness of the significance of cultural resources and eventually led to the development of cultural resource management in the country. In the king's sense, "cultural resources" referred to everything that was old. Thus, it is not surprising that, even at the present time, there is no clear and specific definition of cultural resources used in the legislative context. The commonly used references are "ancient monuments," "ancient objects," and "art objects."

In 1926, six years after the end of King Chulalongkorn's reign, the Bangkok Museum Act was enacted, establishing Thailand's first public museum. In addition, the regulations concerning "transportation of ancient objects and art objects" were enacted in response to the immense trafficking and smuggling of antiquities (Sangruchi 1992:5). At this time, the management of cultural resources mainly involved the protection of archaeological remains.

A remarkable change occurred in the time of Prime Minister Field Marshal Pibunsonggram (1897–1964). Pibunsonggram clarified his role in the government and tried to use elements of culture as tools to cultivate nationalism and patriotism. For example, he encouraged the people to use and buy only Thai products, and required them to dress in what he called "civilized" clothing, such as coats, trousers, blouses, shirts, hats, gloves, and ties (Suwannathat-Pian 1995:135–51; Wyatt 1984:255).

Furthermore, Luang Wichitwathakan (1898–1962), a prominent scholar and prolific history writer in this period, asserted in one of his studies on the ethnic history of the Thai people that the Thais were the most ancient race instead of "one of the most ancient" (Charoenwongsa 1994:1). Kasetsiri (1979:166–68) interpreted Luang Wichitwathakan's history as an ideological weapon of the new ruling elite, particularly the military, to justify ruling the country.

During Pibunsonggram's government, many acts, regulations, and laws that applied to cultural heritage were passed; the most effective ones were the National Culture Act of 1940, the Council of Culture of 1940, and the Act of the Ministry of Culture of 1945. In 1979, when General Kriangsak Chamananda was the prime minister, the Office of the National Culture Commission was established. Later, Prime Minister General Prem Tinnasulanonda announced the national culture policy. Most recently, under the administration of Chuan Leekphai's cabinet, the government declared 1994 as the Thai Culture Promotion Year to promote public awareness of the value of Thai traditions and customs. This nationwide campaign dealt mostly with nonmaterial aspects of the culture such as beliefs, ideologies, religion, and folklore. In regard to the management of archaeological resources, the Fine Arts Department's Office of Archaeology in the Ministry of Culture has taken responsibility since 1926.

The Administration of Archaeological Resources

The management of archaeological resources in Thailand is a government monopoly administered by the Office of Archaeology in the Fine Arts Department (FAD). Under the law, the Office of Archaeology is "the key agency working on the restoration of ancient monuments and archaeological sites. It is also responsible for the preservation and investigation of archaeological remains for the benefit of the nation, for the sake of the study of the nation's history, and for the perpetuation of the cultural heritage of the nation" (FAD 1990:24).

Administratively, the FAD is the only organization responsible for the management of cultural resources in the country. The Office of Archaeology, formed in 1908 as the Antiquity Club, is one of ten agencies in the department. It was gradually reformed and its status was later changed from a private club to a government agency. In its administrative structure, the Office of Archaeology is divided into seven sections: General Affairs, Planning and Evaluation, Research, Restoration and Preservation of Ancient Monuments, Preservation and Restoration of Mural Painting and Non-removable Sculptures, Control and Maintenance, and Historical Park Projects.

Furthermore, according to the law, the Office of Archaeology is given full authority to grant permission or reject proposals for undertaking archaeological investigations on public land. In 1995, the Office of Archaeology was merged with the Office of National Museums into the Office of Archaeology and National Museums, but was later separated as an individual agency under the umbrella of the FAD, as is the Office of National Museums.

Broadly speaking, there are two major groups of archaeologists in Thailand. One group, whose work is mostly concentrated on restoration, preservation, and inventory of archaeological sites, districts, and ancient cities, is associated with the FAD. The other group is associated with academic institutions, such as universities and colleges. In response to the Historical Park Projects, a great number of surveys of archaeological sites and monuments by the FAD's archaeologists during the past ten years were primarily and specifically designed to rescue major archaeological sites and then develop them into "historical parks." Charoenwongsa (1994:2) noted that "administrators/managers take greater pleasure in the restoration of ancient monuments. The situation has not changed very much." This seems ironic because Musigakama (1995:38), a former director of the Office of Archaeology, stated that the Office of Archaeology is not only responsible for survey, maintenance, restoration, and preservation of archaeological heritage, but also for scientific study of archaeological records.

After joint expedition projects with foreign counterparts during the 1960s, Thailand's FAD initiated many mobile projects to counter looting activities in the 1970s. Under the direction of Pisit Charoenwongsa, the Northeast Thailand Archaeological Project was established in 1975 out of its predecessor, the

Ban Chiang Excavation Project, which was a joint effort between the FAD and the University Museum of the University of Pennsylvania, carried out under the coordination of Pisit Charoenwongsa and the late Dr. Chester F. Gorman. With the success of the Northeast Thailand Archaeological Project, the Office of Archaeology (then called the Archaeology Division) created another three regional archaeological projects—Northern, Central, and Southern Thailand.

Following that, regional field projects were brought under the central administration of the Thailand Archaeological Project (TAP). As Director of the TAP and the Research Section of the Archaeology Division, Pisit advised his younger colleagues to choose among themselves their own project directions. In the 1980s, Khemchart Thepchai (the current director of the Office of Archaeology), Tarapong Srisuchart, Bovornvate Rungruchee, Amphan Kijngam, Sathaporn Khanyuen, Sayan Pricharnchit, and Niti Saengwan were directors of these regional projects. To enrich their experiences, some of them moved or rotated from one project to another.

In the 1980s, for the first time, the TAP and its regional field projects produced several hundred site survey reports. With that came a large data collection that resulted in some 50 books being published during the late 1980s and early 1990s.

Joint research projects with foreign colleagues have been carried out with mixed results. Many good elements brought by Western colleagues include the concept of multidisciplinary, problem-oriented research programs and the systematic study of archaeological remains. However, some projects caused misunderstandings and negative feelings between participants, due largely to differences in cultural traditions and personalities.

Legislation Relating to the Protection of Archaeological Resources

As mentioned earlier, the first protection law issued in the reign of King Rama IV was short-lived and was limited to the protection of royal temples. In 1934, the first comprehensive legislation was drafted and was later amended in 1943 and 1961. Called the Ancient Monuments, Ancient Objects, Art Objects, and National Museum Act of 1961, the act was further amended in 1992 during the reign of the present king, Bhumibol Adulyadej (*Royal Gazette* on March 29, 1992). In addition, a number of separate regulations, such as the Act of the Ministry of Education and the Announcement of the Fine Arts Department, have been issued occasionally in line with the act of 1961 (for details, see FAD 2005).

The act of 1961, together with additional amendments and regulations, has broad coverage, including definitions of specific terms, regulations, permit applications, ownership, lists of endangered sites, national museum duties, and penalties for illegal trafficking and the transportation of ancient objects. Unlike other countries such as the United States and Australia, Thailand has no particular law on burial sites and properties belonging to particular ethnic or indigenous peoples. According to the act of 1961, any objects buried or left on public land belong to the nation.

Public Education

Public interest in cultural resources is powerful, as the public becomes the driving force behind efforts to conserve the past. In Thailand, the first formal center for public education in archaeology is the Faculty of Archaeology at Silpakorn University. This institution has been the only center of training and recruitment of archaeologists for over a decade, and most Thai archaeologists have been trained there. The courses focus mainly on Thai archaeology and a basic understanding of archaeological practices, with degrees offered at the bachelor's, master's, and doctoral levels. In 2006, I began teaching an undergraduate course entitled Cultural Resource Management at Silpakorn University's Department of Archaeology; this was the first time that such a course had been taught in Thailand, and I have been teaching the course ever since. In 2008, a master's program in cultural resource management began at Silpakorn University.

During the past decade, many other schools, colleges, and universities—for example, Thammasat University, Khon Kaen University, Chiang Mai University, Srinakharintharawirot University, and several other colleges (mostly former teachers' colleges, which are now known as Rajabhat University Complexes)—have developed archaeology programs and have introduced archaeology courses in their curricula, but none offer degrees in archaeology. Archaeology programs have yet to be introduced in elementary and secondary schools. Therefore, school children learn very little about Thai history and culture in schools.

Besides formal education, knowledge about the past has been transmitted to the public through various kinds of non-formal educational mediums. Museums are one type of non-formal education centers; as of 2009 throughout the country, there are more than 40 public museums operated by the Office of National Museums. In 1995, for example, the Thai government granted a budget of about 2 billion baht (about U.S.$80 million) to build provincial museums throughout the country.

In addition to the government-owned museums, there are a number of private museums and public organizations such as the Museum of the Siam Society, the Ancient City Co. Ltd. (Muang Boran), the Jim Thompson House, the Princess Maha Chakri Sirindhorn Anthropology Centre, and the Museum of Prehistory in Siriraj Hospital of Mahidol University. There are also groups of archaeological volunteers who occasionally organize field trips to archaeological and historic sites around Thailand, as well as to neighboring countries such as Laos, Burma, Cambodia, and Vietnam. This is an indication that archaeological study tours are now becoming popular in Thailand. Since 2001, there has been an increase in the numbers of public magazines promoting natural and cultural tourism in Thailand and neighboring countries, as well.

Major Contemporary Problems

Major problems concerning the management of archaeological resources in Thailand are basically similar to those found in other countries in the world. They include looting, conflicts between government officials and local people, the nature of contract work versus research, and different perceptions about the value of cultural resources.

Looting

Looting seems to be a never-ending problem in Thailand. Through time, many prehistoric and historic archaeological sites have been illegally unearthed. In many cases, merchants from Bangkok hire looters to hunt for antiquities, including pottery, stone bracelets, beads, and bronze weapons. In the case of historic sites, the favored artifact classes are Buddha images and architectural decorative elements such as stone lintels, wooden windows, and doors of Buddhist monasteries.

Surprisingly, a man in a team of looters confessed, when arrested, that he had learned how to dig by observing archaeologists while they were at work. Another woman in the same team said that they had no choice but to hunt for antiquities for money because they were poor and did not own any land (Pumathon 1994:28).

Government Officials versus Local People

Conflicts between government officials and local people arise in the context of restoration of monuments that are currently used as shrines or sacred sites. This may be due to different understandings of the value of archaeological resources. Recently, there was a movement of people in Lopburi Province to protest the restoration of an ancient monument in the city. Archaeologists from the Office of Archaeology wanted to disassemble the monument and restore it by the so-called Anastylosis method, but the people in the province wanted to know why the monument had to be taken apart. They were very concerned about the destruction of the monument because it has great spiritual value for the people in the province (see Suncharoen 1995:8).

In another case, the Office of Archaeology reconstructed a giant pagoda, Wat Chedi Luang, in Chiang Mai, northern Thailand, without enough investigation and public hearings. The inaccurate restoration of the pagoda disappointed the locals and scholars so much that they called a meeting to stop the work (Suksawasdi 1993).

There are few well-trained archaeologists working in government agencies—most government archaeologists have received only basic training and have limited experience in archaeology. They often face problems because, many times, they are assigned to carry out work for which they are not trained.

The Problem of Contract Work

At present, the preservation and restoration of archaeological remains and historic buildings is in the hands of technicians rather than archaeologists. As a practical and academic approach, archaeologists should research essential information before restoration begins, but often that task is left to the technicians. I could not find any sufficient evidence or obtain a clear explanation of why this problem occurs, but it is likely that the research is being left to technicians because there are not enough archaeologists in the country to do the work. It also may have to do with the ethics of practitioners. These technicians lack basic archaeological knowledge, and they may not appreciate the value of cultural resources. They seem to want to finish their work as soon as possible because of time and financial constraints. Thus, much valuable information has been lost. For example, in the restoration of an ancient ruin in Ratchaburi, workers of a contract company reconstructed the ruin by first disassembling it and then reconstructing it. Unfortunately, the workers did not know what the original shape of the monument had been. The result of their work is questionable, both aesthetically and archaeologically.

Different Perceptions of the Value of Cultural Resources

Conflicts between CRM practitioners and the local people have occurred due to different perceptions of the value of cultural resources. Archaeologists or CRM practitioners tend to focus on the informational and economic value of the archaeological resources, while the local people consider the spiritual or symbolic value. A good example is a small simple hillock near a temple in a village of Nakhon Phnom Province. Outsiders may view it as just a normal natural setting in the area, but for people in the village it is a "sacred place" according to their beliefs. Annually, the villagers perform religious rites and celebrations at the place, which has also been an important meeting area between people from Laos and Thailand (Vallibhotama 1992:211).

In 2006, I conducted research on indigenous perceptions and knowledge about archaeology in a remote village in central Thailand, where an archaeological site museum is located. The study revealed that the majority of respondents (41 percent) perceived that archaeology is the study of human skeletal remains, while less than half that number (17 percent) linked it to ancient history or the past (see Table 13.1).

Table 13.1. Public Knowledge and Perception about Archaeology in a Thai Village in Central Thailand

Question: "What do you think of when you hear the word 'archaeology?'" (N=85)

"Archaeology" in villagers' perceptions	Percentage of answers
Human skeletal remains	41.18
Artifacts	23.53
Ancient history/the past	17.65
Ceramics/ancient ornaments (beads, bracelets)	14.12
Ban Chiang[a]	9.41
Ban Pong Manao[b]	2.35

a. Ban Chiang is a widely known prehistoric site in the northeast because it is a cultural World Heritage site.
b. Ban Pong Manao is an Iron Age site where an archaeological site museum is located; it is also the name of the village where the research was conducted.

Conclusions and Recommendations

The management of cultural resources in Thailand is still in the early stages of development. Changes to legislation and policy are crucial to managing these cultural resources. To reduce controversy, the protection law should be open for public participation, providing opportunities for the public to offer input into decisions and actions.

Cooperation between the Fine Arts Department and other private and government agencies and organizations, and public audiences, on both local and national levels (for example, the Ministry of Agriculture, the Ministry of Education, the Department of Highways, the Department of Religious Affairs, the Royal Irrigation Department, amateur cultural heritage conservation clubs, sub-district administration organizations, village heads, and provincial governors) will help improve the quality of the management program.

The Fine Arts Department's Office of Archaeology desperately needs to build nationwide and worldwide networks in the coming years, while a strong public education program should be considered as part of an essential strategy to change public attitudes toward the past.

It should be remembered that the people who live near the sites are the best protectors of cultural resources. Once people have recognized the value and meaning of cultural resources, protection and management will be much more successful.

Lastly, in an era of globalization, the Fine Arts Department's Office of Archaeology should also build global alliances with international organizations and professionals, not only within the United Nations Educational, Scientific and Cultural Organization (UNESCO) and the International Council on Monuments and Sites (ICOMOS), of which Thailand is a member, but also with other nonprofit organizations located in Southeast Asian countries, such as Heritage Watch in Cambodia, and in broader regions of the world, such as the Getty Foundation, the World Archaeological Congress, and the National Park Service in the United States.

Acknowledgments

I gratefully acknowledge comments and suggestions from several individuals, including William D. Lipe, Karl L. Hutterer, Pisit Charoenwongsa, and Rasami Shoocongdej. Any errors, however, are solely my own.

References Cited

Bhumadhon, Phuthorn
1994   The Treasure Hunter at Ban Wang Sai, Lopburi: A Problem of Archaeological Site in Thailand. *Matichon Newspaper*. Sept. 17, pp. 28.

Byrne, Denis
1991   Western Hegemony in Archaeological Heritage. *History and Anthropology* 5:269–76.
1995   Buddhist Stupa and Thai Social Practice. *World Archaeology* 27(2):266–81.

Charoenwongsa, Pisit
1994   Managing Thailand's Archaeological Resources. Paper presented at the 15th Indo-Pacific Prehistory Association (IPPA) Congress, January 5–12, Chiang Mai, Thailand.

Cleere, Henry (editor)
1989   *Archaeological Heritage Management in the Modern World*. Unwin Hyman, London.

Fine Arts Department (FAD)
1968   *A Compilation of Royal Proclamations of King Rama IV, B.E. 2394–2404* (in Thai). Published on the occasion of the royal cremation ceremony of Phra Mahaphodhiwongsacharn Inthachotathern, November 9, Bangkok.
1989   *National Museums in Thailand* (in Thai). Fine Arts Department, Bangkok.
1990   *Theory and Practice in Preservation and Restoration of Ancient Monuments and Archaeological Sites* (in Thai). Technical series n0.1/ 2532(1989), Office of Archaeology, Bangkok.
2005   *Ancient Monuments, Ancient Objects, Art Objects, and the National Museum Act of 1961* (in Thai). Fine Arts Department, Bangkok.

Fowler, Don D.
1982   Culture Resources Management. In *Advances in Archaeological Method and Theory*, vol. 5, edited by Michael B. Schiffer, pp. 1–50. Academic Press, New York.

Glover, Ian
1993   Other People's Past: Western Archaeologists and Thai Prehistory. *Journal of the Siam Society* 80(1):45–53.
Hunter, John, and Ian Ralston (editors)
1993   *Archaeological Resource Management in the U.K.* Alan Sutton Publishing, Dover, N.H.
Hutt, Sherry, Elwood W. Jones, and Martin E. McAllister
1992   *Archaeological Resources Protection.* National Trust for Historic Preservation, Washington, D.C.
Kasetsiri, Charnvit
1979   Thai Historiography from Ancient Times to the Modern Period. In *Perceptions of the Past in Southeast Asia*, edited by Anthony Reid and David Marr, pp. 156–70. Heinemann Educational Books, Singapore.
Kerber, Jordan E.
1994   Introduction. In *Cultural Resource Management*, edited by Jordan E. Kerber, pp. 1–14. Bergin and Garvey, Westport, Conn.
Ketudhat, Pthomrerk
1995   Development of Archaeology in Thailand. *Muang Boran Journal* 21(1–4): 15–44.
Lipe, William D.
1984   Value and Meaning in Cultural Resources. In *Approaches to the Archaeological Heritage*, edited by Henry Cleere, pp. 1–10. Cambridge University Press, Cambridge.
1985   Conservation for What? In *Proceedings 1984*, edited by William J. Mayer-Oakes and Alice W. Portnoy, pp. 1–2. American Society for Conservation Archaeology.
Lipe, William D., and A. J. Lindsay, Jr. (editors)
1974   *Proceeding of the 1974 Cultural Resource Management Conference*, Museum of Northern Arizona, Technical Series no. 14, Flagstaff, Ariz.
McKinlay, J. R., and K. L. Jones (editors)
1979   *Archaeological Resource Management in Australia and Oceania.* New Zealand Historic Places Trust, Wellington.
Musigakama, Nikhom
1995   *A Practical Guide to the Preservation and Restoration of Ancient Monument* (in Thai). Fine Arts Department, Bangkok.
Pumathon, Puthorn
1994   The Treasure Hunter at Ban Wang Sai, Lopburi: A Problem of Archaeological Site in Thailand (in Thai). *Matichon Newspaper.* September 17, p. 28.
Sangruchi, Koranee
1992   Cultural Resource Management. Unpublished paper (in Thai), Faculty of Sociology and Anthropology, Thammasat University, Bangkok.
Smith, George S., and John E. Ehrenhard (editors)
1991   *Protecting the Past.* CRC Press, Boca Raton.

Suksawasdi, Surasawasdi M. L.
1993   The Recent Restoration of Phra Chedi Luang: Problems and Solutions. *Muang Boran Journal* 19(2):155–71.

Suncharoen, Chutima
1995   People of Lopburi Ask for the Return of Ancient Monument (in Thai). *Jud Pra Kai Newspaper*. February 16, p. 8.

Suwannathat-Pian, Kobkua
1995   *Thailand's Durable Premier: Phibun through Three Decades 1932–1957*. Oxford University Press, Kuala Lumpur.

Syamananda, Rong
1993   *A History of Thailand*. 3rd ed. Thai Watana Panish Press, Bangkok.

Vallibhotama, Srisakra
1992   Preservation of Ancient Monuments and Objects: Problem and Solutions. In *3rd Conservation of Natural Resources and Environments of Thailand* (in Thai), edited by Parinya Nutalai, Thongchai Phansawat, and Wanchai Sophonsakulrat, pp. 205–14. FARE, Bangkok.

Vella, Water F.
1978   *Chaiyo!: King Vajiravudh and the Development of Thai Nationalism*. University of Hawaii Press, Honolulu.

Wyatt, David K.
1984   *Thailand: A Short History*. Yale University Press, New Haven.

14

Heritage Resource Management in the United States

HESTER A. DAVIS

Heritage resource management in the United States has its roots in the historic preservation movement. The historic preservation movement has its roots in efforts to commemorate the significant events and the men (and they were largely men) who led the way to the successful American Revolution, and to memorialize the events and heroes of our Civil War, no matter on which side one's ancestors fought. The success of this effort can still be seen in some parts of the South in the statue of a Confederate soldier in the central square of many towns and villages.

Much has been written about what is considered a successful effort to give America a sense of history, starting within 50 years of the creation of the United States. That in the process we destroyed, and are continuing to destroy, the history of another people has not been lost on some of us. That this history has largely been recognized by memorializing bloody conflicts is not unique to our country. Battlefields are our sacred sites, and the places where our heroes were born represent the "living memories" of their lives.

We began the long road to recognition and protection of our nation's history in 1906 with the passage by Congress of the Antiquities Act (although some indicate that it could be said to have begun when Congress created its own library in 1800; King 2008:16). The importance and influence of this seminal piece of legislation was recognized in 2006 by a year-long celebration of its centennial (Harmon et al. 2006). A few individual sites in the Southwest had been purchased by the government prior to 1906, but the Antiquities Act was the first broad sweeping protection of sites on all federal land. It includes a permit system for any investigation of sites on federal land, with penalties (strengthened by recent legislation) for disturbance of sites without permits. Of significance, as it turned out, is the inclusion of a section allowing the president to create national monuments without going through Congress. The National Park Service (NPS) was created in 1916 and in essence created the concept of management of significant sites (now called cultural resources) on federal land.

In 1935, the Historic Sites Act recognized an ongoing effort by the NPS to establish a record of historic properties, largely at first consisting of buildings, that were of national significance. This legislation also officially established the NPS as the lead government agency for historic preservation, a position that it still holds. In 1960, the Reservoir Salvage Act recognized the effort that had begun soon after the end of World War II to recover information from prehistoric and historic sites that were being inundated by the huge federal projects to provide flood control and electricity through damming many of our major rivers. So, congressional activity took place about every 30 years starting in 1906, but the 30 years following 1960 saw a rash of legislation that entirely changed the world of historic preservation in the United States.

Legislation Effecting Cultural Resources after 1960

The National Historic Preservation Act (NHPA) of 1966 and the National Environmental Policy Act (NEPA) of 1969 provide the foundation for our present approach to historic preservation. The Advisory Council on Historic Preservation was created by the act of 1966, and the Council of Environmental Quality by the act of 1969. Both were required to write procedures by which other agencies were to comply with these acts, but neither had any authority over final decisions of other agencies relative to the treatment of cultural resources. So long as agencies or those using federal permits or licenses document that they will "take into account" cultural resources in their planning and have sufficiently justified to the Advisory Council that they will fully document any property that they will destroy, the agencies can do just that—destroy the property. In reality, of course, this has almost never happened. The public outcry would be too great. When push comes to shove, negotiated mitigation has always been the final choice. The act of 1966 also expanded the National Landmarks program (created by the act of 1935) to create a National Register of Historic Places, providing that registered sites on both public and private land be given specific consideration in any federal agency's planning.

The act of 1966 envisioned a nationwide cooperative preservation program between federal and state governments, later amended to include local governments and Native American tribes. Any one of these entities that wishes to participate in the national program must submit a plan and if that is approved (by the National Park Service), it is eligible to receive 50–50 matching grants. The State Historic Preservation Programs are administered by a state historic preservation officer (SHPO) appointed by the governor, assuring the state's commitment to the program. Local governments have preservation programs approved by the SHPO and work under that administrator's guidance. Tribal programs (often called Cultural Preservation Programs), also have an administrating officer and deal directly with the National Park Service. Under section 106 of the act each state has a responsibility to review plans and reports resulting from the compliance efforts of federal agencies, although again, they can only review and comment. They cannot regulate or control what a federal agency can do.

With the passage in 1990 of the Native American Graves Protection and Repatriation Act (NAGPRA) and the amendments of 1992 to the NHPA, there is now a fourth partner in this complicated relationship—federally recognized Native American tribes. Tribes wanting to participate in the opportunity offered them through NAGPRA and the NHPA now do so through the Tribal Historic Preservation Office and they are finally gaining some control over the evidences of their own pasts.

The fine tuning of the mechanisms by which all of these factors are to be considered is still taking place, but the basic wisdom of the preservation process is in the legislation of 1966 and 1969. All other legislation and amendments fix specific problems not covered by the first two acts.

In 1971, for example, President Nixon issued Executive Order 11593, which specifically required all federal agencies to survey their land and nominate any sites to the National Register of Historic Places that met the register's criteria. The order also required this monumental job to be completed within three years. This was a patently impossible task for the majority of agencies since they were given no budgets for this work and, except for the NPS, had no archaeologists or historians on their staffs. The Bureau of Land Management, for example, has responsibility for millions of acres of public land in the west. In 1980, the essence of Executive Order 11593 was included by Congress in amendments to the act of 1966, with no deadline for completion of the surveys.

The Archeological and Historical Preservation Act (AHPA) of 1974 authorized every federal agency to spend its own money to carry out the provisions of the acts of 1966 and 1969. Previously this authority and the funding, particularly for the expensive work of archaeology, had lain solely with the NPS.

The first law recognizing Native American rights relative to sites necessary for their religious practices, the American Indian Religious Freedom Act, passed in 1978. The passage in 1979 of the Archeological Resources Protection Act (ARPA) served to modernize, if you will, the provisions of the Antiquities Act of 1906. The act of 1979 does not, however, replace or amend the act of 1906. It emphasizes agencies' responsibility for protection and greatly increased penalties for disturbing a site, historic or prehistoric, on federal land without a permit.

One extremely useful change in the amendments to the NHPA in 1980 involved the process by which a site became listed on the National Register. Agencies could proceed with their planning after establishing the eligibility of sites for nomination to the National Register, rather than having to wait until the keeper of the register approved the nomination and the property was officially listed, a process that might take months.

Some agencies amended their own enabling legislation and/or their regulations to specify their responsibility for considering natural and cultural resources. Of particular importance to archaeologists was the change in the regulations of the Department of Transportation that required that alternatives be considered if highway plans would destroy sites.

It took until 1987 for all of the differences to be worked out in order for the Abandoned Shipwreck Act to be passed. Consideration of these cultural resources was not specifically mentioned in the act of 1966 or its amendments. This legislation established federal ownership of historic wrecks within the territorial waters of the United States. It gives states certain responsibility for wrecks within three miles of their shores and provides for public access to wrecks for recreational purposes where appropriate. Wrecks are now treated as historic sites under the act of 1966.

In 1992, the act of 1966 was again amended, this time to recognize the partnership of the Tribal Historic Preservation Offices and to include religious and sacred sites as eligible for nomination to the National Register (see National Park Service [NPS] 2002).

More than any other legislation, NAGPRA has changed the world of American archaeology and that of many museums forever (Rose et al. 1996). Not only does NAGPRA protect Native American graves, but it requires any museum, university, or other cultural institution using federal funds or permits to inventory their archaeological collections. The appropriate descendant tribe may then claim all human remains and associated funerary objects, sacred objects, and objects of cultural patrimony.

Until 1974, the NPS had more historians, historic architects, and archaeologists on its staff than any other federal agency and as a consequence it had been the only agency to develop expertise in managing cultural resources. The Archeological and Historic Preservation Act of 1974 created a huge surge in archaeology done by individual federal agencies and, thereby, a huge increase in the number of archaeologists in some of the largest agencies—the U.S. Army Corps of Engineers, the Bureau of Land Management, and the Forest Service, in particular. The federal and state partnership created by the act of 1966 not only forced states to look at their own local interests, but also led to a vast array of state laws recognizing historic properties of local and state interest and protecting sites, objects, buildings, and structures on state land. Many states have also passed laws protecting unmarked graves on state land, thereby protecting graves not included in NAGPRA. A few of these state laws also protect unmarked graves on private property. These are the only laws in the United States that protect what by some are considered archaeological sites, and therefore heritage resources, on private property.

Heritage/Cultural Resource Management

Because the term "cultural resources" first appeared in the act of 1969 (NEPA), "cultural resource management" (or CRM) came into popular use only after

1969. Because archaeologists were the first to recognize that the new laws were going to mean vast changes in their profession, the term is often associated with archaeology and not with the larger preservation concerns with history and historic architecture. All those involved in cultural resource management, however, understand that cultural resources include not just archaeological sites but also buildings, structures, and objects as specified in the act of 1966.

In addition, as time has passed, the term "cultural resources" has come to include traditional cultural properties, sacred sites, and cultural landscapes. It has been difficult for many dealing with issues of compliance to realize that these new "property types" that must be considered may have none of the tangible things that have been used to identify historic and cultural properties—many of these sites are purely natural. For example, the San Francisco Peaks in northwest New Mexico are sacred to the Pueblo communities as the place where the katsinas live.

By 1973, the term "cultural resources management" had come into general use in the archaeological community (Lipe and Lindsay 1974:x). Historians, however, feel that what they are doing is more in the line of general historic preservation. With the increase in employment of historians in "applied" areas, such as government agencies, museums, and as consultants, the term "public history" has come into use to bind together those historians who are not a part of "the academy," as university history faculty are called. Firms specializing in CRM often have a historian on their staffs, but the field of applied history is now so strong that it has an organization of its own, the National Council on Public History.

One other thing to be kept in mind is that archaeologists, historians, and architectural historians working under contract, who say they are doing cultural resource management, are not actually doing management at all. Only those who own or have control of land or property can manage it. What professionals in these fields normally do is to explain to agencies, clients, and state and local governments what is required for them to be in compliance with the many laws affecting their projects. More importantly, perhaps, the professionals can recommend actions to manage the cultural resources in question. The final decision to avoid or mitigate impact—move an historic house or go around it, develop green space or cover over a site with a highway, or any other of a myriad of possibilities for preserving or destroying cultural resources—is in the hands of the landowner (except in those few states that protect burials on private property).

For a federal agency to take into account properties eligible for listing on the National Register, it must now not only listen to the advice of the cultural resource specialist, it must also listen to the public's reaction to its plan and it must consult with appropriate federally recognized Native American tribes. Although seldom taught these useful subjects in graduate school, the specialists in archaeology, history, and historic architecture have learned the intricacies of the laws and the bureaucracy of preservation—they know what and how much needs to be done for their clients to comply with the law and to manage their properties. They consider themselves "CRM professionals." (For a detailed account of the laws, regulations, and the rise of CRM, see King 2008).

Political Action Beginning in the 1970s

Between 1970 and 1980, so much happened that formed what is contemporary CRM that it is difficult to summarize. But I believe the situation that began the multifaceted approaches and activities was the drafting in 1968 of what became the Archeological and Historic Preservation Act of 1974. In the six years between the writing of the first draft of this legislation and its signage into law, archaeologists swung into action. By 1972 in the Southwest and Great Basin, where the bulk of federally owned land is located, archaeologists and representatives of the NPS, the Forest Service, and the Bureau of Land Management were having meetings to figure out what compliance with the laws and regulations was going to involve. Regulations from the Advisory Council did not appear even in draft form until 1973. Such new and sometimes thorny questions as the amount and kind of archaeological work needed to establish significance of a site and therefore its eligibility for nomination to the National Register, and who and where were the archaeologists who would be needed, were major topics of discussion. A large regional meeting was held in Denver in May 1974 to consider these same potential changes (Lipe and Lindsay 1974). Meanwhile, the Society for American Archaeology (SAA) and the NPS sponsored six four-and-a-half day seminars, each attended by six to eight chosen leaders in areas of archaeological concern considered to be in need of review (McGimsey and Davis 1977).

Many troubling questions were considered in these seminars: How will federal agencies know who is a "professional" archaeologist? How much fieldwork and analysis is enough to establish the significance of a site? What makes a site significant? Isn't every site significant until proven otherwise? Would universities, where most of the professional archaeologists of the time were employed, be able to respond to the need? The publication of these seminar deliberations was delayed until 1977, by which time some of the topics were moot. For example, as a result of the seminar on certification, in 1975 the SAA formed a committee to determine the advisability and logistics for the creation of some means of establishing criteria for recognizing who could be considered a "professional" archaeologist. This committee recognized that the SAA's board would need time to deliberate on its suggestions and it felt there was no time to lose. The committee, therefore, met and immediately adjourned itself as an SAA committee, created the Society of Professional Archaeologists on the spot, and drafted standards of research performance and a code of ethics. This organization, known as SOPA, was incorporated in 1976; in 2003 it morphed into the Register of Professional Archaeologists (RPA). The RPA asks those individuals meeting its criteria to sign a pledge to abide by its code of conduct and research standards in their work. In addition, it adopted SOPA's grievance procedure whereby those who are thought to have violated the code or whose performance is considered to be inadequate can be reviewed and, if necessary, go through a due-process hearing. The individual can be disciplined through admonishment, censure, suspension, or expulsion from the RPA. The system is working to the extent that federal agencies, developers, and others needing professional expertise, as well as archaeologists themselves, know that this is the best way to assure that the resources are getting the appropriate attention and the agency or the private developer is getting appropriate advice.

These same six years (1968–1974) also saw the complete turnaround of the profession of archaeology from one consisting of academically employed people, who, during the summer months, would find a site and dig to their heart's content. Now others, usually from federal agencies, were telling archaeologists where to look, when the work must be done, and the amount of time and money they had to find just enough information to establish the eligibility of sites for nomination to the National Register. Because this research might need to be done in the middle of the academic year, by the end of the 1970s, many archaeologists with master's degrees had formed their own companies and set out to look for contracts full time. These archaeologists, who are doing at least 90 percent of the archaeological research being conducted in the United States today, formed a cadre of what are called CRM professionals, a subdiscipline, if you will, of both archaeology and historic preservation. In 1995, these CRM businesses formed an organization, the American Cultural Resource Association (ACRA), which serves its members by providing Internet information on legislation that may affect their "industry," advises them of pending changes in such things as regulations or hourly wages, and a myriad of other problems that might affect their business.

By 1980, most CRM archaeologists considered their specialized part of the profession to be secure. Archaeologists in universities, however, largely considered archaeologists who had gone into business to have abandoned science and to be performing inadequate scientific research in meeting clients' demands. The academic archaeologists complained that reports of work done under contract often lacked enough information to reach the conclusions and recommendations provided the client, much less good scientific advice. All in all, information about the past was not accumulating from the surveys and testing projects being paid for by taxpayers' money. In addition, mitigation projects—or "data recovery," as it is sometimes called, where large sites were given more attention—were often not adequately funded for reports to be widely distributed. And many soon realized that the public was not learning anything about what the archaeologists were finding in their back yards. The amendments in 1980 to the NHPA and the regulations for ARPA included stipulations that information resulting from archaeological projects needed to be distributed in a form that was useful and interesting to the general public. These provisions, along with extremely active public education committees in most of the professional organizations, are now filling this need.

Another thing that makes a general summary about the history of CRM in the United States difficult is that the situation, problems, and experiences in the eastern and western parts of the country are quite different. Most of the federally owned land is in 11 western states. In addition, most Native Americans now live west of the Mississippi River. In the southeast in Arkansas, for example, there were five tribal groups living in the area at the time of first contact by the French. There are no federally recognized tribes in the state now, four having been moved to Oklahoma, and one living in Louisiana. Farther west, in contrast, several tribes are living on at least some small portion of their ancestral lands. Relationships between Native American tribes and archaeologists, therefore, cannot be generalized. As more and more emphasis was put on archaeological sites by the various pieces of legislation, Native Americans saw their chance to tell the world that their past did not belong to everyone, as some archaeologists were saying. Their past belonged to them and they did not wish archaeologists to dig in their sacred sites or particularly to disturb in any way their ancestors' graves. The American Indian Movement (AIM) came into being in 1971. It was aggressive and in some ways quite sophisticated in the use of the media. Archaeologists and federal agencies, both faced with compliance requirements, were ill-equipped to deal with this kind of aggression, justified as it undoubtedly was. In addition, information about what archaeologists were finding was not provided to the descendant groups. There are exceptions, as with everything, particularly in some of the western states with larger and more organized tribes. In the late 1960s and 1970s, for example, university archaeologists in Idaho and Washington were consulting with local tribes and repatriating human remains after study (Thomas J. Green, personal communication, 2006). It has taken at least 20 years and federal legislation for this situation to change elsewhere in the country.

Although relationships between archaeologists and Native American tribes are improving (Dongoske et al. 2000), there are still a few tribes that do not trust archaeologists. Some tribes are demanding the notes, research records, photographs, and reports of all research, citing their intellectual property rights.

Most tribes, however, are taking seriously the opportunity for consultation and understand the power they now have over their ancestral sites, graves, and grave goods. As provided by law, most tribes have created Historic Preservation Offices, and have a tribal historic preservation officer with staff. Archaeologists, too, have learned how to interact with the tribes. In addition, archaeologists have learned that some information they may want or they think their client needs to make a decision about a project may not be available to people who are not members of the tribe; that the sacredness of a site may not be visible, and/ or that oral history is often as useful in telling the story of a site's past as are the artifacts found there.

The Native American Graves Protection and Repatriation Act (NAGPRA) affected Native Americans, archaeologists, and hundreds of museums in the United States. Bioarchaeologists were horrified to find that their unstudied database was about to be reburied and no longer available for study in the future. Archaeologists realized that large collections of artifacts might no longer be available for them to study, and the law provided no guidance to the tribes about what to do with the huge collections of artifacts that they might be entitled to claim. Museum staffs wondered how to deaccession these collections donated to them in good faith, and how to identify unassociated grave goods (that is, records indicating grave goods, but with no skeletal remains in association in the museum). The job of just inventorying these collections was not yet complete for some museums 16 years after the passage of NAGPRA.

Since 1990, however, many human remains have been repatriated and reburied, and some have had forensic studies done before repatriation. The worst fears of museums and archaeologists, that the collections would be unavailable or possibly lost or even sold, has not occurred, to my knowledge. Most tribes realize that they do not have the infrastructure to take care of the collections and are reaching agreements with museums whereby the collections, legally now in the ownership of the tribe, are on loan to the museum, which will continue to curate them.

This brings up an ongoing problem, recognized in the discussions in the 1970s but for which no good resolution has been found in many cases, and that is what we call the curation crisis. In the 1970s, archaeologists recognized that increased fieldwork meant a vast increase in collections needing care. Museums or other kinds of repositories realized they would soon run out of space, even if they started charging for care of the collections. The collections would legally be owned by the federal agency that paid for their recovery. Curation costs were normally not included in budgets prepared by the new cultural resource businesses, nor did agencies want to pay for long-term care. The federal curation standards were finally distributed by the NPS in the mid-1980s, but not all CRM work was or is done by or for federal agencies. In California, for example, there is a state law requiring investigation of a project's area by anyone working with a state permit. Small collections from small projects (for example, oil and gas drilling, or building cell towers anywhere in the country) done by small companies sometimes ended up in someone's garage, the records uncared for, and the artifacts in the bags they came in from the field. This problem is still with us to some degree, partly because some museums have stopped accepting collections, and partly because there are still small survey projects, resulting in small collections.

Conclusion

The basic difference between heritage resource management in the United States and just about all other countries is that objects, sites, buildings, and structures—to say nothing of traditional cultural properties and cultural landscapes—that are on private property in the United States are not subject to any of these federal laws. Most heritage resources are the property of whoever owns the land at the moment. In the eastern United States, where there is relatively little public land and where some of the earliest European settlements occurred, the sites and their contents are extremely vulnerable.

The system created by the Historic Preservation Act of 1966, and supplemented by the Environmental Policy Act of 1969, is working. The four-part partnership has made major changes, not to say upheavals, in the way heritage resource professionals go about their jobs. Periodically there are attacks by Congress, or major projects have problems that hit the papers, or agencies and developers balk at the cost. Cultural resource management in the United States is a frustrating and challenging, yet oftentimes rewarding, endeavor requiring vigilance at all times.

Editor's Note

While archaeology is most commonly spelled with an "ae," U.S. governmental publications employ the spelling "archeology." Throughout this chapter "archaeology" is used, unless referring to particular legislative examples or governmental publications using "archeology."

References Cited

Dongoske, Kurt E., Mark Aldenderfer, and Karen Doehner
2000   *Working Together: Native Americans and Archaeologists.* Society for American Archaeology, Washington, D.C.
Harmon, David, Francis P. McManamon, and Dwight R. Pitcaithley (editors)
2006   *The Antiquities Act: A Century of American Archaeology, Historic Preservation, and Nature Conservation.* University of Arizona Press, Tucson.
King, Thomas F.
2008   *Cultural Resource Laws and Practice: An Introductory Guide.* 3rd ed. AltaMira Press, Walnut Creek, Calif.

Lipe, William D., and Alexander J. Lindsay, Jr.
1974   *Proceedings of the 1974 Cultural Resources Management Conference*, Federal Center, Denver, Colo. Museum of Northern Arizona, Technical Series 14, Flagstaff.

McGimsey, Charles R., III
2005   *CRM on CRM: One Person's Perspective on the Birth and Early Development of Cultural Resource Management*. Arkansas Archeological Survey, Research Series 61, Fayetteville.

McGimsey, Charles R., III, and Hester A. Davis
1977   *The Management of Archeological Resources: The Airlie House Report*. Special Publication of the Society for American Archaeology, Washington, D.C.

National Park Service (NPS)
2002   Federal Historic Preservation Laws. National Park Service, National Center for Cultural Resources, Department of the Interior, Washington, D.C.

Rose, Jerome C., Thomas J. Green, and Victoria D. Green
1996   NAGPRA Is Forever: Osteology and the Repatriation of Skeletons. *Annual Review of Anthropology* 25:81–103.

15

Descendant Communities, Heritage Resource Law, and Heritage Areas

Strategies for Managing and Interpreting Native American Traditional and Cultural Places

DAVID W. MORGAN

In 2004 the International Council on Monuments and Sites (ICOMOS) promulgated the Ename Charter for the Interpretation of Cultural Heritage Sites, a draft document[1] whose goal is to acknowledge that "interpretation of the meaning of sites is an integral part of the conservation process and fundamental to positive conservation outcomes" (Ename Center for Public Archaeology and Heritage Presentation 2007:1). As Gustavo Araoz (2006), the executive director of U.S. ICOMOS, recently put it, "The international heritage community has managed to get by without any detailed guidance on how to articulate a site's significance to the general public . . . , [so] why suddenly now does ICOMOS feel that we need a new doctrinal document, a new set of ethical principles?" The reason is because heritage sites are no longer restricted to a class of patrimonial icons whose interpretation is part of an unchallenged story uniformly accepted by the dominant social class.

Descendant communities are some of those who have challenged the traditional narratives, and here I focus on the peculiarities of the political awakening of Native Americans in the United States and their role in federal heritage resource management. The recognition of subaltern histories, of contradictory interpretations of heritage sites, occurred largely as part of the social upheavals of the 1960s civil rights movement. Of all the subordinate social groups advocating change during the 1960s and 1970s, it was the Native American organizations and tribes who most vigorously advocated recognition of the legitimacy of their heritage. It was the tribes' emphasis on their connection with the natural environment that ultimately transformed them into one of the most important stakeholders in heritage resource management (King 1998:16). Their integral roles were codified over the succeeding few decades in legislation that defined the course of heritage resource management in the United States. Today one of the most significant of these laws with regard to descendant communities, particularly Native Americans, is the National Historic Preservation Act (NHPA; 16 U.S.C. sections 470 et seq. [1966, as amended]).

Because heritage resource laws are sweeping by nature, their implementing guidelines and regulations have to create blanket definitions of what is and what is not in their purview. In the case of the NHPA, this means definitions of what things belong and do not belong on the National Register of Historic Places (NRHP), a list maintained by the National Park Service (NPS). The process of placing cultural resources on the NRHP entails difficult decisions about and definitions of integrity, significance, authenticity, and veracity. This has unintentionally resulted in a static legal perception of Native American history, one whose veracity is largely demonstrated by recourse to Western epistemology. By legally codifying our recognition of Native American heritage in the NHPA and restricting the jurisdiction of the act to federally recognized tribes, we have placed tribes in a paradoxical, ironic situation: as sovereign nations they must appeal to the U.S. government for validation of a heritage resource's significance if they want it afforded consideration under the law. Consequently, tribes are forced to choose between perpetuating the myth of an immutable cultural heritage—an obvious oxymoron—or relinquishing the political and prestige capital available to them through the National Register. One place I believe this paradox is readily apparent is in the guidelines for identifying traditional cultural properties, or TCPs, and nominating them to the NRHP.

Bulletin 38: Traditional Cultural Properties

In amendments to the NHPA in 1980 the secretary of the U.S. Department of the Interior and the American Folklife Center were told to examine ways of preserving and encouraging continuation of traditions underlying American heritage (NHPA section 502; 16 U.S.C. 470a note). What emerged from their examination was a report to Congress in 1983 recommending that traditional cultural resources—with or without ties to tangible real estate—be incorporated into the implementation of the NHPA (Parker and King 1990:2). The secretary of the interior accordingly told the NPS to implement its recommendations to Congress (Parker and King 1990:2), and one of the ways in which it did so was by preparing National Register Bulletin 38, a guidance document prepared two years before the NHPA was actually amended to include TCPs.

According to Bulletin 38, a traditional cultural property "can be defined generally as one that is eligible for inclusion in the National Register because of its association with cultural practices or beliefs of a living community that (a) are rooted in that community's history, and (b) are important in maintaining the continuing cultural identity of the community" (Parker and King 1990:1). The term "traditional" refers to "those beliefs, customs, and practices of a living community of people that have been passed down through the generations, usually orally or through practice" (Parker and King 1990:1). The significance of traditional properties stems from the role they play in sustaining "a community's historically rooted beliefs, customs, and practices," with one example being "a location where Native American religious practitioners have historically gone, and are known or thought to go today, to perform ceremonial activities in accordance with traditional cultural rules of practice" (Parker and King 1990:1).

Some types of TCPs are excluded from the National Register. What Parker and King (1990:3) stressed is that Bulletin 38 "does not address cultural resources that are purely 'intangible'—i.e. those that have no property referents—except by exclusion," despite recommendations to the contrary expressed in the secretary of the interior's report of 1983. They took pains to emphasize that the NPS understands that such properties "may be of vital importance in maintaining the integrity of a social group" and should receive full consideration in the planning and decision making of federal agencies. Nevertheless, "the National Register is not the appropriate vehicle for recognizing cultural values that are purely intangible, nor is there legal authority to address them under section 106 [of the NHPA] unless they are somehow related to a historic property" (Parker and King 1990:3). In short, although TCPs may be quite different than archaeological sites or old buildings, the new guidelines said that the established NRHP evaluation and criteria considerations would still apply to them.

Wyche Fowler, then a senator from Georgia, worked with several tribal organizations—particularly the National Congress of American Indians and the Native American Rights Fund—to incorporate Bulletin 38 into law (King 2003:35–36), and in 1992 amendments to section 101(d)(6) of the NHPA inserted the provision that "properties of traditional religious and cultural importance to an Indian tribe or Native Hawaiian organization may be determined to be eligible for inclusion on the National Register." The amendment also made it mandatory for federal agencies to consult with any "Indian tribe or Native Hawaiian organization that attaches religious and cultural significance" to such properties. These two modifications to the law, along with Bulletin 38, give Native Americans the legal right to list on the NRHP any heritage resource they consider important, so long as it matches the government's defined criteria for inclusion and does not meet the government's defined criteria for exclusion. This creates a relatively narrow sieve through which the tribes and other stakeholders must filter their things and places of significance (see Morgan et al. 2006).

The Gatekeeper Paradox

In my experience in Louisiana it has become clear that there are two aspects of this filtering process that appear particularly alarming to some Native Americans (Morgan 2005; 2007). The first is that the NRHP is a list of "historic" places, hence it can only include properties that are 50 or more years old. The NRHP guidelines, including Bulletin 15 and Bulletin 38, are particularly insistent about this point. If the tribes have begun to ascribe religious and cultural significance to a property within the last five decades it may not be listed on the NRHP. The second and related aspect is the idea of continuity, that is, that TCPs must be, as the name implies, traditional. Notionally, TCPs have been crucial to the maintenance of cultural identity from past to present.

On the surface these two concepts seem to go together quite well. The National Register is for old places, and "valid" TCPs are those that are rooted in history and that help maintain the cultural identity of the community. There is a historical reason these concepts do not work so well in practice: some tribes lost the opportunity to maintain continuity of practice and even familiarity of place as a consequence of the federal Indian policy of the early 1800s. The implications are broad, as Robert Winthrop (1998b:26) succinctly states: "The entire enterprise of traditional use or traditional cultural property studies—at least in the Indian context—is a reflection of a vast cultural dislocation, the disruption of American Indian societies that began in the late fifteenth century, and reached its climax in the United States in the century between 1860 and 1960."

With the passage in the last 30 years of several key federal laws and executive orders, many tribes have made use of the opportunity to reconnect to federal lands from which they were evicted centuries before. For many, however, this entails assigning or ascribing significance to spots on the landscape that stakeholders may never have visited before, or that have not ever been visited in the living memory of the community. This is not necessarily inimical to the NRHP's 50-year criterion, for it is the age of the practice, not necessarily the place, that is under scrutiny. It is this distinction that is fundamental to interpreting the 50-year exclusion criterion (Thomas King, personal communication, November 30, 2004; see also Parker and King 1990:16), and it is one that is often misinterpreted in practice by federal agencies: tribes were removed prior to 50 years ago, ergo they cannot demonstrate continuity of use in the required window of opportunity afforded by the NHPA. The confusion is exacerbated to at least some degree by the insistence in Bulletin 15 that a property cannot be eligible for the National Register if it "has non-contiguous Periods of Significance, one of which is less than fifty years before the nomination" (National Park Service [NPS] 1990a:41; also see Bulletin 22 [NPS (1990b)]).

As has been discussed elsewhere (Morgan 2005:114–20; 2007), another dilemma the NRHP poses to the management and interpretation of descendant communities' heritage is that both the guidelines and the history of Indian law in the United States impose a static view of culture on the NRHP eligibility assessment process. Anthropologists have recognized for decades that culture is partly defined by its mutability and reinvention, for culture, including culture-history, is constantly created, negotiated, and renewed. Looking specifically at Bulletin 38 in the context of a well-known debate over a Chumash property, for example, Brian Haley and Larry Wilcoxon (1997:766) found that the guidelines lack "an appreciation of the constant creation and re-creation of ethnic groups and presume an overly bounded concordance of culture and group identity over time."

In other words, cultural identity is implied to be formed of ancient, immutable properties of the social group, and it is the unmodified character of the cultural content that supposedly forms the backbone of the community's resistance to assimilation (Brown 1997). Anthropologists' efforts in the early twentieth century to capture Native American culture before it "vanished" or was "lost" have crystallized in late twentieth-century and twenty-first century heritage resource management law. Bulletin 38 presumes that cultures are either legitimate or false, and that communities—the undefined analytical unit of cultures in the guidelines (Haley 2004)—either acculturated or did not. Traditions or cultural adaptations outside of this binary framework are potentially spurious (Haley and Wilcoxon 1997). Not only are novelty and adaptability suspect under the evaluation criteria of the NRHP, but the requirements of TCP evaluation grant greater authority to older sources on tradition, which puts contemporary traditionalists in an even more untenable position (Haley and Wilcoxon 1997).

The static perception of culture expressed in the NHPA guidelines arose because of American Indians' status as subject foreign nations and later dependent domestic nations, which has created a complex set of unique legal dilemmas not shared with any other ethnic groups (Brown 1997:778). Two centuries of legal claims have rested on the "assumption that Indian tribes partake of enduring qualities of nationhood, however partial or contested," the consequence of which is that "a certain timelessness has thus become a central feature of how Indians are understood in American law" (Brown 1997:778). Indeed, Klara Kelley (1997) points out that the same immutable presentation of culture—an ideology of imperialism—is to be found in the strictures of the Indian Claims Commission Act of 1946. Given the legal milieu, rediscovering a "lost" culture becomes attractive to tribes for a multitude of social reasons, like pride and vindication, as well as practical reasons, like cultural resources monitoring contracts and gaming concession profits.

To be "legitimate," tribes' corporate definitions of identity are required to be similar to and continuous with a static past, often a past based on primarily older sources on tradition, while self-identification ironically is predicated on the break in cultural continuity that comes from appropriating the past and using its elements to achieve the goals of the present (Geertz 1994). However, speaking candidly about the continual reinvention characteristic of ethnic identity formation would threaten the "primordialist" legal basis of their claims (Brown 1997:778). As one deputy tribal historic preservation officer of a tribe in the New England area once told me, accepting even the popular migration-through-Alaska hypothesis to explain Native Americans' origins in the New World threatens to reduce the tribes to "just another group in a long history of immigrants."

Thus, at some level, arguments over TCP authenticity are subtexts for arguments over sovereignty, power, and epistemology. Some have argued that the criteria of concern here actually are intentionally exclusionary in that they further mask the U.S. government's historical practice of disconnecting living American Indians from their physical past (for example, Nichols et al. 1999:28; Stoffle and Evans 1990a). Regardless of one's view of the intentionality, awareness of the subtext exposes another tension of working with descendant communities in the federal system: the NRHP is declaring the histories of traditionally marginalized, subaltern groups to be part of the mainstream national patrimony, even though federal legislation describes these same groups as sovereign nations. The concepts of Native American cultural property and U.S. patrimony are used interchangeably despite the tacit contradiction. By couching debates over cultural property in this language, says the philosopher Karen Warren (1999:15), it skews any debate in favor of the dominant group:

> Use of the concept or category national patrimony to discuss an entire society's cultural heritage is at least misleading. Surely it is at least an open question whether the concept of national patrimony, like the concepts of property, ownership, utility, and rights, properly captures the relevant information about the relationship of all people to their cultural history. For persons in a cultural context where "the past" is not viewed as property, perhaps not even as "past" (e.g., some Native American cultures), or where talk of property, ownership, utility, and rights do not capture important conceptions of the past (for example, communal kinship with the "living past") . . . what one takes to be the relevant issues . . . will not be captured by the current conception of the debate in terms of the dominant perspective on cultural properties.

In this sense the very language we use becomes a powerful—albeit at times subconscious—tool in a contest for power and sovereignty. Whether elements of culture are appropriated or assimilated depends on the bearers' relationship to the power structure. Thus the claim that the basic TCP definitions and judgment criteria fail to reflect "intangible" property is one based on sovereignty issues (Ziff and Rao 1997:8–9), which is why some tribes have both promulgated their own definition of TCPs and resisted the 50-year exclusion criterion (Morgan 2005). In this light, TCPs become a strong element of cultural identity and are actively used in its construction and reaffirmation. The way this nationalism is construed—on both sides of the legislation—keys back into the very concepts of TCPs as ongoing expressions of static practices that are required to be "historically rooted." The hidden dilemma, as Warren (1999) alludes, is that tribes have accepted the historically static, object-bound perception of culture handed to them by legislators in return for gaining access to political and prestige capital. Go below the surface, however, and it is apparent that they are trying to reappropriate "culture" and negotiate stronger positions of power within a system whose bounds are already defined for them (Handler 1991:67).

The antiquated understanding of culture embedded in our heritage resource legislation creates a gate-keeping dilemma of major proportions. Although King (2003:37, 139–40) now regrets it, Bulletin 38 makes anthropologists the stipulated arbiters of the legitimacy and authenticity of traditions. Cultural outsiders, be it the anthropologists who conduct TCP studies or the NRHP personnel who review the register nomination forms, are placed in the position of being cultural gatekeepers and the delineators of identity, a topic that Winthrop (1998a:447) has discussed in detail in the context of the Chumash debate. The NHPA typically depends on the opinion of scholars to determine the eligibility for the National Register of things like historic buildings. By setting TCPs into the purview of section 106 of the NHPA, Congress in 1992 added to the scholar's view an assessment of legitimacy based on a sense of value that is ascribed to a property within a contemporary social system: what do the stakeholders think about integrity, significance, authenticity, and veracity? This represents a fundamental shift in the relationship between the historic preservation expert and the benefiting community, at least in theory. In practice, says Winthrop (1998a:447), the communities' voices have been taken from them. Communities are treated as "repositories of data" subject to analysis, recording, and inspection by the outside experts. Cultural experience is reduced to a commodity, an ongoing tradition is reduced to a static cultural form, and cultural knowledge is reduced to mental representations housed in resource reports (Winthrop 1998a:447).

The National Heritage Area Approach

What are some solutions? A deceptively obvious one is to reform our understanding of culture as it is expressed in heritage law. This, however, would be a massive undertaking, as the authority of outside experts and the static perception of culture are entrenched in nearly four decades of practice that includes the development of entirely new branches of business, tourism, and preservation. Furthermore, in the case of Native American TCPs, doing so would make those who control mainstream heritage interpretation as it is expressed in the NRHP extremely uneasy because it lodges the significance of these resources "in people's heads" (King 1998:99). People can manipulate and lie about a place's significance to serve their own purposes, which makes cultural outsiders either cynical or extremely anxious (or both). To go to the other extreme, another option that has been considered off and on for decades, even by those who authored Bulletin 38, is to disentangle TCPs from the NRHP and to place them in their own national or tribal registry (King 2003:159; Morgan 2005:122–23; 2007; Parker 1993:3–6; Uebelacker 1984). This is a topic best suited for another venue because of space limitations here.

A third option that I will address, instead, is one that is already becoming accepted in the United States and internationally, and that coexists alongside our entrenched system of cultural resource designations: National Heritage Areas (Morgan et al. 2006). In recent years state governments, the federal government, and local communities have come together to offer National Heritage Areas as an alternate approach to the question of how to best manage the traditional and cultural places of descendant communities. National Heritage Areas are large-scale living landscapes whose preservation is organized by local leaders and residents around a concept of their shared heritage (Barrett et al. 2006). The first national heritage initiative began in 1984, but this type of heritage resource management strategy is part of an international trend in protected areas that has manifested itself over the last 40 years (Mitchell 2003; Morgan et al. 2006; Phillips 2003). At the time of writing Congress has designated 37 regions or corridors National Heritage Areas; another 17 are proposed for designation by Congress, and almost as many may receive further study in the near future.

National Heritage Areas are designated by Congress and receive funds through and technical assistance from the National Park Service, which is currently considering how to programmatically evaluate new bids for congressional designation. The core of the evaluation criteria currently under consideration by the Senate Committee on National Parks says much about what extant National Heritage Areas encompass and what they attempt to recognize. As proposed, a successful bid for National Heritage Area designation would come from places that exhibit a palimpsest of natural, historic, cultural, and other resources that together are nationally significant and represent distinctive aspects of the heritage of the United States. Best candidates would be those areas that reflect traditions, customs, beliefs, and folk life, and that intersect with excellent opportunities for conserving these features in a public venue (Barrett et al. 2006).

What is remarkable is that while National Heritage Areas have a close organizational relationship with the NPS, they are not managed in the National Park Service's traditional, hierarchical way. They are managed through community, grass-roots leadership in a variety of structures that range from federal, state, or local commissions to nonprofit organizations. What they all have in common is that the leaders represent local community interests and expertise, and the hallmark of National Heritage Areas is that they are supported and managed by the people who live there (Barrett 2003; Barrett and Carlino 2003; Barrett et al. 2006; Daly 2003).

National Heritage Areas, in summary, are the province of descendant communities. I suggest that traditional cultural places may be considered and interpreted far more effectively within the framework of National Heritage Areas than that of the NHPA and the National Register for several reasons. First, National Heritage Areas are living landscapes. This means that their approach to heritage is more holistic than one typically thinks of with the NRHP, and this conceptualization is far more analogous to many Native Americans' perceptions of TCPs. The cognitive dissonance and anxiety that often are witnessed when Native Americans are forced to parse their conceptual world into Western analytical units is well known (for example, Carmean 2002; Downer and Roberts 1993; Greiser and Greiser 1993; Kelley and Francis 1994; Parker 1993; Posey and Dutfield 1996; Stoffle and Evans 1990b). As Parker (1993:4) expressed it, the way the National Register "thinks" about the connection between places and the past, present, and future is "decidedly not a Native American way of thinking," and the linear chronology and cause-effect relationship that the NRHP entails and uses to judge membership eligibility "simply are not applicable when dealing with many traditional cultural properties."

Second, and related, is the notion that in National Heritage Areas the individual resources to which we attach superlatives are not the sole focus of management and interpretive consideration. As Carroll Van West, the director of the Tennessee Civil War National Heritage Area, put it when talking about rebuilding the Mississippi Gulf National Heritage Area damaged in 2005 by Hurricane Katrina, National Heritage Areas hold dear not just the iconic landmarks but also the "people, cultural traditions, the commonplace and the seemingly inconsequential markers on the landscape" that serve "as anchors for the region's sense of place and identity" (C. Van West, personal communication, September 14, 2005). To look at another heritage resource to which Katrina has drawn our attention, Kristina Ford, the former city planner of New Orleans, told National Public Radio that what made the city so unique is "the result of 300 years of being built, in which you have a house that was built at this time, another one built at another time, and they're side by side and they haven't been maintained equally" (Chadwick 2005). These haphazard architectural compilations are not, by a large margin, all on the National Register (Morgan et al. 2006), yet Ford emphatically declared that it was this diversity that makes New Orleans so unique, "that make[s] it the place tourists want to come and enjoy and that I love" (Chadwick 2005).

Third, a living landscape perforce requires that the heritage resource managers deal not just with the concept of culture as living, vibrant, and fluid, which the NHPA does not, but also with the people themselves. The managers, in point of fact, are the people themselves. This is why state and local tribes and organizations purposefully ignored by the NHPA fit in so comfortably in the National Heritage Area format. To return to the public radio interview, Ford elaborated that what made the architecture important, and what makes the city truly special even if much of it is destroyed, is New Orleans's diversity of "human beings . . . who have agreed to live sort of provisionally all the time," a diversity that could not be re-created anywhere "without it seeming ersatz" (Chadwick 2005). Physically, she mused, the city could look very different, but "somehow the spirit of the place I think will come back." It is that spirit that National Heritage Areas can capture.

Conclusion

More than anything, National Heritage Areas are a management strategy, and they may prove an effective framework within which to interpret and manage the heritage of descendant communities, including Native Americans. The National Heritage Area model is holistic, locally focused, and directed by the stakeholders themselves. It clearly addresses many of the shortcomings intrinsic to our current approach to preserving national patrimony as individual sites or districts somehow frozen in time. The model may work, but extant designated National Heritage Areas themselves clearly do not encompass most of the traditional cultural places of concern to Native Americans. Consequently we may best be served by fostering the National Heritage Area model, where appropriate, while changing our current approach to traditional cultural property consideration within the existing laws. We should examine communities, rather than places, and we should emphasize tradition and change instead of assumed stasis, essentially blurring the line between history and anthropology. The historian, says King (2003:113), searches for authenticity, while the anthropologist realizes such authenticity is merely a fluid cultural construct.

Note

1. The final version of this document was ratified at the 2008 ICOMOS General Assembly in Quebec, Canada.

References Cited

Araoz, Gustavo
2006 Some Background Musings on the Need for an ICOMOS-ENAME Charter for the Interpretation of Cultural Heritage Sites. *The George Wright Forum* 23(1):40–43.
Barrett, Brenda
2003 Roots for the National Heritage Area Family Tree. *The George Wright Forum* 20(2):41–49.
Barrett, Brenda, and Augie Carlino
2003 What Is in the Future for the Heritage Area Movement? *Forum Journal* 17(4):51–56.

Barrett, Brenda, Nancy I. M. Morgan, and Laura Soullière Gates
2006   National Heritage Areas: Developing a New Conservation Strategy. In *Art and Cultural Heritage: Law, Policy and Practice*, edited by B. Hoffman, pp. 220–33. Cambridge University Press, Cambridge.
Brown, Michael F.
1997   Comments: Anthropology and the Making of Chumash Tradition. *Current Anthropology* 38(5):777–78.
Carmean, Kelli
2002   *Spider Woman Walks This Land: Traditional Cultural Properties and the Navajo Nation*. AltaMira Press, Walnut Creek, Calif.
Chadwick, Alex
2005   Kristina Ford Discusses the Challenge of Rebuilding New Orleans. National Public Radio, *Day to Day*, 4–5 P.M. edition. Interview aired on September 1, 2005, Record no. 200509011604.
Daly, Jayne
2003   Heritage Areas: Connecting People to Their Place and History. *Forum Journal* 17(4):5–12.
Downer, Alan S., and Alexandra Roberts
1993   Traditional Cultural Properties, Cultural Resources Management and Environmental Planning. *Cultural Resource Management* (Special Issue) 16:13–15. Also available online at http://crm.cr.nps.gov/archive/16–si/16–si-5.pdf, accessed May 2, 2008.
Ename Center for Public Archaeology and Heritage Presentation
2007   ICOMOS Ename Charter for the Interpretation of Cultural Heritage Sites. Final version, April 10, 2007. Proposed draft for ratification on file with the Ename Center for Public Archaeology and Heritage Preservation, Oudenaarde, Belgium. Also available online at http://www.enamecharter.org/downloads/ICOMOS_Interpretation_Charter_EN_10-04-07.pdf, accessed May 2, 2008.
Geertz, Armin W.
1994   *The Invention of Prophecy*. University of California Press, Berkeley.
Greiser, Sally T., and T. Weber Greiser
1993   Two Views of the World. *Cultural Resource Management* (Special Issue) 16:9–11. Also available online at http://crm.cr.nps.gov/archive/16–si/16–si-4.pdf, accessed May 2, 2008.
Haley, Brian D.
2004   Review of *Places That Count: Traditional Cultural Properties in Cultural Resource Management*. *Southeastern Archaeology* 23(2):226–28.
Haley, Brian D., and Larry R. Wilcoxon
1997   Anthropology and the Making of Chumash Tradition. *Current Anthropology* 38(5):761–77.
Handler, Richard
1991   Who Owns the Past? History, Cultural Property, and the Logic of Possessive Individualism. In *The Politics of Culture*, edited by B. Williams, pp. 63–74. Smithsonian Institution Press, Washington, D.C.

Kelley, Klara Bonsack
1997   Comments: Anthropology and the Making of Chumash Tradition. *Current Anthropology* 38(5):782–83.
Kelley, Klara Bonsack, and Harris Francis
1994   *Navajo Sacred Places.* Indiana University Press, Bloomington.
King, Thomas F.
1998   *Cultural Resource Laws and Practice: An Introductory Guide.* AltaMira Press, Walnut Creek, Calif.
2003   *Places That Count: Traditional Cultural Properties in Cultural Resource Management.* AltaMira Press, Walnut Creek, Calif.
Mitchell, Brent
2003   International Models of Protected Landscapes. *The George Wright Forum* 20(2):33–40.
Morgan, David W.
2005   *Assessment of Properties of Traditional Religious and Cultural Importance to the Signatory Tribes of the Native American Historical Initiative: Reconnecting to the Lands of the Louisiana Army National Guard.* Northwestern State University's Cultural Resource Office. Submitted to the Louisiana Division of Archaeology, Baton Rouge, and the Louisiana Army National Guard, Camp Beauregard, Pineville.
2007   U.S. National Historic Preservation Act and Indigenous Heritage. In *Interpreting the Past: Who Owns the Past? Heritage Rights and Responsibilities in a Multicultural World*, edited by N. Silberman and C. Liuzza, pp. 234–45. Flemish Heritage Institute, Brussels.
Morgan, David W., Nancy I. M. Morgan, and Brenda Barrett
2006   Finding a Place for the Commonplace: Hurricane Katrina, Communities, and Preservation Law. *American Anthropologist* 108(4):706–718.
National Park Service (NPS)
1990a   *How to Apply the National Register Criteria for Evaluation.* National Register Bulletin 15. U.S. Department of the Interior, National Park Service National Register, Publications. Last revised and updated in 2002. Also available online at http://www.cr.nps.gov/nr/publications/bulletins/nrb15/, accessed May 2, 2008.
1990b   *Guidelines for Evaluating and Nominating Properties That Have Achieved Significance within the Past Fifty Years.* National Register Bulletin 22. U.S. Department of the Interior, National Park Service National Register, Publications. Originally published in 1979. Also available online at http://www.cr.nps.gov/nr/publications/bulletins/nrb22/, accessed September 24, 2009.
Nichols, Deborah L., Anthony L. Klesert, and Roger Anyon
1999   Ancestral Sites, Shrines, and Graves: Native American Perspectives on the Ethics of Collecting Cultural Properties. In *The Ethics of Collecting Cultural Property: Whose Culture? Whose Property?*, edited by Phyllis Mauch Messenger, pp. 27–38. 2nd ed. University of New Mexico Press, Albuquerque.

Parker, Patricia L.

1993   What You Do and How We Think. *Cultural Resource Management* (Special Issue) 16:1–5. Also available online at http://crm.cr.nps.gov/archive/16–si/16–si-1.pdf, accessed May 2, 2008.

Parker, Patricia L., and Thomas F. King

1990   *Guidelines for Evaluating and Documenting Traditional Cultural Properties.* National Register Bulletin 38. U.S. Department of the Interior, National Park Service, Interagency Resources Division, Washington, D.C.

Phillips, Adrian

2003   Turning Ideas on Their Head: The New Paradigm of Protected Areas. *The George Wright Forum* 20(2):8–32.

Posey, Darrell A., and Graham Dutfield

1996   *Beyond Intellectual Property: Toward Traditional Resource Rights for Indigenous Peoples and Local Communities.* International Development Research Centre, Ottawa.

Stoffle, Richard W., and Michael J. Evans

1990a   American Indians and Nuclear Waste Storage: The Debate at Yucca Mountain, Nevada. *Policy Studies Journal* 16(4):751–67.

1990b   Holistic Conservation and Cultural Triage: American Indian Perspectives on Cultural Resources. *Human Organization* 49(2):91–99.

Uebelacker, Morris Leo

1984   *Time Ball: A Story of the Yakima People and the Land—A Cultural Resource Overview.* Shields Bag and Printing Company, Yakima.

Warren, Karen J.

1999   A Philosophical Perspective on the Ethics and Resolution of Cultural Property Issues. In *The Ethics of Collecting Cultural Property: Whose Culture? Whose Property?*, edited by Phyllis Mauch Messenger, pp. 1–25. 2nd ed. University of New Mexico Press, Albuquerque.

Winthrop, Robert H.

1998a   The Making of Chumash Tradition: Replies to Haley and Wilcoxon. *Current Anthropology* 39(4):496–99.

1998b   Tradition, Authenticity, and Dislocation: Some Dilemmas of Traditional Cultural Property Studies. *Practicing Anthropology* 20(3):25–27.

Ziff, Bruce H., and Pratima V. Rao

1997   Introduction to Cultural Appropriation: A Framework for Analysis. In *Borrowed Power: Essays on Cultural Appropriation*, edited by B. H. Ziff and P. V. Rao, pp. 1–27. Rutgers University Press, New Brunswick, N.J.

16

Laws, Language, and Learning

Managing Archaeological Heritage Resources in Europe

WILLEM J. H. WILLEMS

At the outset, it is useful to explain briefly what the subtitle of this chapter is understood to mean because in English discourse there is much terminology in use with sometimes very confusing meanings (see Carman 2002:5–25 for an exhaustive discussion). In addition, there are the various non-English discourses in Europe. First, my subject is "archaeological" as opposed to "architectural," "historic," or the even wider concept of "cultural." In most European discourses, there is a growing recognition that the totality of the historic environment should be considered—much like the holistic American concept of "cultural heritage"—rather than its traditional subdivisions along the lines of academic divisions. Sticking to "archaeological" is for practical purposes because in most of Europe there are academic differences, as well as strong legal and formidable organizational differences, between dealing with archaeology and with architecture or other aspects.

Second, I have kept in the concept of "heritage resource," although in Europe a distinction is generally made between the concepts of heritage and of resource: "heritage" is normally considered to be of concern to society at large; it is also a political and legal term. The same material substance may be described as a "resource" and then is considered to be something that is primarily relevant to archaeologists (see Carman 2002:18; Hunter and Ralston 1993:viii). Nevertheless, it is entirely possible to view heritage as a resource for the public.

Third, there is the concept of "management." By itself, the idea that heritage resources have to be actively managed is not new anymore, but it is different from the more static concept of "taking care of monuments," which is the literal translation of the terminology used in several European languages, for example, in German, *Denkmalpflege* (Willems 1999). It is a concept that is connected to systems of designation that are dominated by legal requirements and administrative procedures and that lead to such things as registers of protected sites, national "stamp collections" of monuments. This is, of course, the oldest form of dealing with the material remains of the past, setting sites, monuments, or objects apart as something special and giving them legal status. It began in Sweden, which has Europe's oldest monuments act, dating back to 1666, and is intimately connected with the formation of nation-states and the need to (re)define national identities in post-Napoleonic Europe (Willems 2001:83–84). This work is still a very important activity in many countries, but it is increasingly supplemented, if not indeed replaced,[1] by various forms of management.

In Europe, there is by no means a universal concept of preserving archaeological heritage resources through management of the historic environment—comprising the material remains of the past—or by any other means, for that matter. That need not surprise, for there are vast differences among the 48 different countries on the continent.[2] There are a number of reasons for this, relating to historical developments over the past century or so, to academic and political traditions, legal systems, and communication or, rather, language.

It is not very useful to go into all of these differences in any detail, as there are some good recent overviews (Biehl et al. 2002; Kobyliński 1998, 2001). It is worthwhile, however, to examine briefly some of the reasons for differentiation in relation to managing heritage resources because these will surely also be relevant at the global level. In addition, this chapter will discuss some recent trends and current issues.

Different Approaches: The Three Ls

Behind the differentiation in approaches to heritage management are any number of causes, some of which are quite specific for particular countries. There are, however, some more general sources of differentiation that can be comprised under three headings: law, language, and learning.

Law

In 1984 Henry Cleere, in the introduction to his *Approaches to the Archaeological Heritage*, observed that until then there had been hardly any international debate on heritage management issues. An important reason for this may have been that until about that time managing the archaeological heritage was traditionally done only by systems of designation that are by definition specific to a country because they are regulated by its laws, administrative traditions, and procedures. That way of dealing with heritage has changed, but it is still true that there are several rather different legal systems (and ways of organizing society) that lead to very different approaches to managing heritage resources. The most evident, though certainly not the only one, is the difference between the Anglo-Saxon common law tradition, where society is self-regulating, and the Roman law tradition, where much depends on the state, which regulates society. A recent discussion between Jean Paul Demoule (2002a, 2002b) and Roger Thomas (2002) provides a wonderful illustration of the consequences of this difference. Through the Napoleonic "civil code," Roman law has become dominant in many countries. Nevertheless, it should not be disregarded that there are still other law traditions, of which the Germanic law tradition that has survived in Scandinavia is equally relevant. For example, the rights of the king in Germanic law, as opposed to private ownership in Roman law, provides decidedly better opportunities for protecting the archaeological heritage.[3] There may be other relevant traditions, and at least one has ended abruptly. After the fall of the iron curtain, rapid privatization, the introduction of raw capitalism, and the abrupt abolishing of Communist laws on communal (cultural) property have in some cases led to catastrophes in heritage management.

Also relevant in this respect is that the European Union does not have a common policy where cultural heritage is concerned. In fact, harmonization of cultural legislation is even specifically excluded under article 128 of the Treaty on the European Union. There is, of course, the highly influential Malta Convention,[4] but that is a voluntary convention by the Council of Europe.[5] For information about the legal and organizational aspects of archaeological resource management in European countries, the Council of Europe maintains the European Heritage Network (HEREIN) website.[6]

Language

There has been regrettably little research into the effect of language on practices in both academic research and heritage management in archaeology.[7] Obviously, the English discourse is so dominant at the global level that it may seem to be the only one—especially to native speakers of English who often tend to have rather poorly developed language skills. An interesting analysis was done by Neustupný (1998), who defined "mainstream" and "minority" research communities in Europe. He terms as "mainstream" the larger groups (German, English, French, Russian, and Spanish). These are the communities that are big enough to have a full internal discourse on all relevant topics, so there is no immediate need to refer to outside sources or to participate in other discourses. For his "minority" communities that is not possible. Indeed, the Scandinavian, Dutch, or Czech "minority" communities traditionally have a very outspoken international orientation. The point is, however, that what happens inside a large community—with the exception of the English one—tends to remain there for lack of communication across the language border. A recent citation analysis of references to academic and professional archaeological literature (Kristiansen 2001) indicates that this phenomenon has been increasing over the past decade or so; there is a clear increase in the geographical constraints on citation, even in the smaller communities. The causes for this[8] may well have to do with the rapid growth of these communities in recent years, which at least in some cases can be attributed to the enormous growth of archaeological heritage resource management.[9] The increase in the number of publications per year is connected to a decrease in their geographical scope and hence in the number and diversity of the international references.

The nature of communication is thus decidedly influenced by language communities and their size, and has given rise to distinct traditions in heritage management.

Learning

Academic traditions vary greatly throughout Europe. Within the European Union there will now be one uniform bachelor-master system,[10] and the EU's Erasmus program facilitates exchange between universities. That does not at all mean, however, that there will be any convergence or common standards in the training of archaeologists working in heritage management. Nor does it mean that the existing power structures in academia at the national level will necessarily change. These aspects are of considerable influence on different ways of thinking about heritage management and on theorizing it (insofar as that is at all an issue). A totally different aspect relates to conservation and restoration, which in Europe are often taught at polytechnics or similar higher educational institutions.[11]

The fact that different approaches to heritage management exist, and will continue to do so, does not mean that there are no discussions at the European level, or that European platforms or standards are lacking. Before turning to some of the trends in heritage management in Europe, it is useful to indicate briefly the latter (see also Willems 1999).

The major standard for heritage resource management was developed by the Council of Europe between 1988 and 1992 as a result of changing views, in the preceding decade or so, on heritage and consequently on how to improve its survival and role in society by incorporation in the spatial planning process.[12] That resulted in the Malta Convention. Some aspects of this standard have been broadened since then by the adoption of the Florence Convention,[13] although this is one of the areas where diversity becomes visible. In some countries this landscape convention is indeed seen as a kind of extension of the Malta Convention, but in many—if not indeed most—countries it appears to be dealt with by departments of agriculture or environment with, at best, limited involvement from the cultural heritage sector (cf. also Clarke 2001:106). Apart from these conventions that set a standard for archaeological heritage management as a whole, practical standards have also been developed by the Council of Europe, such as a core data standard for recording sites and monuments (Council of Europe 1999).

The European Union does not have direct influence on heritage issues, but it may take "incentive measures" to support programs and, more importantly, it has legislative powers that have an indirect impact. For example, since 1997 the EU legislation on environmental impact assessment includes archaeology, so evaluations of the heritage resource potential can now be enforced even if adequate national legislation should be lacking. Although the European Union thus often provides the fuel (financing) for heritage work, the engine is maintained by the Council of Europe, which as an organization is actively concerned with cultural heritage in Europe. One of the latest examples is a forward study that was produced to contribute to the Fifth Conference of Ministers Responsible for the Cultural Heritage in Slovenia in April 2001 (Council of Europe 2001).

Within the discipline of archaeology, a platform for communication was created after the fall of the iron curtain by the founding of the European Association of Archaeologists (EAA) in 1993. The EAA organizes annual meetings, where professional and heritage issues are always major themes, and it publishes a journal and a newsletter.[14] In 1999, this was complemented by the creation of a European organization for state archaeologists called the Europæ Archaeologiæ Consilium (EAC), which is a more formal platform for archaeological heritage issues.[15]

Current Trends and Developments

The above-mentioned "forward planning" study is interesting not only because it expresses the concerns of the Council of Europe with the role of cultural heritage,[16] but also because it contains a table showing what were perceived by some of the experts in its working group to be "broad trends in cultural heritage management." Table 16.1 summarizes some trends as they were perceived in 2000. Many of the same trends are also recognized in the various contributions to a workshop on the future of European archaeology that was organized in 2001 by the European Science Foundation (Kobyliński 2001) and other recent publications (for example, Darvill 2004). The new concepts mentioned in this table are to be added to the older concepts; they are not seen as replacing them. The four main headings provide a useful framework to discuss current trends and developments.

As far as the definition of heritage is concerned, there is indeed a clear development toward contextualizing individual sites and monuments as part of a larger whole—the historic environment—and toward a realization that the sustainability of that larger whole, rather than the conservation of individual monuments or sites, is a key objective of heritage resource management. While the recognition as such, and the conceptual change that it implies, is broadly accepted, the major problem that exists with this approach is that in many countries there are deficiencies both in the legal framework and in the organizational structure to put this into practice. Nevertheless, the approach is being increasingly adopted, as is evident from recent overviews from a sizeable number of European countries.[17] Indeed, the idea that heritage resource management

Table 16.1. Broad Trends in Cultural Heritage Management

Theme	From (old concept)	To (new concept)
Definition of heritage	Monuments	Landscapes
	Buildings	Urban areas
	Sites	Historic environment / cultural heritage
Role of heritage in society	National unity	Respect for cultural diversity
	Generate revenue from visitors	Wider economic benefits/ social benefits
- Decisions	State	Region/locality
	Authoritarian	Democratization
		Participation
- Professionals	Experts	Facilitators
	Single discipline (e.g., buildings, archaeology)	Multi-skilled professionals
	Historical knowledge	Management skills
Significance	Old	Industrial heritage
		Postwar buildings
	Aesthetic	Commemorative value
	National importance	Local distinctiveness
	Monocultural	Values of different cultures
	Narrow range of values	Wide range of values
-Interpretation	Expert led	Community led
-Responsibilities	State led	Communities
		The market/private sector
	Heritage sector	Environmental sector
Management practices	Designation	Characterization
	Separate conservation	Integrated conservation
	Site based	More strategic
	Technical research	Philosophical research

Source: Council of Europe 2001

should in fact be understood as "the management of change" has taken hold and is intimately connected to changes in management practices.

In the 1990s, ideas were developed about the need for a historically founded linking of the management of characteristic landscapes to specific forms of land use and about a rejection of the concept of national parks as a means to preserve some areas at the expense of others: "The idea of the landscape reserve is perhaps one of the clearest mirrors of the western, dissociated and alienated treatment of the past in the landscape" (Kolen 1995:155).[18] The volume edited by Fairclough and Rippon (2002) contains many examples of how site-based heritage protection is rapidly being replaced by more strategic approaches that involve the management of their context and are in alliance with "green" environmental concerns (cf. Macinnes and Wickham-Jones 1992). At the base of this change lies a shift from systems of "designation" to the "characterization of heritage resources." It is not only the individual site or monument any more that is valuated and being dealt with, receiving a status in accordance with its ascribed value. Instead, the historic environment is being studied, evaluated, and defined in terms of its history and its present-day relevance to people. There seem to be two interrelated approaches. One is the "historic landscape characterization" developed as a heritage management tool in the United Kingdom, whereby the historic and archaeological dimension of the present-day landscape is defined in order to explain how and why the landscape is what it is today, to identify its time-depth, and to facilitate sustainable management.[19] Another is the concept of the "cultural biography" of a landscape, monument, or object, an analysis from a long-term perspective on transformations of meaning until the present day, which makes visible all kinds of relationships, causes, effects, and contexts. As was recently concluded on the basis of a study making use of this notion, its potential for heritage resource management has not yet been explored fully, especially for English discourse; its exploration is further advanced elsewhere.[20]

The approaches discussed above have also led to a trend toward integrated conservation projects, where professionals with different expertise, such as architects, landscape architects, archaeologists, or planners, work together on joint projects. This trend would seem to be a preferred option, as the alternative of multi-skilled professionals, advocated by some, seems to be a very questionable development. Integrated projects are still a relative novelty in the countryside; in urban settings there is already much experience with integrated projects (Andrikopoulou-Strack et al. 1997; Council of Europe, ed. 1999; Horn et al. 2004). Recently, a project called APPEAR, which was sponsored by the European Union, focused on the urban heritage.[21] This project studied the conservation, integration, enhancement, and exploitation of urban subsoil archaeological sites in a sustainable way so as to make them available to the population. It produced a "guide" that is essentially an integrated action plan for the completion of accessibility projects at each stage in their development. It includes methodological and practical resources for identifying and implementing specific solutions for the conservation, integration, enhancement, and exploitation of archaeological sites in an urban setting. An "existing practices" database provides end users with a descriptive inventory of European accessibility projects. It offers them examples and references to be used to help them make choices with regard to their own projects. An important part of the project is concerned with the physical conservation of excavated remains.

In recent years, there has also been an increase (also financed by the European Union) in technical research on the preservation of unexcavated, in situ remains, for which the term "environmental archaeometry" is sometimes used (Friberg 1996; Jans 2005; Kars 1997; Kars and Kars 2002). Heritage resources are assumed to be best preserved in situ, but so far this remains a largely untested assumption. Only wetland sites, as a special category, have received much special attention.[22] The same research also provides insight in the conservation of unexcavated sites by using the state of preservation of in situ organic remains as an indicator.

A third development in management practice that should be mentioned is caused by political changes involving increased privatization and belief in allowing market principles to operate in almost all sectors of what used to be the public domain. This has led to the development of standards and mechanisms for quality assurance. In many European countries, the advent of commercial archaeology in the last 10 to 15 years has led to concerns about the quality of archaeological work that were virtually lacking when archaeology was only an academic discipline.[23] The stated reasons for these concerns are similar everywhere. Commercial archaeology becomes possible when there is an obligation to take archaeological remains into account in development projects and at the expense of the developer. The developer thus has an interest in the work being done, but the quality of the result of that work is only relevant in terms of time and money, not in terms of the quality of the end product, which is knowledge about the past.[24]

The absence of private interests in the quality of the end product in combination with the particular character of the archaeological work, a knowledge-based line of business, makes it difficult to use a quality control approach from other types of work. In European archaeology, various approaches are being explored to provide mechanisms that assure quality. One aim is guaranteeing a basic level of performance by quality assurance of the process or methodology. This may include voluntary or enforced standards and guidelines for archaeological contract work, codes of conduct, and the like.[25] A certain level of quality may also be assured by maintaining or creating a state monopoly that excludes a role for the developer and keeps the entire process outside economic competition (Demoule 2002a) or by two types of mixed systems such as in Sweden (Holm 2000; Magnusson 2005; Säfvestad 2004) and in Germany.[26] In Sweden, there is a strong emphasis on providing academic input in private enterprise in archaeology, while "private enterprise" itself is largely limited to a state organization that has to work commercially. Germany represents another type of mixture because it is a federal republic and each of the German states has its own laws and regulations so that fully commercial systems with government agencies responsible for quality control exist side by side with full state monopolies.

Another approach aims at guaranteeing the quality of the product—the content and relevance of the academic output, and its contribution to our knowledge about the past. Where commercial archaeology is kept at bay—either fully or partially—this is normally considered to be the responsibility of the organizations charged with the work. In other systems, a variety of instruments are involved, such as research agendas and peer review systems. A related issue is the way in which systems of quality control are being supervised. They can be almost entirely voluntary, or they can be enforced through a system of certification and accreditation, through a licensing system, through an inspectorate, or by means of a combination of such regulators.

Turning to the role of heritage in society, the most important development that has had a very strong influence on heritage resource management and indeed on society as a whole is decentralization. During the rise of the nation-state in the nineteenth century, existing regional units became less important, often by force, to accomplish national unity. Now, within the European Union, there is a decline in the sovereignty of the states, while regional and local identity and autonomy become increasingly important; this is what in Europe is known as "the Europe of the regions." Concomitant developments are a growing respect for cultural diversity and for local interests. This, of course, is reflected in heritage management, which is now rapidly moving away from fairly authoritarian and centralized decision making toward concerns for social inclusion and involving local stakeholders and communities in dealing with the historic environment. This occurs, not only because stakeholders and communities have a big influence on the sustainable preservation of that environment (Fairclough 1999; McManamon and Hatton 2000:10), but also because it is generally recognized that they have a stake.[27] As it is worded in recent texts by the Council of Europe, this is about "cultural rights" or "rights to the heritage" (Pickard 2002:18). There are instances in Europe where this involves an "indigenous" population, such as the Saami in the Nordic countries, but it can be any minority group or "just" the local population.

This development is in some ways similar to developments in English-speaking continents—North America and Australia—where heritage resource management is coming to terms with its past, and relations with indigenous peoples have undergone fundamental changes. Its roots are different though, and in the United States they go far beyond involving the local/indigenous populations and respecting their interests. At least in continental Europe[28] such developments are often considered with suspicion, especially where "decolonizing the practice of archaeology" seems to entail a flight from objectivity into extremes of cultural relativism for the sake of political correctness.[29] Of course, there remains a difference between respecting the views of the local/indigenous populations and those involved in what Skeates (2000:99) and Schadla-Hall (2004) have recently termed "alternative" interpretations of archaeology. In general, post-processual thinking in archaeology has of course also had an influence on changes in practices and the role of heritage, although the theoretical foundations of heritage resource management seem to remain largely in a more processual perspective.[30]

It should be noted that the process of decentralization has not only led to changes in the role of heritage in society, it has also had some negative effects on heritage management in European countries. For example, it has begun to lead to the demise of central organizations that were able to support specialized expertise that is not commercially viable and cannot be maintained at the local level either. Another—admittedly more disputable—disadvantage is that the authority to decide comes to reside where there is no capacity, competence, or even interest to do so. On average, it seems that middle levels of government (such as the English county or the German Kreis) are better placed than lower levels (municipalities), with the exception of major towns—which in Europe usually have important historic centers.

One aspect of heritage that has become particularly relevant in Europe since the 1990s and the war in the Balkans, where heritage became a target,[31] is that the resource "is always in dispute, between countries, between regions, between different stakeholders" (Howard 2003:212). As Mathers et al. (2005) have recently demonstrated, there are many different aspects to valuing and determining the significance of archaeological heritage. It seems, however, that two issues have become especially important in recent years, incorporating a wide range of values when making a judgment, and including values of different cultures. In "Council of Europe speak," safeguarding the diversity of distinctive European heritage "requires mutual understanding, respect and recognition of the cultural values of others, particularly in relation to the cultural identities and heritage of minority and vulnerable groups" (Pickard 2002:19). In addition, there is increasing attention for heritage resources representing conflict and/or contested symbols. Often that is a very difficult task. It is one thing for English Heritage to develop policies for recent "monuments of war" in England (Schofield 1998), which broadened the horizon for archaeological heritage management but at the same time—in principle—still fits into a "nationalistic" or in any case traditional approach to heritage. It is quite another for German heritage managers to deal with buried remains of Third Reich buildings and installations in Berlin in a sensitive manner (Kernd'l 2002). Recognizing their significance as a token from an unpleasant past takes both courage and sensitivity because it is easily confused with other aims or (consciously) misinterpreted as such.

Of course the trends and developments discussed in this chapter represent only a limited number of aspects of archaeological resource management in Europe. There are characteristic traits and presumably specific issues in each country that could enrich the international discourse, but very often remain at the national level. Contrary to what might have been expected, there is in particular a lack of discussion between southern and northern Europe, rather than between eastern and western Europe. Achieving a higher level of participation in discussions of pan-European and indeed global interest may well require another decade of international cooperation.

Notes

1. My own country, the Netherlands, has recently become a case in point when the new government in 2004 declared a moratorium on new archaeological and built monuments; the usefulness of the current register is to be examined, and management through the instruments of spatial planning is strongly advocated.

2. There are 46 member states (and one candidate member) of the Council of Europe, plus the Vatican.

3. For example, in countries that have been influenced by the French Code Civile, anything below the surface belongs to the owner, in theory extending down to the center of the earth, unless a specific exception is made by law. In countries that have retained Germanic law, anything below the surface in principle belongs to the Crown.

4. The official title is European Convention on the Protection of the Archaeological Heritage (Revised). It was opened for signature in 1992 and has currently been ratified by 26 countries.

5. It is important to note that the Council of Europe is a purely intergovernmental organization of all European countries. The European Union is very different: it is a supranational body with common institutions to which its 25 member states have delegated part of their sovereignty. On the role of the Council of Europe with respect to cultural heritage, see Pickard 2002.

6. The European Heritage Network (Réseau Européen du Patrimoine) can be found at http://www.europeanheritage.net/sdx/herein/index.xsp. Other additional countries are covered by http://www.planarch.org. See also http://www.heritagelaw.net.

7. Since this was written, the subject has received considerable attention. In 2007, the *European Journal of Archaeology* 10(2–3) published a special double issue on "Communication in Archaeology," with several relevant papers. In addition, in 2008, a forum discussion was published in *Archaeologies* 4(1):164–200, on "Global Languages of Archaeology," with eight different contributions on the subject.

8. See also the discussion in Kobyliński 2001:44–46.

9. Published examples are the Netherlands, where the number of full-time equivalents (FTEs) in jobs for archaeologists has quadrupled in the last decade (Bloemers 2005; Willems and Brandt 2004: introduction), and Ireland (O'Sullivan 2003).

10. This is the result of the so-called Bologna process that started in 1999 (see, for example, http://www.bologna-bergen2005.no/). For some implications, see Bloemers 2005; Eggert 2005.

11. For an overview not covering the whole of Europe, see http://www.encore-edu.org/.

12. See Council of Europe 1987 and 1989 for conference reports and 1992 for the text and explanatory report of the convention. Many texts are downloadable through the portal at http://www.coe.int. Although an attempt was made in the 1980s, the Council of Europe never succeeded in producing a convention on the underwater cultural heritage.

13. For the European Landscape Convention, see Council of Europe 2000. The

convention was opened for signature in 2000 and has meanwhile been ratified by 18 countries. Other relevant European conventions are the European Convention on Offences Relating to Cultural Property (Delphi Convention) and the Convention for the Protection of the Architectural Heritage of Europe (Granada Convention), both of 1985.

14. See http://www.e-a-a.org; Marciniak 2000; Willems 2002. The *European Journal of Archaeology* (*EJA*) has been published since 1993 and there is a regular newsletter, *The European Archaeologist* (*TEA*).

15. See Willems 2000. The EAC does not yet have a website.

16. As explicitly worded by its director general for culture, see Weber 2001. It was a U.K. group that drafted the table (Clarke 2001), so it contains some elements that may well reflect particular Anglo-Saxon or U.K. views or concerns, but in my opinion it is most certainly of general relevance for trends in Europe.

17. See Fairclough and Rippon 2002 for overviews from a substantial number of European countries with many further references. A discussion of legal frameworks is in Prieur 2002.

18. Kolen 1995:155. On this subject, see also Kristiansen 1992, both with further references.

19. See Fairclough et al. 2002; Darvill 2004, both with further references.

20. Yates 2005:134; see however Kolen 2005 and Bloemers 2002:94 on a research program developed to do just that. For earlier discussion (in English) on the notion of cultural biography, see various contributions in the *Archaeological Dialogues* 6(2) (1999).

21. http://www.in-situ.be./A_pres_overview.html.

22. For an excellent overview of the management of wetland heritage resources in Europe, see Coles and Olivier 2001. Of particular relevance for this aspect is also the Ramsar Convention (Ramsar Convention 2004), which nowadays gives much more attention to the cultural aspects of wetlands; see http://www.ramsar.org/.

23. For a recent overview, see Willems and van den Dries 2007.

24. See Cumberpatch 2000 for a critique of the U.K. system with its primacy of the interests of the developer.

25. The most developed systems are those in the United Kingdom and in the Netherlands (Institute of Field Archaeologists 1999; Willems and Brandt 2004).

26. For Germany, which is a federal state, see Verband der Landesarchäologen in der Bundesrepublik Deutschland (1994) (this is the standing conference of state archaeologists in Germany).

27. While this has become increasingly common, it does not mean that there is agreement on views that "everyone, whatever their interest, has a stake" (Fairclough 1999:131) (cf. note 28).

28. In England, the appropriation of monuments and their interpretation by New Age groups seems to have received at least some measure of official recognition.

29. See Arnold 2000 for an insightful comparative analysis of American and European (in particular, German) perspectives. Also Skeates 2000: chapter 5.

30. See the recent discussion between Moss 2005 and Hegmon 2005, which also relates to theory and CRM.

31. Golden 2004 offers an analysis of similar situations.

References Cited

Andrikopoulou-Strack, Nora, Brigitte Beyer, and Bernd Päffgen (editors)
1997   *Bodendenkmäler in der Stadt: Beispiele für Erhaltung und Präsentation aus dem Rheinland* (Archaeological monuments in towns: Examples for conservation and presentation from the Rhineland). Rheinland Verlag GmbH, Köln.

Arnold, Bettina
2000   A Transatlantic Perspective on German Archaeology. In *Archaeology, Ideology and Society: The German Experience*, edited by H. Härke, pp. 398–422. Series Gesellschaften und Staaten 7. Fritz Lang Verlag, Bern and Frankfurt.

Biehl, P. F., A. Gramsch, and A. Marciniak (editors)
2002   *Archäologien Europas/Archaeologies of Europe: Geschichte, Methoden und Theorien/History, Methods and Theories.* Tübingen Archäologische Taschenbücher 3. Waxman, Münster.

Bloemers, Tom J. H. F.
2002   Past- and Future-Oriented Archaeology: Protecting and Developing the Archaeological-Historical Landscape. In *The Netherlands, Europe's Cultural Landscape: Archaeologists and the Management of Change*, edited by G. Fairclough and S. Rippon, pp. 89–96. EAC Occasional Paper 2. Europæ Archaeologiæ Consilium, Exeter.
2005   *Die Umsetzung der Konvention von Valletta in den Niederlanden: Anregungen zur Neukonzeptualisierung von Forschung, Denkmalpflege und Lehre* (The implementation of the Valletta Convention in the Netherlands: Inspiration for rethinking research, heritage management, and academic training). *Archäologisches Korrespondenzblatt* 10:199–210.

Carman, John
2002   *Archaeology and Heritage, an Introduction.* Continuum, London and New York.

Clarke, Kate
2001   From Regulation to Participation: Cultural Heritage, Sustainable Development and Citizenship. In *Forward Planning: The Function of Cultural Heritage in a Changing Europe*, edited by the Council of Europe, pp. 103–12. Council of Europe Publishing, Strasbourg.

Cleere, Henry (editor)
1984   *Approaches to the Archaeological Heritage: New Directions in Archaeology.* Cambridge University Press, Cambridge.

Coles, Bryony, and Adrian Olivier (editors)
2001   *The Heritage Management of Wetlands in Europe.* EAC Occasional Paper 1. Europæ Archaeologiæ Consilium, Exeter.

Council of Europe

1992   *European Convention on the Protection of the Archaeological Heritage (Revised) and Explanatory Report.* European Treaty Series 143. Council of Europe Publishing, Strasbourg.

1999   *Core Data Standard for Archaeological Sites and Monuments/Fiche D'indexion Minimale Pour les Sites Archéologiques.* Council of Europe Publishing, Strasbourg.

2000   *European Landscape Convention and Explanatory Report.* European Treaty Series 176. Council of Europe Publishing, Strasbourg.

Council of Europe (editor)

1987   *Archaeology and Planning: Report of the Florence Colloquy.* Architectural Heritage Reports and Studies 5. Council of Europe Publishing, Strasbourg.

1989   *Archaeology and Major Public Works: Report of the Nice Colloquy.* Architectural Heritage Reports and Studies 12. Council of Europe Publishing, Strasbourg.

1999   *Report on the Situation of Urban Archaeology in Europe/Rapport Sur la Situation de l'archéologie Urbaine en Europe.* Council of Europe Publishing, Strasbourg.

2001   *Forward Planning: The Function of Cultural Heritage in a Changing Europe.* Council of Europe Publishing, Strasbourg.

Cumberpatch, Christopher G.

2000   Some Problems in Contemporary English Archaeology. *Archaeologia Polona* 38:225–38.

Darvill, Timothy

2004   Public Archaeology: A European Perspective. In *A Companion to Archaeology,* edited by J. Bintliff, pp. 409–34. Blackwell, Oxford.

Demoule, Jean Paul

2002a   Rescue Archaeology, the French Way. *Public Archaeology* 2:170–77.

2002b   Reply to Roger Thomas. *Public Archaeology* 2:239–40.

Eggert, Manfred K. H.

2005   Archäologie im Umbruch: Einführung in die Thematik (Changes in archaeology: Introduction to the theme). *Archäologisches Korrespondenzblatt* 10:111–24.

Fairclough, Graham

1999   The "S" Word—or Sustaining Conservation. In *Conservation Plans in Action,* edited by C. Clarke, pp. 127–31. English Heritage, London.

Fairclough, Graham, G. Lambrick, and D. Hopkins

2002   Historic Landscape Characterisation in England and a Hampshire Case Study. In *Europe's Cultural Landscape: Archaeologists and the Management of Change,* edited by G. Fairclough and S. Rippon, pp. 69–83. EAC Occasional Paper 2. Europæ Archaeologiæ Consilium, Exeter.

Fairclough, Graham, and S. Rippon (editors)

2002   *Europe's Cultural Landscape: Archaeologists and the Management of Change.* EAC Occasional Paper 2. Europæ Archaeologiæ Consilium, Exeter.

Friberg, Gunnel (editor)
1996   *Deterioration of Archaeological Material in Soil.* Central Board of National Antiquities, Stockholm.

Golden, Jonathan
2004   Targeting Heritage: The Abuse of Symbolic Sites in Modern Conflicts. In *Marketing Heritage: Archaeology and the Consumption of the Past,* edited by Y. Rowan and U. Baram, pp. 183–202. AltaMira Press, Walnut Creek, Calif.

Hegmon, Michelle
2005   No More Theory Wars: A Response to Moss. *American Antiquity* 70(3):588–90.

Holm, L.
2000   Swedish Cultural Heritage Management: Retrospect and the Current Situation. *Archaeologia Polona* 38:69–86.

Horn, Heinz-Günther, Hansgerd Hellenkemper, Gabriele Isenberg, and Harald Koschik (editors)
2004   *Stadtentwicklung und Archäologie* (Urban development and archaeology). Klartext, Essen.

Howard, Peter
2003   *Heritage: Management, Interpretation, Identity.* Continuum, London and New York.

Hunter, John, and Ian Ralston (editors)
1993   *Archaeological Resource Management in the UK: An Introduction.* Alan Sutton Publishing Ltd., Stroud.

Institute of Field Archaeologists
1999   *By-laws, Standards and Policy Statements of the Institute of Field Archaeologists* [with partial updates in later years]. Institute of Field Archaeologists, Reading.

Jans, Miranda M. E.
2005   Histological Characterisation of Diagenetic Alteration of Archaeological Bone. Institute for Geo- and Bioarchaeology, Free University, Amsterdam.

Kars, Eva A. K., and Henk Kars (editors)
2002   *The Degradation of Bone as an Indicator for the Deterioration of the European Archaeological Property, Final Report.* Rijksdienst voor het Oudheidkundig Bodemonderzoek, Amersfoort.

Kars, Henk
1997   Conservation Science and the Archaeological Property. In *Archaeological Heritage Management in the Netherlands,* edited by W. J. H. Willems, H. Kars, and D. P. Hallewas, pp. 173–91. Van Gorcum, Assen.

Kernd'l, Alfred
2002   Archäologie des 20. Jahrhunderts: Das Beispiel Berlin (Archaeology of the twentieth century: The case of Berlin). In *Menschen, Zeiten, Räume—Archäologie in Deutschland* (Men, times, regions—Archaeology in Germany), edited by W. Menghin, pp. 389–91. Theiss, Stuttgart.

Kobyliński, Zbigniew (editor)

1998   *Ochrona dziedzictwa archeologicznego w Europie* (Protection of the archaeo-
        logical heritage in Europe). Scientific Society of Polish Archaeologist and
        Commissioner General for Historical Monuments, Warsaw. (Most of the texts
        were published in English in 2000 in *Archaeologia Polona* 38).

2001   *Quo vadis archaeologia? Whither European Archaeology in the Twenty-first
        Century*. European Science Foundation/Polish Academy of Sciences, Warsaw.

Kolen, Jan

1995   Recreating (in) Nature, Visiting History: Second Thoughts on Landscape Re-
        serves and Their Role in the Preservation and Experience of the Historic En-
        vironment. *Archaeological Dialogues* 2(2):127–59.

2005   *De biografie van het landschap: Drie essays over landschap, geschiedenis en
        erfgoed* (The biography of landscapes: Three essays on landscape, history, and
        heritage). Ph.D. dissertation, Free University, Amsterdam.

Kristiansen, Kristian

1992   From Romanticism through Antiquarianism to an Historical View of Na-
        ture: The Case of Denmark. In *All Natural Things: Archaeology and the Green
        Debate*, edited by L. Macinnes and C. Wickham-Jones, pp. 52–64. Oxbow, Ox-
        ford.

2001   Borders of Ignorance: Research Communities and Language. In *Quo vadis
        archaeologia? Whither European Archaeology in the Twenty-first Century*, ed-
        ited by Z. Kobyliński, pp. 38–43. European Science Foundation/Polish Acad-
        emy of Sciences, Warsaw.

Macinnes, Leslie, and C. Wickham-Jones (editors)

1992   *All Natural Things: Archaeology and the Green Debate*. Oxbow, Oxford.

Magnusson, Å.

2005   An Agenda for the Renewal of Swedish Heritage Management. *Archäologisches
        Korrespondenzblatt* 10:194–98.

Marciniak, Arek

2000   Protection and Management of Archaeological Heritage: The Importance and
        Achievements of the European Association of Archaeologists. *Archaeologia
        Polona* 38:205–14.

Mathers, Clay, Tim Darvill, and Barbara J. Little (editors)

2005   *Heritage of Value, Archaeology of Renown: Reshaping Archaeological Assessment
        and Significance*. University Press of Florida, Gainesville.

McManamon, Francis P., and A. Hatton (editors)

2000   *Cultural Resource Management in Contemporary Society*. Routledge, London.

Moss, Madonna L.

2005   Rifts in the Theoretical Landscape of Archaeology in the United States: A
        Comment on Hegmon and Watkins. *American Antiquity* 70(3):581–87.

Neustupný, Evzen

1998   Mainstreams and Minorities in Archaeology. *Archaeologia Polona*
        35–36:13–23.

O'Sullivan, Jerry (editor)
2003   *Archaeology and the National Roads Authority.* National Roads Authority, Dublin.
Pickard, Robert
2002   *European Cultural Heritage.* Volume II, *A Review of Policies and Practice.* Council of Europe Publishing, Strasbourg.
Prieur, M.
2002   Legal Provisions for Cultural Landscape Protection in Europe. In *Cultural Landscapes: The Challenges of Conservation*, World Heritage Papers 7, edited by P. Ceccarelli and M. Rössler, pp. 150–55. UNESCO World Heritage Centre, Paris.
Ramsar Convention
2004   *The Ramsar Convention Manual: A Guide to the Convention on Wetlands* (Ramsar, Iran, 1971). 3rd ed. Ramsar Convention, Gland.
Säfvestad, Ulf
2004   Preface. In *Stone Age Scania: Significant Places Dug and Read by Contract Archaeology*, edited by M. Andersson, P. Karsten, B. Knarreström, and M. Svensson, pp. 5–6. National Heritage Board, Lund, Sweden.
Schadla-Hall, Tim
2004   The Comforts of Unreason: The Importance and Relevance of Alternative Archaeology. In *Public Archaeology*, edited by N. Merriman, pp. 255–71. Routledge, London and New York.
Schofield, John (editor)
1998   *Monuments of War: The Evaluation, Recording and Management of Twentieth-Century Military Sites.* English Heritage, London.
Skeates, R.
2000   *Debating the Archaeological Heritage.* Duckworth, London.
Thomas, Roger
2002   Comment on *Rescue Archaeology, the French Way*, by Jean-Paul Demoule. *Public Archaeology* 2:236–38.
Verband der Landesarchäologen in der Bundesrepublik Deutschland
1994   *Archäologische Denkmalpflege und Grabungsfirmen: Kolloquium im Rahmen der Jahrestagung 1993, Bruchsal, 10.-13. Mai 1993* (Archaeological heritage management and commercial archaeology: Colloqui at the annual meeting 1993, Bruchsal, May 10–13, 1993). Landesdenkmalamt Baden-Württemberg, Stuttgart.
Weber, R.
2001   Role of Heritage in a Changing Europe. In *Forward Planning: The Function of Cultural Heritage in a Changing Europe*, edited by the Council of Europe, pp. 5–7. Council of Europe Publishing, Strasbourg.
Willems, Willem J. H.
1997   Archaeological Heritage Management in the Netherlands: Past, Present and Future. In *Archaeological Heritage Management in the Netherlands*, edited by W. J. H. Willems, H. Kars, and D. P. Hallewas, pp. 3–34. Amersfoort, Assen

1999   *The Future of European Archaeology.* Oxbow, Oxford.
2001   Archaeological Heritage Management and Research. In *Quo vadis archaeologia? Whither European Archaeology in the Twenty-first Century*, edited by Z. Kobyliński, pp. 83–91. European Science Foundation/Polish Academy of Sciences, Warsaw.
2002   The Role of Archaeological Societies in Preserving Cultural Memorials. In *Encyclopedia of Life Support Systems, Social Sciences and Humanities, Archaeology, Preserving Archaeological Sites and Monuments.* UNESCO/EOLSS, Oxford. Electronic document, http://www.eolss.net, accessed September 16, 2009.
Willems, Willem J. H. (editor)
2000   *Challenges for European Archaeology.* Ministry of Culture, The Hague.
Willems, Willem J. H., and Roel W. Brandt
2004   *Dutch Archaeology Quality Standard.* Rijksinspectie voor de Archeologie, Den Haag, Amsterdam.
Willems, Willem J. H., and Monique H. van den Dries (editors)
2007   *Quality Management in Archaeology.* Oxbow Books, Oxford.
Yates, Brian
2005   Review of F. Gerritsen, *Local Identities, Landscape and Community in the Late Prehistoric Meuse-Demer-Scheldt Region, CRM. The Journal of Heritage Stewardship* 2(2):133–34.

17

Cultural Heritage in the Global Policy Arena

Issues, Institutions, and Resources in the Policy Mix

WILLIAM H. JANSEN II

Recent gatherings focused on cultural heritage issues have highlighted both the compelling need to consider current archaeological issues on a global stage and to recognize the increasingly complex array of factors that will ultimately affect the success of preserving the world's cultural heritage in the face of enormous pressures (for example, see Smith et al. 2004, as well as the introduction to this volume). The international policy environment is a crucial part of the global arena that currently affects the conduct of cultural heritage preservation internationally and will continue to do so in the future.

To date, much of the international policy dialogue for the cause of cultural heritage preservation has been focused in a relatively limited arena that is most influenced by the United Nations Educational, Scientific and Cultural Organization (UNESCO). The broadest policy issues on the global stage tend to be influenced by such sweeping topics as poverty reduction, economic growth, the war on terrorism, expanding democracy, HIV/AIDS, and child survival.

On such a global policy stage, cultural heritage may not, at first glance, loom large among the issues competing for international policy attention. The big multinational organizations play major roles in the establishment of the international policy agenda, and the financial might of these large organizations can determine the weight that specific issues receive in international dialogue. Ultimately, financial resources become an important indicator of the seriousness with which specific policy issues are addressed as well as the durability of an issue over time. Historically, the finances available in the international arena for cultural heritage issues have been quite modest.

Nevertheless, cultural heritage issues have been receiving increasing attention and there now are new opportunities for raising the policy profile of cultural heritage preservation on the international scene. Cultural resource preservation and management policy issues have tended to fall into two general categories: (1) preservation or protecting a site from harm; and, (2) combining cultural heritage and economic interests (such as cultural resource management and tourism).

Examples of Major Policy Institutions and Current Policy Themes: Institutions Focused Specifically on Cultural Heritage

Arguably, the most consistent force for recurrently raising cultural heritage issues to the international policy forefront has been the United Nations Educational, Scientific and Cultural Organization. The World Heritage Convention of 1972 linked the concepts of nature conservation and the preservation of cultural properties and has guided fundamental policy dialogue on cultural heritage issues in the international arena for more than three decades (United Nations Educational, Scientific and Cultural Organization [UNESCO] 1972). As of October 2006, 184 countries had signed the convention and are listed as participating states in the accord. Interestingly, the concept of nature conservancy and cultural heritage preservation remained linked in this policy forum.

In 1992, UNESCO established the World Heritage Centre, which serves as an action arm within UNESCO for the coordination of the World Heritage Convention. By organizing annual sessions of the World Heritage Committee, the centre plays a lead role in setting significant policy issues related to heritage preservation across the globe. The centre also maintains the World Heritage List, a compendium of cultural and natural properties that are considered the most outstanding heritage sites in need of preservation and protection from an international perspective. In 2007, there were 851 properties on the World Heritage List: 660 cultural properties, 166 natural properties, and 25 mixed natural properties in a total of 141 countries.

General International Institutions Relevant to the Policy Arena

Other players in the international policy arena have equal or even more substantial roles in the process of defining the global issues deserving attention. The international organizations that identify global development issues and priorities generate serious attention from national governments and the global community. Such organizations include the World Bank, the United Nations Development Program (UNDP), and the U.S. Agency for International Development (USAID). These organizations are the custodians of literally billions of dollars of resources and their policies can have major impacts on governmental direction and activities at a national or sub-national level.

These general development organizations, however, rarely have a major policy agenda that specifically identifies cultural heritage preservation as a goal or policy priority. The UNDP, for example, currently focuses its policy direction on the Millennium Development Goals, including "halving extreme poverty, cutting child deaths, providing all of the world's children with an education, rolling back infectious disease and forging a new global partnership to deliver results" (United Nations Development Programme [UNDP] 2005b:1). Typical of the life cycle of policy agendas, the UNDP embarked upon the policy of supporting the Millennium Development Goals in 2000. This policy direction is scheduled to be in effect until 2015, when significant progress toward the goals is anticipated (UNDP 2005a). The Millennium Development Convention in 2000 attracted the signatures of 189 countries and continues to shape general development policies internationally.

The World Bank, as well, is influenced by the Millennium Development Goals. However, the World Bank's annual report of 2004 describes the following themes in its approach to lending: reducing poverty and improving economic management; investing in people; addressing the challenges of sustainable development; revitalizing infrastructure; supporting private sector development; building strong financial systems; and, promoting modern legal and judicial systems (World Bank 2004).

The U.S. Agency for International Development (USAID), in contrast, has a somewhat different policy approach. In 2002, USAID adopted a policy posture to international assistance that is in the U.S. national interest and designed to promote freedom, security, and opportunity (U.S. Agency for International Development [USAID] 2002). The policy interests articulated by USAID at that time focused on promoting democratic governance, driving economic growth, improving people's health, mitigating conflict, providing humanitarian aid, and accounting for private foreign aid (USAID 2002:iv). By 2006, USAID's policy framework for foreign aid had five core goals: promote transformational development; strengthen fragile states; support strategic states; provide humanitarian relief; and address global issues and other special self-sustaining concerns (USAID 2006:4–5). Although differing in language, some of USAID's policy agenda includes similar issues to those on the UNDP's Millennium Development Goals list or the thematic interests of the World Bank.

Even if the general policy agendas of the major international development funding agencies do not list cultural heritage as a specific policy priority, these same organizations can still be active players in the cultural heritage arena, particularly at the national level. Often, cultural heritage activities can emerge under the policy rubric of economic growth or poverty reduction in the big multinational development arena. For example, the UNDP and USAID recently provided funding for a cultural resource management effort with the Palestinian Authority that combined cultural heritage preservation interests with the prospect of developing tourism and related income-generation potential (Abu Aita 2004).

In July 2006, the World Bank produced the Operational Policy (OP 4.11) on Physical Cultural Resources. The objective of this policy is to "avoid or mitigate adverse impacts on physical cultural resources from development projects" that the World Bank finances (World Bank 2006a). As the policy title suggests, the definition of cultural resources is oriented to heritage that has physical form, and to policy specifying that the assessment of risk to cultural resources is to be undertaken within a broader environmental assessment process (see also Fleming and Campbell, this volume).

The World Bank goes further than implementing a "do no harm" policy when it comes to cultural heritage sites. It also has begun tracking specific development projects and lending that contain cultural heritage activities. However, monitoring investments in cultural heritage work is complicated by the fact that a wide variety of projects (urban development, electrification, roads, and so forth) can include a component or activity that finances cultural heritage preservation or management efforts. Often, projects with an orientation to tourism can contain a more direct reference to, and investment in, broader cultural heritage resource management activities than simply avoiding harm.

Resources and Funding Levels as an Expression of Policy Imperatives

Just as important as articulated policy positions or policy interests in the international arena, patterns of allocation of financial resources represent one of the most quantifiable expressions of organizational interest and international priorities for action. When one examines the conceptual leaders of the international cultural heritage policy dialogue, it is quickly evident that the amount of financing controlled by the leading policy agencies is relatively modest.

For example, the total resources approved for UNESCO's main programmatic areas for 2006–2007 totaled about U.S.$762.6 million worldwide. The total resources available for programming at UNESCO include both direct budgetary appropriations and extra budget resources. Of all programmatic resources, about U.S.$87.3 million, or about 11 percent, was slated to support cultural efforts or efforts related to cultural heritage (UNESCO 2006). The remainder of UNESCO's operational budget supports other interests and policy initiatives (see Figure 17.1). The organization's largest dollar-value programs for 2006–2007 were Education and the Natural Sciences, representing about 30 percent and 32 percent, respectively, of the total programmatic resources approved (UNESCO 2006).

Over the period from 2002 to 2006, the portion of UNESCO's direct budget appropriation for its Culture Program area changed little. For the 2002–2003 operational period, the budget appropriated for the Culture Program was U.S.$43.8 million or about 14.3 percent of the total for programs (UNESCO 2002). The same figure for 2006–2007 had grown to around U.S.$50.6 million, a growth in absolute dollars of 15.5 percent. However, the portion of the total programmatic budget shrank slightly to 13.4 percent (UNESCO 2006).

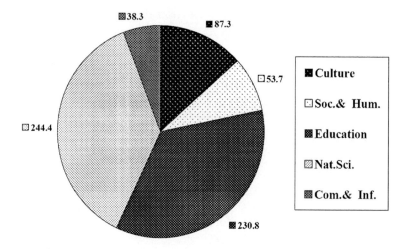

Figure 17.1. Total UNESCO resources (U.S.$ millions) by program. Culture: $87.3M;
Social Sciences and Humanities (Soc & Hum): $53.7M; Education: $230.8M; Natural
Sciences (Nat Sci): $244.4M; Communications and Information (Com & Inf): $38.8M.
Source: UNESCO 2006.

The World Heritage Fund focuses all of its resources on heritage issues; however, its annual operational budget ranges only between U.S.$4 million and $8
million per year. Financing from the World Heritage Fund for a specific initiative can reach as much as U.S.$200,000, but more commonly such financing is
in the range of U.S.$15,000 to $80,000 (World Heritage Committee 2006; World
Heritage Fund 2002). The fund distributes its resources across a number of regions of the world (see Figure 17.2). The regions of Africa and Latin America/
Caribbean consumed about half of the World Heritage Fund's financial allocations for 2002.

By contrast, the annual funding levels of the major international development agencies range in the billions of dollars, giving even minor policy initiatives the potential of being the recipients of relatively large amounts of money.
The UNDP, for example, for the 2004–2005 operational period, expected to
allocate about U.S.$5.9 billion dollars for development initiatives worldwide
(UNDP 2003:12) and U.S.$8.1 billion for 2006–2007 (UNDP 2005c:12). In its
appropriations request to the U.S. Congress for fiscal year 2006, USAID requested around U.S.$9.14 billion for its international efforts—about 50 percent
more than the value of the UNDP's global programs the previous year (USAID
2005).

For total funding and the capacity to martial financial resources behind specific policy initiatives, the World Bank is in a league of its own. During the
period 1996 to 2006, total lending by the World Bank averaged around U.S.$21.4

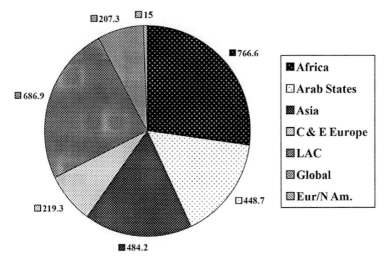

Figure 17.2. World Heritage Fund international assistance (U.S.$ thousands) by region. Africa: $766,600; Arab States: $448,700; Asia: $484,200; Central and Eastern Europe (C & E Europe): $219,300; Latin America and Caribbean (LAC): $686,900; Global: $207,300; Europe and North America (Eur/N Am): $15,000. Source: World Heritage Fund 2002.

billion annually, with a cumulative lending for those 11 years reaching nearly U.S.$235 billion (World Bank 1999, 2000, 2006b). During a similar time frame (1996–2007), the World Bank identified 68 projects that include or included cultural heritage components and involved a direct investment in cultural heritage totaling more than U.S.$782 million (World Bank 2007).

The total direct investment in cultural heritage at the World Bank during the period from 1996 to 2007 represents less than one-third of 1 percent of the total value of the bank's loans for the same time frame. From this pattern, it is clear that the World Bank currently is investing a minute portion of its total development resources in cultural heritage activities. However, even investments of less than 1 percent of the World Bank's annual lending resources represent a sum that is about 10 times the annual budget of the World Heritage Fund and about 1.5 times greater than UNESCO's total cultural program.

Cultural heritage spending at the World Bank is linked to its economic growth or poverty-reduction policy objectives. The main rationale for funding and lending strategies will continue to reflect those general development objectives. Nevertheless, countries in some regions appear to see more frequently economic development or other interests in seeking financial resources linked to cultural heritage issues. For example, during 2003–2004, variations in the relative frequency of cultural heritage themes in World Bank lending appear (see Figure 17.3). Countries in the Middle East and North Africa accounted for 44 percent of the lending related to cultural heritage, followed by East Asia

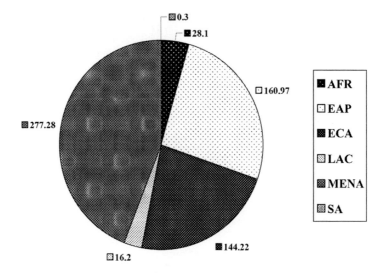

Figure 17.3. Variation of World Bank lending (U.S.$ millions) for cultural heritage by region. Africa (AFR): $28.1M; East Asia and Pacific (EAP): $160.97M; Europe and Central Asia (ECA): $144.22M; Latin America and Caribbean (LAC): $16.2M; Middle East and North Africa (MENA): $277.28M; South Asia (SA): $0.3M. Sources: World Bank 2003; World Bank 2004.

and the Pacific (26 percent), and Europe and Central Asia (23 percent). These regional differences may reflect variations in how much importance national governments place on tourism and the role of cultural heritage sites in developing tourism potential.

Emerging Policy Themes for Cultural Heritage Preservation and Management

The World Heritage Centre and UNESCO have been successful in raising awareness about cultural heritage and promoting the principles of the World Heritage Convention. By 2002, however, the international assistance effort from the centre was at a "turning point" in which the requests from countries for assistance with new sites exceeded the resources available (Phares and Guttman 2002:8–9). Phares and Guttman document that the ability to respond to demands for assistance for heritage sites declined from 30 percent before 1992 to around 16 percent in 2002 (2002:21). Consequently, while country awareness and willingness to do more in cultural resource management has grown, the financial resources within UNESCO and the World Heritage Centre have been unable to meet that demand.

Acknowledging this fact, recent policy issues addressed in the international arena have included how to best expand the resources available to organizations active in cultural heritage. In 2002, a conference by the World Heritage Centre helped identify opportunities to develop new partnerships with civil society and corporations for cultural heritage efforts. Among the suggestions made were the development of public-private partnerships, and the "mainstreaming" of world heritage into the development processes of the World Bank and the United Nations (World Heritage Centre 2003:144).

Among the initiatives being pursued by UNESCO is the building and maintaining of new systems of international cooperation for cultural heritage. Marcio Barbosa calls for new partnerships for heritage conservation that will involve "South-South" (developing country to developing country) cooperation and wider "North-South" (developed country to developing country) relationships that extend beyond traditional donor-recipient agreements (Barbosa 2003:21). The deputy director general of UNESCO envisions involving corporations, research institutions, trust funds, foundations, and individuals in international heritage conservation efforts (Barbosa 2003:21).

Increasingly, cultural heritage preservation is being woven within economic strategies and interests. Yang and Phares, for example, acknowledge the inseparability of heritage preservation and economic development. They outline protocols for including heritage management within poverty-reduction efforts, sustainable tourism, and job-creation interests at even the city level (Yang and Phares 2003:12–14). Nicola Bono, the Italian undersecretary for culture, emphasizes the important role that countries and communities can play in identifying sites of heritage significance to indigenous cultures, while also recognizing the importance of linking cultural heritage interests with common interests in tourism, private enterprise, and job creation (Bono 2003:22–23).

Development and economic interests, almost by necessity, are defined by countries and localities within countries. Consequently, the policy issues associated with economic development and cultural heritage are increasingly being defined in terms consistent with the perspectives of national, district, or even city governments. Sharon Sullivan outlines some of the significant advantages of empowering local communities in the cultural heritage management process. To strengthen the policy environment for heritage preservation, she advocates involving all stakeholders and actively addressing the economic and social interests of local communities (Sullivan 2004:54).

With national governments empowered to define the economic growth and poverty-reduction priorities and policies that development agencies (such as the World Bank, USAID and the UNDP) tend to follow in their development financing, country-level and sub-national entities are well placed to play a much more active role in the future international policy arena for cultural heritage preservation. Increasingly, the policies of development agencies need to evolve and become more sophisticated in the ways that cultural heritage preservation is integrated within economic growth policies and programs. The World Bank appears to have progressed further in terms of cultural heritage management issues within the general development setting than USAID or the UNDP. The World Bank's "do no harm" policy, for example, could be replicated in other organizations. However, the World Bank could be and is doing more.

Tracking development spending for cultural heritage at the World Bank is a good start. However, recent meetings hosted by the bank actually invited experts to give presentations to help think expansively about further cultural heritage measures. At a gathering in March 2005, for example, Walter Santagata advocated including development financing that directly supports the revitalization of cultural heritage as part of the existing economic and social systems of interest to the bank and development organizations (Santagata 2005). Michelle Trimarchi presented the concept of culture as having substantial economic impact so that investment in culture is, in effect, an investment in a better economy (Trimarchi 2005). These presentations further the policy rationale that financing cultural heritage preservation and management is not just a related activity that could have an indirect economic benefit. Rather, cultural resource management programs could be a fully qualified, mainstream economic growth investment. If policy thinking progresses along these lines, substantial new resources could become available for cultural heritage work.

Realizing Policy Opportunities and Implications for the Future

With ongoing discussion about what constitutes an economic growth initiative and the growing emphasis internationally on poverty reduction, new opportunities in the international policy dialogue for cultural heritage appear destined to include new linkages between cultural preservation, job creation, and the economic benefits of cultural resource management. Policy advocacy, however, will need to be both at the country level and in the major economic development donor organizations. At the country level, policies will be needed that clearly articulate a place for cultural heritage preservation within the economic growth strategies of national governments. These policies may require refining tourism policies and the role of cultural resource management in long-term plans for tourism over time.

Significant opportunities exist at the country level to rethink national policies related to cultural heritage management and longer-term national economic growth interests. Hamdan Taha provides a recent example from Palestine where, in 2002, the government took steps to combine antiquities functions at the Ministry of Tourism and cultural heritage functions at the Ministry of Culture and created a new government department—the Department of Antiquities and Cultural Heritage (Taha 2004:31–32). In the process of reexamining the role of cultural heritage in the national interest, Palestinian officials found new ways of linking economic development funding being received from USAID and the UNDP to help finance cultural heritage preservation efforts as a contributor to economic growth.

Within international economic development organizations, new policies will be needed to ensure that spending does no harm to known cultural heritage sites. Development organizations will need help from cultural heritage experts to develop policies on financing heritage preservation efforts and also for creating an appropriate cultural resource management policy niche within economic growth or poverty-reduction priorities.

In 2000, the Italian Trust Fund for Culture and Sustainable Development was established at the World Bank to "assist the Bank in the implementation of initiatives that advance the preservation, promotion and management of cultural assets and enhance cultural heritage related activities in developing countries" (World Bank 2005c:1). Although the fund operates with only about U.S.$4.5 million in assets, it has been successful in drawing investments from other parts of the World Bank for cultural heritage activities and, in the future, may help define new strategies and policies for cultural heritage preservation in the context of development efforts.

New opportunities for technical exchange in cultural resource management will emerge in which agencies with a historically domestic focus (such as the U.S. National Park Service) can provide proven cultural resource management and asset management expertise to the global community. Technical assistance partnerships with countries like Egypt or Tunisia, which have a strong tradition of melding national cultural heritage management programs with a vibrant and important tourism industry, can provide important successful models for combined cultural heritage and economic growth strategies on a national scale.

Another new area of need will be the development of measurement indicators that will help governments and donor organizations know if growing investments in cultural heritage preservation are having the desired impact, both on heritage conservation and on economies. Economists and archaeologists may need to work together to formulate new models for defining policy outcomes that link cultural heritage and economic growth goals.

Conclusion

The most exciting prospect for the future is that cultural heritage conservation interests continue to grow and evolve on the global scene. Perhaps most heartening is the prospect for the wider application of a broader array of internationally available financial resources for the important work of cultural heritage preservation.

To fully realize this potential, cultural heritage and responsible management of cultural resources will need a vibrant and effective advocacy on the stage of world opinion. Advocacy for cultural heritage preservation within the economic development arena, where the financial resources at stake are huge, remains in its early stages. The development of new and evolved heritage policies will be required to take cultural heritage management to the level of global attention that it deserves.

Policy advocacy champions for cultural heritage are still needed within the global policy context. These policy champions will have to be able to communicate convincingly with policymakers, using arguments that can link the issue with economic goals and other programmatic imperatives of broad global concern. To date, cultural resource management professionals have not been effective or significantly present within the policy-formation arena of organizations that wield substantial financial resources. Perhaps, although time will tell, the most effective policy advocates for cultural heritage will be committed and informed laypersons with a cultural resource management perspective who are experienced with the global policy dialogue process and who can champion cultural heritage issues knowledgeably within the policy formation process (Ian Campbell, personal communication, 2007). This means that future advancements of cultural heritage issues within the international policy arena probably will need to be based on active collaboration between cultural heritage and development or other professionals who work within international and multilateral funding organizations.

References Cited

Abu Aita, H. E. Mitri
2004   Guest Column. *Focus* (United Nations Development Program, Jerusalem) 1:3.
Barbosa, Marcio
2003   Keynote Presentation. In *World Heritage 2002: Shared Legacy, Common Responsibility*. UNESCO World Heritage Centre, Paris.
Bono, Nicola
2003   A National Perspective on World Heritage. In *World Heritage 2002: Shared Legacy, Common Responsibility*. UNESCO World Heritage Centre, Paris.
International Centre for the Study of the Preservation and Restoration of Cultural Property (ICCROM)
2003   *Programme and Budget 2004–2005*. XXIIIrd General Assembly of the International Centre for the Study of the Preservation and Restoration of Cultural Property, Rome.
Phares, Jehanne, and C. Guttman
2002   *Investing in World Heritage: Past Achievements, Future Ambitions; A Guide to*

International Assistance. World Heritage Papers 2. UNESCO World Heritage Centre, Paris.

Santagata, Walter

2005   Material Cultural Heritage and Sustainable Economic Development. Presentation at a World Bank Workshop, World Bank, Washington, D.C.

Smith, George, D. Jones, and T. Wheaton

2004   Working Together: Archaeology in Global Perspective. *International Journal of Heritage Studies* 10(3)(July):321–27.

Sullivan, Sharon

2004   Local Involvement and Traditional Practices in the World Heritage System. In *Linking Universal and Local Values: Managing a Sustainable Future for World Heritage*, edited by E. Merode, R. Smeets, and C. Westrik, pp. 49–55. World Heritage Papers 13. UNESCO World Heritage Centre, Paris.

Taha, Hamdan

2004   Managing Cultural Heritage in Palestine. *Focus* (United Nations Development Program, Jerusalem) 1:30–31.

Trimarchi, Michelle

2005   The Economic Impact of Culture. Presentation at a World Bank Workshop, World Bank, Washington, D.C.

United Nations Development Programme (UNDP)

2003   *UNDP Budget Estimates for the Biennium 2004–2005*. Executive Board of the United Nations Development Programme and of the United Nations Population Fund, New York.

2005a   A *Time for Bold Ambition: Together We Can Cut Poverty in Half*. United Nations Development Programme, New York.

2005b   *International Cooperation at a Crossroads: Aid, Trade and Security; Human Development Report*. United Nations Development Program Annual Report, New York.

2005c   *UNDP Budget Estimates for the Biennium 2006–2007*. Executive Board of the United Nations Development Programme and of the United Nations Population Fund, New York.

United Nations Educational, Scientific and Cultural Organization (UNESCO)

1972   *Convention Concerning the Protection of the World Cultural and Natural Heritage*. UNESCO (Adopted by the General Conference at its Seventeenth Session), Paris.

2002   Approved Programme and Budget, 2002–2003. UNESCO, Paris.

2006   Approved Programme and Budget, 2006–2007. UNESCO, Paris.

U.S. Agency for International Development (USAID)

2002   *Foreign Aid in the National Interest: Promoting Freedom, Security, and Opportunity*. U.S. Agency for International Development, Washington, D.C.

2005   *Congressional Budget Justification FY 2006*. U.S. Agency for International Development, Washington, D.C.

2006   Policy Framework for Bilateral Foreign Aid: Implementing Transformational

Diplomacy through Development. U.S. Agency for International Development, Washington, D.C.

World Bank

1999   Annual Report. World Bank, Washington, D.C.

2000   Annual Report. World Bank, Washington, D.C.

2003   *Culture and the Corporate Priorities of the World Bank: Report on Progress from April 1999 to December 2002.* World Bank, Washington, D.C.

2004   Annual Report. World Bank, Washington, D.C.

2005a   *Management of Cultural Property in Bank-Financed Projects.* World Bank Operational Policy Note no. 11.03. World Bank, Washington, D.C.

2005b   *World Bank Investment in Cultural Heritage and Development: Summaries of Investment Projects under Implementation and in Preparation.* World Bank, Washington, D.C.

2005c   *Italian Trust Fund for Culture and Sustainable Development.* World Bank, Washington, D.C.

2006a   Operational Policies OP 4.11, Physical Cultural Properties. The World Bank Operational Manual. World Bank, Washington, D.C.

2006b   Annual Report. World Bank, Washington, D.C.

2007   Cultural Heritage in Sustainable Development, Cultural Heritage Projects. Electronic document, http://go.worldbank.org/BGVU4HCY30, accessed December 14, 2007.

World Heritage Centre

2003   *World Heritage 2002: Shared Legacy, Common Responsibility.* UNESCO World Heritage Centre, Paris.

World Heritage Committee

2006   *Convention Concerning the Protection of the World Cultural and Natural Heritage.* World Heritage Committee, Thirtieth Session. UNESCO, Paris.

World Heritage Fund

2002   *Provision of International Assistance.* UNESCO, World Heritage Fund, Paris.

Yang, Minja, and J. Phares

2003   Safeguarding and Development of World Heritage Cities. In *Partnerships for World Heritage Cities: Culture as a Vector for Sustainable Urban Development*, pp. 10–14. World Heritage Papers 9. UNESCO World Heritage Centre, Paris.

18

Cultural Heritage and the Development Process

Policies and Performance Standards of the World Bank Group

ARLENE K. FLEMING AND IAN L. CAMPBELL

Public and private sector infrastructure development throughout the world is a multi-trillion dollar industry. The acceleration in pace, volume, and scale of construction projects requires increased attention and rapid action by cultural heritage proponents. In the face of this challenge, individuals, organizations, and institutions responsible for cultural heritage must evolve from mere custodians of the past to become an integral part of the modern construct for socio-economic development and environmental management.

Development in an Environmental Context

The nexus of development and environment was acknowledged and elaborated in pioneering legislation, the National Environmental Policy Act (NEPA), created by the U. S. Congress in 1969 (see Environment, Health and Safety Online 1969). Cultural heritage is included in NEPA's definition of environment, along with biophysical and social factors. The act requires assessments of environmental impacts to be completed prior to authorization of construction projects undertaken on land owned by the U.S. government or financed with government funds. This involves collection and analysis of data by a multidisciplinary team as well as documented consultation with the public and other relevant stakeholders (see also Davis, this volume). The concepts and provisions of NEPA have spread throughout the world.

The relationship between environmental protection and economic development received international attention during the 1980s through the work of the World Commission on Environment and Development (also known as the Brundtland Commission), which promoted the concept of a holistic approach to the management of the planetary environment. The commission's report to the United Nations in 1987, entitled *Our Common Future*, spoke of an environmental "Global Commons," comprising a whole that is larger than the sum of the parts (World Commission on Environment and Development 1987). It advocated sustainable development wherein human activities are undertaken in harmony with the natural environment.

Cultural Heritage in Environmental Impact Assessment

The process of environmental impact assessment (EIA) has gained widespread use as a method for achieving a balance between development and environmental protection at the individual project level. It is designed to determine the geographical area likely to be affected by a project; to identify the biophysical, social, and cultural features within the area; and to assess a proposed project's impact. The EIA investigation thus involves a variety of specialized disciplines and skills in a spatial approach, as a multidisciplinary endeavor to collect, organize, and analyze, as comprehensively as possible, information on human and natural conditions in the designated impact area.

A variety of technical tools are helpful in this spatial analysis, including geographic positioning systems (GPS), geographic information systems (GIS), and remote sensing (RS), as well as a host of other rapidly developing advances in information collection, organization, management, display, and analysis. Detailed maps, surveys, and inventories of spatially defined areas also are important resources. Against this baseline, using various analytical techniques, including computer-based models in order to predict possible impacts such as air pollution and hydrological changes, the anticipated effects of a development project are determined. Steps are then taken in project design and implementation to avoid or mitigate any potentially negative effects.

During the past three decades, EIA has become established in virtually every country of the world. It is required by national laws and regulations, and adopted as a quid pro quo for investment by multilateral and bilateral financing agencies. Harking back to NEPA, and similar legislation in other industrially developed countries, EIA practice and legal provisions usually include cultural heritage together with biophysical and social factors. However, since the advent of EIA in most developing and transition[1] countries was enabled by natural science professionals and newly formed governmental agencies for environmental protection, individuals and institutions responsible for cultural heritage were generally not consulted or included. As a result, in many countries, there is a knowledge and communication gap between environmental and cultural heritage authorities. Hence, the cultural heritage component of EIA often has been treated in a cursory fashion, or even neglected.

The World Bank Group

Since its creation to enable reconstruction following World War II, the World Bank has expanded to become a significant source of financial and technical assistance to the world's developing and transition countries. At present, the World Bank Group has 184 member countries, including donors and borrowers, and consists of 5 entities that collaborate to reduce poverty through loans, credits, guarantees, technical assistance, and a host of other activities. The component organizations of the World Bank Group are the World Bank, which consists of the International Bank for Reconstruction and Development (IBRD) and the International Development Association (IDA); the International Finance Corporation (IFC); the Multilateral Investment Guarantee Agency (MIGA); and the International Centre for Settlement of Investment Disputes (ICSID).

To its credit, the World Bank Group has since 1986 incorporated cultural heritage (also termed cultural property or cultural resources) into its requirements for safeguarding the environment. As described below, two of the entities in the World Bank Group—the World Bank and the IFC—have policies requiring that cultural heritage be included in the EIAs required for investment projects.

The World Bank Operational Policy 4.11—Physical Cultural Resources

The IBRD, founded in 1944, is the oldest of the World Bank Group organizations. Its objective is to reduce poverty in poor and middle-income countries through loans, guarantees, risk management initiatives, and analytic and advisory services. During fiscal year 2006, the IBRD lent U.S.$14.1 billion to 33 countries for 112 new operations. The other component of the World Bank, the IDA, was established in 1960 to serve the 81 poorest countries in the world by providing financing at highly concessional rates. The interest-free credits and grants provided by the IDA are financed through contributions from donor countries and net income transfers from the IBRD. Commitments during fiscal year 2006 totaled U.S.$9.5 billion for 167 operations in 59 countries (World Bank 2006a).

Loans and grants provided by the World Bank to its client countries must comply with the provisions of 11 safeguard policies: Environmental Assessment (which covers the World Bank's EIA requirements), Natural Habitats, Forests, Pest Management, Physical Cultural Resources, Involuntary Resettlement, Indigenous Peoples, Safety of Dams, International Waterways, Disputed Areas, and Use of Country Systems. The policy for cultural heritage, issued in 1986 as Operational Policy Note (OPN) 11.03—Management of Cultural Property in Bank-financed Projects, was actually one of the first, and predated Environmental Assessment (Operational Policy [OP] 4.01) by three years. In April 2006, the World Bank replaced OPN 11.03 with OP 4.11—Physical Cultural Resources, which explicitly states that cultural resources must be a component of Environmental Assessment (see World Bank 2006b).

In formulating the Physical Cultural Resources safeguard policy, the World

Bank conducted extensive consultations in its client countries, with government officials, cultural heritage experts, and representatives of civil society. International cultural heritage organizations and the general public also were consulted, as were staff members of the World Bank. These investigations demonstrated a willingness among the various categories of respondents to include cultural heritage in assessing the environmental impact of development projects, but specific guidance was lacking. A second significant finding was the existence of a gap in communication and knowledge between the environmental protection and cultural heritage authorities in every one of the ten borrowing countries where consultations were held.

This evidence from the consultations stimulated creation of two guidance tools designed to aid in implementation of the World Bank's policy. The first is the Physical Cultural Resources Safeguard Policy Guidebook, which provides instructions for the various categories of professionals who are involved in considering cultural heritage within the EIA process, and examples for applying the policy to different types of projects. The second tool under development is the set of Physical Cultural Resources Country Profiles. Each profile is a compendium of information for a client country of the World Bank. The profile provides an introduction to cultural heritage in the country concerned, including typologies, general locations and inventories, information on administrative and legal management provisions and institutions, and information on professional experts and organizations. It also contains information on environmental laws and regulations, including those for EIA. The guidebook and the profiles together serve to orient World Bank staff, client country personnel, and EIA practitioners to the task of completing the cultural heritage component of EIA for development projects.

The World Bank's Physical Cultural Resources safeguard policy applies only to tangible, or physical, cultural resources, which are defined as movable or immovable objects; sites; structures; and groups of structures and natural features and landscapes that have archaeological, palaeontological, historical, architectural, religious, aesthetic, or other cultural significance. They may be located in urban or rural settings, and they may be above or below ground, or underwater. Their cultural interest may be at the local, provincial, or national level, or within the international community. The policy acknowledges that these resources are important as sources of valuable scientific and historical information, as assets for economic and social development, and as integral parts of a people's cultural identity and practices.

The objective of the policy is to help borrowing countries avoid or mitigate adverse impacts on cultural heritage in projects financed by the World Bank, while adhering to the host country's national legislation and its obligations under relevant international environmental treaties and agreements. Incorporating cultural heritage into EIA means that the conventional steps of the EIA process are to be followed in implementing the cultural heritage component. This includes provisions for consultation with stakeholders and disclosure of the EIA report, except where such disclosure would endanger either the resources (for example, revealing the location of unexcavated archaeological material) or individuals with knowledge of the resources.

Instructions for managing cultural heritage during implementation or operation of a project must be included in the project's Environmental Management Plan. Provisions for management of any chance finds, or cultural material uncovered during construction or other project activities, are to be clearly determined in accordance with the country's laws and regulations pertaining to such finds. The policy provides for technical assistance or other means of strengthening a country's capacity to manage cultural resources as required by a specific project, and also indicates the possibility that the World Bank could incorporate broader capacity-building assistance into its country assistance program.

The International Finance Corporation Policy on Social and Environmental Sustainability—Performance Standard 8: Cultural Heritage

The IFC lends to private sector borrowers in contrast to the two entities of the World Bank that finance projects for governments. The IFC provides equity, long-term loans, structured finance, and risk management products, as well as technical assistance and advisory services, to clients operating in regions and countries with limited access to capital. During fiscal year 2006, the IFC committed U.S.$6.7 billion for 284 projects in 66 countries (World Bank 2006a).

In 1998, the IFC adopted a group of environmental and social safeguard policies, which included an adaptation of the World Bank's policy (OPN 11.03), for the management of cultural property. A review of the IFC's policies in 2003 led to revisions and restructuring in order to make them more comprehensive, effective, and relevant to the IFC's business plan, as well as to the needs of its private sector clients. The revision process included extensive international consultations with the IFC's government shareholders, staff, and clients, as well as with civil society organizations and the general public. In February 2006, the IFC adopted its Policy on Social and Environmental Sustainability with eight performance standards designed to help the IFC and its clients manage their social and environmental performances with an outcomes-based approach. The IFC also adopted its Policy on Disclosure of Information in the interest of improved transparency (International Finance Corporation [IFC] 2006a).

The eight performance standards are as follows: (1) Social and Environmental Assessment and Management System; (2) Labor and Working Conditions; (3) Pollution Prevention and Abatement; (4) Community Health, Safety and Security; (5) Land Acquisition and Involuntary Resettlement; (6) Biodiversity

Conservation and Sustainable Natural Resource Management; (7) Indigenous Peoples; and (8) Cultural Heritage (IFC 2006a). The performance standards provide objectives and specific requirements to assist clients in meeting the objectives through measures consistent with the social and environmental risks and impacts of a specific project. Each performance standard has an accompanying guidance note that serves as an aid to implementation and a source of additional information (see IFC Environmental and Social Standards). In addition to providing requirements for projects financed by the IFC, the policy, performance standards, and guidance notes are intended to assist its private sector clients in making their business operations more sustainable.

Performance Standard 8: Cultural Heritage recognizes the importance of cultural heritage for current and future generations, aims to protect it from adverse impacts of development projects, and intends to support its preservation. The standard also promotes the equitable sharing of benefits derived from the use of cultural heritage. Thus, in contrast to the World Bank's safeguard policy for physical cultural resources, the IFC's performance standard covers intangible cultural resources. In this regard, a provision is included for protecting the economic rights of communities in instances where their cultural heritage is appropriated for commercial gain (see IFC 2006b).

In practice, the applicability of Performance Standard 8 is determined during the Social and Environmental Assessment Process. Cultural heritage involved in a project is then managed through the client's Social and Environmental Management System as required by the IFC's Performance Standard 1. Corresponding to the World Bank's OP 4.11, Performance Standard 8 mandates compliance with a country's national law and with relevant international standards; requires consultation with stakeholders, including affected communities; and stipulates that provisions be made for chance finds that may appear during construction. The standard establishes conditions for removal of cultural heritage when absolutely necessary. It also provides instruction on handling "critical cultural heritage," defined as "(i) the internationally recognized heritage of communities who use, or have used within living memory the cultural heritage for long-standing cultural purposes; and (ii) legally protected cultural heritage areas, including those proposed by host governments for such designation" (IFC 2006b).

The Equator Principles and Financial Institutions

As a lender to the private sector, the IFC has ties to commercial banks throughout the world. Acting on a growing imperative to avoid social and environmental damage from development projects, several of the world's leading commercial banks approached the IFC to explore the use of its safeguard policies as a model for the commercial banking industry. This resulted in formulation of the Equator Principles, adopted in 2003 by a group of major financial institutions as voluntary guidelines for the categorization, assessment, and management of social and environmental risks in investment projects.

A new version of the Equator Principles, issued in July 2006, reflects the revised IFC Policy on Social and Environmental Sustainability and the eight performance standards, including the provisions for safeguarding cultural heritage, as well as concerns raised by environmental groups and other nongovernmental organizations (see The Equator Principles 2006). Changes include a lowering of the threshold for applicable projects from U.S.$50 million to U.S.$10 million, adoption of stronger social and environmental standards, and a commitment to periodic reporting. Sixty financial institutions had adopted the Equator Principles as of February 2008. Taken together, these institutions operate in over 100 countries (see The Equator Principles 2006).

A Challenge for Cultural Heritage Professionals

With the inclusion of cultural heritage in their policies for safeguarding the environment, major international financial institutions acknowledge that cultural heritage is a key component of the resource base. This recognition enables heritage institutions and professionals to play an integral role in the development process. It also provides opportunities to vastly augment the inventory of cultural resources through investigations and analyses carried out in EIAs. However, as noted above, there is in many countries a communication gap between the cultural heritage authorities and the environmental protection agency. This is symptomatic of a general lack of awareness on the part of cultural heritage professionals about the EIA process and its critical importance in the preservation and management of cultural heritage. Furthermore, as techniques for identifying and mitigating the biophysical and social impacts of projects increase in sophistication and become progressively mainstreamed into the project development process, there is a danger of the gap widening.

It is thus important for professionals in the field of cultural heritage management to work toward closing this gap by integrating their work more fully into environmental impact assessment and related planning instruments. This should include the wider application of existing analytical tools for safeguarding cultural heritage, the development of new techniques and methodologies, and a closer engagement with the strategic planning process that gives rise to national development project portfolios.

National governments, nongovernmental organizations, academic institutions, and individual cultural heritage professionals throughout the world are at different stages in the process of conceptual reorientation and readiness to manage cultural heritage in the development process. Effective strategies and approaches will vary from country to country depending on many factors, including political, economic, cultural, and social conditions.

Note

1. Transition countries are those countries formerly under Communist governments.

References Cited

Environment, Health and Safety Online
1969   United States National Environmental Policy Act, as amended. Electronic document, http://ehso.com/Laws_NEPA.htm, accessed December 26, 2007.
The Equator Principles: A Benchmark for the Financial Industry to Manage Social and Environmental Issues in Project Financing.
2006   Electronic document, http://www.equator-principles.com/, accessed February 29, 2008.
IFC Environmental and Social Standards
2008   Electronic document, http://www.ifc.org/ifcext/enviro.nsf/Content/EnvSoc-Standards, accessed March 3, 2008.
International Finance Corporation (IFC)
2006a   Policy and Performance Standards on Social and Environmental Sustainability and Policy on Disclosure of Information. April 30. IFC, Washington, D.C.
2006b   IFC Performance Standard 8. International Finance Corporation's Performance Standards on Social and Environmental Sustainability, April 30. Electronic document, http://www.ifc.org/ifcext/enviro.nsf/AttachmentsBy Title/pol_PerformanceStandards2006_PSIntro_HTML/$FILE/PS_Intro.pdf, accessed March 3, 2008.
Mekay, Emad
2006   Finance: Banks Adopt Fortified Green Principles. Inter Press Service Agency, July 6. Electronic document, http://www.ipsnews.net/news.asp?idnews=33890, accessed March 19, 2008.
World Bank
2006a   Annual Report. World Bank, Washington, D.C.
2006b   The World Bank Operational Manual. Electronic document, http://www.worldbank.org/opmanual, accessed December 26, 2007.
World Commission on Environment and Development
1987   *Our Common Future.* Oxford University Press, New York.

19

International Laws, Treaties, and Organizations

PATRICK J. O'KEEFE

Over the past 50 years, the international community has developed a legal framework to preserve the world's cultural resources. This is still very much a work in progress. To date, it has concentrated on tangible heritage—sites, monuments, and objects—and largely ignored the intangible—stories, songs, myths, language, religion—even when these are associated with the former. Moreover, development of the framework is uneven, with certain aspects receiving more attention than others. States, the principal players on the world stage as far as cultural preservation is concerned, do not give this a high priority and often prefer to do as little as possible to fulfill their obligations.

Organizations

The United Nations Educational, Scientific and Cultural Organization (UNESCO) is the main body concerned with the preservation of cultural resources worldwide. It is one of the group of organizations known as the United Nations Specialized Agencies—organizations associated with, but independent of, the United Nations Organization. Culture is listed third in the title and this is the role it occupies in the working of the body, where it is the smallest division—just ahead of social sciences. However, it must be recognized that this is the decision of states. The secretariat may propose budgets and programs, but it is the states that decide what funds will be voted and how they are to be allocated. Of course, the secretariat has great power in that it is represented by one person—the director general—while the states are split into various power groups with their own agendas.

The UNESCO framework for preserving cultural resources consists of conventions and standard-setting recommendations.[1] The former are international legal instruments carrying rights and obligations for those states that become party to them. The latter have little legal weight—states should observe their requirements and report to the general conference of UNESCO at regular intervals on action taken to implement them. Recommendations have a value to nongovernmental organizations and individuals who, concerned at the action of a governmental authority, can contact the UNESCO secretariat to complain. The secretariat can then bring a relevant recommendation to the attention of the authority who may then be prepared to take it into account when establishing policy or taking specific action.

States members of UNESCO have adopted the following conventions (numbers of states parties to each convention are listed as of October 2009):

- Convention on the Protection of Cultural Property in the Event of Armed Conflict 1954 (123 states parties—"Hague Convention") together with two protocols of 1954 (100 states parties) and 1999 (55 states parties) respectively;
- Convention on the Means of Prohibiting and Preventing the Illicit Import, Export and Transfer of Ownership of Cultural Property 1970 (118 states parties—"1970 Convention");
- Convention Concerning the Protection of the World Cultural and Natural Heritage 1972 (186 states parties—"World Heritage Convention");
- Convention on the Protection of the Underwater Cultural Heritage 2001 (26 states parties—"Underwater Convention");
- Convention on the Safeguarding of the Intangible Cultural Heritage 2003 (116 states parties—"Intangibles Convention"); and
- Convention on the Protection and Promotion of the Diversity of Cultural Expressions 2005 (103 states parties—"Cultural Expressions Convention").

A number of UNESCO's recommendations deserve special mention in the current context:

- Recommendation on International Principles Applicable to Archaeological Excavations 1956;
- Recommendation Concerning the Safeguarding of the Beauty and Character of Landscapes and Sites 1962;
- Recommendation Concerning the Preservation of Cultural Property Endangered by Public or Private Works 1968;
- Recommendation Concerning the Protection at National Level of the Cultural and Natural Heritage 1972; and
- Recommendation Concerning the Safeguarding and Contemporary Role of Historic Areas 1976.[2]

The role of UNESCO in promoting these instruments has been challenged. For example, during negotiations on the Underwater Convention, Norway reserved its position as to whether UNESCO was the appropriate forum for negotiation and adoption of the convention. It would have liked the negotiations removed to the United Nations in New York, presumably on the grounds that there the law of the sea arguments would be more likely to prevail. However, it was difficult to see the real basis for Norway's objections. In June 2005, during the negotiations of governmental experts on what was to become the Cultural Expressions Convention, the delegation of the United States of America walked out of the concluding speech of the meeting's chairman. The delegation stated, "The draft Convention produced by this Working Group is deeply flawed and fundamentally incompatible with UNESCO's constitutional obligation to promote the free flow of ideas by word and image." The United States took the view that the draft convention was about trade and not culture.

The conventions of UNESCO are public law instruments in that they deal with their subjects on an inter-state level. It was felt that there should be a convention that allowed action for recovery of stolen objects at the private level. Thus, UNESCO requested the International Institute for the Unification of Private Law (UNIDROIT) to draft such an instrument. The resulting UNIDROIT Convention (Convention on Stolen or Illegally Exported Cultural Objects 1995 [29 states parties—"UNIDROIT Convention"]) is regarded as complementary to the Convention of 1970.[3]

The United Nations Organization has produced resolutions on restitution of cultural property for many years, but its most important one is Resolution 1483 of May 22, 2003, which includes a paragraph requiring states to take appropriate steps to facilitate the return of cultural property to Iraq. This has been implemented by legislation in states such as Australia, Switzerland, the United Kingdom, and the United States.

The most important regional organization involved in matters of resource preservation is the Council of Europe. This body is responsible for promoting the cultural development of Europe along with economic and social progress. It has produced some significant conventions in the field of cultural resource preservation:

- European Cultural Convention 1954 (49 states parties);
- European Convention on Protection of the Archaeological Heritage (revised) 1992 (35 states parties—"European Archaeological Convention");
- European Landscapes Convention 2000 (25 states parties—"Landscapes Convention"); and
- Council of Europe Framework Convention on the Value of Cultural Heritage for Society 2005 (1 state party; needs 10 to come into force—"Framework Convention").[4]

The Parliamentary Assembly of the Council of Europe has also produced a number of recommendations addressed to the Committee of Ministers indicating desirable action on specific matters. Among these are

- Underwater Cultural Heritage 1978;
- Metal Detectors and Archaeology 1981;

- Protecting the Cultural Heritage Against Disasters 1986;
- International Protection of Cultural Property and the Circulation of Works of Art 1988;
- Maritime and Fluvial Cultural Heritage 2000; and
- Tax Incentives for Cultural Heritage Conservation 2003.

The Committee of Ministers has also issued recommendations addressed to member states. Of significance in the present context is Recommendation No. R(98)4 on Measures to Promote the Integrated Conservation of Historic Complexes Composed of Immoveable and Moveable Property

The European Union, until recently not particularly involved in cultural resources preservation, has produced a directive (93/7/EEC of March 15, 1993) titled The Return of Cultural Objects Unlawfully Removed from the Territory of a Member State and a regulation (No. 3911/92) titled The Export of Cultural Goods. These are legally binding on member states and must be implemented in local law.

Shaping Cultural Resource Preservation

There is no room here to discuss all the ways in which cultural resource preservation is shaped by the above conventions, recommendations, resolutions, and regulations. Certain aspects have been selected and the impact on them of some of the international instruments will be examined.

Archaeology Underwater and in the Development Process

The two instruments most directly relevant to archaeology are the Revised European Convention and the Underwater Convention. Part of the latter consists of an annex setting out "Rules Concerning Activities Directed at Underwater Cultural Heritage." This is an integral part of the convention and thus has the same standing in international law. The original draft was done by the International Council on Monuments and Sites (ICOMOS), but was renegotiated by governmental experts to be part of the convention.

Both instruments state that archaeological sites should be preserved in situ. This is not an inflexible rule. Rule 1 of the annex to the Underwater Convention requires in situ preservation to be considered "as the first option." States party to the European Archaeological Convention must make provision, as circumstances demand, "for the conservation and maintenance of the archaeological heritage, preferably in situ." They must also undertake to conserve "in situ when feasible" elements of the archaeological heritage found during developmental work. It is obvious that public policy as represented by these two instruments favors in situ preservation.

The major reason for revising the European Archaeological Convention in

1992 was to ensure that there was an archaeological input into the developmental planning process from the very beginning—that archaeologists not be consulted only when something was found. States parties have to ensure that archaeologists and town and regional planners work together in a systematic way to modify developmental plans where necessary and to allow time and resources for study of the site and publication of the results. Where activities incidentally affect the underwater cultural heritage, states parties to the Underwater Convention must use the best practicable means at their disposal to prevent or mitigate adverse effects.

Both of these instruments require states parties to take certain measures to ensure that archaeological work does not adversely affect the heritage. For example, both state that non-destructive techniques must be used whenever possible. Both deal with the vexed issue of publication. The European Archaeological Convention requires the production of surveys, inventories, and maps, as well as "a publishable scientific summary record before the necessary comprehensive publication of specialized studies." The annex to the Underwater Convention states that interim and final reports shall be made available according to a timetable established at the commencement of the project and that a final synthesis shall be made public as soon as possible.

Archaeology in Occupied Territory

Recent years have seen a number of situations where territory of one state has been occupied by the armed forces of another. Two long-standing occupations are those of Northern Cyprus and the West Bank of Palestine. Can the occupying state conduct archaeological survey and/or excavation in the occupied territory? This question was addressed in UNESCO's recommendation of 1956, which said that states should refrain from any excavations, and that any chance finds should be handed over to the authorities of the territory at the termination of hostilities.

The matter was taken up again in the Second Protocol to the Hague Convention in 1999. Under article 9, states parties that are in occupation must prohibit and prevent any archaeological excavation "save where this is strictly required to safeguard, record or preserve cultural property." Also to be prohibited and prevented is "any alteration to, or change of use of, cultural property which is intended to conceal or destroy cultural, historical or scientific evidence." Public policy is clearly to stop states in occupation from conducting archaeological excavations. It would seem that less intrusive activities such as surveying and photography would be permitted.

Site Preservation

The goal of preserving sites obviously underlies many of the provisions of the European Archaeological Convention and the Underwater Convention. It is also inherent in other international instruments such as the World Heritage Convention. In general, the latter applies to monuments, groups of buildings, and sites of outstanding universal value. The duties of states under this convention are set out in broad terms. For example, states have a "duty of ensuring the identification, protection, conservation, presentation and transmission to future generations of the cultural and natural heritage." Some have argued that the convention is too vague to create legal obligations on the part of states. However, this was rejected by the High Court of Australia in *Commonwealth v. Tasmania* (see Commonwealth of Australia 1983).

Here the Commonwealth of Australia was attempting to use powers derived from the World Heritage Convention in order to override action by the government of the state of Tasmania in constructing a dam that would have destroyed significant natural areas but also Aboriginal habitation sites of great antiquity. A majority of the judges held that the convention imposed an obligation on Australia, as a state party, to take effective and active measures for the protection, conservation, presentation, and transmission to future generations of its cultural and natural heritage, "including the taking of legal measures to this end." One of the judges, Anthony Mason, said, "Unless one is to take the view that over 70 nations have engaged in the solemn and cynical farce of using words such as 'obligation' and 'duty' where neither was intended or undertaken, the provisions of the Convention impose real and identifiable obligations and provide for the availability of real benefits" (see Commonwealth of Australia 1983).

The World Heritage Convention establishes a list on which are placed monuments, groups of buildings, and sites of outstanding universal value. As part of the process of inscribing one of these on the list, the state on whose territory it lies should show that a management plan is in place to provide for its preservation. There have been exceptions such as in the case of Angkor in Cambodia, but in general there is compliance. This has more immediate effect than the very general provisions of the convention provided that states do actually implement the requirements of the management plan and keep it up to date.

The definition of "sites" in the World Heritage Convention refers to "the combined works of nature and of man." From this has evolved for the purposes of the convention the concept of "cultural landscape," which, according to the operational guidelines, consists of three categories: those defined and intentionally created by man, those that have evolved organically, and those that have an associative nature. The European Landscape Convention goes further and refers to an area "perceived by people, whose character is the result of the action and interaction of natural and/or human factors" (article 1). But in both contexts the intent is to preserve significant areas involving cultural resources.

Illicit Traffic

Theft and smuggling of cultural heritage items often damages them and the cultural record. Smuggling in many cases flows from clandestine excavation, which, by its very nature, destroys context as well as objects already damaged or those with little or no commercial value. Encompassed within the general term of illicit traffic, this activity is seen as a major threat to preservation of cultural resources.

The United Nations Educational, Scientific and Cultural Organization has tried to fight illicit traffic with its Convention of 1970. This was the culmination of a process that began during the period between the two world wars when a convention was drafted in the context of the League of Nations but was halted by the advent of war. Unfortunately, acceptance of the convention by the major art market states has been slow in coming, although recent years have seen acceptance by states such as Japan, Sweden, Switzerland, and the United Kingdom. It is under active consideration in Belgium and Germany, to name but two. However, there are significant differences in how states have implemented the convention.

Objects stolen from "a museum or a religious or secular public monument or similar institution" are to be prohibited entry into a state party, provided the object is "documented as appertaining to the inventory of that institution." There is no problem with states' implementation of this provision. The problem is with the much broader issue of other theft and smuggling in general. The convention provides in article 3 that "the import, export and transfer of ownership of cultural property effected contrary to the provisions adopted under this Convention by the States Parties thereto, shall be illicit." Another provision, article 9, refers to cultural patrimony in jeopardy from pillage of archaeological or ethnological materials. Australia and Canada, in reliance on article 3, have implemented the convention broadly. The United States, in reliance on article 9, has a narrow implementation relying on presidential declarations and additional bilateral agreements. However, all three countries will take action on behalf of a foreign claimant. In contrast, Switzerland, in its legislation of 2003 implementing the convention, also requires bilateral agreements with other states. Japan has a much more restricted implementation. Indeed, it must be questioned whether Japan has effectively become party to the convention. Its law of 2002 really only applies to objects stolen from a museum or similar institution as described above, and then only when Japanese authorities are notified before the objects enter Japan.

The public policy underlying the UNIDROIT Convention of 1995 is quite clear: "The possessor of a cultural object which has been stolen shall return it." Moreover, "a cultural object which has been unlawfully excavated or lawfully excavated but unlawfully retained shall be considered stolen" provided this is consistent with the law of the state where the excavation took place. This makes clear a situation that has been much debated in international law circles particularly as it appertains to the United States. Private persons can use these provisions of the convention to claim stolen objects—a great advantage when the state refuses to take action because of matters that may be entirely unconnected with the claim. The convention also permits a state party to claim, in the courts of another state party, a cultural object that has been unlawfully exported. The court has to return the object if the claimant state establishes one or more of four specified grounds or, more generally, "that the object is of significant cultural importance for the requesting state."

Intangible Heritage

Intangible heritage can be closely tied to the preservation of cultural resources. There may be a connection between myth and a site, between religion and a monument, between song and a building. The United Nations Educational, Scientific and Cultural Organization has attempted to deal with this aspect of the heritage in its Intangibles Convention, but that, in the opinion of many people, is flawed since it contains little in the way of duties or obligations on the part of states members. Work being done in the World Intellectual Property Organization may have a more successful outcome, but that organization is limited by its constitution to matters of intellectual property.

The definition of intangible cultural heritage in the Intangibles Convention is complex and is not really a definition, consisting as it does of part description. To come within the terms of the convention, intangible cultural heritage must be compatible with international human rights "as well as with the requirements of mutual respect among communities, groups and individuals, and of sustainable development." The convention requires the establishment of the Representative List of the Intangible Cultural Heritage of Humanity. The purpose of this list is to ensure better visibility of intangible cultural heritage and awareness of its significance, as well as to encourage dialogue that respects cultural diversity. This is a laudable objective, but hardly one requiring an international convention to achieve.

Historic Complexes

The Council of Europe is the only international organization that has tried to deal specifically with the relationship between a structure and its contents where there is a heritage value in the relationship itself exceeding the individual values. In the case of industrial archaeology, for example, the value of discarded machinery may be enhanced if the place where it worked is still in existence and the connection can be maintained. In its recommendation on the matter, the Council of Europe sought to encourage owners to maintain that connection by various incentives, including tax exemptions.

The issue is controversial as it inhibits the ability of an owner to dispose of movable property. This is particularly significant in those jurisdictions where the eldest son inherits the immovable property and only the movable may be distributed among other children. It can result in one child inheriting an empty building. Where the family wants to maintain the connection between the building and the furniture, for example, some children have to forgo their right of possession. The situation becomes more complex as generation follows generation.

Conclusion

International conventions, recommendations, and resolutions on preservation of cultural resources are not just for lawyers. All of these documents represent a considerable investment by states in terms of time and money. They cannot be lightly dismissed. They are often the result of lengthy debate and hard fought compromises. They provide a guide to how states view various matters and what they are likely to accept if proposals on public policy are put forward. The information is there, but principles in terms of public policy have to be extracted from the texts, the process that led to adoption, and what has happened since.

Notes

1. There are also instruments such as declarations and guidelines that are significant in interpreting the law and applying it in practice.

2. The text of all of these instruments can be found at United Nations Educational, Scientific and Cultural Organization, http://portal.unesco.org/en/ev.php-URL_ID=12024&URL_DO=DO_TOPIC&URL_SECTION=201.html.

3. The text is available at International Institute for the Unification of Private Law [UNIDROIT] 1995.

4. Texts are available at Council of Europe, Complete list of the Council of Europe's treaties.

References Cited

Brown, Michael
2005   Heritage Trouble: Recent Work on the Protection of Intangible Cultural Property. *International Journal of Cultural Property* 12(1):40–61.
Chamberlain, Kevin
2004   *War and Cultural Heritage*. Institute of Art and Law, Leicester.
Commonwealth of Australia
1983   *Commonwealth v. Tasmania* (The Tasmanian Dam Case), 158 CLR 1, 46 ALR 625. Electronic document, http://law.ato.gov.au/atolaw/view.htm?DocID=JUD%2F158CLR1%2F00004, accessed April 18, 2009.

Council of Europe
2009   Complete list of the Council of Europe's treaties. Electronic document, http://
        conventions.coe.int/Treaty/Commun/ListeTraites.asp?CM=8&CL=ENG, ac-
        cessed April 18, 2009.
International Institute for the Unification of Private Law (UNIDROIT)
1995   Convention on Stolen or Illegally Exported Cultural Objects (Rome). Elec-
        tronic document, http://www.unidroit.org/english/conventions/1995cultural
        property/main.htm, accessed April 18, 2009.
Musitelli, Jean
2002   World Heritage, between Universalism and Globalization. *International
        Journal of Cultural Property* 11(2):323–36.
O'Keefe, Patrick
1997   *Trade in Antiquities: Reducing Destruction and Theft.* UNESCO Publishing,
        Paris; Archetype Publications, London.
2002   *Shipwrecked Heritage: A Commentary on the UNESCO Convention on
        Underwater Cultural Heritage.* Institute of Art and Law, Leicester.
2007   *Commentary on the UNESCO 1970 Convention on Illicit Traffic.* 2nd ed. Insti-
        tute of Art and Law, Builth Wells, Wales.
Prott, Lyndel
1997   *Commentary on the UNIDROIT Convention.* Institute of Art and Law, Leices-
        ter.
United Nations Educational, Scientific and Cultural Organization (UNESCO)
2009   Standard-Setting Instruments. Electronic document, http://portal.unesco.org/
        en/ev.php-URL_ID=12024&URL_DO=DO_TOPIC&URL_SECTION=201.
        html, accessed April 18, 2009.
Voon, Tania
2006   UNESCO and WTO: A Clash of Cultures. *International & Comparative Law
        Quarterly* 55(3):635–52.

20

Archaeological Looting and Economic Justice

NEIL BRODIE

The Problem

The illegal and destructive appropriation and trade of archaeological heritage is a well-documented phenomenon. It causes economic loss and cultural dislocation for the dispossessed "source" communities and countries, balanced by corresponding economic and cultural gains for the acquiring communities and countries. States and international NGOs have developed legal and other normative instruments aimed at controlling the trade, and relevant professional bodies are beginning to explore the ethical dimension. Nevertheless, laws and ethics have fallen short of their purpose, and the problem persists. The design of more appropriate legal and ethical responses is hampered by a poorly developed conceptual framework (with an imprecise terminology to match) founded upon a patchy evidence base of uncertain reliability. There is an urgent need for more empirical research and some innovative theoretical input.

The problem can be theorized as one of value. There are various stakeholder interests in archaeological heritage: the interests of those who trade in it, those who study it, those who collect it, and those who have a religious, ethnic, or other attachment to it. These interests give rise to the differently constructed composites of cultural (symbolic, spiritual, aesthetic, educational) and economic value that are assigned to heritage (Lipe 1984; Throsby 2001:28–29) and expressed as sometimes contradictory claims for property rights.

Recent research into what has been called subsistence digging has drawn attention to the economic value of archaeological heritage and emphasized the economic interest of all stakeholders, even though that interest is sometimes obscured or denied. The economic value of archaeological heritage is also being exploited through cultural tourism and has provided the incentive for some recent traveling museum exhibitions. Yet despite these manifestations, existing ethical and legal approaches to the protection of archaeological heritage overlook or ignore its economic dimension, and this might be one reason why they have not been totally effective. In view of this possibility, this chapter will investigate the economic value of archaeological heritage and make some tentative suggestions as to how it might be utilized in such a way as to improve the current protective regime.

Subsistence Digging

The term "subsistence digging" was introduced by Staley (1993) in his study of St. Lawrence Islanders and is used to describe the undocumented and usually illegal[1] excavation of artifacts from archaeological sites that are then sold for subsistence purposes (Hollowell 2006a, 2006b; Matsuda 1998, 2005). Any effort to stop such digging in order to maintain the integrity of archaeological sites can then be construed as valuing archaeological heritage over human life. Meanwhile, cultural "specialists," whether they be administrators, lawyers, archaeologists, museum curators, or art historians, may also derive economic benefit from their legitimate access to archaeological heritage while at the same time ignoring or denying its economic value, a point not lost on subsistence diggers (Barkan 2002:35; Matsuda 1998:93; Rao and Walton 2004:21). Thus it is argued that the characterization of subsistence digging as "looting" criminalizes what are already deprived communities, and subsistence diggers should instead be regarded as legitimate stakeholders in archaeological heritage. In fact, in situations of extreme poverty the digging and selling of artifacts might even be construed as a human right, as was debated at the World Archaeological Congress in 2003 (Hollowell 2006a:73–74).

The financial returns from subsistence digging can be significant. It has been estimated, for example, that the hypothetical sale of all artifacts that might be obtained from Roman-Byzantine tombs in northern Jordan would raise in total U.S.$10–18 million (Rose and Burke 2004:8). The sale of material from Bronze-Age tombs would add to this figure. It is important to remember, however, that this is a total figure and not an annual one, so that if the tombs were emptied over a ten-year period, for example, they would generate U.S.$1–2 million worth of artifacts annually. Recent work on St. Lawrence Island has suggested that digging generates U.S.$1.5 million per year for the island, or about U.S.$1,000 per person (Hollowell 2006b:105). These sums are substantial and go a long way to explaining the prevalence of subsistence digging and illicit trade. Nevertheless, though substantial, they are finite, limited by the facts that eventually the sites are worked out and the artifacts are exported.

The argument in favor of subsistence digging is one of economic justice, but subsistence digging is not an equitable enterprise, nor is it a long-term solution to economic deprivation. Subsistence diggers typically receive only a small portion of the final sales price of an object and the income is not sustainable. Atwood (2004:36) talks of the "neglected, embittered communities" in Peru, where now "there is nothing to show for it except tales of a few looters who struck it rich, bought a fancy pick-up, and moved out of town."

Economic Value

Economic value is usually held apart from cultural value, not because it is not a cultural value, but because economists have developed sophisticated techniques of measuring it. Thus economic value has the appearance of being an objective or at least quantitative attribute, as opposed to the apparently more subjective and qualitative cultural values (Mason 2002:12, 15). The economic value of archaeological heritage derives from its conjunct private and public utility, which means that the economic value of its cultural content can be measured directly in financial terms and indirectly by contingent valuation methodologies designed to measure public "willingness-to-pay" (Darvill 1995; Mason 2002).

There is a growing literature on the economic importance of archaeological heritage and of decisions that relate to the heritage's definition, conservation, and use. Most work to date, however, has focused on public utility in situations where the economic outcomes (costs and benefits) of archaeological projects are contained within a single economic domain (for example, a country or a municipality). The economic assessment of projects carried out across economic domains, whether officially in source countries by archaeologists from acquiring countries, or illicitly to provide artifacts for the international market, is more complex for two reasons: first, because the artifacts present in an unplundered archaeological site have value as commodities and can be bought and sold, but they also have asset value because of the flow of services that they may generate; and second, because the costs and benefits of exploitation are distributed transnationally but unequally among the countries involved. Nevertheless, any resolution of the problems posed by looting and subsistence digging will probably need to take account of these broader economic contexts. As a very preliminary step toward providing those contexts, in what follows comparative accounts are provided of what might be the salient economic characteristics of official and illicit excavations, and a provisional assessment is made of the respective economic outcomes for both source and acquiring countries.

The Economics of an Illicit Excavation

When artifacts are taken from a site by unrecorded excavation and sold locally, their value as commodities is realized monetarily. Repeat sales within the same country will generate more money. This money is ultimately derived from acquiring countries abroad, and, as already described, can make a substantial contribution to a source community's economy. The magnitude of the contribution is ultimately limited by the export of material abroad, after which time it is no longer available for transacting within the country of origin. Once in the acquiring countries, artifacts provide long-term economic benefit through their continuing circulation as commodities and also by their curation in museums. In museums, artifacts are taken out of commerce, gathered together, and conserved and displayed, with a view to attracting visitor income and public and private subsidies. In effect, they become a capital resource. They also comprise the subject matter of academic research and of specialist and popular publications, which produce further income streams. These economic benefits are not limited in time so long as the artifacts remain within the acquiring country, and so, in the long term, they can be substantial. Against these benefits must be set the equally long-term costs of storage and curation.

The comparative public utilities of illicit excavations are harder to assess. Research has shown that public utility is positively correlated with income and educational attainment (Mourato and Mazzanti 2002:61), so that a priori it would be expected that consumers in developed acquiring countries would benefit more than those in developing source countries. Art museums have public utility in acquiring countries. In source countries, archaeological sites and monuments that have been vandalized or destroyed must have only minimal public utility, if any at all, and the same can be said of artifacts that have been lost through illegal export.

In sum, although in the short term a source country's economy might profit from illicit digging, in the long term the economic benefits are experienced mainly in the acquiring countries. It is one of the inequities of the trade, and one typical of the global economic process, that at the source the economic potential of archaeological heritage is realized through unsustainable commodity production, while in the developed acquiring countries, the durability of artifacts and their accumulation in museums as physical capital generate sustainable economic flows.

The Economics of an Officially Sanctioned Excavation

The situation with archaeological sites in source countries that are legally excavated to a professional standard by foreign archaeologists is harder to assess. In general, all artifacts recovered remain in the source country. Some might be displayed in museums and, together with archaeological monuments and excavated sites that are conserved and presented for public viewing, generate income through tourism. Again, though, many artifacts will remain in storage, and the relative costs of storage are probably higher in source countries than in acquiring countries, because typically source-country museums will be expected to curate all excavation finds, while many museums in acquiring countries will only be curating high-quality objects acquired on the market.

In the acquiring countries, museums derive no direct economic benefit from official excavations abroad, as none of the excavated artifacts will actually be acquired, but academics will be employed and the academic press will thrive. The intellectual product can be marketed through the popular media. There are no empirical studies that have measured the monetary value of these activities, but they are likely to be significant and might outweigh any financial benefits that accrue to the source country from retaining control over the excavated material, particularly when storage costs are taken into account.

Public benefits are probably more equally distributed; the material products of excavation, in the form of revealed architecture and curated artifacts, are available within the source country for public viewing and are able to provide the subject matter of educational programs and media productions. They might also promote social cohesion.

The economic outcomes of official and illicit excavations are provisionally compared in Tables 20.1 and 20.2 under the headings of Sales (sales of artifacts), Visitor (visitor and tourist income), and Academic and media. These comparative tabulations are preliminary at best and are in urgent need of empirical substantiation and quantification, but they do suggest that although any excavation will produce economic benefits for both source and acquiring communities, in the long term those benefits accrue disproportionately in favor of the acquiring communities. In the short term, for the source countries, there is a significant financial gain to be made from illicit digging, though in the long term, the potential economic benefits of official excavation probably outweigh those of illicit excavation. The costs of curating material might be significant, however, and eat into any revenue generated by other means. What confounds this comparison is that within source countries income streams generated through different agen-

Table 20.1. Economic Outcomes of an Illicit Excavation (✓ = benefit; x = cost; size of symbols indicates relative magnitude)

	Acquiring country	Source country
Sales	✓	✓
Visitor	✓ x	
Academic and media	✓	

Table 20.2. Economic Outcomes of an Official Excavation (✓ = benefit; x = cost; size of symbols indicates relative magnitude)

	Acquiring country	Source country
Sales		
Visitor		✓ x
Academic and media	✓	✓

cies benefit different constituencies. The proceeds from illicit excavation flow through the black market, while licit excavations tend to benefit government employees and academics and, more diffusely, the public at large.

Recent thinking in development economics has added another dimension to the problem. Social connectedness (theorized as social capital) has an important role to play in improving public welfare by facilitating flows of information and material. It improves access to markets and employment, and it offers insurance against economic shortfall. It has been argued that the goal of development projects is now moving away from improving material well-being toward inculcating what Rao and Walton (2004:3) term "equality of agency" through initiatives aimed at increasing social capital. The possible uses of archaeological heritage for generating social capital have hardly been explored, though social cohesion was listed above as a possible public benefit of official excavation. Nevertheless, there are projects that, deliberately or not, do seem aimed at increasing social capital. At the site of Kuntur Wasi in northern Peru, for example, an archaeological museum built in 1994 with the participation of local people now acts as a community center and library and forms the focus of a community association. In 1997, the United Nations Development Program drew attention to the political empowerment that had been articulated around the archaeological site and its museum (Onuki 1999, 2007). Thus, while illicit excavation depletes what might be a viable source of economic capital, it might also attenuate social capital.

It is increasingly being argued that it should be an ethical prerogative of good archaeological practice to ensure that the cultural and thus economic value of excavated sites is maximized for public benefit by combining appropriate site conservation and presentation with curation and display of the associated artifacts. There are many successful examples of this type of project, but also of projects that fall short of the ideal. One reason for this failure is that project directors do not always have the expertise and/or resources necessary to conceive and to implement the necessary arrangements. It is easier to attract funding for a project with a recognizable product of intellectual significance (an excavation report) than for associated conservation and educational initiatives that have a less well-defined public utility. The importance of the contingent valuation methodologies described above, however, is that they are quantifiable, and when they are quantified by economists they do provide measures of public utility (defined as economic value) that are finding increasing acceptance. It may well be that if archaeological project proposals itemize economic as well as research outcomes, it will enable funding agencies, particularly those with a development slant, such as the World Bank, to assess more accurately the returns on their investments. Crucially, it might then allow project directors to obtain the necessary funding to enhance the cultural and thus economic value of archaeological sites.

Cultural Property Law

National and international "cultural property" law has grown ad hoc since the nineteenth century. As its name suggests, cultural property law is framed in terms of ownership. It is designed to ensure that objects of cultural importance remain in the exclusive possession and control of their rightful owners, whether private or public.[2] It has taken this form because of the historical circumstances of its formation: to prevent or to rectify the illegal transport of objects by military or market forces.

There is a developing opinion that cultural property law has fallen short of its purpose in that it does not prevent the destruction and depredation of cultural heritage in war or in peace (Lowenthal 2005; Merryman 2005; Nafziger and Paterson 2004; O'Keefe 1997:18; Shapiro 2005:3). Many reasons are given for this shortfall. One reason is poor subscription, as major acquiring countries have not or have only recently acceded to the relevant international conventions (O'Keefe 1997:23). Another reason is poor enforcement of existing laws. Although many states have acceded to the major conventions, and enacted national laws, they have done nothing to enforce them. A major problem is that cultural heritage is usually not a funding priority, so that the resources necessary for effective law enforcement are simply not available (O'Keefe 1997:18–20).

There is also much disagreement about what should be the fundamental philosophy of cultural property law. Although there is a general consensus that the trade in archaeological artifacts as it is presently constituted is inequitable and causing irreversible harm to the archaeological heritage, there is considerable dispute about how best to resolve the problem, whether by placing the trade under what might be characterized as "weak regulation," or under "strong regulation." According to proponents of weak regulation, the apparent failure of cultural property law is due to the simple fact that it tries to place too much control on the international market. They argue that, with the exception of a limited number of exceptional or otherwise significant pieces, most cultural objects should be made freely available for international trade. Free trade would increase the amount of cultural material in circulation, thereby improving public access, and profits generated at the source could be used to protect important cultural sites. The strong regulation perspective is that a free market would not assure an equitable circulation of cultural objects, nor would it increase public access. Instead it would cause a flow of cultural objects into a limited number of acquiring communities. The trade would not be sustainable, any money generated at the source would need to pay for oversight, and none would "trickle down" to site protection. In effect, the debate over regulation is about whether the conservation of archaeological heritage would be best served by public ownership or by private ownership. There is hardly any common ground for constructive dialogue, and with discursive recourse to emotive appeals to "common sense" or "morality," that either betray a personal conceit or are designed to mobilize public and political support, the problem persists.

As far as the economic value of archaeological heritage is concerned, the weak regulation perspective recognizes it, but only in a limited sense, in terms of its commodity value. Weak regulation has nothing to say about the full economic value of heritage and makes no recommendations about how it should be preserved, realized, or apportioned. The strong regulation perspective seems to discount economic value altogether. One way out of this public versus private impasse might be to admit discussion of economic value, in its broadest sense, and this would entail discussion of what alternative property regimes might be available.

What distinguishes cultural property from ordinary property is its designated cultural value, so that the exclusion of economic value from legislative consideration is probably deliberate. Paul Bator, for example, wrote about it in his influential book *The International Trade in Art* (1983). Bator had served as a member of the U.S. delegation that participated in the drafting the United Nations Educational, Scientific and Cultural Organization (UNESCO) Convention of 1970, and he wrote his book in support of the United States ratifying articles 7(b) and 9 of that convention, which it subsequently did as the Convention on Cultural Property Implementation Act (CCPIA) of 1983. Bator acknowledged the public value of art and recognized the economic imbalance of the international trade, specifically noting that "private vendors are highly unlikely to include the social costs of losing national art in their selling price" (1983:27 n. 55). He concluded, however, that world trade generally might be unfair, but to consider the economic dimension alone would be an "incomplete" characterization of the problem. His interest was cultural conservation (Bator 1983:28).

Bator's opinion was probably typical of the time, and it would probably be the same today. In 2004, for example, the International Law Association (ILA) suggested eight draft principles for "cooperation in the mutual protection and transfer of cultural material" (Paterson 2005). The express purpose of these principles is to achieve a compromise between the positions characterized here as weak regulatory and strong regulatory, and thus provide less adversarial methods of dispute resolution (Nafziger and Paterson 2004). Again, however, the principles make no allowance for the economic dimension. It was suggested in their support that "most disputes over cultural property . . . reveal concerns . . . that go beyond those of monetary value" (Paterson 2005:70).

Bator was right that the outcomes of the trade cannot be measured simply in economic terms, and the ILA is correct to say that there are concerns apart from monetary ones, but, equally, the economic value of heritage cannot simply be ignored. When this happens, it becomes a covert value, helping to shape proprietorial attitudes and claims, while at the same time preventing their legitimate expression. This means that disputes over economic access might be obscured and confounded through their negotiation in an inappropriate cultural idiom. It is a curious feature of the literature on subsistence digging, for example, that while the outsider research perspective emphasizes the economic rationale, the diggers themselves are often reported using identity claims to legitimize their actions by describing artifacts as an ancestral bequest (Hollowell 2006b:104; Matsuda 1998:8).

Part of the problem is that cultural property law is anachronistic in terms of its economic context. The UNESCO Convention of 1970 remains the benchmark for cultural property law because it sets out general principles of protection and cultural equity that continue to have contemporary relevance. The recent ratifications by countries such as the United Kingdom and Switzerland have emphasized that, more than 30 years after its adoption, the convention is still a viable and important piece of international legislation. But the convention was drafted in the late 1960s and since then there have been many theoretical advances in developmental and environmental economics that are relevant to archaeological heritage, including some of the concepts and metrics that have been discussed here. For example, although the concept of a public good was described in 1951, it was not until the 1990s that the contingent valuation methodologies used to measure public utility achieved some measure of general acceptance among economists (Throsby 2001:25). The importance of social connectedness was first noted in the 1970s (Douglas and Isherwood 1979:63–65) and later formalized as the concept of social capital (Bourdieu 1997). It is possible that the full economic value of cultural property was not recognized by the convention because at the time it could not be measured. But that is no longer the case.

A Comparative Perspective

Just how or even if economic value should be admitted into cultural property law remain open questions, but there are perhaps legislative lessons to be learned from the United Nations Convention on Biological Diversity (CBD) of 1992, which aims to regulate the intellectual exploitation of animal and plant resources for their genetic content. At first sight, the purpose of the CBD might seem far removed from the issues being discussed here, but at least one expert in the field has included genetic resources under the heading cultural property (Posey 1998:42), and the motivating issue for legislation was again the exploitation of source communities and countries for the economic and sociocultural benefit of the developed world.

The demand for new biological materials developed in the 1980s as pharmaceutical and agricultural companies began to explore the scientific and economic potential of new gene-sequencing technologies. By the 1990s, numerous expeditions around the world were searching (bioprospecting) for previously unknown (to the researchers at least) organisms (Parry 2004:31). Many of these expeditions made use of local or indigenous knowledge to identify and locate suitable material, and concerns were expressed within the scientific community that the one-time monetary payments made to source communities in return for their expertise were out of all proportion to the profits that could be made from the long-term commercial exploitation of genetic information. It was argued that there should be mechanisms in place to ensure that the source communities continued to profit from long-term commercial successes, perhaps through royalty payments (Parry 2004:40). At the same time, it was obvious that successful bioprospecting depended upon the existence and thus conservation of native flora and fauna, even as large areas of land were being made over to agricultural production. Thus conservation and ultimately bioprospecting would require viable economic alternatives to farming (Posey 1998:46), and they could be provided in part by a fairer distribution of commercial income.

It was against this background that the CBD was agreed upon at the United Nations Conference on Environment and Development in 1992. The CBD has three main objectives: the conservation of biodiversity; sustainable use of the components of biodiversity; and sharing the benefits arising from commercial and other utilization of genetic resources in a fair and equitable way. It is not hard to see that these objectives, redefined toward archaeological heritage, would be a desirable component of any new cultural property law.

Experience gained from the legal and ethical regulation of bioprospecting has confirmed that conservation at source is improved by a fair distribution of income. Another important point is that a lot of bioprospecting takes place on land that is communally owned by source communities, and agreements have to be negotiated that will benefit the community, as opposed to individual persons or regional or national governments. By customary law, heritage resources in sub-Saharan Africa, and among indigenous peoples more generally, have been common property, and they cannot be sold or surrendered without communal agreement (Shyllon 1998:105–10). Communal ownership of archaeological artifacts also seems to have been recognized by the U.S. Native American Graves Protection and Repatriation Act of 1990. John Carman has discussed the positive implications of common property regimes for archaeological conservation at some length (Carman 2005:81–99), but it is enough to note here that they offer a "third way" between the polarized opposites of public and private ownership, although communal ownership of resources may be at odds with the presumed public ownership of the national or regional governments (Hayden 2004:120).

Communal ownership has not worked to protect archaeological sites from subsistence digging on St. Lawrence Island. St. Lawrence Island is owned by the Sivaqaq and Savoonga Native Corporations, which allow their members to dig and sell any artifacts they can find, while excluding outsiders (Hollowell

2006b:105). But communal ownership is only one part of the equation. There also needs to be equitable distribution of long-term economic benefit, and in the case of St. Lawrence this does not seem to be happening. Material is sold direct to dealers for one-time payments (Hollowell 2006b:105), and at that point the islanders lose control of economic potential of the material.

Ways Forward

Cultural (including archaeological) tourism has been suggested as one possible solution to the underemployment and deprivation that drives people to dig up saleable artifacts, and seems particularly appropriate in the archaeologically rich areas where illicit excavation and/or subsistence digging is endemic. In theory, cultural tourism is a sustainable strategy of economic exploitation, though there are material and sociocultural costs to be mitigated, and for it to draw people away from digging, any revenues would need to be fairly distributed through the relevant community and not siphoned off by socially or geographically distant authorities.

Nevertheless, in theory, the income derived from cultural tourism might be substantial. The previously mentioned site of Kuntur Wasi—along with sites such as Sipán and Batan Grande—is one of the archaeological sites constituting the archaeology-focused northeastern tourism circuit of Peru. In 2003, the circuit attracted 69,000 foreign tourists and 1.2 million Peruvians, with a projected annual growth of 3 percent. The average length of stay was five days.[3] In 2001 it was estimated that international visitors spent U.S.$119 per day while domestic visitors spent U.S.$19 per day (Goodwin and Nizette 2001). Thus in 2003, the input into the northern Peruvian economy from foreign tourism would have been in the area of U.S.$40 million, with Peruvian visitors adding more. This figure sits well with a rough estimate made in 1999 that archaeological tourism generated U.S.$14 million per year for Chiclayo, the largest town on the circuit (Watson 1999).

In 2000, the International Council of Museums (ICOM) held workshops in Peru and Bolivia in an effort to impose order on the rapidly expanding and, from the museums' point of view, potentially disruptive commercial environment of cultural tourism, and the Charter of Principles for Museums and Cultural Tourism was proposed (International Council of Museums [ICOM] 2000). While reaffirming that a museum is a not-for-profit institution, and that preservation of cultural and natural heritage should take precedence over economic interests, the charter also develops the innovative "economic point of view" that cultural tourism should include "profitability in its economic, social and environmental dimensions" (principle 5), provided that there is local involvement and that socioeconomic benefits are distributed fairly in the community (principle 1). The ICOM charter, perhaps for the first time in the cultural property arena, has broached the issue of fair distribution of economic proceeds. Perhaps it offers a framework that could be developed to guide museums through other commercial involvements.

One involvement might consist of museums in acquiring countries renting material for display from source communities or countries. Loan or exchange agreements as they are presently constituted between museums or other cultural institutions in acquiring countries and those in source countries typically involve material and expertise, but not money (Heilmeyer 1997). For museums in acquiring countries, borrowing material for display eliminates the need to acquire material on the market, and presumably it also makes financial sense as constantly changing exhibitions will attract more repeat visitors than permanent ones. Source countries receive in exchange comparable material or "payment-in-kind" in the form of technical or educational support. But while such loan agreements provide a less destructive and perhaps more profitable route than the market for museums to acquire material, there is no real economic incentive for source countries or communities to participate. Some recent international "loan" exhibitions, however, have gone beyond the exchange of material and expertise, and have been more in the nature of rental or lease agreements, with the source countries receiving hard cash in return for their artifacts.

In June 2005, for example, a five-month exhibition of artifacts from the ancient Egyptian tomb of Tutankhamun opened at the Los Angeles County Museum of Art. About 300,000 advance tickets had been sold at up to U.S.$30 each, and the museum hoped to attract 800,000 or more visitors during the exhibition's stay. More money was made through gift marketing with unusual items such as King Tut candy and a Tut tissue box offered for sale in the museum's shop. After Los Angeles, the exhibition moved on to the Fort Lauderdale Museum of Art, the Field Museum of Chicago, and the Franklin Institute in Philadelphia. Part of the income from the 27-month tour was destined for Egypt, with Zahi Hawass, the secretary general of Egypt's Supreme Council of Antiquities, estimating that Egypt would receive about U.S.$35 million, to be spent on training staff and improving the country's museums (Haithman 2005; Reynolds 2005).

The Tutankhamun tour was organized by a commercial company in collaboration with the National Geographic Society and other organizations. Commercially organized exhibitions are not without their critics, however, who include some important ones within the museum community of the United States. The Association of Art Museum Directors (AAMD), for example, has expressed concerns that an increasing flow of private income might undermine the charitable and public (and tax-exempt) philanthropy that has traditionally supported museums, and that the commercial requirement to attract visitors might undermine curatorial standards and adversely affect the museum's mission by placing an inappropriate emphasis on entertainment (Association of Art

Museum Directors [AAMD] 2006). The domestic perspective of the AAMD is different from the international one being articulated here, so it is not surprising perhaps that the AAMD has little to say about the ultimate destination of exhibition revenue, or the economic justice of the arrangement. Nevertheless, it does emphasize that there are two separate issues. One is the role of commercial organizations in arranging museum exhibitions, as addressed by the AAMD. The other is the practice of renting artifacts for display. The AAMD's silence on the second issue might be taken as a sign of tacit approval—or not. Either way, exhibitions such as the Tutankhamun one open up prospects for source communities to raise money by entering into commercial agreements with foreign museums, with or without the intercession of a commercial company, and there are already precedents. The museum at Kuntur Wasi, for example, was paid for with money raised through an exhibition of site finds that toured Japan in the early 1990s (Onuki 1999:43; 2007).

The use of museum exhibitions to raise money for source communities suggests a further strategy—that museums in acquiring countries should rent (rather than borrow) material for extended periods of time. This strategy would achieve three things: first, it would meet the museums' need to acquire new and interesting material for display (and thus keep up the number of visitors); second, it would not deprive source communities or countries of their property; third, it would constitute a sustainable, long-term mechanism of income generation for the source communities or countries, and thus be in accord with the principles developed in the ICOM cultural tourism charter. The rent to be paid would depend upon a full assessment of the economic benefits to be gained by the renting museum, with due consideration of the costs involved in transport, insurance, and conservation. There would need to be at least two provisos, and probably more: first, the material provided for display should conform to an acceptable standard of provenance; second, source country museums should not be emptied simply to attract foreign currency. While it is unrealistic to expect that the sums of money involved would be anything like those generated by the Tutankhamun exhibition, they might still be worthwhile from the perspective of a source country.

What might be wanted now to govern the kind of international leasing arrangements suggested here is a charter of the type proposed by ICOM for cultural tourism. It could include an explicit statement of the socioeconomic rationale and justice underpinning such agreements; an agreed-upon set of standards to govern curatorial aspects of exhibition; guidance as to what might constitute acceptable provenance; and perhaps guidance about financing. Such a charter would go a long way toward allaying fears within the museums community about the possible negative consequences of rental agreements.

While these suggestions are fine in theory, and the example of Kuntur Wasi confirms that they can work in practice, it is hard to see how they would benefit the St. Lawrence Islanders. Many museums will not buy St. Lawrence artifacts, even though they are legally for sale, for fear of stimulating the market. But even if any good-quality objects that are found in the future are offered for rent to interested museums, in the short term, the income obtained would not match that to be made through digging. One reason Kuntur Wasi seems to have succeeded is because of the willingness of an international partner, in this case the Tokyo University Archaeological Mission, which since 1998 has excavated the site, to work constructively with the local community. But perhaps the bottom line is simply that the gold and exposed architecture of Kuntur Wasi are more enticing for tourists than the middens and ivories of St. Lawrence Island.

Conclusion

In the age of the global economy, it is perhaps inevitable that the economic value of cultural heritage will achieve a greater salience (Baram and Rowan 2004:3). Unless the economic benefits that flow from archaeological heritage can be properly characterized and quantified, and unless steps are taken through law and ethical practice to ensure that those benefits are maximized over the long term for the benefit of source communities, the problem of illicit excavation and trade will persist and, presumably, grow worse. Any new cultural property law that makes no provision for fair economic distribution stands the chance of being perceived by a large constituency as irrelevant at best and oppressive at worst.

Notes

1. However, this is not the case for St. Lawrence Island.
2. The term "cultural property," despite its enshrinement in two major international legal instruments and their ensuing national laws, remains a controversial one. Because of its property connotations of alienation and trade, the term "cultural heritage" is often preferred, with its different, and anti-market, heritage connotation of preservation (Blake 2000; Prott and O'Keefe 1992; Shapiro 2005:4–5).
3. Figures quoted in Inter-American Development Bank 2004 were obtained from the Centro Turistíco Nor-Oriental del Perú and the Centro de Estudios para el Desarollo y la Participación.

References Cited

Association of Art Museum Directors (AAMD)
2006   Exhibition Collaborations between American Art Museums and For-Profit Enterprises. Electronic document, http://www.aamd.org/papers/documents/ Comercialcollaborations_FINAL.pdf, accessed April 2, 2009.

Atwood, Roger
2004   *Stealing History: Tomb Raiders, Smugglers, and the Looting of the Ancient World*. St. Martin's Press, New York.

Baram, Uzi, and Yorke Rowan
2004   Archaeology after Nationalism: Globalization and the Consumption of the Past. In *Marketing Heritage*, edited by Yorke Rowan and Uzi Baram, pp. 3–26. AltaMira Press, Walnut Creek, Calif.

Barkan, Elazar
2002   Amending Historical Injustices: The Restitution of Cultural Property—An Overview. In *Claiming the Stones/Naming the Bones*, edited by Elazar Barkan and Ronald Bush, pp. 16–50. Getty Research Institute, Los Angeles.

Bator, Paul
1983   *The International Trade in Art*. University of Chicago Press, Chicago.

Blake, Janet
2000   On Defining the Cultural Heritage. *International and Comparative Law Quarterly* 49:61–85.

Bourdieu, Pierre
1997   Forms of Capital. In *Education, Culture, Economy and Society*, edited by A. H. Halsey, H. Lauder, P. Brown, and A. S. Wells, pp. 46–58. Oxford University Press, Oxford.

Carman, John
2005   *Against Cultural Property*. Duckworth, London.

Darvill, Timothy
1995   Value Systems in Archaeology. In *Managing Archaeology*, edited by M. A. Copper, A. Firth, J. Carman, and D. Wheatley, pp. 40–50. Routledge, London.

Douglas, Mary, and Baron Isherwood
1979   *The World of Goods*. Routledge, London.

Goodwin, Harold, and Peter Nizette
2001   An Assessment of the Economic Development Potential for a Northern Tourism Circuit. Electronic document, http://www.haroldgoodwin.info/resources/Peru%20Scoping.ppt, accessed April 2, 2009.

Haithman, Diane
2005   The Return of King Tut. *Los Angeles Times*, June 16:E30.

Hayden, Cori
2004   Prospecting's Public. In *Property in Question*, edited by Caroline Humphrey and Katherine Verdery, pp. 115–38. Berg, Oxford.

Heilmeyer, Wold-Dieter
1997   The Protection of Archaeological Cultural Property from an Archaeological Perspective. *Law and State* 56:96–105.

Hollowell, Julie
2006a   Moral Arguments on Subsistence Digging. In *The Ethics of Archaeology*, edited by Chris Scarre and Geoffrey Scarre, pp. 69–93. Cambridge University Press, Cambridge.

2006b   St. Lawrence Island's Legal Market in Archaeological Goods. In *Archaeology, Cultural Heritage, and the Antiquities Trade*, edited by Neil Brodie, Morag M. Kersel, Christina Luke, and Kathryn Walker Tubb, pp. 98–132. University Press of Florida, Gainesville.

Inter-American Development Bank

2004   Developing the Northeastern Tourist Circuit (NTC) to Enhance MSME Competitiveness. Electronic document, http://www.iadb.org/projects/project.cfm?language=English&project=PE-M1009, accessed April 2, 2009.

International Council of Museums (ICOM)

2000   Proposal for a Charter of Principles for Museums and Cultural Tourism. Electronic document, http://icom.museum/tourism_engl.html, accessed April 2, 2009.

Lipe, William D.

1984   Value and Meaning in Cultural Resources. In *Approaches to the Archaeological Heritage*, edited by Henry Cleere, pp. 1–11. Cambridge University Press, Cambridge.

Lowenthal, David

2005   Why Sanctions Seldom Work: Reflections on Cultural Property Internationalism. *International Journal of Cultural Property* 12:393–424.

Mason, Randall

2002   Assessing Values in Conservation Planning. In *Assessing the Values of Cultural Heritage*, edited by Marta de la Torre and Randall Mason, pp. 5–30. The Getty Conservation Institute, Los Angeles.

Matsuda, David

1998   The Ethics of Archaeology, Subsistence Digging, and Artifact Looting in Latin America: Point, Muted Counterpoint. *International Journal of Cultural Property* 7:89–97.

2005   Subsistence Diggers. In *Who Owns the Past?*, edited by Kate Fitz Gibbon, pp. 255–68. Rutgers University Press, New Brunswick, N.J.

Merryman, John H.

2005   Cultural Property Internationalism. *International Journal of Cultural Property* 12:11–39.

Mourato, Susana, and Massimiliano Mazzanti

2002   Economic Valuation of Cultural Heritage: Evidence and Prospects. In *Assessing the Values of Cultural Heritage*, edited by Marta de la Torre and Randall Mason, pp. 51–76. The Getty Conservation Institute, Los Angeles.

Nafziger, James A. R., and Robert Paterson

2004   A Blueprint for the Development of Cultural Heritage Law Introduction. *Art, Antiquity and Law* 9:1–2.

O'Keefe, Patrick

1997   *Trade in Antiquities*. UNESCO, London; Archetype, Paris.

Onuki, Yoshio

1999   Kuntur Wasi: Temple, Gold, Museum . . . and an Experiment in Community Development. *Museum International* 51(4):42–46.

2007   The Archaeological Excavations and the Protection of Cultural Heritage in Relation with the Local Society: Experiences in Peru. *Archaeologies* 3:99–115.

Parry, Bronwyn

2004   Bodily Transactions: Regulating a New Space of Flows in "Bio-information." In *Property in Question*, edited by Caroline Humphrey and Katherine Verdery, pp. 29–48. Berg, Oxford.

Paterson, Robert K.

2005   The "Caring and Sharing" Alternative: Recent Progress in the International Law Association to Develop Draft Cultural Material Principles. *International Journal of Cultural Property* 12:62–77.

Posey, Darrell A.

1998   Can Cultural Rights Protect Traditional Cultural Knowledge and Biodiversity? In *Cultural Rights and Wrongs*, pp. 42–56. Institute of Art and Law, Paris; UNESCO, Leicester.

Prott, Lyndel V., and Patrick J. O'Keefe

1992   "Cultural Heritage" or "Cultural Property"? *International Journal of Cultural Property* 1:307–20.

Rao, Vijayendra, and Michael Walton

2004   Culture and Public Action: Relationality, Equality of Agency, and Development. In *Culture and Public Action*, edited by Vijayendra Rao and Michael Walton, pp. 3–36. Stanford University Press, Stanford, Calif.

Reynolds, Christopher

2005   Crowds Greet Return of the King at LACMA. *Los Angeles Times*, June 17: B2.

Rose, Jerome C., and Dolores L. Burke

2004   Making Money from Buried Treasure. *Culture without Context* 14:4–8.

Shapiro, Daniel

2005   Cultural Property and the International Cultural Property Society. *International Journal of Cultural Property* 12:1–5.

Shyllon, Folarin

1998   The Right to a Cultural Past: African Viewpoints. In *Cultural Rights and Wrongs*, pp. 42–56. Institute of Art and Law, Paris; UNESCO, Leicester.

Staley, David P.

1993   St. Lawrence Island's Subsistence Diggers: A New Perspective on Human Effects on Archaeological Sites. *Journal of Field Archaeology* 20:347–55.

Throsby, David

2001   *Economics and Culture*. Cambridge University Press, Cambridge.

Watson, Peter

1999   The Lessons of Sipán: Archaeologists and Huaqueros. *Culture without Context* 4:15–20.

21

Funding Strategies for World Heritage Sites in Least Developed Countries

BRIJESH THAPA

The designation of World Heritage sites by the United Nations Educational, Scientific and Cultural Organization (UNESCO) was a major outcome of the Convention Concerning the Protection of the World Cultural and Natural Heritage. This international treaty was adopted during a general conference on November 16, 1972, and as of September 2009, 186 states parties have ratified it (United Nations Educational, Scientific and Cultural Organization [UNESCO] 2009), including 46 of the 50 least developed countries (LDCs) as classified by the United Nations Economic and Social Council. While it does not nominate sites, UNESCO encourages member states to identify and submit nominations on an annual basis to the World Heritage Committee. The prospective sites are evaluated on their "outstanding universal value" merit, regulatory framework, management plans, and authenticity. Approval of designation is classified under the culture, natural, and mixed categories based on one or more of the 10 established criteria (see Table 21.1). A mixed category (cultural landscapes) is the newest designation, instituted in 1992, and reflects sites that meet both natural and cultural criteria. Each member state is responsible for maintenance and management of respective sites, as UNESCO does not provide operational funds (Leask 2006; UNESCO 2009).

The number of inscriptions to the World Heritage List has grown substantially with new sites being added annually. As of September 2009, there were 890 World Heritage sites inscribed under the cultural (n=689), natural (n=176), and mixed sites (n=25) categories in 148 countries (UNESCO 2009). However, since the inscription of the first World Heritage sites, a majority constituted built heritage largely in Europe; and as expected, this region has the highest concentration of sites. Nevertheless, since 1994, there has been a steady increase in natural and mixed designations in developing countries (Leask 2006; Smith 2003). Among the LDCs, currently there are 66 sites inscribed in 26 countries (UNESCO 2009) (see Table 21.2).

With the growth in designations, the World Heritage site brand is becoming increasingly significant. This accolade is desired by numerous countries due to

Table 21.1. World Heritage Site Inscription Criteria

	Criteria
i.	to represent a masterpiece of human creative genius;
ii.	to exhibit an important interchange of human values, over a span of time or within a cultural area of the world, on developments in architecture or technology, monumental arts, town-planning or landscape design;
iii.	to bear a unique or at least exceptional testimony to a cultural tradition or to a civilization which is living or which has disappeared;
iv.	to be an outstanding example of a type of building, architectural or technological ensemble or landscape which illustrates (a) significant stage(s) in human history;
v.	to be an outstanding example of a traditional human settlement, land-use, or sea-use which is representative of a culture (or cultures), or human interaction with the environment especially when it has become vulnerable under the impact of irreversible change;
vi.	to be directly or tangibly associated with events or living traditions, with ideas, or with beliefs, with artistic and literary works of outstanding universal significance. (The Committee considers that this criterion should preferably be used in conjunction with other criteria);
vii.	to contain superlative natural phenomena or areas of exceptional natural beauty and aesthetic importance;
viii.	to be outstanding examples representing major stages of earth's history, including the record of life, significant on-going geological processes in the development of landforms, or significant geomorphic or physiographic features;
ix.	to be outstanding examples representing significant on-going ecological and biological processes in the evolution and development of terrestrial, fresh water, coastal and marine ecosystems and communities of plants and animals;
x.	to contain the most important and significant natural habitats for in-situ conservation of biological diversity, including those containing threatened species of outstanding universal value from the point of view of science or conservation.

Source: http://whc.unesco.org/en/criteria/.

various perceived and actual benefits accrued from designation, such as international recognition, improved protection and management, political and ethnic recognition, new partnerships and projects, economic and social improvement, and increased tourism activity. Of all these, increased economic benefits via tourism appears to be the underlying factor most sought by member states (Leask 2006). The economics of tourism based on the influx of visitors and subsequent increases in income, tax, and job creation are highly touted and desired. Also, the designation is likely to be more important for developing countries as they tend to capitalize by utilizing the brand and iconic logo for the purposes of marketing in order to attract visitors (Boyd and Timothy 2006).

Table 21.2. World Heritage Sites in Least Developed Countries

Country	World Heritage Site	Year of Inscription
Afghanistan	Minaret and Archaeological Remains of Jam	2002
	Cultural Landscape and Archaeological Remains of the Bamiyan Valley	2003
Bangladesh	Historic Mosque City of Bagerhat	1985
	Ruins of the Buddhist Vihara at Paharpur	1985
	The Sundarbans	1997
Benin	Royal Palaces of Abomey	1985
Burkina Faso	Ruins of Loropeni	2009
Cambodia	Angkor	1992
Cape Verde	Cidade Velha, Historic Centre of Riberia Grande	2009
Central African Republic	Manovo-Gounda St. Floris National Park	1988
Democratic Republic of the Congo	Virunga National Park	1979
	Garamba National Park	1980
	Kahuzi-Biega National Park	1980
	Salonga National Park	1984
	Okapi Wildlife Reserve	1996
Ethiopia	Rock-Hewn Churches, Lalibela	1978
	Simien National Park	1978
	Fasil Ghebbi, Gondar Region	1979
	Aksum	1980
	Lower Valley of the Awash	1980
	Lower Valley of the Omo	1980
	Tiya	1980
	Harar Jugol, the Fortified Historic Town	2006
Gambia	James Island and Related Sites	2003
	Stone Circles of Senegambia	2006
Guinea	Mount Nimba Strict Nature Reserve	1982
Haiti	National History Park and Citadel, Sans Souci, Ramiers	1982
Lao People's Democratic Republic	Town of Luang Prabang	1995
	Vat Phou and Associated Ancient Settlements within the Champasak Cultural Landscape	2001
Madagascar	Tsingy de Bemaraha Strict Nature Reserve	1990
	Royal Hill of Ambohimanga	2001
Malawi	Lake Malawi National Park	1984
	Chongoni Rock-Art Area	2006
Mali	Old Towns of Djenné	1988
	Timbuktu	1988
	Cliff of Bandiagara (Land of the Dogons)	1989
	Tomb of Askia	2004
Mauritania	Banc d'Arguin National Park	1989
	Ancient Ksour of Ouadane, Chinguetti, Tichitt and Oualata	1996
Mozambique	Island of Mozambique	1991

continued

Country	World Heritage Site	Year of Inscription
Nepal	Kathmandu Valley	1979
	Sagarmatha National Park	1979
	Royal Chitwan National Park	1984
	Lumbini, the Birthplace of Lord Buddha	1997
Niger	Air and Ténéré Natural Reserves	1991
	W National Park of Niger	1996
Senegal	Island of Gorée	1978
	Djoudj National Bird Sanctuary	1981
	Niokolo-Koba National Park	1981
	Island of Saint-Louis	2000
	Stone Circles of Senegambia	2006
Solomon Islands	East Rennell	1998
Sudan	Gebel Barkal and the Sites of the Napatan Region	2003
Togo	Koutammakou, the Land of the Batammariba	2004
Uganda	Bwindi Impenetrable National Park	1994
	Rwenzori Mountains National Park	1994
	Tombs of Buganda Kings at Kasubi	2001
United Republic of Tanzania	Ngorongoro Conservation Area	1979
	Ruins of Kilwa Kisiwani and Ruins of Songo Mnara	1981
	Serengeti National Park	1981
	Selous Game Reserve	1982
	Kilimanjaro National Park	1987
	Stone Town of Zanzibar	2000
	Kondoa Rock-Art Sites	2006
Yemen	Old Walled City of Shibam	1982
	Old City of Sana'a	1986
	Historic Town of Zabid	1993
Zambia	Mosi-oa-Tunya / Victoria Falls	1989

Note: Classification is based on the United Nations Economic and Social Council. For more information, visit http://www.un.org/esa/policy/devplan/profile/.

Least Developed Countries (LDCs) that have not ratified the World Heritage Convention: Djibouti, Equatorial Guinea, Somalia, Timor-Leste, Tuvalu.

LDC that do not have any World Heritage sites: Angola, Bhutan, Burundi, Chad, Comoros, Djibouti, Equatorial Guinea, Eritrea, Guinea-Bissau, Kiribati, Lesotho, Liberia, Maldives, Myanmar, Rwanda, Samoa, Sao Tomi & Principe, Sierra Leone, Somalia, Timor-Leste, Tuvalu, Vanuatu.

Source: Compiled from http://whc.unesco.org/en/list/.

However, there is a paucity of empirical research that actually confirms the correlation that designation of a World Heritage site truly results in increased visitation. The key limitation has been the lack of access to reliable data, including for sites in developed countries (Hall 2006; Leask 2006). Also, the comparison of visitor numbers at pre- and post-designation at individual sites does not accurately measure the relationship, as there are other factors that can influence visitation. In China, the town of Lijang, a World Heritage site, has witnessed a dramatic increase of largely Chinese visitors since the designation. However, according to Duang, the increase has been largely attributed to the construc-

tion of an airport, and China's recent policy of promotion and advocacy of leisure holidays and vacations (as cited in du Cross 2006:209). In Australia, Ralf
Buckley (2004) concluded that World Heritage sites do receive large numbers
of visitors, and listing also increases international visitation. However, a major
limitation to the study was lack of reliable and pertinent data.

Given visitation trends to World Heritage sites, sustainability in resource
management needs to be at the forefront due to the growing challenge of bal-
ancing conservation and generating revenues (Shackley 2006). More importantly, for tourism to be sustainable at World Heritage sites in LDCs, major
initial investment is needed for restoration, and improvement in visitor and site
management. Generally, financing for cultural heritage resource management,
including World Heritage sites, is problematic and a major managerial issue
that is faced by even wealthy countries (Hall 2006). In an era of government
funding cutbacks as well as lower priority toward cultural heritage resources,
alternative sources of funding are needed. Financial resources are critical for
maintaining the integrity of heritage resources as economic sustainability is
desired by heritage resource managers. While World Heritage sites have been
the beneficiaries of additional protection and funding, not all sites have experienced this approach. In most cases, nongovernmental organizations (NGOs)
and foreign monies have aided in the preservation of certain monuments and
historic sites (Timothy and Boyd 2006). Besides World Heritage sites, other
cultural and natural national treasures have also suffered neglect largely due
to the lack of skilled human resources, financial capital, and political will of
governments. The purpose of this chapter is to outline potential funding strategies, such as debt swaps, user fees, conservation taxes, and departure taxes, for
sustainable conservation and management of World Heritage sites in LDCs.

World Heritage Sites: Issues and Challenges

The designation of World Heritage sites is a major tool for conservation and
protection of global cultural and natural assets. World Heritage sites are also
symbolic manifestations of local and national pride that can potentially mobilize support to protect and preserve historic and religious monuments, and
cultural and natural landscapes (Smith 2003). While some World Heritage sites
have been able to collectively rally support among local communities, other
sites have received mixed reviews, or designation has been largely symbolic
and strictly promoted for tourism by national governments. A general concern
among local communities in LDCs is a lack of public awareness and consequent
support for the significance of designation. In Nepal, site designations have
been symbolic with lack of public appreciation and interest. World Heritage
sites appear to be strictly used by the Nepal Tourism Board for external marketing and promotional purposes (Thapa 2007). In St. Lucia, the recently inscribed

Pitons Management Area as a World Heritage site has received mixed reviews by local communities and the national government. Local community members largely lack understanding or awareness of the significance of designation (Nicholas, Thapa, and Ko 2009). Also, while the government is obliged to protect the site, the opportunity costs of economic benefits from hotel and resort development at the site have led public officials to question the designation (Nicholas, Thapa, and Pennington-Gray 2009). World Heritage sites are global icons and resources with outstanding universal value; however, there is a need to connect individual sites to their local communities in order to be sustainable. Overall, community involvement and a sense of local ownership are essential to connect local and universal values of World Heritage sites (Millar 2006).

In addition to outreach and support among the key stakeholders, there are major internal issues such as site and visitor management that require immediate attention at World Heritage sites (Pederson 2002), especially in LDCs. Capacity building with staff training and professional development, interpretation resources and techniques, and structural repair and restoration are necessities at most sites. Collectively, management plans in all World Heritage sites in LDCs that address site and visitor management are in dire need of being formulated and implemented. Besides such issues, there are other monumental challenges for World Heritage sites in LDCs. Increases in population growth, urbanization, modernization, development pressures, armed conflict, and insurgency are key factors that limit the ability of communities and countries to maintain the integrity and authenticity of World Heritage sites. These issues are ubiquitous and need to be addressed, or the maintenance of World Heritage site mandates will be compromised.

In Nepal, encroachment and development have plagued sites in the Kathmandu Valley, largely due to conflicting core and buffer zones at the respective sites. The deterioration of the monuments and related authenticity issues are extremely problematic. Besides cultural sites, natural sites have also been affected due to political instability and internal domestic insurgency (Thapa 2004, 2007).

Armed conflicts have created crises in cultural heritage and natural resources management, along with serious challenges in protecting and preserving World Heritage sites. In Ethiopia, Simien National Park, a World Heritage site inscribed in 1978, was inaccessible from 1984 to 1991. During an armed conflict, all park infrastructures were destroyed (Jacobs and Schloeder 2001). Perpetual armed conflict in the Democratic Republic of Congo has dramatically affected the biodiversity and indigenous cultures at all five natural World Heritage sites. All five sites are at high risk due to ongoing conflict (Hart and Mwinyihali 2001). Current armed conflict and its consequences for cultural and natural resources, including World Heritage sites in Iraq and Afghanistan, are further testament to the issue.

Due to the inability of member states to maintain the integrity and authenticity of the sites, such sites are listed on the World Heritage in Danger List. Each listed site is evaluated annually, and with demonstrable improvements the respective site can be removed from the danger list. While removing a site from the World Heritage List is rare, two sites have been de-listed. In 2007, the Arabian Oryx Sanctuary in Oman was the first site to be removed, followed in 2009 by Dresden Elbe Valley in Germany. Some sites have been on the danger list for numerous years, such as the Chan Chan Archaeological Zone in Peru, which has been listed since 1986. As of September 2009, 31 sites in 25 countries were on the danger list, with the Democratic Republic of Congo leading with 5 natural sites. Collectively, the LDCs host 13 sites (4 cultural and 9 natural) in 8 countries on the danger list (UNESCO 2009), and this number is likely to increase given the challenges facing LDCs.

The danger list is a constructive tool to draw attention about a respective site to the member state of UNESCO. In addition, the sites on the danger list are provided technical assistance and some monies from the World Heritage Centre, which administers the World Heritage List and the World Heritage Fund. The World Heritage Fund has an annual budget of approximately U.S.$4 million, which is a meager amount given the number of World Heritage sites. This amount can still provide some assistance to much needed sites. In addition to the World Heritage Fund, there are five other funding sources (for example, Japanese Funds-in-Trust) that are donations offered by individual countries earmarked for specific projects (UNESCO 2009).

It is evident that funding for World Heritage sites by UNESCO is a luxury, and the responsibility lies with individual member state. Since financial resources are extremely limited and prioritized in LDCs, external donor agencies, organizations, foundations, and foreign governments are sought for financial and technical resources (Timothy and Boyd 2006). Nevertheless, sites should not rely totally on external donors, but should be proactive in approaching local and national governments for increased funding. In addition to supplemental monies, other potential self-funding strategies need to be explored and implemented. The following sections will discuss potential funding strategies in order to secure additional funding for World Heritage sites, and cultural heritage resources management in general.

Debt Swaps: Nature and Culture

Debt-for-nature swaps have been an innovative instrument for numerous developing countries to reduce their foreign debt and simultaneously raise revenues for conservation and protection of natural resources. The concept derived from debt-for-equity swaps "involves a mechanism of exchange in which a certain amount of the debtor's foreign debt is canceled or forgiven, in return for local currency from the debtor government to invest in a domestic environmental protection project" (Thapa 1998:269). The environmental project can range from designation and management of protected areas to park personnel training and environmental education programs.

Debt-for-nature swaps may involve official bilateral debt between two governments or trilateral official and private debt between two governments and an international nongovernmental organization (INGO). Debt swaps are usually facilitated by an INGO (for example, Conservation International, World Wildlife Fund, and Nature Conservancy) that has identified a need for a specific environmental project. Also, the INGO is usually in partnership with a domestic NGO that is actually responsible for the administration and implementation of the identified project (Thapa 1998). Typically, the INGO seeks a potential donor, which could include governments, commercial banks, organizations, and private foundations. The international secondary market for second-hand debts is also sought for deeply discounted debts. Once the respective debt is identified, the INGO could either buy it from the secondary market, or receive it as a donation from commercial banks or governments. Monetary donations are also requested from charitable foundations to buy discounted debt. The purchased debt is exchanged to the indebted country for local currency investments in environmental conservation projects (Thapa 1998, 2000).

Since it was proposed by Lovejoy (1984), the first debt-for-nature swap was officially conducted in 1987, in which U.S.$650,000 of Bolivian foreign debt was bought by Conservation International at a discounted price of U.S.$100,000. In return, Bolivia agreed to invest U.S.$250,000 in local currency toward protection and management of the Beni Biosphere Reserve. Since the first swap, numerous countries (for example, Costa Rica, Mexico, the Philippines, and Madagascar) have participated, especially those with high debt burdens and rich biodiversity (Thapa 1998). In recent years, the frequency and swap amounts have steadily increased, while additional countries such as Panama, Bangladesh, El Salvador, Paraguay, Jamaica, Botswana, Cameroon, Colombia, and Peru have become involved.

The most recent debt-for-nature swap was conducted in October 2007 between Costa Rica and the United States, and it was the largest (U.S.$26 million) in history (Lacy 2007). Similarly, in September 2006 Guatemala was a major beneficiary with U.S.$24 million in debt owed to the United States waived in exchange for Guatemalan investment in local currency in four designated areas for conservation and environmental protection during the next 15 years (Nature Conservancy 2006).

The United States has been active in debt swaps largely due to the Tropical Forest Conservation Act (1998), which permits eligible countries to exchange their debt to finance tropical forest conservation initiatives. Twelve countries have been beneficiaries of the act, which has generated more than U.S.$135 million for tropical forest conservation (U.S. Agency for International Development [USAID] 2008). For example, U.S.$8.3 million in debt payments by Botswana were exchanged for conservation and restoration of tropical forests in the Okavango Delta and Chobe National Park regions. For Peru, U.S.$6.6 million were exchanged for preservation of more than 27.5 million acres of rain forests (USAID 2008). Europe also has been active in debt swaps that are beyond environmental conservation and protection. In June 2006, France offered 100 percent debt relief of the 570 million euros owed by Cameroon. In exchange, Cameroon would be required to invest in education, health, infrastructure, and natural resources management over the next five years. Of the total debt relief amount, 20 million euros were earmarked for preservation and conservation of the Congo Basin, the world's second largest tropical forest (News from France 2006). Similarly, Germany's recent debt swap with Indonesia, worth 73.6 million euros, was earmarked largely for education and nature conservation. In exchange, Indonesia is required to fund several targeted areas (education, capacity building, and nature conservation projects) with 50 percent of the total swap value in local currency (*Jakarta Post* 2004).

The Paris Club, an informal group founded in 1956 of official creditors composed of 19 permanent members from major industrialized countries, also has been progressive in debt elimination, debt restructuring, and debt swaps for various programs beyond nature conservation. Sectors such as health, education, and other poverty reduction programs have all received attention (Paris Club 2006). Of these, cultural heritage resources have received little or no attention; hence, there are opportunities for involvement, and this should be addressed by indebted and creditor countries.

Currently, some aspects of cultural heritage resource protection already are prevalent within debt-for-nature swaps, given that some of the protected natural areas are also cultural landscapes. In the context of World Heritage sites, natural and mixed sites potentially could qualify under the framework of the debt-for-nature swap. A potential application has been supported for sites in Nepal (Thapa and Thapa 2002). Recent data indicates that there are 27 World Heritage sites in LDCs classified under the natural category, and one as a mixed site (UNESCO 2009). A majority of these sites are vulnerable and could use an infusion of financial resources.

Debt swapping is a tool to reduce foreign debt, generate revenues for conservation and management of cultural and natural resources, and create sustainable development programs locally (see Figure 21.1). Based on the current framework, LDCs have opportunities to engage in debt-for-cultural-heritage-conservation swaps. Creditor nations would potentially be interested in protecting and preserving World Heritage sites as they are of global value. However, debtor LDCs need to establish priorities and a willingness to engage in such swaps for conservation of local and global heritage. More importantly, similar

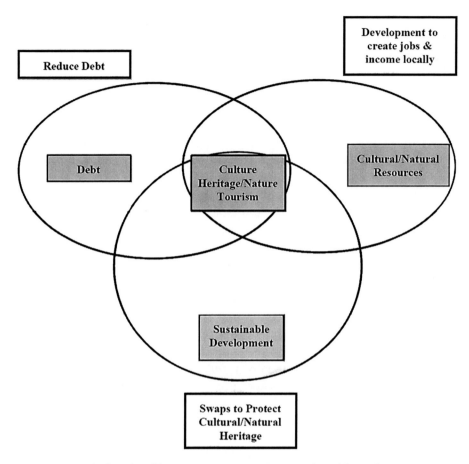

Figure 21.1. Debt for cultural heritage conservation. Source: Adapted from Thapa 2000.

to the nature conservation movement, the advocacy of INGOs that specialize in the cultural heritage sectors should also be proactive for such swaps. Besides INGOs, organizations such as UNESCO, including the World Heritage Centre, could play a major role in promoting this specific swap concept for cultural heritage conservation among member states. Debt swaps have been able to protect vulnerable natural areas by establishing protected areas and consequently creating an economic base for local communities. With the growth in ecotourism and cultural tourism, it is beneficial for LDCs to capitalize by conserving and protecting their natural and cultural resources.

User Fees

User fees are a standard method to generate revenues for World Heritage sites. Compounded with the lack of financial resources, and due to the potential to generate income, even traditional non-fee sites have been forced to adopt a user-pay principle. In the Philippines, at the Tubbataha Reef Marine Park, a World Heritage site inscribed in 1993, a two-tiered diving fee was implemented in 2000, largely to generate revenues. Additionally, a revenue-sharing scheme is practiced by the park so that local communities also benefit (Tubbataha Reef Marine Park 2006). In the Galapagos Islands, a renowned World Heritage site (currently listed on the World Heritage in Danger List) inscribed in 1978, tourists are required to pay an entry fee of U.S.$100 per person while citizens of Ecuador pay U.S.$6 per person. Galapagos National Park receives 40 percent of the entry fees. According to legislation, 90 percent of the collected revenues must be spent to fund community and conservation initiatives on the island (Galapagos Conservation Trust 2006). Other national parks and protected areas in Kenya, Tanzania, Uganda, and Botswana, some of which are World Heritage sites, also have two-tiered fees from U.S.$20 and above per person. However, sites in developing countries and LDCs typically tend to charge far lower entry fees compared to what international visitors would be willing to pay. Generally, visitors are inclined to pay more, provided the money flows directly into conservation and management of resources at the respective site (Spergel 2001).

User fee pricing is an important issue for World Heritage sites. In LDCs, willingness to pay, elasticity of demand, and political considerations need to be taken into account to generate a pricing mechanism that will not deter visitation by local or international visitors. In addition, a differential pricing mechanism for local, domestic, and international visitors should be implemented (Cochrane and Tapper 2006).

Generally, in LDCs, the current system based on legislation mandates that all user fees be collected and reported to national coffers. Then, annual allocations are distributed to each site. New legislation in numerous developing countries, including some LDCs, has experimented with allowing individual sites to keep all or some percentage of their user fees. For example, in Nepal, individual protected areas, including two natural World Heritage sites, are allowed to keep 50 percent or more of their entry fees (Spergel 2001).

Distribution of user fee revenues is important for individual World Heritage sites, as each site is unique, with various needs. Due to the benefits accrued from this system, more countries have participated, including the United States with its Recreation Fee Demonstration Program. Although user fees are not likely to cover all operating costs, revenue-sharing mechanisms for World Heritage sites in LDCs should be promoted. In addition, user fees should act as supplementary revenues and not replace traditional funding sources.

Another major challenge for LDCs is the process of collecting user fees due to various constraints, notably unethical and corruptive practices. A potential solution could be for each LDC to promote a "one pass" system that would allow the visitor access to all of the World Heritage sites and other cultural sites and natural protected areas. The single card-pass would alleviate local cash management problems and creates efficiency in revenue collection. The card could also be used as a monitoring tool for such activities as visitor counts to individual sites.

In addition, there are other related sources to generate income for World Heritage sites in LDCs. Depending on the site, revenues from concession fees from businesses (for example, stores, restaurants, tour companies) that operate within the site boundaries can be lucrative. However, fees need to be at true market value and a transparent method of awarding contracts to concession companies is a necessity (Cochrane and Tapper 2006). Other revenues include permit fees usually linked to natural World Heritage sites, which can be substantial. Nepal generates more than U.S.$2 million per year for expeditions to Mt. Everest within Sagarmatha National Park (inscribed in 1979), and other Himalayan peaks. Teams are charged U.S.$50,000 per expedition to Mt. Everest, the world's highest mountain (Spergel 2001).

Conservation Taxes and Departure Taxes

Taxes are usually controversial, but in order to generate revenues for natural and cultural resources, a conservation tax between 1 and 5 percent levied to all inbound international travelers (leisure and business) could be a feasible option. Since domestic tourism in LDCs is usually very minimal, such taxes should only be assessed to international visitors. The income generated from this tax should be strictly assigned for conservation of natural and cultural heritage resources, including World Heritage sites. Generally, the tourism industry is usually opposed to extra taxes on tourists, hence support should be garnered from this key stakeholder group. However, the industry should be supportive of a "reasonable" conservation tax or fee assessed to visitors, as natural and cultural resources are principal tourism products that need to be conserved and managed sustainably.

Belize is a pioneering case study that could be employed as a model to generate revenues for the natural and cultural sectors, including World Heritage sites. In Belize, under an innovative program administered by the Protected Areas Conservation Trust, each passenger that visits by plane or cruise ship has to pay a conservation fee of U.S.$3.75, which is earmarked for programs that support conservation and management of natural and cultural sites. The conservation fee generates almost 81 percent of the total income for the trust. The trust also receives 20 percent of the passenger head taxes paid by cruise ships, and 20 percent commission from recreation fees, license fees, and concession fees from protected areas. In addition, the trust encourages individual and business donations from local and international markets. Collectively, the trust has annual financial resources of U.S.$750,000 (Protected Areas Conservation Trust

2006). The example of Belize is encouraging, but to put something similar into place in other LDCs would require LDC governments to muster political will to authorize legislation.

The creation of a conservation trust is an optimal method for administration of a conservation tax or fee. The collection mechanism for these funds would need strong monitoring, transparency, accountability, and enforcement. Three aspects of money management by the trust would need to be formulated and implemented: 1) it could only be used for a specified purpose or purposes; 2) it must be kept separate from other sources of money, such as a government agency's regular budget; and 3) it would be managed and controlled by an independent board of directors (Spergel 2001:8).

Conservation trusts have become popular since the mid-1990s, as more than 40 developing countries have created them for various biodiversity conservation projects. Revenues for trusts have been largely derived from grants issued by governments and international donors, and to a lesser degree from taxes and fees designated for conservation. Some successful conservation trust programs in LDCs with major multimillion dollar endowment funds are in Bhutan, Madagascar, and Uganda (Spergel 2001).

The natural resource sector (parks and biodiversity conservation) has been the major beneficiary of such funds from conservation trusts, including a few natural World Heritage sites. However, the cultural sector also has an opportunity to be the recipient of trust funds, especially if the generated revenue is a result of tourist conservation taxes. Legislation could be created to integrate the natural and cultural sectors, as in most LDCs they are not usually mutually exclusive, especially with respect to World Heritage sites.

In addition to conservation taxes, most LDCs have a two-tiered airport departure tax for residents and visitors. Departure taxes have enabled them to raise substantial revenues, in which a certain percentage is usually allocated to their national tourism organizations, or other earmarked projects. For example, in the Republic of Cook Islands, 20 percent of the U.S.$10 departure tax for tourists is channeled to an Environmental Protection Fund (Spergel 2001).

Also, tourism development taxes (for example, hospitality or bed taxes) are imposed by local communities in addition to a sales tax for each individual who rents a room in a lodging facility. The tax rate fluctuates between 1 and 20 percent and is collected by lodging operators, who are required to submit the funds to local governments. Depending on respective legislation of the tourist development tax, the monies are usually designated for specific reallocation, such as local tourism promotion organizations or other identified projects. For example, the Turks and Caicos Islands increased room taxes by 1 to 9 percent, with the increase allocated to finance a protected area conservation trust (Spergel 2001).

Similar to conservation and departure taxes, income generation schemes such as bed taxes require political will, as legislation, collection, and enforcement mechanisms need to be instituted. In Luang Prabang (a World Heritage site), an emerging cultural heritage destination in Laos, the community had recommended a U.S.$2 bed tax for all tourists using a lodging facility. The potential revenues from the bed tax were earmarked for conservation and management of heritage resources in the community. However, this never materialized, largely due to the lack of political will and a revenue resource management manual. Due to lack of implementation, local businesses and the tourism industry adopted their own income generating initiatives, largely through visitor donations to support conservation of heritage resources in their community (Aas et al. 2005). This example demonstrates that the private sector—that is, the tourism industry—also has a major stake in cultural heritage resources and is an active contributor to conservation.

Overall, local communities that have World Heritage sites should be proactive and institute bed taxes as another stream of revenue. For LDCs that do not currently have a departure tax, it may be a feasible option to generate revenues for national tourism organizations, and conservation of natural and cultural heritage resources. Additionally, for LDCs that do not wish to institute a conservation tax, an increase in the departure tax could be an option. Based on the percentage increase, monies should be strictly earmarked for conservation of cultural and natural resources, including World Heritage sites.

Debt swaps, user fees, conservation taxes, and departure taxes have been identified as potential funding strategies for World Heritage sites in LDCs. However, there are also other additional funding mechanisms that potentially could be explored, such as corporate sponsorships or in-kind donations. Similar to the imposition of new taxes, corporate sponsorships or donations can be controversial, but they are beneficial tools. Corporate sponsorship could be analyzed with strict guidelines about the type of desired company, promotional materials, and funding mechanisms in order to avoid commercialization and commodification of sites. At the local level, key major businesses should be sought for potential cash and in-kind sponsorship. Also, legislation in LDCs could promote sponsorship of cultural and natural resources via certain tax subsidies as incentives.

Conclusion

Although the designation of World Heritage sites has been promoted as a conservation instrument to protect nature and culture, the economics of tourism have increasingly pushed to the forefront. Tourism has been employed as a tool to promote conservation due to its potential to generate revenues for the communities and respective World Heritage sites. Given the demand and additional marketing, World Heritage sites in LDCs will experience added physical stress. Since the primary objective is sustainability, balance should be achieved between conservation goals and overuse with increased visitation.

World Heritage sites in LDCs face numerous challenges, with limited financial resources to combat issues. It is apparent that monies from international governments and external donors are limited and competitive among LDCs due to the priority of issues. Hence, LDCs need to engage in income-generating mechanisms from previously untapped sources to fund the cultural heritage sector, including World Heritage sites. This chapter has outlined selected funding strategies, such as debt swaps, user fees, conservation taxes, and departure taxes for sustainable conservation and management of World Heritage sites in LDCs and other developing countries. Overall, the key issue is that LDC governments need to demonstrate political will, commitment, and legislation to protect and conserve natural and cultural heritage resources, including World Heritage sites.

References Cited

Aas, Christina, Adele Ladkin, and John Fletcher
2005   Stakeholder Collaboration and Heritage Management. *Annals of Tourism Research* 32(1):28–48.
Boyd, W. Stephen, and J. Dallen Timothy
2006   Marketing Issues and World Heritage Sites. In *Managing World Heritage Sites*, edited by A. Leask and A. Fyall, pp. 56–68. Butterworth-Heinemann, Burlington, Mass.
Buckley, Ralf
2004   The Effects of World Heritage Listing on Tourism to Australian National Parks. *Journal of Sustainable Tourism* 12(1):70–84.
Cochrane, Janet, and Richard Tapper
2006   Tourism's Contribution to World Heritage Site Management. In *Managing World Heritage Sites*, edited by A. Leask and A. Fyall, pp. 98–109. Butterworth-Heinemann, Burlington, Mass.
Du Cross, Hilary
2006   Managing Visitor Impacts at Lijiang, China. In *Managing World Heritage Sites*, edited by A. Leask and A. Fyall, pp. 206–14. Butterworth-Heinemann, Burlington, Mass.
Galapagos Conservation Trust
2006   Entry Fees. Electronic document, http://www.gct.org/faq.html#entryfee, accessed November 9, 2006.
Hall, C. Michael
2006   Implementing the World Heritage Convention: What Happens after Listing? In *Managing World Heritage Sites*, edited by A. Leask and A. Fyall, pp. 21–34. Butterworth-Heinemann, Burlington, Mass.

Hart, Terese, and Robert Mwinyihali
2001   *Armed Conflict and Biodiversity in Sub-Saharan Africa: The Case of the Democratic Republic of Congo (DRC).* Biodiversity Support Program, Washington, D.C.

Jacobs, J. Michael, and A. Catherine Schloeder
2001   *Impacts of Conflict on Biodiversity and Protected Areas in Ethiopia.* Biodiversity Support Program, Washington, D.C.

Jakarta Post
2004   Indonesia, Germany to Sign $60m Debt Swap Deal. Electronic document, http://www.thejakartapost.com/yesterdaydetail.asp?fileid=20041108.L05, accessed October 29, 2006.

Lacy, Marc
2007   U.S. Forgives Costa Rican Debt to Help Environment. Electronic document, http://www.nytimes.com/2007/10/17/world/americas/17costa.html, accessed October 29, 2007.

Leask, Anna
2006   World Heritage Site Designation. In *Managing World Heritage Sites*, edited by A. Leask and A. Fyall, pp. 6–19. Butterworth-Heinemann, Burlington, Mass.

Lovejoy, Thomas
1984   Aid Debtor Nations' Ecology. *New York Times* October 4:A31.

Millar, Sue
2006   Stakeholders and Community Participation. In *Managing World Heritage Sites*, edited by A. Leask and A. Fyall, pp. 38–54. Butterworth-Heinemann, Burlington, Mass.

Nature Conservancy
2006 $24 Million of Guatemala's Debt Now Slated for Conservation. Electronic document, http://www.nature.org/wherewework/centralamerica/guatemala/work/art19052.html, accessed October 29, 2006.

News from France
2006   France and Cameroon: Debt-for-Nature Swap. Electronic document, http://www.ambafrance-us.org/publi/nff/NFF0608.pdf, accessed October 29, 2006.

Nicholas, N. Lorraine, Brijesh Thapa, and Pennington-Gray
2009   Public Sector Perspectives and Policy Implications for the Pitons Management Area World Heritage Site, St. Lucia. *International Journal of Sustainable Development and World Ecology* 16(3):205–16.

Nicholas, N. Lorraine, Brijesh Thapa, and Yong Jae Ko
2009   Residents' Perspectives of a World Heritage Site: The Pitons Management Area, St. Lucia. *Annals of Tourism Research* 36(3):390–412.

Paris Club
2006   What Does the Paris Club Do? Electronic document, http://www.clubdeparis.org/en/, accessed October 29, 2006.

Pederson, Arthur
2002   *Managing Tourism at World Heritage Sites: A Practical Manual for World Heritage Site Managers.* UNESCO World Heritage Centre, Paris.

Protected Areas Conservation Trust

2006   Protected Areas Conservation Trust of Belize. Electronic document, http:// www.pactbelize.org, accessed November 9, 2006.

Shackley, Myra

2006   Visitor Management at World Heritage Sites. In *Managing World Heritage Sites*, edited by A. Leask and A. Fyall, pp. 84–93. Butterworth-Heinemann, Burlington, Mass.

Smith, Melanie

2003   *Issues in Cultural Tourism Studies*. Routledge, London.

Spergel, Barry

2001   *Raising Revenues for Protected Areas: A Menu of Options*. WWF Center for Conservation Finance, Washington, D.C.

Thapa, Brijesh

1998   Debt-for-Nature Swaps: An Overview. *International Journal of Sustainable Development and World Ecology* 5(4):1–14.

2000   The Relationship between Debt-for-Nature Swaps and Protected Area Tourism: A Plausible Strategy for Developing Countries. In *Proceedings of the 1999 Wilderness Science in a Time of Change Conference*, edited by S. McCool, D. Cole, W. Borrie, and J. O'Loughlin, pp. 268–72. Rocky Mountain Research Station, U.S. Department of Agriculture, Fort Collins, Col.2003

2004   Tourism in Nepal: Shangri-la's Troubled Times. *Journal of Travel and Tourism Marketing* 15(2):117–38.

2007   Issues and Challenges of World Heritage Sites in Nepal. In *World Heritage: Global Challenges, Local Solutions*, edited by R. White and J. Carman, pp. 23–27. Archaeopress, Oxford.

Thapa, Srijesh, and Brijesh Thapa

2002   Debt-for-Nature Swaps: Potential Applications in Nepal. *International Journal of Sustainable Development and World Ecology* 9(3):239–55.

Timothy, J. Dallen, and W. Stephen Boyd

2006   World Heritage Sites in the Americas. In *Managing World Heritage Sites*, edited by A. Leask and A. Fyall, pp. 240–49. Butterworth-Heinemann, Burlington, Mass.

Tubbataha Reef Marine Park

2006   Management Plan. Electronic document, http://tubbatahareef.org/index/?id= 29, accessed November 1, 2006.

United Nations Educational, Scientific and Cultural Organization (UNESCO)

2009   World Heritage List. Electronic document, http://whc.unesco.org/en/list, accessed September 20, 2009.

U.S. Agency for International Development (USAID)

2008   Introduction to the Tropical Forest Conservation Act. Electronic document, http://www.usaid.gov/our_work/environment/forestry/intro_tfca.html, accessed October 29, 2008.

Contributors

Neil Brodie is director of the Cultural Heritage Resource at Stanford University's Archaeology Center in California. Previously he coordinated the Illicit Antiquities Research Centre at the McDonald Institute for Archaeological Research, University of Cambridge, England. He conducts research on the commercial misappropriation of cultural heritage and has published several books on the illicit antiquities trade, including *Archaeology, Cultural Heritage and the Antiquities Trade*, which he coedited with Morag M. Kersel, Christina Luke, and Kathryn Walker Tubb (UPF, 2006).

Heather Burke is associate professor at Flinders University in South Australia. Prior to her appointment at Flinders, she worked as a cultural heritage manager for government agencies and as a private consultant for more than fifteen years. She is coauthor, with Claire Smith, of *Digging It Up Down Under: A Practical Guide to Doing Archaeology in Australia*.

Ian L. Campbell, a development economist specializing in environmental and cultural heritage issues, is a consultant to the World Bank. During his 42-year career, he has held senior advisory positions in governments, international agencies, and nongovernmental organizations. He has been a team leader for many environmental impact assessments.

Hong Chen is a Ph.D. candidate at Fudan University in Shanghai, focusing on paleolithic archaeology. She has published on public archaeology in China.

Jack Corbett is associate professor of public administration at Portland State University, Oregon, and professor of planning and regional development at the Instituto Tecnológico de Oaxaca, Mexico. He has authored numerous articles on heritage management and community development, and he is a member of an international panel of the President's Committee on the Arts and Humanities to develop a sister park system between the United States and Mexico.

Hester A. Davis was state archaeologist of Arkansas from 1967 to 1999 and professor of anthropology at the University of Arkansas until her retirement in

1999. She has been an officer in most national archaeological organizations in the United States and has served on the Cultural Property Advisory Committee for six years. She is preparing a biography of the archaeologist and ethnohistorian Mildred Mott Wedel.

Janette Deacon has worked as an archaeologist specializing in the Stone Age in South Africa since the early 1960s. As the archaeologist at the National Monuments Council in the 1990s, she contributed to the drafting of new cultural resources legislation and associated policies and guidelines. She is an honorary professor at the University of South Africa in Pretoria and the coordinator of the South African Rock Art Project, a program of the Getty Conservation Institute.

Paulo DeBlasis is associate professor at the Museu de Arqueologia e Etnologia, University of São Paulo, Brazil, where he has served as the scientific director and head of the postgraduate department. He has conducted cultural resources management and public archaeology development projects throughout Brazil for more than twenty years.

María Luz Endere is a researcher for CONICET (Consejo Nacional de Investigaciones Científicas y Tecnológicas) and an adjunct professor in law and cultural heritage management in the Department of Archaeology at the Universidad Nacional del Centro de la Provincia de Buenos Aires (UNICEN), Argentina. She is currently in charge of the academic secretariat of its Ph.D. in Archaeology program. She has done consultancy work on heritage legislation in Argentina with the World Bank, UNESCO, and other agencies.

Arlene K. Fleming is a cultural resource and development specialist who serves as a policy advisor at the World Bank on such issues as the cultural heritage component of environmental impact assessment and the use of cultural assets. She has done archaeological fieldwork in Turkey and Italy, served on the curatorial staff of the Smithsonian Institution, and worked as the director of evaluation at the National Endowment for the Humanities in the United States.

William H. Jansen II has devoted the bulk of his career to understanding international issues and making improvements in the human condition around the globe. He served as a foreign service officer with the U.S. Agency for International Development (USAID) for more than twenty years. He is a research associate professor of anthropology at the University of North Carolina at Chapel Hill and is currently serving as a technical advisor to U.S. development assistance programs in Zimbabwe.

Habil. Zbigniew Kobyliński is a professor in the Department of Historical and Social Sciences, Cardinal Stefan Wyszynski University, Warsaw, Poland, where he is director of the Institute of Archaeology. He is also a research scholar at the Institute of Archaeology and Ethnology of the Polish Academy of Sciences. In 2007 he became the president of the Scientific Society of Polish Archaeologists. He has authored books and papers on the theoretical foundations of cultural heritage management.

Thanik Lertcharnrit (formerly Sawang Lertrit) is an associate professor in the Department of Archaeology, Silpakorn University, Thailand. His archaeological research interests and publications address the prehistory of Thailand and Southeast Asia and cultural and archaeological resource management, including public perceptions of archaeology.

Andrew R. Mason is a senior archaeologist as well as an associate with Golder Associates in British Columbia, Canada. He is also vice president (North America) for the International Committee on Archaeological Heritage Management (ICAHM) for the International Council on Monuments and Sites (ICOMOS).

Akira Matsuda is a Handa Japanese archaeology fellow at the Sainsbury Institute for the Study of Japanese Arts and Cultures in the United Kingdom and is completing his Ph.D. in public archaeology at the Institute of Archaeology, University College London. His research interests include the relationship between archaeology—and more broadly cultural heritage—and contemporary society, and local people's engagement with excavations in Somma Vesuviana, Italy. He is the membership secretary of the World Archaeological Congress.

Phyllis Mauch Messenger serves as a grants consultant for the Institute for Advanced Study at the University of Minnesota, and she was the founding director of the Center for Anthropology and Cultural Heritage Education at Hamline University, St. Paul, Minnesota. She is the editor of *The Ethics of Collecting Cultural Property* and coeditor of *Heritage Values*.

David W. Morgan is director of the U.S. National Park Service's (NPS) Southeast Archeological Center in Tallahassee, Florida. He served as the chief of archeology and collections at the National Center for Preservation Technology and Training (NCPTT) from 2005 to 2009, after serving as an assistant professor at Northwestern State University of Louisiana. His research and publications focus on the archaeology of prehistoric and historic North America.

Katsuyuki Okamura works in the museum managerial section of the Osaka City

Cultural Properties Association. Previously, he worked as a field archaeologist and museum curator for over 20 years. His research interests include archaeology and modern society. He is currently the senior representative for Eastern Asia in the World Archaeological Congress (WAC) Council and a member of the WAC Executive.

Patrick J. O'Keefe, a specialist in the law and management of cultural heritage, has had a distinguished career in the Australian Public Service and the University of Sydney. He has been a consultant to the Parliamentary Assembly of the Council of Europe and numerous national governments on cultural heritage issues. A prolific author, he was the founding chair of the Heritage Law Committee of the International Law Association and coauthored, with Lyndel Prott, *Law and the Cultural Heritage* (1984).

S. B. Ota is regional director of the Central Region for the Archaeological Survey of India. He has directed the structural conservation of national protected monuments and managed several World Heritage sites in India, as well as publishing on various archaeological topics, including heritage management.

Nick Petrov is an assistant professor in the faculty of the History of World Culture at St. Petersburg State University of Culture and Arts in Russia. Since 1994, he has managed the field research of medieval sites in eastern Novgorod, and in 2003 he coordinated the Annual Meeting of the European Association of Archaeologists at St. Petersburg.

David Pokotylo is an associate professor in the Department of Anthropology at the University of British Columbia, Vancouver, Canada. He has carried out regional and national studies on public perceptions and attitudes toward archaeology and archaeological heritage management in Canada.

Nelly M. Robles García is an archaeologist with the National Institute of Anthropology and History (INAH) in Oaxaca, Mexico, and the director of the Archaeological Sites of the Valley of Oaxaca. In 2009 she was appointed president of the Archaeological Council, the scientific advisory organism of the INAH. She has authored six books on the archaeology of Oaxaca and has been designated by ICOMOS as an expert for assessment of the state of preservation of World Heritage sites in Latin America.

Chen Shen is the Bishop White Curator of Far East Archaeology at the Royal Ontario Museum, Canada. He has been conducting archaeological fieldwork in

China, the United States, and Canada since 1984 and has published widely on Chinese Pleistocene archaeology and current archaeological practices in China.

Jorge E. Silva is a professor of archaeology at San Marcos University School of Archaeology in Lima, Peru. Previously he served as director of the School of Archaeology at the Museum of Archaeology and Ethnology and as dean of the Social Sciences Faculty of San Marcos University. He has published widely on the archaeology and ethnohistory of the Inca Empire in Peru, including *Origen de las civilizaciones Andinas*, in Historia del Perú: Culturas Prehispánicas (2007).

Claire Smith is an associate professor at Flinders University in South Australia and president of the World Archaeological Congress. She has ongoing research projects with the Aboriginal communities in the Barunga region of the Northern Territory, and with Ngadjuri people in South Australia. She has published widely, including *Indigenous Archaeologies: Decolonising Archaeological Theory and Method*, coedited with H. Martin Wobst (2005).

George S. Smith retired as the associate director of the Southeast Archaeological Center (SEAC) in Tallahassee, Florida. He holds a faculty appointment in the Department of Anthropology at Florida State University where he teaches cultural heritage management. He is the co-editor of the book *Heritage Values in Contemporary Society* and the Cultural Heritage Management section of the *Encyclopedia of Global Archaeology*. He helped establish the Public Education and Curriculum committees at the Society for American Archaeology and received honorary doctorate degrees from the University of South Florida and the University of Alaska for his work in cultural heritage management.

Brijesh Thapa is an associate professor in the Department of Tourism, Recreation, and Sport Management at the University of Florida, Gainesville. He is also director of the Center for Tourism Research and Development at the university.

Willem J. H. Willems is a professor of archaeological resource management and of Roman archaeology at the University of Leiden, the Netherlands, where he is dean of the faculty of Archaeology. He is the former inspector general for archaeology in the Netherlands, and he participated in the Council of Europe's committee that drafted the Malta Convention. He was the founding president of the Europæ Archaeologiæ Consilium, the international association for European state archaeologists.

Index

Lightning Source UK Ltd.
Milton Keynes UK
UKOW04f1310270415

250419UK00001B/4/P